W9-CUU-044

# The 2016 Solo and Small Firm Legal Technology Guide

## CRITICAL DECISIONS MADE SIMPLE

Sharon D. Nelson, Esq., John W. Simek and Michael C. Maschke

INTRODUCTION BY JAMES A. CALLOWAY, ESQ.

**ABA LAW PRACTICE DIVISION**
The Business of Practicing Law

**Commitment to Quality**: The Law Practice Division is committed to quality in our publications. Our authors are experienced practitioners in their fields. Prior to publication, the contents of all our books are rigorously reviewed by experts to ensure the highest quality product and presentation. Because we are committed to serving our readers' needs, we welcome your feedback on how we can improve future editions of this book.

Facebook®, Twitter®, LinkedIn®, Google®, Pinterest®, and YouTube® are registered trademarks of their respective corporations.

Cover design by RIPE Creative, Inc.

Nothing contained in this book is to be considered as the rendering of legal advice for specific cases, and readers are responsible for obtaining such advice from their own legal counsel. This book and any forms and agreements herein are intended for educational and informational purposes only.

The products and services mentioned in this publication are under or may be under trademark or service mark protection. Product and service names and terms are used throughout only in an editorial fashion, to the benefit of the product manufacturer or service provider, with no intention of infringement. Use of a product or service name or term in this publication should not be regarded as affecting the validity of any trademark or service mark.

The Law Practice Division of the American Bar Association offers an educational program for lawyers in practice. Books and other materials are published in furtherance of that program. Authors and editors of publications may express their own legal interpretations and opinions, which are not necessarily those of either the American Bar Association or the Law Practice Division unless adopted pursuant to the bylaws of the Association. The opinions expressed do not reflect in any way a position of the Division or the American Bar Association.

© 2016 American Bar Association. All rights reserved.

Printed in the United States of America.

20  19  18  17  16    5  4  3  2  1

ISBN: 978-1-63425-392-5

Discounts are available for books ordered in bulk. Special consideration is given to state bars, CLE programs, and other bar-related organizations. Inquire at Book Publishing, American Bar Association, 321 N. Clark Street, Chicago, Illinois 60654.

www.ShopABA.org

# *Dedication*

SHARON NELSON AND John Simek dedicate this book to their children, Kelly, Sara, Kim, JJ, Jason, and Jamie, and to their grandchildren, Samantha, Lilly, Henry, Tyler, Evan, Jordan, Cash, and Parker—here's to many more vacations together on the Outer Banks.

Michael Maschke dedicates this book to his amazing wife, Summer, and their expanding family, especially to Lily and Sutton! The past few years have been the best of my life. God couldn't have blessed me more than with you three.

# Contents at a Glance

# Contents

xiiContents

# About the Authors

## Sharon D. Nelson, Esq.

 Sharon D. Nelson is the president of Sensei Enterprises, Inc. Ms. Nelson graduated from Georgetown University Law Center in 1978 and has been in private practice ever since. She now focuses exclusively on electronic evidence law.

Ms. Nelson, Mr. Simek, and Mr. Maschke are the coauthors of the nine most recent editions of this book (2008–16). Ms. Nelson and Mr. Simek are also coauthors of *Locked Down: Information Security for Lawyers* (American Bar Association, 2012). Additionally, Ms. Nelson and Mr. Simek are coauthors of *The Electronic Evidence and Discovery Handbook: Forms, Checklists, and Guidelines* (ABA, 2006). Ms. Nelson is a coauthor of *How Good Lawyers Survive Bad Times* (ABA, 2009). Ms. Nelson and Mr. Simek's articles have appeared in numerous national publications, and they frequently lecture throughout the country on digital forensics and legal technology subjects.

Ms. Nelson is a cohost of Legal Talk Network's *The Digital Edge: Lawyers and Technology and Digital Detectives* podcasts. Ms. Nelson and Mr. Simek have a regular legal tech column called "Hot Buttons" in the ABA Law Practice Division magazine *Law Practice*. Ms. Nelson was a member of the American Bar Association's Cybersecurity Task Force and serves on its Standing Committee on Technology and Information Systems. She is now the chair of the Law Practice Division's Professional Development Board and serves on its governing Council. She is a member of the Editorial Board of Law Technology News.

Ms. Nelson is a Past President of the Virginia State Bar (2013–14). She is a past president of the Fairfax Bar Association and past president of the Fairfax Law Foundation, past chair of the ABA's TECHSHOW Board, and past chair of the ABA's Law Practice Management Publishing Board. She is a graduate of Leadership Fairfax and served for many years on the Governing Council of the Virginia State Bar and on its Executive Committee. She is the former chair of the Virginia State Bar's Unauthorized Practice of Law Committee and served on both its Technology Committee and its Standing Committee on Finance. She is currently the chair of the Virginia State Bar's Future of Law Practice Committee, of its Better Annual Meeting Committee, and of VSB TECHSHOW 2016. She is a member of the ABA, the Virginia Bar, the Virginia Bar Association, the Virginia Trial Lawyers Association, the Virginia Women Lawyers Association, and the Fairfax Bar Association.

In 2015, Ms. Nelson was named by *Virginia Lawyers Weekly* as a member of the Class of 2015's Leaders in the Law. This honor recognizes attorneys and professionals in law-related fields who made outstanding contributions to the practice of law in Virginia, who made significant achievements through the practice of law, who provided leadership in improving the justice system, and who made important contributions to Virginia's legal community and/or the community at large.

Ms. Nelson has served as a Court Appointed Special Advocate (CASA) for Abused and Neglected Children for the past five years.

## John W. Simek

 John W. Simek is the vice president of Sensei Enterprises, Inc. He is a Certified Information Systems Security Professional (CISSP) and a nationally known testifying expert in the area of digital forensics. Mr. Simek holds a degree in engineering from the United States Merchant Marine Academy and an MBA in finance from Saint Joseph's University. After forming Sensei, he ended his more than twenty-year affiliation with Mobil Oil Corporation, where he served as a senior technologist, troubleshooting and designing Mobil's networks throughout the Western Hemisphere.

In addition to his CISSP designation, Mr. Simek is an EnCase Certified Examiner (EnCE), a Certified Handheld Examiner, a Certified Novell

Engineer, a Microsoft Certified Professional + Internet, a Microsoft Certified Systems Engineer, an NT Certified Independent Professional, and a Certified Internetwork Professional. He is also a member of the High Tech Crime Network, the Fairfax Bar Association, and the American Bar Association. In addition to coauthoring the books cited in Ms. Nelson's biography, he also serves on the 2016 ABA TECHSHOW planning board of the Law Practice Division. He currently provides information technology support to more than 250 area law firms, legal entities, and corporations. He lectures on legal technology and digital forensics subjects throughout the world.

He is a cohost of Legal Talk Network's *Digital Detectives* podcast and blogs at **youritconsultant.com**.

Mr. Simek also serves as a Court Appointed Special Advocate (CASA) for Abused and Neglected Children.

## Michael C. Maschke

Michael C. Maschke is the Chief Executive Officer and a digital forensics examiner at Sensei Enterprises, Inc. He is a Certified Computer Examiner (CCE), an EnCase Certified forensic technologist (EnCE), and a Certified Information Systems Security Professional (CISSP).

Mr. Maschke holds a degree in telecommunications from James Madison University. He has significant experience with network troubleshooting, design and implementation, systems integration, and computer engineering. Prior to becoming the Chief Information Officer, Mr. Maschke oversaw Sensei's information technology department, which provided support to hundreds of area law firms and corporations.

He has spoken at the American Bar Association's TECHSHOW conference on information security and is a coauthor of *Information Security for Lawyers and Law Firms* as well as the last eight editions of this book, all published by the American Bar Association.

# Acknowledgments

ONCE AGAIN, WE WELCOME our good friend Jim Calloway as the author of the introduction to this book. Jim is the director of the Oklahoma Bar Association's Management Assistance Program. He frequently writes and speaks on legal technology issues, Internet research, law office management and organization, and legal ethics. He is often on the faculty with us at ABA TECHSHOW and is Sharon's co-host on the Legal Talk Network's *Digital Edge: Lawyers and Technology* podcast.

We are very happy that our friend and colleague Jennifer Ellis again agreed to be a contributing author. She has updated her marvelous "Social Media for Law Firms" chapter for this edition of our book. Jennifer is a social media maven par excellence. You couldn't possibly get better advice.

Thanks to good friends Tom Mighell and Paul Unger, who generously updated their excellent "iWin: iPad for Litigators" chapter in the book— iPad aficionados will find a wealth of information in that chapter.

We are again indebted to our long-time friend Dave Bilinsky. Dave is a Practice Management Consultant and lawyer for the Law Society of British Columbia. He contributes an annual chapter, and an invaluable one, on taking your firm paperless.

Thanks to Denise Constantine who revved this edition up as our Manager of Book Publishing at the Law Practice Division. We wish you much success in your new endeavors! We also thank Jeff Salyards, who took over for Denise as our book was submitted—and we thank the as yet unknown folks who will bring this book to production!

And thanks to Richard Ferguson, our long-time friend and Project Manager for this edition of the book. Richard, we will salute with a "wee dram" when we see the book in print! Thanks for everything, one and all!

Finally, we again thank our colleagues here at Sensei, who carried the load while we were writing and were never too busy to deliberate over recommendations and to offer insightful comments. We don't come to work every day; we come to play, and we really like the folks we play with. Thanks, one and all!

Mike Maschke, Sharon Nelson, John Simek

# Introduction

## by James A. Calloway, Esq.

*"The first rule of any technology used in a business is that automation applied to an efficient operation will magnify the efficiency. The second is that automation applied to an inefficient operation will magnify the inefficiency."*

—*Bill Gates*

*"Once a new technology rolls over you, if you're not part of the steamroller, you're part of the road."*

—*Stewart Brand*

Legal work is about the management, analysis, and processing of information.

Today it is practically impossible to effectively manage information without the use of information technology.

And so we find members of the legal profession, many of whom believe that they handled their information quite well for generations, using books on shelves, 3" × 5" note cards, and file cabinets stuffed full of folders and paper, pressed into an era of constant change fueled by today's rapidly changing technology. Of course, many lawyers became lawyers because they didn't like math, science, or engineering. Now they stare at a computer or smartphone screens for most of their working days. Life truly is what happens when you are making other plans.

Law firms cannot operate today without Internet access, computers, mobile devices, and other technology tools. There has been a growing focus on the extent to which a lawyer can competently and ethically practice without understanding the role of technology today.

It was in August of 2012 that ABA revised its Model Rules of Professional Conduct to reference the need for a lawyer to be competent with the technology tools the lawyer uses and have an awareness of cyber security and data protection issues. The official comment to Rule 1.1 on Competence was amended to add the italicized language below:

"To maintain the requisite knowledge and skill, a lawyer should keep abreast of changes in the law and its practice, *including the benefits and risks associated with relevant technology*, engage in continuing study and education and comply with all continuing legal education requirements to which the lawyer is subject."

Fifteen states have now adopted this rule change, and it is likely by the time this book is printed more will have joined that group.

Many small firm lawyers have long understood the importance of technology in a way that many of their counterparts in large firms have not. Large firms have IT departments to help them navigate technology purchasing decisions and processes focused on making certain that lawyers maximize their billable hours rather than worry about which operating system is best. The small firm lawyer often makes the purchasing decision and very directly feels the economic impact of the purchases.

The discussion is continuing as to whether and how a lawyer can be ethical and competent while paying only minimal attention to the technology tools that the lawyer uses.

In April 2015, the Professional Ethics Committee for the State Bar of Texas issued Ethics Opinion 649 which stated that, while a lawyer can generally communicate confidential information by e-mail, certain circumstances may cause the lawyer to have a duty to advise the client whether it is prudent to use encrypted e-mail or another form of communication entirely. **http://tinyurl.com/o9utok9**

On June 30, 2015, the State Bar of California issued an ethics opinion stating that lawyers who handle litigation have an ethical duty to be competent in e-discovery or associate with others who have that competence. **http://tinyurl.com/nau3h77**

At this point, there seems to be no doubt that lawyers and technology will be heading into the future walking hand in hand, even if some of the lawyers believe it to be a "shotgun marriage."

*The 2016 Solo and Small Firm Legal Technology Guide* will not replace a law firm IT director, but annually it provides the information required for the solo or small firm lawyer who *is* the firm IT director, like it or not. It also will serve as an indispensable guide for a local consultant who has the ability to manage a law firm's technology infrastructure but is not aware of all of the legal-specific technology products that are available today. Some of this book will be read and reread, while other portions will be skimmed or skipped depending on the immediate technology needs of the firm. No law firm can avoid dealing with technology issues today. Lawyers in all practice settings can greatly benefit from this guide.

This guidebook can serve as a law firm's trusted source of basic information as well as in-depth information. It is a quick reference guide to understanding where a new product or software release fits into a law firm's overall strategy. The authors of this guide bring their long experience working with the legal profession to the pages of this volume. It is certainly the most cost-effective technology resource that any budget-conscious law firm could hope to obtain.

Lawyers are facing changes that impact most aspects of their professional lives. Many of the changes relate to technology advances and the changing expectations of consumers because of their experiences with technology. Four days to prepare a three-page document in correct form sounded fine in the age of the IBM Selectric typewriter, but it seems ridiculous to many consumers today. They want it done right, but they also want it now. People's lives are more intertwined with technology today—as a glance around any public gathering will verify.

Lawyers produce documents as the evidence and result of their work. While many members of the public may not appreciate the value of legal documents and deride "paper pushers," lawyers will always understand the value of a well-drafted contract or settlement proposal presented to opposing counsel. But the basic tools that a lawyer would use to prepare documents are changing as the use of the many "hidden" advanced features of word processors becomes commonplace and document assembly tools improve in affordability and ease of use. Lawyers whose keyboarding skills are less than adequate now rely on speech recognition software. Siri and other mobile speech recognition tools allow one the ability to dictate directly to digital text anywhere.

Most business executives are faced with the challenge of constantly improving their operations and efficiency. They will require similar improvements from the law firms serving them in the same way they require their suppliers, employees, and outside contractors to continue to innovate and improve.

A law firm's technology infrastructure and reasonable skill in using the day-to-day technology tools clearly is important for good professional business operations.

Today a litigator must understand e-discovery, a family lawyer must understand social media, and a lawyer advising businesses must have a broad understanding of data security and the specific technology tools that an industry or a sector uses. A lawyer may generally rely on an assistant to do e-filing, but must have the training, ability, and confidence to personally e-file an important pleading should the need arise.

*The 2016 Solo and Small Firm Legal Technology Guide* can help you purchase new tools to replace those that have become outdated or broken. But the highest and best use of the *Guide* is to use it to create change and set your law firm on a path to success by using the tools profiled and information provided in this book to secure your law firm's place in our uncertain future.

James A. Calloway is the Director of the Oklahoma Bar Association Management Assistance program and a former chair of ABA TECHSHOW. He blogs at **http://www.lawpracticetipsblog.com** and tweets at @jimcalloway.

# CHAPTER ONE

# Computers

## Desktop Computers

### Personal Computers (PCs)

The Dell OptiPlex line of computers continues to offer the perfect combination of performance and business-grade hardware at just the right price. All Dell computers can be purchased with a three-, four-, or five-year warranty and offer a large selection of available options for protecting your investment. They offer both hardware and software warranty protection of varying levels, along with same-day or next-business-day response for the replacement of failed computer hardware or software.

We strongly recommend the purchase of a three-year warranty—the average life span of a business computer system—with any new computer. Purchasing software technical support, in our judgment, is generally not worth the additional cost, especially when most firms have an IT provider who is familiar with their software and setup and can assist when help is needed, rather than having to rely on Dell for assistance.

Dell also offers accidental damage protection for its computer systems, which covers damage caused by spilled liquids, drops, falls, and electrical surges for a period of three to five years, at an additional cost ranging from $34 to $55. This cost is much lower than in previous editions of this book.

Another option from Dell worth noting is its Keep Your Hard Drive program. Typically, if a hard drive crashes while under warranty, Dell will take the failed hard drive and replace it with a new or refurbished one. Citing privacy concerns—with all the continuing data breaches in the news—Dell now offers its users the ability to keep their hard drives, even in the event a replacement is needed, but at an additional cost. The cost for this option ranges from $7 to $21, depending on the length of the warranty (one to five years), and it is a small price to pay to maintain total control over and responsibility for the sensitive and confidential data on the hard drive. For recommendations on how to securely remove data from a hard drive before disposal, check out the Utilities chapter.

Below, we provide you with our recommendations for a Dell OptiPlex business-grade computer system with all of the hardware components included.

## Windows-Based Desktop Computer

| Hardware Component | Recommendation |
| --- | --- |
| *Computer Model:* | Dell OptiPlex 9020 Mini Tower |
| *Operating System:* | Microsoft Windows 7 Professional 64-Bit (Includes Windows 8.1 Pro license); eligible for free Windows 10 Upgrade |
| *Processor:* | 4th Gen Intel Core i7-4790 Processor (Quad Core, 3.6 GHz Turbo, 8 MB, w/HD4600 Graphics) |
| *Memory:* | 8 GB 1600 MHz Memory DDR3 Memory |
| *Video Card:* | AMD RADEON RS 240 |
| *Hard Drive:* | 1 TB 3.5-Inch SATA Hard Drive |
| *Optical Drive:* | 16X DVD+/−RW |
| *Network:* | Intel Gigabit LAN 10/100/1000 Ethernet |
| *Warranty:* | 3-Year Basic Hardware Service with 3-Year Onsite Service After Remote Diagnosis |
| *Other Notes:* | No mouse and keyboard required; no out-of-band systems management; USB 3.0 ports included |

The fourth-generation Intel Core i7-4790 Quad Core 3.4 GHz processor will provide more than enough power to support both current and future versions of business-grade software, including the next version of the Windows Operating System, throughout the life cycle of the machine. The Intel Core i7 has replaced the Intel Core 2 Duo processor and has become the standard for business-grade systems. The Intel Core i7 Quad Core processor is offered with varying levels of clock speeds, with the 3.6 GHz version currently in the upper range of processor clock speeds offered by Dell for this model of computer system. The faster the processor, the higher the premium for having cutting-edge technology. The amount of memory included in this system is enough to support your business applications, handling even "memory hungry" applications with ease. Eight gigabytes (GB) of memory has become the recommended standard for the minimum amount of memory in business-grade computers, given the low cost and high gain in performance for the upgrade. This upgrade is a must-have option when purchasing a 64-bit system, which can actually take advantage of the additional resources.

The video card included in this system provides dual-link digital visual interface (DVI) outputs. By providing dual interfaces, this graphics adapter allows you to have dual monitors, an option we will never go without when purchasing a new computer system. John calls his current setup 2¾ monitors since there are two 20-inch wide screen monitors and the 15½-inch display on the laptop. (Monitors, keyboards, and other peripherals are discussed in subsequent chapters.)

A hard drive plays an important role in the configuration of your computer system because it is the hardware component where your information (files) is actually stored. In short, the better the hard drive is, the faster your computer can read and write your data. This system comes with a 1 TB Serial ATA (SATA) hard drive, which will provide enough storage space for the average lawyer user. The 6 GBps SATA interface allows for more throughput and higher cache than the previous revisions of the SATA specification. In fact, Dell no longer offers earlier versions of SATA hard drives as an option when configuring an OptiPlex desktop or smaller capacity drives. We wouldn't be surprised if, in the near future, the usage of 3.5-inch hard drives is discontinued due to the large power requirements to operate them and their propensity to fail, especially as the cost of solid-state hard drives continues to fall. In fact, Dell now offers many choices for notebook-sized (2.5-inch) drives and solid-state drives for the OptiPlex model line.

Dell does offer the ability to configure your OptiPlex computer with separate boot and data drives. By selecting a solid-state hard drive for the boot drive and a standard SATA hard drive for the data drive, your system performance may be even better, especially when powering on your computer (startup time). However, given the limited sizes offered by Dell for the solid-state drives, many lawyers would quickly fill them up, causing problems with the computer's operation. Further, some versions of Office 365 can only be installed to the local C: volume (boot), otherwise causing errors if attempting to install it to a secondary data drive.

When configuring an optical drive for the system, choosing the 16X DVD+/–RW drive will allow you to burn and read data from both CDs and DVDs. We used to recommend that you purchase your computer with a FireWire 400 or 800 Mbps (megabits per second) adapter, but that is no longer the case. Newer interfaces have come out within the past few years, such as USB 3.0 and Thunderbolt, a serial data interface primarily found on Apple computer systems, and are now beginning to be offered on a small number of Windows-based computers. Now that these technologies have been out for a few years, especially USB 3.0, it is time to jump on board—especially if you transfer a lot of data to external hard drives. In actuality, it's becoming harder to find USB 2.0 external hard drives, so you might as well take advantage of the increased speed. The Dell OptiPlex 9020 Mini Tower now includes four USB 3.0 ports (two on front, two on back) and six USB 2.0 ports.

Dell currently offers its computers preinstalled with the Windows 7 or Windows 8 operating systems. Even for die-hard techies like us, it would be a reach to think about using Windows 8 *(or 10, more on that later in the book)* at this time in a business environment, especially without a touch-screen monitor—remember the problems with Windows Vista and hardware drivers? Windows 8 hasn't caught fire with businesses as many industry analysts predicted it would, and given the current lack of implementation, it is considered by many to be another Microsoft failure, just like Microsoft Vista. It remains to be seen, but at this time, we have no plans to upgrade our systems from Windows 7 to Windows 8 and are currently waiting on Windows 10 to work the kinks out, planning to assess whether to adopt it in early 2016. The exception would be for touch devices like tablets or all-in-one computer systems, where Windows 8 would be a better alternative. Microsoft released the Windows 10 operating system as a free upgrade, and this system would be eligible for the upgrade when the time is right. The free upgrade offer for the Windows 10 operating system is valid until July 2016, and hopefully, all of the kinks will have been worked out by then.

The three-year onsite parts and labor warranty will cover hardware defects and failures of the computer system at a relatively small cost. The cost of this warranty is built into the cost of the recommended system and should be considered a requirement when purchasing a new computer for your business or firm. Dell provides the consumer with a toll-free phone number to call for technical support, and if any hardware needs to be replaced, Dell will send a support technician to your location to replace the defective part after remote diagnosis. The hardware replacement and labor cost is covered by the warranty, so there should be no additional out-of-pocket costs.

There are some additional pointers to consider when configuring this desktop system. First, most users already have their own wireless keyboard and mouse and don't need another basic USB keyboard and mouse taking up space in the desk drawer. This can be avoided by removing them from the default configuration of this system, and you'll save about $10. For those of you who don't have a wireless keyboard and mouse—you should be looking at upgrading immediately. Our recommendations for a wireless desktop suite can be found in the Computer Peripherals chapter.

Another tip: Dell also includes by default an out-of-band management device, which shouldn't be necessary. Again, just removing this piece of hardware can save you approximately $30. If you consider yourself to be technically challenged, you may want to leave the management device for remote diagnostics by the support personnel.

For those users who are looking to purchase a new monitor or two, Dell does offer the ability to bundle monitors when configuring your new computer system. If you need a new monitor or two, it may be a good idea to save a few bucks and bundle them with the purchase of your new computer system. Based on a price comparison, it appears that you save about $50 or more per monitor when selecting them at the time of your computer purchase, and we're always looking for ways to save you money! As of this writing, one of the options for monitors is $100 less than Dell's online retail price when bundled—talk about hidden savings!

Keep in mind that, on average, the expected life cycle of a new business computer system is around three years, which is covered by the three-year warranty you purchased. The recommended Dell OptiPlex 9020 Mini Tower desktop computer can be configured and purchased from Dell's website starting at around $960.

Remember that the "sweet spot" in buying computers changes regularly. Our specs will get you close, but they will shift slightly during the lifespan of this publication. You can receive a courtesy copy of our current specs (for workstations, laptops, and servers—PC or Mac) by e-mailing sensei@senseient.com and simply making a request. We are generally able to get our current specs to you within twenty-four hours during the workweek. We are happy to report that many, many readers are taking advantage of this offer, so don't be shy. We are always pleased to help.

## Apple Computers (Macs)

In the past, Apple computers (Macs) were used primarily by businesses with a need for multimedia functions, such as video editing and graphic design—both areas in which Apple systems have always excelled. Usually, Apple's appearance in an office environment was the result of someone having a personal preference for the Macintosh operating system over the Windows-based system.

Macs are still not as widely used in law offices as Windows-based computers are, but Apple's shift to using Intel-based processors in all of its systems, and the continued popularity of the iPad and iPhone mean they are chosen more frequently now by solo and small firm lawyers. As a result of the change in processors, Macs can now run both the Mac OS X and Windows operating systems on the same computer. In a way, it's like having two systems in one.

A Mac computer can be easily configured to connect to and function on a Windows-based network, including communicating with and authenticating a Windows domain controller.

For those concerned with computer security, Mac systems are perceived to be more secure than their Windows-based counterparts since they are not targeted as often by malware, due to the overall smaller number of Mac users. Some Mac users scoff at the suggestion that their computer should be running some kind of security software for protection. However, they would be wrong; Macs absolutely need security software—Apple itself now says so. Remember, the bad guys who write browser exploits (pieces of malware that take advantage of vulnerabilities in Internet browsers such as Firefox) don't care what operating system the computer is running. In fact, security companies consistently warn that malware writers who attack browsers are increasingly becoming the real threat, as vulnerabilities in operating systems are less frequently targeted.

In 2014 alone, Mac users battled viruses and Trojans that have been used in a number of targeted attacks against governments ("Appetite Trojan"); malware that spreads via spam messages—posing as an undelivered parcel notification from FedEx that steals documents from the local computer system ("LaoShu Trojan"); and finally the CoinThief Trojan, malware designed to steal login credentials related to various Bitcoin-related exchanges using malicious browser add-ons.

In 2015, Mac users dealt with zero-day exploits targeting the latest version of the Mac OS X operating system ("Yosemite"), adware/spyware such as MacKeeper that installs unwanted adware on a user's systems, and other exploits targeting QuickTime and Safari.

So Apple users, please don't be naive—you, too, need virus and malware protection. In 2012, Apple removed from its website the language suggesting that you didn't need this type of protection, and for the past three years, it has been actively encouraging the use of security software.

Apple's continuing release of security patches, even for the latest version of its operating system, is a clear sign of just how targeted this software and its applications are by the developers of malware. For years, we have recommended that security protection suites be installed on all computers, regardless of the operating system.

While they are still not the majority, we are beginning to see Apple computers make their way into smaller law offices, especially in the solo, stand-alone environment. Now that Apple computers use Intel chipsets, users are taking advantage of the opportunity to better integrate their systems with the Windows world. Some users run Windows on their Mac computers as the primary operating system. Others use Boot Camp, a free utility provided by Apple at no charge with each system, to dual-boot between Windows and Mac OS. With Boot Camp, users can install Microsoft Windows 7, 8.1, or 10 operating system right alongside Apple's OS X on any Intel-based Macintosh computer. Setting up a dual-boot system would be our recommendation, as opposed to running Windows within a virtual machine on a Mac computer.

To run the Windows 7 or newer operating system, you must upgrade your version of Boot Camp to version 4.0 or newer. The most current release of Boot Camp is version 6, which added support for Windows 10. Boot Camp 6 includes support for the following features of your Mac in Windows 10: USB 3.0, USB-C, Thunderbolt, built-in SD or SDXC card slot, USB Apple SuperDrive and the Apple keyboard, trackpad, and mouse.

The Boot Camp software guides users through the processes of creating a new partition of the local hard drive on which to install the Windows operating system and also provides all of the necessary Windows drivers required for hardware functionality. As an alternative to dual-booting with Boot Camp, some users have even purchased third-party products like Parallels Workstation or downloaded Oracle's VM VirtualBox, which allows them to run Windows, Linux, and other operating systems within the Mac OS itself. Virtual Machine (VM) software is described in more detail in a later section of this book.

The iMac desktop systems combine performance and ergonomics by putting the hardware components that make up the system in the same casing as the monitor, eliminating the need for separate components like a tower unit sitting underneath your desk. As a result, the space-saving design allows you to free up both desk and floor space without giving up performance. Below, we provide our recommendation for an iMac business-grade desktop system with all of the hardware components outlined.

**Macintosh-Based Desktop Computer**

| <u>Hardware Component</u> | <u>Recommendation</u> |
| --- | --- |
| *Computer Model:* | 21.5-inch iMac |
| *Operating System:* | Mac OS v10.10 Yosemite |
| *Processor:* | Intel Core i5 Quad Core 2.7 GHz (Turbo Boost up to 3.2 GHz) |
| *Memory:* | 8 GB 1600 MHz DDR3 SDRAM |
| *Video Card:* | Intel Iris Pro Graphics |
| *Hard Drive:* | 1 TB (5400-rpm) Hard Drive |
| *CD/DVD-ROM:* | 8X SuperDrive (DVD+R DL/DVD±RW/CD-RW) |
| *Network:* | 10/100/1000 Base-T Gigabit Ethernet Port, 802.11 ac Wi-Fi wireless networking (802.11a/b/g/n compatible), Bluetooth 4.0 |
| *Warranty:* | 3-year AppleCare Protection Plan for iMacs |
| *Other:* | FaceTime HD Camera, Built-in 21.5-inch Monitor and Stereo Speakers, Dual Microphones, two Thunderbolt Ports, four USB 3 Ports, Mini Display-Port, Apple Wireless Keyboard and Magic Mouse, SDXC Card Slot, and Kensington Lock Slot |

The 21.5-inch iMac comes with an Intel Core i5 Quad Core 2.7 GHz processor, 8 GB of memory, and the Mac OS v10.10 Yosemite operating system. For an additional $200, this system can be configured for up to 16 GB of memory, which may be overkill for basic business usage—unless you are running a Windows virtual machine from within Mac OS X. If you choose to dual-boot, which is our recommendation, 8 GB of memory should be plenty. The 1 TB 5400 RPM SATA hard drive comes standard and will provide more than enough storage space and hard drive performance for the average lawyer. However, if you feel that you need additional storage space or performance speed, the hard drive can be configured with 256 GB or 512 GB of flash storage or Apple's 1 TB Fusion Drive—a combination flash storage and regular hard drive. The flash storage media

will contain the files necessary to boot and load the operating system, dramatically increasing the speed with which the computer system starts up. The hard drive can be upgraded to 3 TB in size, but this option is only available for the 27-inch version of the iMac.

The standard Ethernet adapter and 802.11 ac Wi-Fi wireless networking adapter will allow your computer to connect to the business network, whether over a wired network or wireless, even if it's Windows-based. The AirPort wireless adapter is also backward compatible with 802.11a/b/g/n wireless networks.

The other standard hardware included with the iMac is the built-in Face-Time HD camera, stereo speakers, 21.5-inch LED-backlit display with IPS technology, four USB 3.0 ports, two Thunderbolt ports, and one SDXC memory card slot. This system also includes one Mini DisplayPort, which allows users to add a second external monitor to their computer system if needed, and the standard Apple wireless keyboard and Magic Mouse. The 21.5-inch iMac computer weighs 12.5 pounds and has a depth of about 7 inches, so finding room on your desk for one of these systems is very easy.

Apple's standard warranty with a new iMac provides you with ninety days of telephone support and one year of service coverage. We recommend that you upgrade the warranty to the extended AppleCare Protection Plan for iMac, which provides you with telephone and service support for three years. The cost to extend the warranty plan is $169 and is well worth it. The 21.5-inch iMac computer can be purchased from Apple's webstore starting at $1,099, and the pricing of the 27-inch iMac starts at $1,799.

## Laptops

### Personal Computers (PCs)

The Dell Latitude line of laptop computers continues to combine performance and mobility in a laptop system that remains at the top of its class. These business-grade laptops are thin and extremely light, weighing less than 4½ pounds. They are a perfect fit for the mobile lawyer and provide an ideal mobile computing solution. Below, we provide you with our recommendations for a Dell Latitude business-grade laptop with all of the hardware components included.

**Windows-Based Laptop Computer**

| Hardware Component | Recommendation |
|---|---|
| *Computer Model:* | Dell Latitude E6440 |
| *Processor:* | 4th Gen Intel Core i7-4610M 3.0 GHz 4M Cache |
| *Operating System:* | Microsoft Windows 7 Professional 64-Bit |
| *Memory:* | 8 GB DDR3 1600 MHz SDRAM |
| *Video Card:* | AMD Radeon HD 8690M |
| *Hard Drive:* | 2.5-inch 500 GB Solid State-Hybrid Drive |
| *CD/DVD-ROM:* | 8X DVD+/−RW drive |
| *Network:* | 10/100/1000 Mbps Ethernet adapter, Intel Centrino Advanced-N 6235 802.11AGN Dual Band Wi-Fi Half-Mini Card |
| *Warranty:* | 3-Year Basic Hardware Service with 3-Year Next-Business-Day Limited Onsite Service after Remote Diagnosis |
| *Other:* | 14-Inch Wide HD+ LED screen, 90W AC power adapter, 9-cell/97 WHr primary battery, weighs 4.68 lbs., four USB 3.0 ports, VGA, HDMI, Memory Card Reader, Noise-Cancelling Digital Array Microphone and Light Sensitive Webcam, Fingerprint reader, and contactless smartcard reader |

The Dell Latitude E6440 comes with a fourth-generation Intel Core i7-4610M 3.0 GHz processor and 8 GB of memory, which should be sufficient to run all of the business applications of a mobile lawyer. The system also comes preinstalled with Microsoft Windows 7 Professional 64-bit. Microsoft released the Windows 10 operating system as a free upgrade, and this system would be eligible for the upgrade when the time is right.

The system's fingerprint reader provides the level of security needed to protect your personal files and confidential data. When it's enabled, you can restrict user logon access to either the biometric access or to a user name and password. A fingerprint reader keeps data on the hard drive secure through encryption, with the hardware requiring successful authentication before the data contents can be decrypted. Enabling a start-up or hard drive password in the system's BIOS is a great way to add an extra layer of protection to your system and is highly recommended if you're storing sensitive client data on your laptop.

The AMD Radeon HD 8690M graphics card supplies crisp, clear graphics to the 14-inch wide LED display. The 500 GB hard drive will provide more than enough storage space for the mobile user, with a hard drive speed that will supply faster drive performance. The DVD+/–RW drive will allow you to burn and read both CDs and DVDs without the need to attach an external burner. The Ethernet adapter will allow you to connect your laptop to your network when you're in the office, and the wireless network adapter will allow you to stay connected when on the move. The Intel wireless adapter provides connectivity to 802.11a/b/g/n wireless networks, supporting dual-band operation (2.4 and 5 GHz) with data rates up to 300 megabits per second (Mbps). The 9-cell battery is an upgrade that will supply the laptop with power longer than the standard 6-cell battery and should charge faster as well. This battery upgrade is a must-have if you plan to use the wireless network adapter when running the laptop off of the battery, although this will add some slight weight to the unit. The 9-cell battery will provide you with approximately three hours more battery life than the standard 6-cell battery, which will save you from searching for electrical outlets wherever you go. Finally, the integrated HD video webcam and digital microphone is great for videoconferences or recording audio, such as podcasts.

The three-year, next-business-day onsite parts and labor warranty is the same warranty described in the Desktop Computers section. The Dell Latitude E6440 can be purchased from Dell's website starting at around $1,549.

If you are particularly clumsy or accident-prone, you may want to consider adding the CompleteCare Accidental Damage Protection Plan to your purchase. This plan covers any damage to the laptop, including such things as liquid spills (one client has used this plan multiple times to cover the unwelcome effects of spilling red wine), surges, and dropping the device. Obviously, it does not cover intentional damage, theft, or normal wear and tear. For the additional $76 to $111, depending on the length of the warranty (three- to five-year options), you will have peace of mind when you set your coffee cup (or wineglass) on the keyboard.

## Apple Computers (Macs)

The Apple MacBook Pro is perfect for the mobile lawyer who requires a powerful notebook in a compact and lightweight design. The MacBook Pro laptop comes standard with a wide-screen Retina display, built-in FaceTime HD camera, wireless network adapter, and much more. The

MacBook Pro laptop is available with 13- or 15-inch screens. Apple no longer sells a 17-inch version of this model. In prior editions of this book, Apple offered the Retina display only in the upgraded 15-inch model of the MacBook Pro. This is no longer the case. Now all versions of both the 13- and 15-inch MacBook Pros come standard with the Retina display. The MacBook Pro is available only in the aluminum case with glass LED display. The MacBook Pro can be fully integrated into any Windows-based network without too much overhead and configuration. Below, we provide our recommendations for an Apple MacBook Pro business-grade laptop with all of the hardware components included.

**Macintosh-Based Laptop Computer**

| Hardware Component | Recommendation |
| --- | --- |
| *Computer Model:* | 15-Inch MacBook Pro |
| *Operating System:* | Mac OS v10.10 Yosemite |
| *Processor:* | Intel Core i7 Quad Core 2.2 GHz |
| *Memory:* | 16 GB 1600 MHz DDR3 |
| *Video Card:* | Intel Iris Pro |
| *Hard Drive:* | 256 GB Flash Storage |
| *CD/DVD-ROM:* | 8X SuperDrive (DVD+R DL/DVD±RW/CD-RW) |
| *Network:* | 10/100/1000 Base-T Gigabit Ethernet Port, AirPort Extreme Wi-Fi (802.11a/b/g/n), Bluetooth 4.0 |
| *Warranty:* | 3-year AppleCare Protection Plan |
| *Other:* | FaceTime HD Camera, Built-in 15.4-Inch LED-Back-lit Display with IPS Technology, Stereo Speakers, two USB 3 Ports, two Thunderbolt Ports, SDXC Card Slot, and HDMI |

The base 15-inch MacBook Pro laptop comes with 16 GB of memory (minimum amount available) and the Mac OS v10.10 Yosemite operating system. The Intel Iris Pro video card provides perfect high resolution to the 15.4-inch-wide Retina LED display, with a maximum resolution of 2880 × 1800 pixels. The 256 GB flash storage hard drive provides enough space to store all of your documents, pictures, and music. The 8X SuperDrive will allow you to burn and play both CDs and DVDs. The built-in 802.11 ac Wi-Fi wireless networking adapter will keep you connected on the road, and it supports the 802.11n standard. The adapter is also backward compatible with 802.11a/b/g wireless networks. The aluminum body MacBook is very light, weighing just 4.49 pounds.

If you need more processing power, this model can be upgraded to an i7 2.5 or 2.8 GHz quad-core processor—for a pretty penny!

The new Force Touch trackpad gives you precise cursor control and supports two-finger scrolling, tap, double-tap, and drag capabilities. It also now supports pressure-sensing capabilities. If you have been a lifelong Windows user, be forewarned: There is no right-click button on the trackpad. To right-click on a Mac, you must hold down the Control key while clicking. A tip for former Windows users: Don't want to hold down the Control key to initiate a right-click with the mouse? You can tap the trackpad with two fingers rather than holding down the Control key—you just have to enable the option within the Keyboard & Mouse settings.

Have you ever tripped over a power cord and had your laptop come flying off the desk? With the 85W MagSafe 2 power adapter, you no longer have to worry. The magnetic power connector will cleanly disengage from the side of the laptop and cause no damage to the computer or the power cord. This a great gift to those of us who are occasionally less than graceful.

The sleek and elegant design of the MacBook Pro is what sets it apart from the competition. The design and celebrated ease of use makes the Mac Book Pro a smart choice when purchasing a laptop for yourself or your firm. The MacBook Pro configured above can be purchased from Apple's webstore for $1,999.

## Netbooks/Ultrabooks

Netbooks and ultrabooks continue to be very popular among mobile users, including lawyers. Essentially, these devices are highly portable mini-laptops. They are much smaller, cheaper, and lighter than most traditional laptops. As with the other computer recommendations, it is impossible to mention all of the available manufacturers and models of ultrabooks and netbooks.

More recently, netbooks have taken a backseat to the class of laptops called ultrabooks. Ultrabooks, which are becoming increasingly popular, are paper-thin laptops (nearly weightless when compared to a traditional laptop). Ultrabooks have more robust hardware specifications than netbooks, but they also command a higher price.

Apple released the MacBook Air, an ultrabook considered the first of its class, long before PC manufacturers released the first competitor. Much as the iPad has dominated Android-based tablets, in part because it was first to the market, the MacBook Air continues to be an extremely popular alternative to the regular laptop for a mobile user, and starts at a cost of $899 or so.

The MacBook Air is offered in both 11- and 13-inch models, with configurable internal flash storage capacity available from 128 to 256 GB. The 1.6 GHz Dual Core Intel Core i5 processor is more than capable of handling web browsing and document editing, but not a lot more than that, which is perfect for the mobile lawyer. For more power users, the processor can be upgraded to a 2.2 GHz dual-core Intel Core i7. When purchasing the MacBook Air, users should choose to upgrade the memory to 8 GB for the extra $100 cost. This upgrade is well worth the price for the performance increase that will be received. The battery of the 11-inch model lasts up to nine hours when surfing the Internet, with the battery of the 13-inch model lasting up to twelve hours.

If you were to hold an 11-inch model, weighing just 2.38 pounds, you'd never go back to using a standard laptop. The MacBook Air is available for purchase on Apple's website starting at $900.

## Tablets

Most users would expect to see the iPad recommended in this section, but keep in mind the iPad is much more of a personal device than it is a "true laptop replacement." You will find our recommendations and thoughts on the iPad later in this book, so please don't worry.

Business-grade tablets, those that can truly replace a laptop, are quickly becoming the next big thing in solo and small firm technology. Sharon and John are being bombarded with questions on this very topic at many of the presentations that they give throughout the country—is there a tablet that can actually replace my laptop, while maintaining all of the functionality?

The answer is, yes there is. You can now leave your 4.5-pound laptop and clunky travel bag at home when you need to hit the road.

The Microsoft Surface Pro 4 is truly considered a laptop replacement. The tablet boasts a 12.3-inch display with a resolution of 2736x1824. The sixth-generation Intel Core processor (i3, i5, i7) is the same processor that you will find in your laptop computer system, and it provides this tablet with more than enough horsepower to run your business applications smoothly. The tablet comes preloaded with Microsoft Windows 10, which means that you can load and run any of your necessary business software—allowing you to get the same functionality out of this device as you can out of your laptop—at just a fraction of the weight!

The device can be configured with 4, 8, or 16 GB of memory and anywhere from 128 GB to 1 TB of storage space. For network connectivity, this device comes with a wireless adapter supporting 802.11a/b/g/n and Bluetooth 4.0 wireless technology. It has both a front- and rear-facing camera, as well as a stereo microphone perfect for videoconferencing. We would recommend that you give serious consideration to the 16 GB memory, 256 GB storage, i7 unit.

The Microsoft Surface Pro 4 tablet can be purchased online from Microsoft's webstore (**www.microsoft.com**) or from your local electronics retailer starting at $899.

# CHAPTER TWO

# Computer Operating Systems

**O**LDER VERSIONS OF THE Microsoft Windows operating system (Windows Vista and older) are no longer addressed in this book, mainly because most of the versions are no longer relevant and the majority (Vista is the exception) are not supported by Microsoft, which means they should not be used by business or individuals due to the insecurity of these operating systems.

## Microsoft Windows 7

Windows 7 is the successor to Windows Vista and was made available to the general public on October 22, 2009. Microsoft was ready to move on from the epic failure that was Vista, and finally got it right with the release of Windows 7. It is more "XP-like," emphasizing performance improvements and eliminating the compatibility issues that plagued Microsoft Vista. We have been running the various versions of Windows 7 since it was first released as a beta and absolutely love it—as do many of our clients.

Windows 7 is available in six editions, but only a few of those are worth mentioning to the solo and small firm market:

**Starter Edition**—is primarily for small notebooks, such as a netbook. The Starter Edition is 32-bit only, supports only a single processor, and does not support multiple monitors, such as dual displays. This edition was not designed for business use.

**Home Premium Edition**—comes bundled with Internet Explorer 10, allows for a connection to a home network, and is for home use only. The upgrade (from a previous operating system) retail cost for this edition is $149.99 per license, and the full retail cost for this edition is $199.99 per license.

**Professional Edition**—includes all the features of the Home Premium Edition, plus allows connection to a company network, such as a domain, and includes a backup-and-restore utility to protect your system. The upgrade retail cost for this edition is $199.99 per license, and the full retail cost for this edition is $299.99 per license.

**Ultimate Edition**—includes all the features of the Professional Edition, plus BitLocker encryption to help secure your data. The upgrade retail cost for this edition is $219.99 per license, and the full retail cost for this edition is $319.99 per license.

All of these editions are available for purchase and download from Microsoft's website, and for an additional $14.95, you can elect to have a physical disk shipped to you as a backup.

For your business, you will need to purchase either the Professional or Ultimate Edition to install on your computer systems. Obviously, upgrading is less expensive than purchasing a full license. If you have computer systems running Windows XP, the time to upgrade has long passed. As author Nelson notes, it is likely unethical to use Windows XP, as it cannot adequately protect your confidential information—and that fact is well known.

Users may also upgrade their computer systems to Windows 7 from both Windows XP and Windows Vista. However, for users upgrading from Windows XP, you must be careful when performing an upgrade. This upgrade path actually performs a "clean" installation, and the user must back up all programs and data because the upgrade will not retain any of the information. There isn't a prompt during the upgrade process to notify users to back up their data, so this step must be performed before beginning the upgrade process. In other words, there is no direct upgrade path from XP to Windows 7. It is probably best to do a clean install anyway to clean up any past "sins" and remove any leftover files from applications that didn't completely uninstall in the past. You can get some advice about your hardware and software compatibility by running the free Windows Upgrade Advisor (**http://www.microsoft. com/en-us/download/details.aspx?id=20**). This utility will tell you if your hardware is compatible and what software may need to be upgraded.

If you are upgrading from Windows Vista, most of you will not have to worry about the process deleting all of your information. As was the case when upgrading from Windows XP to Windows Vista, you need only perform a clean install if you are going to a version that is lower on the food chain (e.g., Windows Vista Ultimate to Windows 7 Home Edition).

Regardless of the upgrade path you take, we always strongly recommend that you back up your system and data before upgrading.

The only other installation scenario with a clean installation is an upgrade from a 32-bit version to a 64-bit version operating system, regardless of the edition. Microsoft released the first Service Pack for this operating system (SP1) to the public in February 2011, and at the time of its release, it was not a mandatory update. This Service Pack addressed a number of security issues and fixed a few bugs related to HDMI audio and the printing of XPS documents.

Please note that Windows 7 can no longer be purchased online at the Microsoft Store, but it is still available when configuring a new system from Dell and from other third-party retailers, both online and in brick-and-mortar locations.

## Microsoft Windows 8

Windows 8 is the successor to Windows 7 and became available to consumers in early fall of 2012.

The Windows 8 user interface is built based on the Metro design language, featuring a new start screen, Internet Explorer 10, support for USB 3.0, and a new Windows Defender. Windows 8 has also added support for UEFI SecureBoot, which is a feature used to prevent unauthorized firmware, operating systems, or drivers from running at boot time.

There has been much controversy over the new Metro look, replacing the all-too-familiar Windows Start button. The Metro UI environment is tile-based, similar to the Start screen seen on the Windows Phone operating system. The Start button had originally been removed from the taskbar, but was later reinstated with the update, Windows 8.1, released in October 2013.

Windows 8 is available in four editions, three of which are focused on business-grade computers: Windows 8, Windows 8 Pro, and Windows 8 Enterprise. The Windows RT edition is built to run solely on tablet hardware.

Windows 8 has been available for a few years now as of this writing, and it appears very likely that it is headed toward a fate similar to Windows Vista. The adoption of this operating system by businesses has been very slow, and even that may be a generous description. We have no plans to upgrade our systems to Windows 8, and we continue to purchase new computers for our clients with Windows 7 preinstalled—as long as it's offered as an option. The one exception is for a touchscreen device, like a tablet. The tile interface is really made for touch and is similar to the iPad. Several of our colleagues have rolled out Windows 8, but only on tablets. It is not very practical to be reaching across your desk to touch your monitor.

## Microsoft Windows 10

Windows 10, the latest operating system from Microsoft, is the successor to Windows 8 and was released to the public on July 29, 2015. Windows 10 is being offered as a free upgrade for those computers running Windows 7 Service Pack 1 or Windows 8.1 until July 29, 2016. Otherwise, Windows 10 Pro is also offered in retail packaging priced at $199.

Microsoft introduced a universal application architecture across all Microsoft product families including computers, tablets, smartphones, and Xbox One, allowing for applications to be designed and run across all of the devices—similar to the iOS environment. One of the main features that was included was an updated Start Menu (combination of Windows 7 and 8), a new web browser named Microsoft Edge, and integrated support for fingerprint and face recognition logins. Microsoft's Edge browser is now the default browser in Windows 10 and has adopted the HTML5 specification, dropping much of the support for legacy Internet Explorer releases (meaning websites developed for IE6 or IE7 won't render in this new browser).

Also new to this operating system is the inability for users to be able to selectively install Windows updates. Microsoft now installs all Windows updates automatically. The release of this software has been positively received by the public, but one of the initial criticisms, and a valid one, involves privacy concerns. By default, the system transmits user data to Microsoft or its partners, a troubling setting. For now, it's not easy to restrict what Windows collects. The data can be restricted—it's easier if users don't use the Express Settings during setup, but rather select the "custom install" to turn off some of the data collecting options. As an alternative, you can try one of the free tools to change the settings in a more user-friendly interface (**bgr.com/2015/08/14/windows-10-spying-prevention-privacy-tools/**).

There is no doubt that Windows 10 looks promising. According to one recent survey, 73 percent of respondents polled stated that they planned to adopt Windows 10 within two years of its launch. This number is surprising, because neither Windows 7 nor Windows 8 had such high planned adoption rates. For now, until all of the inevitable bugs are worked out, we still purchase our new computer systems with Windows 7 preinstalled. Generally, this process of debugging can take upwards of six months to a year, so please check back with us throughout the coming year to see if our recommendations have changed.

## Mac OS X Version 10.8 (Mountain Lion) Operating System

Released to the public on July 25, 2012, Mac OS X 10.8 was the ninth major release of Apple's OS X operating system. Many of the features included in this version of the operating system were migrated from Apple's iOS software, including Notes, Reminders, and Messages. This version also includes the latest version of the Safari web browser, Safari 6.

Some of the additional features in Mountain Lion include the Game Center, Notification Center, AirPlay Mirroring, Dictation, and full Facebook and Twitter integration within the operating system.

While users can still download the Mountain Lion upgrade from the Mac App Store for $19.99, it makes more sense to upgrade to Yosemite, the latest operating system.

## Mac OS X Version 10.9 (Mavericks) Operating System

Released to the public in late 2013, Mavericks was the tenth major release of the OS X operating system. Some of the new features include integration with iBooks, a new Maps application (Google Maps competitor), a reworked Calendar application, an updated version of Safari, the introduction of an iCloud Keychain, improved notifications, Finder Tabs, and improved battery and performance-boosting technologies.

The cost to upgrade to this version is the best part—it's free. Users can download this update from the Mac App Store; however, it makes more sense to upgrade to Yosemite, the latest operating system.

## Mac OS X Version 10.10 (Yosemite) Operating System

Released to the public in October 2014, Yosemite is the newest (eleventh) major release of the OS X operating system. With Yosemite, Apple introduced a revision to the operating system's user interface, with all of the graphics inspired by iOS 7. While it still possesses the desktop appearance, the inclusion of new icons, light and color schemes, and even new default fonts, Apple has put a lot of effort into the upgrading of the look and feel of the software.

Some of the new features of this operating system include the Handoff functionality, which allows the operating system to integrate with iOS 8 devices over Bluetooth LE and Wi-Fi. The Notification center has been revamped and includes new features, such as a "Today" view, and the Spotlight feature is now a more prominent part of the operating system.

This operating system is installed on newly purchased Macs by default. If you're using a Mac that is running an older version of the Mac OS X operating system and your system meets the technical requirements to upgrade, we recommend that you do so for the added features and security improvements. And on top of that—there's no cost to do so. That's a no-brainer!

# CHAPTER THREE

## Monitors

NOW THAT YOU HAVE your brand new computer or shiny new laptop, you are ready for the task of picking out that brand new monitor—and you can have all the real estate your heart desires these days. The era of 14-inch monitors is long gone. You might even be able to reclaim some territory on your desk—and actually see some wood for a change—even if you choose to have two or three monitors. We have standardized on two monitors for clients and ourselves, although John has recently started asking for a full-sized third instead of the "partial size" laptop screen!

Choosing a monitor can be an overwhelming task because of all the options and bells and whistles to choose from. If you don't know what you're looking for, you can be inundated with all of the technical jargon that advertisers use to get you to purchase their monitors.

Previously, we had separate sections for all the different types of monitors, but with this edition, we've grouped them all into one—because there really is only one type of monitor you should be looking for. We will walk you through the process and explain how to weed through all of the technical jargon, providing you with a solid recommendation for purchasing a monitor.

First and foremost, the days of CRT monitors are over. Charities won't even take these monitors as donations anymore, so they can only be recycled at this point. The flat-panel monitor has taken over.

Flat-panel, wide-screen monitors have a flat viewing surface that provides a better viewing angle than CRT monitors did. They are also less bulky, taking up only a fraction of the desktop space and weighing next to nothing when compared to the weight of the ancient CRT dinosaurs. Flat-panel monitors have come down significantly in price over the past few years and are very affordable.

Flat-panel monitors, like computers, come in all different sizes, resolutions, and performance. The flat-panel monitor that we recommend is the Dell P2214H 22-inch wide-screen (16:9) LED monitor. This monitor offers an optimal resolution of 1920 × 1080 at 60 Hz, which will provide you so much desktop real estate that you won't know what to do with it all, especially if you follow our recommendation and get two of them. The higher resolution will enable you to view documents, images, and videos with stunning detail, vivid colors, and seamless motion. The display can be rotated and viewed horizontally or vertically, depending on your preference.

This monitor accepts video graphics array (VGA), DisplayPort (version 1.2a), and digital visual interface (DVI) inputs and offers a contrast ratio of 1000:1 and maximum viewing angle of 178 degrees. It also includes four built-in USB 2.0 ports (three downstream ports, one upstream port) for connecting your peripheral devices, and it only weighs about 7 pounds. If needed, this device can be mounted on a wall using a standard VESA wall mount. The Dell P2214H 22-inch wide-screen monitor can be purchased online from Dell's website for $229 and comes with a standard three-year hardware warranty. If bundled with the purchase of a new computer from Dell, you may be able to get a much better deal on the price.

If you need a larger viewing area, you may want to consider using dual wide-screen monitors. Of course, your computer must have dual-monitor support, which most of the newer computers have by default. Usually, you will find that purchasing dual monitors, or in some cases three monitors, will be cheaper than purchasing a single large one. And anecdotally, we have found that folks who move to dual monitors never want to go back. Certainly, none of the authors would accept anything less than dual monitors—and we are all beginning to covet a third, although we would really need bigger desks, if not a special built-in shelf. We can dream . . .

# CHAPTER FOUR

# Computer
# Peripherals

IF YOU THOUGHT PURCHASING the right computer and monitor was tough, wait until you realize how many options there are when it comes to selecting computer peripherals. Having the right computer peripherals can make your computing faster, more comfortable, and a better overall experience. Wireless devices have brought peripherals into a new dimension, getting rid of that Gordian knot mess of wires that we all used to struggle to untangle. Below, we provide recommendations for portable mice, wireless desktops, external storage devices, and speakers. As always, bear in mind that there is a universe of choices. These are our top picks.

## Portable Mouse

For portability, those users who travel with laptops and want a nifty little wireless travel mouse should consider the excellent Microsoft Wireless Mobile Mouse 4000. Using 2.4 GHz wireless technology, this mouse connects to your computer with a reliable connection range of up to 15 feet. The nano transceiver that you plug into the USB port of your computer has a slot inside the mouse to store it when on the go. This mouse uses Microsoft's BlueTrack technology to smoothly track the mouse movements on virtually any surface. This notebook mouse also includes the standard back button and scroll wheel, in an ergonomic design that we've all become accustomed to. If you are concerned about the current battery life, the mouse includes an indicator light that will glow red when the batteries need to be replaced—and it only requires a single AA battery, which is included. The battery should last ten months or more before needing replacement. Of course, you do need to look at the light periodically so that you don't end up with a dead mouse and have to scramble for a new battery. This mouse is compatible with both Windows and Mac computers, including the Windows 10 operating system, and can be purchased online from Microsoft's website for $34.95.

## Wireless Keyboard Desktops

With the introduction of wireless technology, wireless keyboard desktops have become extremely popular—so popular that it's almost impossible to find a USB keyboard and mouse. In fact, it's been so long since we purchased a stand-alone mouse or keyboard that we no longer provide recommendations for each of these individual devices. We recommend the purchase of a wireless keyboard desktop set instead. A wireless keyboard desktop is a keyboard and mouse desktop combination that connects to your computer using radio frequency (RF) technology. The keyboard and mouse are powered with standard or rechargeable batteries and transmit their signals to a desktop receiver that is connected to the computer. It requires very little setup to install, and it eliminates the need for cables, which have plagued computer users since the first PC came into existence.

Our recommendation when purchasing a wireless keyboard desktop is the Logitech Wireless Wave Combo MK550. This wireless keyboard desktop comes with a wave key design that provides superior comfort with full-size and full-travel keys designed for quiet operation. The slight regular curve of the keyboard features consistently sized keys, which lets you type with confidence and ease. The keyboard uses the standard QWERTY layout, so you don't have to relearn how to type, as you do with some of the other curved keyboards. The height of the keyboard is adjustable, with three options for leg height, allowing you to choose the position that's most comfortable for you. The keyboard uses 128-bit AES encryption to secure data as it's transmitted from the keyboard to the receiver, and both the keyboard and mouse use the 2.4 GHz wireless spectrum to connect to the receiver. Logitech claims that the keyboard can operate up to three years before the batteries need to be replaced, and if true, the batteries should last the expected lifetime of the keyboard. The package includes four AA batteries, with both the keyboard and mouse requiring two each.

Logitech's wireless laser mouse M510, which is part of the MK550 combination, should operate for up to two years before the batteries will need to be replaced. The laser mouse uses a small infrared laser instead of an LED, which increases the resolution and sensitivity of the mouse. The laser mouse keeps your hands pain-free with the integration of contoured sides and soft rubber grips. The Logitech Wireless Wave Combo includes a three-year limited hardware warranty. This wireless desktop system is compatible with Windows 7 or Windows 10. The Logitech Wireless Wave Combo MK550 can be purchased for around $79.99 from your local electronics retailer or online at **www.logitech.com**.

## External Storage Devices

External storage devices are pieces of hardware that connect to your computer using USB, FireWire, eSATA, or some other type of interface and are used to store electronic data. These devices come in all sizes, shapes, colors, and volumes of storage space. They have all but replaced the CD-ROM, DVD, and backup tapes as the leading means to store electronic data because of their portability, low cost, and vast amount of storage space. Be sure to consider some type of secure authentication or encryption for external storage, especially if confidential client information is backed up or stored on these devices. Most products now come with some sort of built-in hardware or software encryption that can be enabled at no additional cost. Just be sure to remember your passphrase, because if you forget it, there's no way to recover your data.

### External Hard Drives

External hard drives are great devices for storing media such as videos, pictures, music and for backing up the data from your internal hard drive. These devices are very easy to install and use. Most external hard drives are plug-and-play devices, which means you simply have to plug them in to your computer to use them—and nothing else! The drivers necessary for these devices to work are loaded automatically by the operating system. For the volume of information they can store, they are a very good, inexpensive backup solution. Also, lawyers who are otherwise technically challenged seem to do well with this form of backup, which can really be reduced to the push of a button or an automated method that so many lawyers seem to prefer—set it and forget it.

The Seagate Backup Plus Desktop Drive is the external hard drive that we recommend for all lawyers and users. The Backup Plus Desktop Drive comes with available capacities of 2 and 8 TB of storage space. These capacities allow you to select the amount of storage space that best meets your requirements and may provide enough storage capacity to contain backups from more than one computer system. The Backup Plus Desktop Drive comes with backup software that can be used to automatically back up your data to the device, and it is Windows 10 compatible. You can now even use the Seagate Mobile Backup App to easily back up photos and videos on the go directly from your mobile device to the Backup Plus Desktop Drive.

All of the available models should provide enough storage space to back up all of the data required by most lawyers. If you're looking to back up multiple computers and/or a server, then you probably will need to purchase one of the larger-sized drives—and make sure that you purchase more than one. We recommend that if you're using this external hard drive to back up your company data and files, then you should rotate drives on a weekly or more frequent basis—keeping one onsite and the other one offsite. This will allow your firm to recover its information in the event of a disaster such as a fire in the office. With the recent rise of ransomware infections, we recommend disconnecting the drive when it is not being used. That way if your computer gets infected with ransomware such as CryptoLocker, your data won't get encrypted and can be used to restore your information.

These devices connect to your computer through the USB 3.0 interface (backward-compatible with USB 2.0) and can be placed flat or on their side. The drive is whisper quiet and relatively small in size, so it can sit on your desk or on top of your computer without taking away valuable space. Compatible with both Windows and Mac computers, the drive includes an NTFS driver for Mac that will allow interoperability between systems without the need to reformat the drive. The Backup Plus Desktop Drive can be purchased online at **www.seagate.com** for between $99 and $249, depending on the storage capacity, and it comes with a two-year standard warranty.

### Flash Drives

USB flash drives (thumb drives) are small, portable storage devices that use flash memory to store electronic data. Currently, they are offered with storage volume sizes ranging from 4 GB to 1 TB. For the most part, USB flash drives with capacities of 4 GB and smaller have been discontinued—in fact, when shopping for flash drives at our local computer supply store, they have all but gotten rid of any USB flash drive less than 8 GB in size! USB flash drives offer many advantages over other portable storage devices, such as the floppy disk, CD-ROM, and DVD. In particular, they are smaller, are more durable, are faster, and can hold more data. Unfortunately, these devices also pose a great security risk for small businesses and law firms because their small size makes them absurdly easy to lose. This risk can be minimized, however, by purchasing the SanDisk Ultra USB 3.0 flash drive.

This model is available with 16, 32, 64, 128, or 256 GB of storage space for your files and comes standard with 128-bit AES hardware encryption to keep your data secure. Using the SanDisk SecureAccess software, a user can protect access to private files with password protection and encryption. The software creates a file vault (protected folder) on the USB drive, creating a secure storage location for the user to place and keep all sensitive and confidential data. This flash drive is also fast, featuring transfer speeds of up to 100 Mbps.

The SanDisk SecureAccess software is compatible with the Windows 10 and Mac OS X v.10.5+ operating systems, although Mac users will have to download the supporting software from the App Store.

The SanDisk Ultra USB flash drives can be purchased online at **www .sandisk.com** for between $35 and $130, depending on the storage capacity, and all come with a five-year limited warranty. Some of the other online retailers that SanDisk may refer you to purchase its products may have lower retail pricing—so check carefully.

For those users who require top-of-the-line security, look no further than the 4 GB Personal S250 Secure Drive from IronKey, which also comes in 2, 8, 16, and 32 GB versions. The D250 model does come in a 64 GB version, but we prefer the more robust S250 model. A comparison of the two models is provided in the following graphic from IronKey's website:

As outlined in Figure 4.1, the main difference between the two models is the speed with which data can be read or written to and from the device.

This USB device is designed for the needs of sensitive military, government, and enterprise networks and includes AES hardware encryption that has been validated to meet government Federal Information Processing Standard (FIPS) requirements, specifically FIPS 140-2 Level 3. The security features require no software or drivers to enforce, with all the security being handled by the device hardware, and the features are always on.

**Figure 4.1** IronKey Secure Drive Comparison

The device requires that a user authenticate with a password before encryption keys are enabled and data can be accessed. This device is even waterproof! As they tend to be inadvertently placed in washing machines while in the pocket of your pants, this is an excellent feature, though we've not yet put it to the test.

This device has a self-destruct mechanism (think *Mission: Impossible* without the smoke) that will wipe (i.e., permanently and irretrievably remove) the data contents if a user or thief tries to break into the IronKey and enters ten incorrect passwords. The Password Manager and Password Generator applications are also included. The Password Generator application will generate very secure passwords of whatever length and complexity you desire. The Password Manager securely stores your passwords on the IronKey along with the associated web address. Merely insert your

IronKey device in your computer and go to a website that requires a user ID and password. The IronKey will prompt you to save the credentials if it is the first time the IronKey has "seen" the website. If the logon credentials are already stored on the IronKey, a dialog box will be presented to confirm that the ID and password should be retrieved from the secure Password Manager application. Make sure you back up your password "vault" to the IronKey website in case your IronKey is lost or damaged. Unfortunately, the current version of the Identity Manager (password vault) does not work with the latest versions of Firefox or Internet Explorer. An update is being worked on, but was not available as we went to publication. You may want to consider using a different password manager since delivery of updates has been very slow over the last several years.

The password information is backed up to IronKey in a secure encrypted fashion. If you ever lose your IronKey device, just retrieve your password information from the IronKey website. The device even comes preloaded with a portable version of Firefox, which, when launched and used with the provided Secure Sessions Service, encrypts and keeps all of your Internet traffic private and secure. The IronKey Personal S250 Secure Drive can be purchased online from IronKey's website (**www.ironkey.com**) for from $93 to $510, depending on the storage capacity.

## Speakers and Headphones

Lawyers (and their staff) often tell us that the most important peripheral device they need for their computer is a pair of speakers. They like to be able to listen to music while they work and are adamant about fidelity. Without breaking the bank, reasonable quality desktop speakers can be purchased to provide the user with a clear, true sound. Logitech, a leading provider of speaker systems for computers, makes the LS21 speakers. They offer 2.1 stereo sound with a subwoofer, providing enhanced bass, and the speakers come in a slim, stylish profile. These speakers offer quality audio at a reasonable price. The speakers have a stereo headphone jack, an auxiliary input where you can connect your iPod or MP3 player and integrated controls located on a wired remote. They even include a cable-management system to help reduce the clutter of wires. The Logitech LS21 speakers can be purchased online for around $30 from **www.logitech.com**.

If you purchase one of the recommended Dell flat-panel monitors, consider adding a sound bar. The sound bar clips onto the bottom edge of the

Dell flat-panel and gets its power from the monitor itself. It provides a clean installation and doesn't take up any additional desk space. The model of the sound bar will vary depending on the Dell monitor that you wish to attach the speakers to, so be sure to check out Dell's website to ensure that you select the appropriate model.

Be careful of speaker "wars" in the office as people battle for the loudest music. Consider headphones to provide a quieter office environment.

If you use a laptop, a desktop computer system, or a smartphone that supports Bluetooth and wish to keep your music to yourself, a number of wireless headphone options are available. Jabra makes the Revo Wireless headphones, solidly built with a lightweight aluminum frame and shatterproof headband. The headphones are very comfortable with a padded headband and memory foam ear cups. The device includes a rechargeable battery that lasts up to twelve hours on a single charge, provides up to 240 hours of standby time, and weighs only 8.47 ounces. This device only takes three or fewer hours to fully charge. The wireless device supports Bluetooth 3.0, including Audio/Video Remote Control Profile (AVRCP), which allows you to control your music from this device when it's streaming from your phone. This headset can be purchased online or from your local electronics retailer starting at $199.

# CHAPTER FIVE

# *Printers*

EVEN IN THE ERA of the "paperless" office, most law firms still print a lot of documents on a daily basis, probably more than any other type of business. To say that the practice of law tends to be less than green is a massive understatement—at least most firms have implemented a recycling program. Nonetheless, it is certainly critical to have a good, reliable printer to ensure that your firm is printing quality documents in the shortest amount of time. Below, we discuss and recommend printers for stand-alone systems, network systems, and multifunctional printers/copiers.

## Stand-Alone Printers

The most basic type of printer is the stand-alone printer. This type of printer connects directly to a computer and is not placed on the network. It only has to be capable of handling a single user's print jobs. Even in environments where networked printers are used and recommended, there can be valid reasons to have stand-alone printers—perhaps so the bookkeeper can keep financial records from inadvertently being picked up by someone else. Senior partners may feel their information is so confidential that they want a printer in their office (though their staff often mutter that they are just too lazy to walk down the hall). Many makes and models of stand-alone printers are available to choose from, and each has different performance specifications, features, and available fonts.

The question about whether to use an ink-jet printer is dead. No more ink-jet. We highly recommend going with a laser printer. Ink-jet printers typically result in a higher cost of ownership over the long haul, with ink cartridges printing at a higher cost per page than the average laser printer. There are even studies that show a cost of $3,000–$5,000 per gallon for name-brand ink cartridges. Human blood is cheaper. Laser is better quality and more economical—case closed.

A stand-alone printer can be shared through enabling File and Print Sharing on your local computer, but we strongly counsel against this practice. It creates a host of security vulnerabilities that could compromise not only your system but also your entire network, and it causes a lot of management and configuration headaches for the IT administrator.

When discussing printers with our clients, we are frequently asked, "Should I purchase a color or a black-and-white laser printer?" You will pay a slight premium for a color laser printer, and in most instances, it is not worth the cost when purchasing a stand-alone printer. It is usually more cost-effective to purchase a color laser printer to be placed on the local computer network and shared so that more than one user can print to it.

The Hewlett-Packard (HP) LaserJet Pro M201dw black-and-white laser printer is the perfect solution for the stand-alone or network (up to five users) printer. The printer has a built-in Ethernet connection, along with USB and wireless support for network connectivity, and prints in duplex (two-sided) mode by default. This printer prints as many as 26 pages per minute, comes standard with a paper input capacity of 250 sheets, and has a recommended monthly volume of up to 2,000 pages but can support a monthly duty cycle of up to 15,000 pages if needed. The printer has a first-page-out speed of 8 seconds and supports all the common page types, such as letter, legal, executive, and envelopes. This printer comes standard with 128 MB of memory and can connect to your computer using the USB interface. It should be noted that the printer does come with a USB cable, which previous HP models we've recommend have not. For mobile users, this printer is compatible with Apple's AirPrint service, which allows users to print to the device from their iPad, iPhone, or iPod touch—a feature that is quickly becoming a necessity with the increasing number of iPads and iPhones being used in the workplace.

This black-and-white printer was designed for quick business printing and offers a cost-effective solution for personal printing. The printer is both Mac and Windows compatible, including Windows 8 and Windows 10. It also comes standard with a one-year limited warranty. The HP LaserJet Pro M201dw printer can be purchased online for around $199.99 (before discounts) from **www.hp.com**. At the time of writing, this printer was discounted to a cost of $149.99 on HP's webstore.

If you're looking for tips on how to reduce the frequency with which you have to purchase replacement laser cartridges, there are a few things you can do. First, look into software that automatically removes wasted pages from printing jobs, especially common when printing out content from websites using your Internet browser. This printer comes with software called HP Smart Web Printing that you can install on your local computer, which reduces the wasted pages and space when printing from websites.

Another great tip is to change the print quality to "Draft" if the document is just going to be discarded shortly after printing and not something official that you're going to submit to court. This alone can save you lots of toner.

## Networked Printers

Networked printers are used to provide a printing resource to multiple users. Networked printers are generally installed in a central location and then shared throughout the local network. The administration and security of these printers can be integrated into your network's security infrastructure, such as through Windows Active Directory for a Windows-based network, and networking a printer is much more secure than sharing it through the File and Print Sharing service. You should consider disabling the remote administration function (via a web browser) for the printer. Remote administration typically means that a specialized website is running on the printer. These web services are rarely secure and fairly easy to compromise. It is recommended to install the printer in a central location, which simplifies the management, administration, and security of these devices. Network printers can be shared with the various computers and users that make up your network with very little overhead and effort. Many types of networked printers are available, and depending on your need—low volume, high volume, color—your options will vary. A popular request from many law offices is to have multiple trays for the printer. The capability to have multiple paper types loaded is usually available in the mid-range to higher-end printer models.

### Low-Volume Network Printers

Low-volume network printers are designed for workgroups of users having a small to moderate print volume, as high as 5,000 pages per month. These printers are moderately priced and are primarily used to segment printing within offices based on user group or physical location. Network printers have more robust hardware than stand-alone printers to handle multiple jobs from different users at the same time.

The HP LaserJet Pro 400 Printer M401dw black-and-white network-based laser printer is great for a small law firm because it provides users with a highly reliable, cost-effective printer that is capable of handling the expected volume produced by an average small firm. The HP LaserJet Pro 400 Printer M401dw prints as many as 35 pages per minute and has a recommended monthly print volume of up to 3,000 pages. This model also has a monthly duty cycle of up to 50,000 pages. It comes standard with an input capacity of 300 sheets and 256 MB of memory, and it handles all paper sizes. This printer has a first-page-out speed of 8 seconds. As an added feature, the printer allows for automatic duplexing for printing double-sided documents. The printer has an embedded gigabit Ethernet network adapter to attach the printer to your local network and a built-in Wi-Fi 802.11 b/g/n adapter for wireless connectivity. This printer also supports Apple's AirPrint service, allowing users to print directly from their iPad, iPhone, or iPod Touch device. For additional security, this printer can prevent unauthorized access with management features including 802.1x authentication and password protection. This model does come with a USB cable.

The memory of this printer can be upgraded if desired, and the printer's drivers are compatible with both Mac and Windows-based systems, including Windows 8 and Windows 10. The printer comes with a standard one-year warranty and includes a CD-ROM with the drivers and software necessary to configure the device. The HP LaserJet Pro 400 Printer M401dw black-and-white laser printer can be purchased online for around $400 (before any discounts) from **www.hp.com**. At the time of writing, this printer was discounted to a cost of $299.99 on HP's webstore.

### High-Volume Network Printers

High-volume network printers are designed for businesses that need the capacity to print a large volume of pages on a monthly basis, and they are usually considered when your firm needs a printer that can produce more than 5,000 pages per month. These devices contain hardware that can handle the volume load and are built to print constantly.

The HP LaserJet Enterprise MFP M630f multifunction printer is ideal for firms that print large volumes of documents on a monthly basis. This printer has a recommended monthly printing volume of 5,000 to 28,000 pages and prints up to 60 pages per minute. The printer comes with a standard input capacity of 1,100 sheets, three paper trays, 1.5 GB of memory, and an embedded gigabit Ethernet network adapter to attach the printer to your local network. The network connectivity can be upgraded to support wireless networks, a must-have option for those firms that use a wireless infrastructure for their local network. It should be noted that the printer doesn't come with a USB or network cable, which will have to be purchased separately if you want to connect the printer directly to a computer. This printer also supports Apple's AirPrint service, allowing users to print directly from their iPad, iPhone, or iPod Touch device if you purchase the wireless option.

For future compatibility, this printer is IPv6-ready, although we have yet to see any clients running IPv6 only. For added security, this printer supports network authentication (LDAP, SMTP) that lets administrators control device access and secure print jobs through user authentication.

The printer comes with a one-year, next-business-day onsite warranty. It is compatible with both Mac and Windows-based networks, including Windows 8. A CD-ROM that contains both printer driver files and software necessary to manage and configure the device is included; in addition, the necessary software can be downloaded from HP's website. The HP LaserJet Enterprise MFP M630f multifunction printer can be purchased online for around $3,499.99 from one of HP's resellers, and it comes with a standard one-year warranty. At this cost, you may want to investigate using your digital copier as a printer, depending on your anticipated monthly print volume and cost per page.

## Color Network Printers

Color network printers are essential for any law firm or small business that wants to print a significant volume of documents in color. If the color printer is networked, multiple users can have access to the shared resource, which is far more cost-effective than giving everyone a color printer. HP is still the leading manufacturer of color printers in terms of value, selection, overall reliability, and performance. Its color LaserJet printers are reasonably priced and produce high-quality color documents.

For a small business or law firm, the HP Color LaserJet Enterprise CP4025dn printer is perfect for everyday color printing. This printer prints up to 35 pages per minute for both black and white and color and has a recommended monthly volume of 2,000 to 7,500 pages. Its first-page-out speed of less than 9.5 seconds means that the color print job starts almost as soon as it has been sent to the printer. The standard input capacity is 600 sheets, and the printer supports all paper sizes and can be upgraded with an envelope feeder.

The printer comes standard with 512 MB of memory and an embedded gigabit Ethernet network adapter that enables the printer to connect to your local network. If necessary, the memory can be upgraded to a maximum of 1 GB. The printer's drivers support both Mac and Windows-based systems, including Windows 8, and the printer can be networked for easy accessibility. Windows 8 and Windows 8.1 drivers are also available for download from the HP website. The printer comes with a one-year onsite limited warranty. So far, there is no indication of a driver for Windows 10, but there should be one available by the time this publication goes to print.

The HP Color LaserJet CP4025dn printer can be purchased online for around $1,300 (before discounts) from one of HP's resellers. It should be noted that the printer doesn't come with a USB or network cable, which will have to be purchased separately. That shouldn't be a problem since you will probably connect this printer to a network and not directly to a computer.

The largest operational cost for a color laser printer is the consumables. Color cartridges are not cheap, and color prints can be very expensive. One configuration point to make on all computers networked to your color printers: Change the default color setting to black. This will save on the printing and subsequent waste of color cartridges for unnecessary color copies. Users can always override the setting when a color printout is required.

Digital copier manufacturers are beginning to take over the task of color printing. Investigate using a color copier for your color print needs versus a stand-alone color printer, or if you have a large-scale color print job, you may want to consider the costs of outsourcing the project to your local copier store. You might be surprised at the amount of money you could save.

Typically, lawyers lease their copiers. As you work with your copier lessor, which normally provides your supplies, make sure you negotiate a low cost per color copy and only pay for the number of pages that you print. Don't pay for the consumables (e.g., toner cartridges) or maintenance, as these should be included as part of the per-page cost.

## Multifunctional Printers/Copiers

Don't you wish there was a single device that you could install on your local network that could do everything your office needs—printing, faxing, scanning, and copying? Happily for lawyers, such devices are becoming a standard fixture today. Multifunctional printers (MFPs) offer the capability to print, scan, copy, and fax from the same device, combining the functions of multiple devices into just one and eliminating the need to purchase them separately. In the long run, purchasing or leasing an MFP can save you the time and money often expended to upgrade and service multiple devices.

MFPs are very expensive and are generally leased because of the high cost to purchase. When looking at whether to buy or lease MFPs, keep some functionality questions in mind:

- Do you want the ability to print in color and black-and-white?
- Do you need duplex printing?
- Do you want to scan documents to your hard drive, user box, or e-mail?
- Do you want incoming faxes to be sent to e-mail as an image file or just printed?
- Do you want to be able to link the use of the MFP to the firm's billing program?
- What printing capacity do you need?
- Do you need any finishing capabilities (e.g., stapling, folding, three-hole punch, etc.)?
- Can users print to the device using their tablet or mobile phone?
- Do you need to implement any security on the unit, and if so, what?
- At the end of your lease, can the hard drive be securely wiped or erased?

The answers to these questions will give your vendors enough detail to provide you with the MFP device that best meets the firm's needs. Your digital copier may already have some of these features installed but not configured. Check with your vendor to see what capabilities your current copier has. In our office, we have a Konica Minolta Bizhub C224e MFP device. It allows us to print both in color and in black and white at speeds up to 22 pages per minute; to scan to hard drive, user box, e-mail, or FTP;

and to fax documents, although we do not use that feature. We are able to download our scanned documents from a built-in secure internal website as JPG, PDF, XPS, or TIFF files, as well as scan to an internal e-mail address—which we constantly use. This device has a 3,650 sheet max capacity with dual scanning speeds up to 160 pages per minute.

The Bizhub has advanced security features such as job erase, hard drive sanitizing and lock, user authentication and account tracking, IP address filtering, and secure print and scan encryption. Plus, there are options for biometric and HID proximity card authentication, should we ever need these advanced security features. Needless to say, the Bizhub provides us with a secure MFP option. We are huge fans—as this is our second model of one of these devices.

# CHAPTER SIX

## *Scanners*

ALMOST AS COMMON AS printers, scanners have become a necessary piece of equipment in most offices, as more paper documents are being scanned and stored electronically. The drive to a paperless office is still very much under way. The setup and operation of scanners has become simple to the point where even the most novice computer user can do it. Many of the tasks that once had to be performed manually are now automated, and in most cases, the hookup entails connecting a single wire.

Not often do we have to insert a CD to install software anymore, now that preloaded drivers are prevalent. Network scanners, however, are a little more complex to set up, and configuring them may require the assistance of your IT staff or your IT consultant.

Most desktop scanners communicate with the computer through the USB interface and come with a variety of software to assist in the scanning and file conversion process. Some models come standard with optical character recognition (OCR) software that will read the scanned image and produce a document that is editable and searchable. Fujitsu is a manufacturer of home and business-grade scanners that have been constantly rated the best models for businesses. In the following sections, we make recommendations for both low-volume and high-volume scanners from Fujitsu.

Some law firms may already have scanning capability in their digital copier. As we previously stated, check with your vendor to see if scanning with your copier is a more cost-effective solution than purchasing a stand-alone unit.

## Low-Volume Scanner

The Fujitsu ScanSnap iX500 Desktop Scanner is a great value for a solid automatic document feeder (ADF) scanner. This desktop scanner scans up to 25 color pages per minute, has an ADF capacity of 50 sheets, and can handle both legal- and letter-sized paper. The scanner has a maximum scanning resolution of 600 × 600 dpi and connects to the computer via the USB 3.0 interface, which is responsible for the increase in scanning speed. This scanner also comes with a built-in wireless adapter, allowing you to scan directly to a computer or mobile device without the need of a cable. This scanner is compatible with Microsoft Windows 7 and Windows 8 (32-bit and 64-bit) and Mac OSX v.10.6 or newer. This scanner comes with bundled software that includes Adobe Acrobat XI Standard Edition (Windows version of software), ScanSnap Organizer v5.0, ABBYY FineReader Express Edition, ABBYY FineReader for ScanSnap 5.0, Scan to Microsoft SharePoint v3.4, and CardMinder v5.0.

Adobe Acrobat XI Standard software allows you to automatically convert scanned data into searchable PDF files. Some of the automatic features of this device include auto paper-size detection, auto de-skew, and auto blank-page removal. The auto blank-page removal eliminates the need to edit scanned documents because the scanner has the ability to recognize the deleted blank pages. The ABBYY FineReader software allows you to scan documents directly to applications such as Microsoft Word, Excel, and PowerPoint.

A new feature of this scanner is the ability to scan to the cloud. With the free ScanSnap Connect app, users can link their ScanSnap to their iPad, iPhone, or Android mobile device for viewing on the go. Users also have the ability to scan to Evernote, Google Docs, Salesforce, SugarSync, and SharePoint. Again, as with all cloud services, please use caution and seek the advice of your IT staff when moving client data to the cloud to ensure that your documents are secure.

The scanner comes with a standard one-year limited warranty that can be upgraded to the Advanced Exchange Service program. The Fujitsu ScanSnap iX500 Desktop Scanner can be purchased online from Fujitsu's website (**www.fujitsu.com**) for $495 and comes with a one-year limited warranty. The inclusion of Acrobat Standard makes this a very worthwhile purchase.

## High-Volume Scanner

The Fujitsu fi-5530C2 is perfect for legal professionals who need a high-speed scanner on a modest budget and are serious about scanning documents. The built-in automatic document feeder (ADF) holds 100 pages and scans up to 50 pages per minute (100 images) in 200 dpi in color, monochrome, and grayscale. This scanner comes standard with 64 MB of memory and advanced software tools to allow administrators to centrally manage the scanner more productively and cost effectively.

Using the Fujitsu fi-5530C2 scanner, you can convert any document to Adobe PDF using Adobe Acrobat software, which is not included with the purchase of this scanner. Luckily, most lawyers already have access to this software. This scanner can handle a vigorous duty cycle of up to 4,000 documents per day and can handle documents ranging in size from a business card to a legal document without issue. The Ultra SCSI and USB 2.0 interface allows for simplified connectivity to your computer. The scanner is compatible with Microsoft Windows 7 and 8 computer systems. It should be noted that this scanner is not compatible with Macs. The Fujitsu fi-5530C2 scanner can be purchased online through one of Fujitsu's resellers for around $2,500 and comes with a three-month onsite limited warranty.

This amount of money is a lot for a solo or small firm operation to spend, especially on a scanner. We're sure that your digital copier could provide a less expensive solution for your scanning needs, especially if you have a newer unit that will provide a convenient ability to scan to e-mail—which none of these ScanSnap devices do. Consider that before you make a purchasing decision and you might be able to save yourself a lot of money.

# CHAPTER SEVEN

## Servers

ONE OF THE BIGGEST, most important and expensive decisions you will have to make regarding technology for your firm is which server to purchase. A server is the mother ship of the network, so the purchase decision should be made very carefully. It is absolutely not the time to be penny wise and pound foolish. The choice of a server is a business decision—make no mistake about that—and if made with great consideration and thought, it will allow your business to be more efficient from a technology perspective.

Like workstations and laptops, servers come in every make, model, and flavor. Unlike workstations, however, servers are expensive and can consume a large chunk of your technology budget rather quickly. Your firm will need to plan carefully when selecting a server—including discussing future needs and goals—so that the desirable hardware and software components can be identified. Be careful when planning, because you don't want to have to buy a new server every other year. The average life span of a server is four to five years—so start planning (and budgeting) well in advance!

### Solo—File and Printer Sharing

The most simple and basic reason for getting a server is for file and printer sharing. Centralizing electronic file storage and administration and installation of printers will save you time, money, and headaches when it comes to maintaining and managing your network. Some servers are designed specifically for the purpose of sharing files, documents, and printers. These servers come with the basic hardware and software and are relatively inexpensive when compared to the mid-range to higher-end servers.

The Dell PowerEdge T320 server was designed for the small business to provide the most basic file-and printer-sharing capabilities. A listing of the server's hardware and software components, along with some technical specifications, is provided below.

### File and Printer Sharing Server

| Hardware Component | Recommendation |
|---|---|
| *Model:* | Dell PowerEdge T320 |
| *Chassis:* | Tower |
| *Operating System:* | Windows Server 2012 R2, Standard Edition |
| *Processors:* | Intel Xeon E5-2430L, 2.00 GHz, 15 MB Cache |
| *Memory:* | 16 GB RDIMM, 1600 MT/s, Low Volt, Dual Rank |
| *Primary Controller Card:* | PERC H310 Integrated RAID Controller |
| *Hard Drive Configuration:* | RAID-5 |
| *Hard Drives:* | Three 1 TB 7.2K RPM Near-Line SAS 6 Gbps Hard Drives |
| *Network Adapter:* | Onboard Broadcom 5720 Dual Port 1 GB LOM |
| *Warranty:* | 3-Year ProSupport and Next Business Day Onsite Service |
| *Other:* | DVD+/-RW Drive |

This Dell PowerEdge T320 was customized through Dell's website (**www.dell.com**) and contains an Intel Xeon 2.00 GHz processor with 16 GB of RAM. This server comes with the Windows Server 2012 R2 Standard Edition operating system. CALs (client access licenses) are needed for each device or user that accesses the server. The three SAS (serial-attached SCSI) 1 TB hard drives are configured in a RAID-5 (redundant array of independent disks) hard drive configuration for increased performance and fault tolerance. In a RAID-5 hard drive configuration, if one of the hard drives were to fail, the server would continue to operate until the failed hard drive could be replaced. In most other hard drive configurations, if a server's hard drive were to fail, the server would be inoperable until the disk was repaired or replaced. The RAID-5 configuration offers both fault tolerance with the parity hard drive and better performance than most other RAID or mirrored disk configurations. RAID-5 hard drive configurations are strongly recommended for all law firm servers.

In total, this server has about 2 TB of hard drive space available for the storage of electronic data, programs, and other applications. You used to be able to save a little bit of money by reducing the number of hard drives purchased and setting up a RAID-1 hard drive configuration, but since hard drives have come so far down in price, we no longer recommend this as an option. Also, RAID-5 is a more fault tolerant and flexible configuration.

The onboard dual gigabit network adapters will allow clients to connect to the server at gigabit speeds, assuming the rest of your network components (switches, cabling) are gigabit as well.

One of the most important features to consider when purchasing a server is the warranty. In most cases, you will not need both the hardware and software support. At a minimum, you must include a hardware warranty that will cover the hardware and labor cost to replace any of the components that may fail during the server's life cycle. This Dell PowerEdge server comes with a three-year, next-business-day onsite parts and labor warranty at an included cost of about $400 when bundled with the server hardware. Having a hardware warranty for your server is critical to protecting your equipment, data, and business. This is no time to be miserly. This Dell PowerEdge T320 server was quoted on Dell's website for approximately $3,200 at the time of this writing.

## Small Firm—File and Printer Sharing/Hosting Services

When purchasing a server for your network, you must decide what function the server will have in your day-to-day business operations. In addition to file and printer sharing, it's common for small firms to host their company's e-mail. Although you can also host a website, we recommend that you outsource that to a website hosting provider because of potential security, administration, and resource issues. The added hosting services (e-mail and/or web) will require a server with upgraded hardware to be able to provide the necessary resources for the services to operate reliably.

Previously, our server recommendations included those running Microsoft Small Business Server 2011, which, depending on the edition/add-on (Standard or Premium), included Microsoft Exchange Server and Microsoft SQL Server. As of July 1, 2013, in response to small business market trends and behavior, such as moving in the direction of cloud computing for applications and e-mail, Dell no longer offers this operating system as an option, and it has since been discontinued. The Microsoft Exchange Server software will have to be purchased separately for those firms that wish to host their own e-mail. An alternative is to order the hardware without an operating system and obtain the Microsoft Small Business Server 2011 software from another source.

The Dell PowerEdge T630 was designed for small firms or businesses that are looking for a cost-effective solution to hosting their own e-mail or website. The server's hardware and software components, along with some technical specifications, are provided.

### File and Printer Sharing/Hosting Services

| Hardware Component | Recommendation |
|---|---|
| Model: | Dell PowerEdge T630 |
| Chassis: | Tower |
| Operating System: | Windows Server 2012 R2, Standard Edition |
| Processors: | Dual Intel Xeon E5-2640 v3 2.6 GHz, 20 M Cache, 8.0GT/s QPI |
| Memory: | 32 GB RDIMM, 2133 MT/s, Dual Rank |
| Primary Controller Card: | PERC H730 RAID Controller |
| Hard Drive Configuration: | RAID-5 |
| Hard Drives: | Three 2 TB 7.2K RPM Near-Line SAS 6 Gbps 3.5-Inch Hard Drives |
| Network Adapter: | Onboard Intel i350-AM2 Dual Port 1 GB LOM |
| Warranty: | 3-Year ProSupport and Mission Critical 4HR 7x24 Onsite |
| Other: | Redundant Power Supply, DVD+/-RW Drive |

The Dell PowerEdge T630 listed here was customized through Dell's website. It contains Dual Intel Xeon 2.6 GHz processors with 32 GB of memory. The server specified above was customized in a tower chassis; however, the same model is available in a rack mount chassis at no additional cost. The rack mount chassis is for those firms and small businesses that maintain their servers and networking equipment in a rack. The processors will supply more than enough horsepower to configure the server as an e-mail or web server, and the 32 GB of memory will allow these services to run smoothly and will prevent the server from lagging or becoming bogged down.

The server comes with Windows Server 2012 R2 Standard Edition preinstalled. CALS will need to be purchased for each device and/or user that wishes to connect to the server. Dell offers a five-pack of device or user CALS bundled with the server purchase for a price of $136.86.

The three 2 TB SAS hard drives are configured in a RAID-5 hard drive configuration and provide about 4 TB of storage space for your firm's applications and data. Again, this PowerEdge server comes with the three-year Pro-Support 4HR 7x24 onsite hardware warranty, which provides three years of four-hour, same-day parts and labor warranty. The Dell PowerEdge T620 server was quoted on Dell's website for approximately $7,365 at the time of this writing.

Don't forget to consider backup software and any additional applications (e.g., antivirus, antispyware, antispam, etc.) when configuring the server, because you might get a better discount from the vendor if they are bundled and purchased with the server hardware.

## Small Firm—Database/Applications Server

Your firm's software requirements, current and future, will play a big role in determining what hardware and software components your server will need to adequately support your firm in the coming years. So far, we have discussed the hardware and software specifications for a server used primarily for file and printer sharing and one capable of handling basic hosting services, such as e-mail and a website. When planning to use a server to host a database application, case management software, or e-discovery software, you must look at the minimum requirements for each piece of software and then go above and beyond the specifications that vendors provide. What vendors list should be regarded cautiously as a bare minimum. To run well and reliably, the software almost always requires more horsepower.

The recommended Dell PowerEdge T630 server is capable of handling most database and software applications as long as it's configured with advanced hardware to handle the powerful and robust database applications. The server's hardware and software components are provided below:

### Database/Applications Server

| Hardware Component | Recommendation |
| --- | --- |
| *Model:* | Dell PowerEdge T630 |
| *Chassis:* | Tower |
| *Operating System:* | Windows Server 2012 R2, Standard Edition |
| *Processors:* | Dual Intel Xeon E5-2690 v3 2.6 GHz, 30 M Cache, 9.6GT/s QPI, Turbo |
| *Memory:* | 128 GB RDIMM, 2133 MT/s, Dual Rank |
| *Primary Controller Card:* | PERC H730 RAID Controller |
| *Hard Drive Configuration:* | RAID-5 |
| *Hard Drives:* | Three 2 TB 7.2K RPM Near-Line SAS 6 Gbps 3.5-Inch Hard Drives |
| *Network Adapter:* | Onboard Intel i350-AM2 Dual Port 1 GB LOM |
| *Warranty:* | 3-Year ProSupport and Mission Critical 4Hr 7x24 Onsite |
| *Other:* | Dual, Hot-plug, Redundant Power Supply 1100W, DVD+/-RW Drive |

The PowerEdge T630 server was customized through Dell's website and contains Dual Intel Xeon E5-2690 v3 2.6 GHz processors and 128 GB of memory. The processor is faster than the processor included with the server discussed in the previous section.

This server comes with the Windows Server 2012 R2 Standard Edition operating system with Hyper-V capability for virtualized environments.

The three 2 TB hard drives are configured in a RAID-5 hard disk configuration and provide about 4 TB of storage space for applications and data. If more storage space is needed, this upgrade can be made when the server is configured to meet your needs, especially if you plan to use virtualization (explained in the following section).

The redundant power supply allows the server to stay powered on in the event that one of the power supplies fails. The server comes with dual embedded Broadcom Ethernet adapters, providing connectivity for up to two networks. The PowerEdge server comes with a three-year ProSupport Mission Critical 4HR 7x24 onsite hardware warranty, which provides three years of a four-hour, same-day parts and labor warranty. The Dell PowerEdge T620 server was quoted on Dell's website for approximately $11,283 at the time of this writing. You can save a little money if you want the next day warranty instead of the four-hour response warranty.

## Virtual Servers

The large push within the IT industry continues to be toward virtualization bundled with cloud services. Microsoft continues to sell more licenses for virtual machines than it does for physical hardware. This is one trend that isn't going to reverse.

Simply put, virtualization means that a single piece of hardware contains and hosts multiple server or desktop images, otherwise known as machines. Virtualization enables the consolidation of data and applications onto a single physical hardware server. The reduction in hardware saves energy, management, and administration effort and reduces overall hardware and software costs, along with rack space, especially if your firm needs multiple servers.

Virtualization is used to separate hosting services and applications, creating independent machines, which allows for one virtual server to be down for maintenance without affecting the others. For example, if

Windows Updates were downloaded onto a virtual server hosting file and print sharing services, this virtual server could be rebooted and have the updates applied without having to bring down or affect the entire host system, keeping other virtual servers online and available to users. It also means that you can quickly "spool up" a virtual machine for testing new applications or services without investing in additional hardware. Virtual servers are also very flexible and can be modified on the fly. Resources (e.g., RAM, disk space, processing power, etc.) can be modified while the virtual machine is running. Running short on disk space? No problem. Just go to the management console and add a few hundred gigabytes to the virtual machine's dynamic disk.

Previously, virtualization was not implemented due to the costs, expertise, and the large budget required. It was not typically found in a small firm environment; however, this is no longer true. We are recommending that small firms consider virtualization technologies when making server hardware and software purchasing decisions, especially in scenarios where the client is hosting services such as e-mail internally.

Is server virtualization the best choice for your network environment? Probably, but you will need to answer a number of questions before making this determination.

First, what services and applications are running on your network? If your network is running Microsoft Exchange Server, SQL Server, and a case management application, most likely you will need multiple servers to host all of these services and software. Most case management applications now require a separate server to run on. By using virtualization, you can avoid purchase of another physical hardware server by installing the case management software on its own virtual server, as long as your virtual server meets, if not exceeds, the host specifications required by the vendor of the software.

When purchasing a host system (the server hosting the virtual servers), the most critical hardware options to consider are the amount of memory, number and type of processors, and amount of storage space. For each virtual server, 8 GB or more of memory must be allocated for the virtual server to operate. A larger amount of memory will be needed if the virtual server is hosting a database or other memory-hungry service. This does not account for the amount of memory that the host system will require. For example, if you have a host server running three virtual servers, you will need a minimum of 32 GB or more of memory installed in the host server to supply the host and all of the virtual servers with enough memory resources to operate. To accommodate the necessary hardware, the host system must be running at least the Windows Server 2012 Standard Edition operating system.

When running virtual servers, you will need to ensure that the host system has enough processing capability to handle the processing load. At a minimum, you will want the system to contain Intel Xeon processors with a processing speed of 2.53 to 3.6 GHz. The optimum solution for stand-alone servers is to use Intel Xeon processors with the same speed range, and in virtualization solutions, you will need to have multiple processors with multiple cores. The Xeon processors that are in the servers recommended previously were designed by Intel for virtualization solutions, providing increased virtualization security, reduced storage and network latencies, and acceleration of fundamental virtualization processes throughout the system. The multicore processors combine two or more cores onto a single integrated circuit, providing multiprocessing capabilities to the chip. Multiprocessing allows the execution of multiple concurrent software processes in a system, which is vital in a virtualization solution.

The amount of storage space required to run all of the virtual servers and the host system will vary from solution to solution. When determining the amount of storage space the systems will require, you need to consider the services and applications that will be hosted. For example, a virtual server hosting Microsoft Exchange Server will require enough disk space to account for the current size and future growth of the Exchange Database stores along with the program files and operating system. If more space is needed at a later time, the amount of storage space allocated to each virtual server can be independently configured and modified in real time. For ease of configuration and setup, bearing the cost of additional hard drive storage up front makes more sense than waiting to add more hard drives later. Plus, it's always recommended that the host system and virtual servers have available more than enough hard drive space, so problems with low disk space can be avoided. We have clients who have terabytes of disk space available just for their File and Printer Sharing virtual server. As an alternative to purchasing host-based storage, you may want to look into a Storage Area Network (SAN) device that would provide locally attached storage over a dedicated network, usually over Fibre Channel or iSCSI.

Microsoft offers free server virtualization solutions for Windows Server 2008 and Server 2012. For host systems running Windows Server 2008 or

2012, Microsoft has included the Hyper-V virtualization system with the base installation of the operating system, and this role is installed through the Server Roles interface. Hyper-V enables the consolidation of multiple server roles as separate virtual servers running on a single host system, allowing for different operating systems such as Linux, Windows, and others to run in parallel. For more information regarding Microsoft's virtualization solutions, you can visit Microsoft's website at **http://www. microsoft.com/en-us/server-cloud/solutions/virtualization.aspx**.

Hyper-V was designed with enhanced security features in mind, providing an architecture that is less vulnerable to attack. This software includes a set of management and administration tools that can be used to manage the host and virtual systems' hardware from the same interface. It even allows administrators to migrate live systems from server to server. Windows Server 2012 has an updated version of Microsoft's Hyper-V, which includes such new features as network virtualization, multitenancy, storage resource pools, and cloud backup. The new version of Hyper-V also increases the amount of memory and storage and the number of virtual processors that each machine can be allocated. For more information regarding Microsoft's Hyper-V 2012 R2, you can visit Microsoft's TechNet website at **https://technet.microsoft.com/en-us/library/hh833684.aspx**.

Depending on the operating system of the host system, a few Microsoft-based software options are available for server virtualization, and they are fully supported. We have observed that the free Hyper-V implementations may have some issues sharing peripheral devices across the virtual machines. As an example, you may not be able to share the USB ports of the hardware with a virtual machine without some kind of workaround, which means that you can't copy files from a USB flash drive from the host system to the virtual system.

Software licensing will also play a role in determining your firm's ability to move to a virtualization environment. To say the licensing is easy to figure out when it comes to virtualization would be a flat-out lie. Microsoft has muddied the waters when it comes to virtualization licensing, because it varies depending on the type of server operating system and the number of processors. Some operating system editions allow you to use the license key on the host and on up to two virtual machines. If you're running a host with Windows Server 2012 Datacenter Edition, you get a feature called Automated Virtual Machine Activation. With this feature, any virtual machine on this host running Windows Server 2012 R2 Datacenter/Standard/Essentials will automatically activate.

There are other alternatives to Microsoft's virtualization solutions, such as VMware's vSphere Hypervisor (ESXi). If you are investigating alternative virtualization solutions, you will need to work with your IT vendor to see what other options might be available. We currently recommend and use the VMware solution instead of Microsoft's Hyper-V solution. VMware has been in the virtualization game a lot longer than Microsoft, and you can share those USB ports with the virtual machines. VMware Tools also offers some other useful and time-saving administration capabilities. The stability of Hyper-V continues to be a concern among several of our clients, although it has improved with the 2012 R2 version of Hyper-V.

What we do know is this: The cost to purchase the hardware and software necessary to implement a virtualization environment for your network will be significantly less than the cost of purchasing multiple physical servers to fill the necessary roles your applications and services require.

## Peer-to-Peer

Many small firms use the built-in peer-to-peer network capabilities of their computer systems as an alternative to purchasing a server. A peer-to-peer network, in its simplest form, is two or more computers that are able to communicate with one another to share files and folders, printers, and applications without using a server to accomplish these tasks. Peer-to-peer networks are commonly used in solo or small firm offices with only two or three computers. The computers, located on the same local network and belonging to the same Workgroup (Microsoft's name for a peer-to-peer network), can access shared resources in the Workgroups to which they are joined. Unless a computer is joined to a domain, it belongs to a Workgroup. By default, on Windows XP computers, the Workgroup name is MSHOME, and in older versions of Windows, the default Workgroup is WORKGROUP. Just to complicate matters, Microsoft has changed the default Workgroup name in Windows 7, 8, and 10 back to the original WORKGROUP.

Peer-to-peer networks may sound like a good solution for small firms that have only a few computers, but this type of network has some significant disadvantages compared to purchasing a server. First, when networking computers together, you are going to experience a slowdown and incon-sistency in your system's performance. Workstations are not capable of handling concurrent access to their files by other computers. When this occurs, the system's resources are severely taxed, causing disruption to the users. Think of this as a tug-of-war for data. Your computer is trying to use data at the same time that someone else needs it. Because of the inconsistency and unreliability of the peer-to-peer network, corruption of shared files, such as case management and billing systems, occurs frequently. Since computers in a peer-to-peer network can be running different operating systems, software incompatibilities between the systems can occur. Management of user accounts, along with implementing the proper security controls to protect sensitive and confidential data, becomes a nightmare—and even more difficult should a breach occur that requires investigation.

The decentralization of critical firm data can lead to unnecessarily complex data backup scenarios, often resulting in important data not being backed up or protected. On top of all the issues above, the need to manage and administer multiple copies of the same software, such as antivirus protection on each individual computer, becomes needlessly tiresome. Software that is centrally managed is much more cost-effective to purchase and maintain, as opposed to managing each computer's software suites independently. Just figure in the added administration costs that your firm will pay its IT provider; this will more than cover the cost of a server—and then some!

There is an inaccurate perception that peer-to-peer networks save money and cost less than client/server networks. However, in the end, this is never the case. Yes, purchasing a server—even a lower-end unit—might seem expensive at first, but the costs of managing and maintaining a peer-to-peer network will always be higher than the costs you would have incurred if you had implemented a server/client network in the first place. The software licensing costs for peer-to-peer networks can be higher because you are purchasing single licenses. Software that is administered and maintained on independent computers will take more time than if it were centrally managed from a server. Technical support and consulting costs will be much higher in a peer-to-peer environment, a fact that is usually not considered when making the initial decision to purchase and use a peer-to-peer network. For most small network environments, even those involving as few as two computers, purchasing a server to centralize applications and data can save time and money—and the number of headaches you will have to endure—in the long run.

# CHAPTER EIGHT

# Server Operating Systems

CHOOSING THE HARDWARE COMPONENTS is just one step in selecting the right server for your business. The next step is determining what operating system and software will best meet the current and future needs of the firm. There are many variations of server operating systems currently available for both Windows and Mac servers, and they are described in detail below.

## Microsoft Windows Server 2003—Any Edition

Any server running the Microsoft Windows 2003 Server operating system should be replaced or upgraded immediately. As of July 14, 2015, Microsoft discontinued support for this version. If you are a lawyer, this means you cannot ethically use this operating system because it is no longer receiving security updates and you cannot reasonably protect your firm's confidential data!

## Microsoft Windows Server 2008 R2

Microsoft Windows Server 2008 R2 is the successor to Windows Server 2003. It was officially launched in late February 2008 and built from the same code base as Windows Vista, however, without all the problems that Vista had. Microsoft Windows Server 2008 and 2008 R2 are both now in extended support from Microsoft, which ends on January 14, 2020. Keep this in mind as you discuss and plan your firm's future technology decisions.

This operating system includes a lot of new features and enhancements, such as native support for IPv6, new security features such as BitLocker, and an improved Windows Firewall with a more secure default configuration. Also, the manner in which this operating system handles processors and memory is different from previous versions. Processors and memory are now treated as plug-and-play devices, meaning they are "hot-swappable." They can now be removed and replaced without shutting down the server, although sticking your hands into a hot, running server is probably not a very bright idea.

Windows Server 2008 includes expanded Active Directory functionality and a major upgrade to Terminal Services. Terminal Services now supports Remote Desktop Protocol 8.0, which provides the ability to share a single application over a Remote Desktop connection rather than the entire desktop, as was the case in previous versions. It also provides additional support for multiple monitors and stronger encryption algorithms for keeping data traffic secure.

In previous versions of the Windows operating system, if corruption or errors were found on a new technology file system (NTFS) volume, the volume would have to be dismounted and taken offline for the errors to be corrected. Windows Server 2008 supports a self-healing NTFS format that can detect and fix errors while online without having to bring down the entire system. Microsoft Windows Server 2008 is offered in both 32- and 64-bit versions.

Windows Server 2008, like previous versions, is offered in the following editions:

- Standard Edition
- Enterprise Edition
- Datacenter Edition
- HPC Server
- Web Server
- Storage Server
- Small Business Server
- Essential Business Server

Most of the editions listed above would not be considered when purchasing a server solution for a small business or law firm and will not be discussed in more detail in this book. However, the Standard, Enterprise, and Small Business Server editions are described below.

In February 2011, Microsoft released Service Pack 1 for Windows Server 2008 R2, which introduced two new features and addressed a number of security issues in this version of the operating system. The two new features, RemoteFX and Dynamic Memory, add support for 3-D graphics within a Hyper-V-based virtual machine, as well as dynamic memory allocation based on the resources the virtual machine requires at any given time. It is recommended that if you're running Windows Server 2008, you download and install the latest Service Pack from Windows Updates as soon as possible.

## Microsoft Windows Small Business Server 2008 Standard and Premium Editions

Windows Small Business Server (SBS) 2008 is based on Windows Server 2008 and includes Microsoft Exchange Server 2007 Standard Edition, Windows SharePoint Services 3.0, and trial subscriptions for Microsoft's new security products, such as Forefront Security for Exchange.

The SBS 2008 operating system was officially launched on November 12, 2008. Like previous editions of SBS, the 2008 version is offered in both Standard and Premium editions. The Standard Edition is regarded as a single server solution for small businesses, your all-in-one operating system.

In one server, you get file and printer sharing, e-mail, web hosting, and the ability to set up a domain for up to seventy-five users and/or devices. The Premium Edition contains all of the features and software the Standard Edition has, plus a license for the Microsoft SQL Server 2008 Standard Edition. The Premium Edition requires two separate servers, one for Windows Server 2008 with Exchange and the other solely for SQL Server. This requirement is going to be a problem for small firms on a tight budget, but it may be more affordable if used in a virtualized environment.

Windows SBS 2008 is offered only in a 64-bit version due to the requirements of Microsoft Exchange Server 2007, whose production version is 64-bit. This distinction is important when considering your hardware purchase. Make sure you have 64-bit hardware if you are considering using these new server operating systems.

On a more positive note, Microsoft has finally changed the way CALs are purchased for SBS. In earlier editions, CALs could be purchased only in groups of five, ten, or twenty licenses, but not anymore. CALs for SBS 2008 can now be purchased individually.

Dell has discontinued the option of configuring servers with the Microsoft Windows Small Business Server option, so we recommend using the Windows Server 2012 Standard Edition option at this time or purchasing the operating system from another supplier, but understand that it will go out of support much sooner than the more recent versions.

## Windows Server 2008 Standard Edition

The Windows Server 2008 Standard Edition was designed to increase the reliability of your server infrastructure while simultaneously saving time and reducing costs when it comes to server maintenance.

Standard Edition comes with enhanced security features to help protect your data and network and includes powerful tools that give you greater network control. Windows Server 2008 Standard Edition comes with IIS 7.5, a powerful web hosting and services platform. The operating system also includes Windows Server Hyper-V—virtualization software designed to support machine virtualization—and an upgraded version of Terminal Services that supports Remote Desktop Protocol 8.0.

In terms of security, Standard Edition includes tools to improve auditing and secure startup, and it enables disk encryption using BitLocker. Standard Edition supports up to 32 GB of memory, 4 multicore processors, and up to 250 concurrent Terminal Service connections.

## Windows Server 2008 Enterprise Edition

Microsoft Windows Server 2008 Enterprise Edition, like its predecessor, is an operating system that is aimed at medium to large-sized businesses looking for a server capable of handling enterprise-level services.

Microsoft Server 2008 Enterprise Edition provides mission-critical applications through such features as failover clustering, fault-tolerant memory synchronization, and cross-file replication. This edition also features the latest advancements in security and is extremely scalable to support mission-critical applications.

This operating system is recommended for servers that will be hosting database applications, case management applications, or other software that requires more processing power and memory addressing than the Standard and SBS operating systems can support.

## Microsoft Small Business Server 2011 Standard and Essentials

Microsoft Small Business Server 2011 (SBS 2011) is the successor to SBS 2008 and is offered in two versions: Standard and Essentials. A separate SBS Premium add-on is available for small firms that require SQL Server.

The Standard Edition is designed for small businesses and supports up to seventy-five users and/or devices. Like the previous SBS versions, this edition provides a single server solution for small businesses that includes e-mail, remote access, and file and printer sharing. This edition includes both Microsoft Exchange Server 2010 and SharePoint Foundation Server 2010.

The Essentials Edition is designed for small businesses and supports up to twenty-five users and/or devices. This edition is integrated with Microsoft's cloud services and doesn't require the end user to purchase any CALs. This edition, unlike the Standard Edition, does not include Microsoft Exchange Server or SharePoint Foundation Server 2010.

For those small businesses that need to deploy additional servers on their network to run SQL Server 2008 R2 Standard, the Premium Add-on license is the component that they'll need to purchase. Additional server and SQL CALs are required with this component and will add cost to the purchase, depending on the number of users and computers that need to access this system.

Dell has discontinued the option of configuring servers with the Microsoft Windows Small Business Server option, so we recommend using the Windows Server 2012 Standard Edition option at this time or purchasing the operating system from another supplier.

## Microsoft Windows Server 2012

In September 2012, Microsoft released this version of its operating system software to coincide with the release of Windows 8. Server 2012 is offered in four editions, only three of which (Essentials, Standard, and Datacenter) would be considered when purchasing a server for a small business.

Server 2012 includes a number of new and enhanced features that IT administrators will love, including:

- A newly redesigned user interface with a focus on easing server management tasks, including the administration of multiple servers from within the same window
- An updated version of Windows PowerShell with over 2,300 commands, compared to about 200 in Windows Server 2008
- A new version of Windows Task Manager
- IP Address Management (IPAM) role for discovering, monitoring, auditing, and managing IP address space used on the local network
- An updated version of Windows Active Directory, including simplified upgrading of the Domain Functional Level to Server 2012, a new graphical user interface (GUI), the ability to set multiple password policies within the same domain, and the ability to safely clone virtualized domain controllers
- An updated version of Hyper-V, which includes such new features as network virtualization, multitenancy, storage resource pools, cloud backup, support for an increased number of virtual processors, greater storage capacity, and more memory
- A new version of Internet Information Services (IIS) (version 8.0) used to host websites
- A new file system, Resilient File System (ReFS), that is intended for file servers and improves the features of NTFS

## Microsoft Server 2012 R2

Windows Server 2012 R2 is the latest version of Windows Server, released in October 2013—it should be the operating system of choice when configuring a new server. This edition, like Windows Server 2012, was released in four editions: Foundation, Essentials, Standard, and Datacenter.

Some of the changes from Windows Server 2012 that were introduced in Windows Server 2012 R2 include:

- Automated tiering of frequently accessed files on the fastest physical media
- De-duplication for Virtual Hard Drives
- New version of Windows PowerShell (v4)

+ Integrated Office 365 support
+ Return of the Windows Start Button
+ UEFI-based virtual machines
+ Boot from SCSI device option
+ Faster VM deployment (50 percent increase in speed reported)

We are currently running this operating system on some of our servers and include this operating system when configuring new servers for our clients. It has our stamp of approval at this time.

## X64 Operating Systems

Until about eight years ago, 32-bit processors dominated the commercial marketplace, and 64-bit processors were found only in supercomputers or very high-end and expensive servers. Now, however, 64-bit processors are standard rather than an option when configuring a server or a desktop computer prior to purchase. The 64-bit operating systems have been developed to run on these processors and offer many advantages over their 32-bit counterparts. In fact, the newer versions of Microsoft's server operating systems are offered only in 64-bit versions.

First, these systems process more data per clock cycle, and second, they offer direct access to more virtual and physical memory than 32-bit systems. These advantages provide for more scalable, higher-performing computing solutions, which is a requirement when running a virtualized environment. There are far fewer device driver issues with X64 operating systems now than when 64-bit systems first appeared on the market; however, it's always important to make sure everything is compatible before migrating from a 32-bit environment to a 64-bit environment.

The current versions of Windows desktop-based operating systems and server-based operating systems are all offered in 64-bit versions, and with most editions, that is the only option.

## Mac OS X Server 10.7 (Lion)

Apple released Mac OS X Server 10.7, code-named Lion, in 2011. This version of Mac OS X Server includes an application called the Server app, which is a simplified configuration process for setting up and administering the most critical functions of the server, including file sharing, e-mail, contacts, backups, and remote access, to name a few. The software also includes Apple's equivalent of Microsoft's Active Directory and a new feature that provides wireless file sharing for iPad devices that allows access to documents on the server.

Lion Server also includes updated versions of the iCal Server 3, Wiki Server 3, Mail Server 3, and Xsan software. This software requires a base purchase of OS X Lion from the Mac App Store and is actually purchased as an add-on or a bundled group of apps sold as Mac OS X Lion Server. While this edition can be purchased and downloaded from the Mac App Store, we recommend that if you upgrade, you upgrade to the latest operating system, Mac OS X Server 10.10.

## Mac OS X Server 10.8 (Mountain Lion)

With the release of the Mountain Lion desktop software, Apple released its server counterpart. Mac OS X Server 10.8, nicknamed Mountain Lion, has several features that should appeal to small businesses and enterprises alike. This product, now an add-on from the Mac App Store, had new and enhanced features, including:

- ♦ Advanced administration through the Server app
- ♦ Profile Manager that provides one-stop administration of all Apple devices within an organization, including both Mac and iOS devices
- ♦ The ability for iOS users to self-enroll their devices for system management through an internal web portal
- ♦ Revamped wiki service, providing collaboration and document and project management capabilities
- ♦ Renaming of various services to match their Mountain Lion desktop equivalents, e.g., iChat Server is now Messages Server, iCal Server is Calendar Server
- ♦ iPad/iWork integration
- ♦ Push notifications
- ♦ Active Directory integration

While this edition can be purchased and downloaded from the Mac App Store, we recommend that if you upgrade, you upgrade to the latest operating system, Mac OS X Server 10.10.

## Mac OS X Server 10.9 (Mavericks)

Mac OS X Server 10.9, nicknamed Mavericks, was released in the fall of 2013 as a downloadable package from the Mac App Store, just like Mountain Lion was. This Server app costs only $19.99 for the upgrade; however, you should upgrade to the latest Mac OS X server software, Yosemite, if your current hardware meets the necessary requirements.

One of the new features in the Mavericks operating system is a XCode Server used in iOS development—Caching Server 2, which speeds up the download and delivery of software through the App Store, Mac App Store, and iTunes Store so that copies can be downloaded faster to computers and iOS devices from the local cached resource. Some of the additional new features include Profile Manager—simplifying the deployment and configuration of new Mac computers and iOS devices; File Sharing—using SMB2, sharing files and folders between Macs, PCs, or iPads is significantly faster and easier to set up; and Time Machine Backups—the server can act as a designated Time Machine Backup location for all the Mac computers on the network.

## Mac OS X Server 10.10 (Yosemite)

Mac OS X Server 10.10, nicknamed Yosemite, was released in October 2014 as a downloadable package from the Mac App Store, just like the previous versions of the Server software have been. This Server app costs only $19.99 for the upgrade and should be the server operating system of choice at this point.

Some of the new features include an easier than ever ability to share data and folders between Mac, iPad, and PCs using the new superfast protocol for sharing files in OS X Server, SMB3. This new protocol helps protect against data tampering and eavesdropping by encrypting and signing data while in transmission, adding another layer of security protection to your server.

The new Profile Manager simplifies deploying, configuring, and managing Mac computers and iOS devices, including user accounts, and allows administrators the ability to perform push installs of OS X enterprise apps and iOS media assets including PDF, ePub, and iBooks Author files.

The Caching Server automatically speeds up the downloads and delivery of software updates through the App Store, Mac App Store, iTunes Store, iTunes U, and iBooks Store to users on the network whose apps need updating.

## Linux-Based Operating Systems

Linux-based operating systems are similar to Unix-based operating systems and are built on an open-source kernel packaged with system utilities, software, and libraries. The underlying source code of the operating system can be freely modified, used, and redistributed, and it is supported by a community of programmers and volunteers.

Linux is now packaged for different uses, primarily servers, which contain modified kernels along with a variety of software packages tailored to different requirements. Some of the commercially available distributions that are backed by corporations are Fedora (Red Hat), SUSE Linux (Novell), Ubuntu (Canonical Ltd.), and Mandriva Linux. Each of these distributions has versions specifically designed and programmed to run on server-based hardware to provide management, web and e-mail hosting services, and file and printer sharing, along with other services and functionality that are available in both Mac and Windows-based server operating systems. There are also desktop and mobile versions for each of these versions of Linux, which only hold a microscopic fraction of the desktop operating system market share.

Unless you're a serious technologist, you don't want to go anywhere near Linux-based operating systems.

# CHAPTER NINE

# Networking Hardware

NETWORKING HARDWARE TYPICALLY REFERS to equipment that allows network devices to communicate with one another, but not always. Other types of networking hardware include server racks, cabling, and other devices that help make up the computer network. Here we provide descriptions and recommendations for the most common types of networking hardware that you will require in a solo or small firm computer network.

## Switches

A switch is a piece of networking hardware that connects network segments (discrete sections of the network), allowing multiple devices to communicate with one another. For example, if two or more computers are connected into the same switch and are located within the same defined network, the switch will allow these devices to communicate. Switches inspect data packets as they are received and, based on the source and destination hardware addresses, will forward the data packet appropriately. By delivering the packet of information only to the device it was intended for, network bandwidth is preserved, as well as confidentiality, and the information is delivered much more quickly. In comparison, network hubs send the traffic to all ports, irrespective of the destination device, and are rarely seen in a production environment anymore. In fact, eBay may be the only place that you can purchase a hub these days. Unlike network hubs, switches are "intelligent" devices that can operate on more than one layer of the Open Systems Interconnection (OSI) model, such as a multilayer switch. Switches allow traffic to pass through them at speeds of 10 Mbps, 100 Mbps, 1 Gbps, or 10 Gbps, depending on the speeds of the ports.

The International Organization for Standardization created the OSI model as a way of subdividing a communications system into seven layers: Physical, Data Link, Network, Transport, Session, Presentation, and Application. We could write a whole book on the OSI model, but others already have.

Most solo and small law firms will not need expensive high-end network switches for their computer infrastructure. In the majority of situations, a switch is needed only to connect computer workstations to the server and to the router for Internet access. NETGEAR offers reasonably priced switches in a variety of configurations to meet almost any solo or small firm need. The ProSAFE Gigabit Plus Switches series is a good choice for the solo or small law firm because of the low cost, ease of setup, and reliability. Setup of these devices requires no configuration—just plug in the power and network cables and you're ready to go.

When purchasing a switch for your firm, you will need to determine the number of connections or ports the switch will need. Next, you will have to determine the speeds of the ports that you will require. Will all of your computers need the ability to connect to the server at gigabyte speeds, or will just a handful of devices need that kind of speed? Remember, you certainly will pay more for a 48-port switch with 48 gigabit ports than if you buy a 48-port switch with only two gigabit ports and 46 10/100MB ports. Given the bandwidth of today's networks and applications, it's almost a requirement to purchase a switch with gigabit ports, and the added speed is worth the additional cost. The ProSAFE Gigabit Plus Switches from NETGEAR can be found on its website at **www.netgear.com**.

These switches are also offered in a 1U rackmount solution that will fit standard 19-inch racks and are backed by a NETGEAR ProSAFE lifetime hardware warranty.

For those law firms that require or desire tighter security controls over their computer systems and users, a managed switch may be the solution. A managed switch, unlike an unmanaged switch, is a device that can be administered or controlled. Advanced features include the ability to limit how computer systems can "talk" with one another at the physical level (private virtual LANs), advanced performance monitoring, Layer 3–based prioritization, and increased bandwidth control. These switches also support Quality of Service (QoS), which can be used to prioritize certain network traffic over other functions, such as VoIP phones. A good cost-effective managed switch for small to medium-sized law firms is the ProSafe Gigabit Smart Switch from NETGEAR. This managed switch can be found on NETGEAR's website (**www.netgear.com**) starting at around $200 and can be purchased with differing numbers of ports and connection speeds, depending on the requirements.

As an alternative, Dell manufactures some very cost-effective switches for network connectivity. It has managed and unmanaged versions as well as multi-gigabit port models.

## Entry-Level and Intermediate-Level Routers

A router is a computer networking device that connects two or more independent networks—e.g., your firm's local computer network and your Internet service provider's (ISP) network. A router's job is to determine the proper path for data to travel between the networks and to forward data packets to the next device along the path—basically to get your data from point A to point B. Routers come in all shapes and sizes and can have different features. For a solo or small firm, the most basic router will often be sufficient to connect the local network to the Internet, as well as to protect computers and other hardware devices on the local network from outside attacks (though there is no silver bullet solution). A basic router will require some configuration from the default values to communicate with the ISP's network, as well as to strengthen the security and protection it provides to your information systems. Most basic routers are capable of handling only broadband Internet connections, such as cable and DSL, by using the Ethernet port coming from the cable or DSL modem. If your firm has a T-1 or any variant of this Internet connection, your ISP will probably provide you with a router.

The increasing number of data breaches has created a lot of discussion recently about which router a solo or small firm should use. Whichever router your firm chooses, it must have a built-in firewall and logging capabilities. There can be no exceptions. Previously, we recommended a Linksys router as a basic routing solution for solo and small firms. When configured correctly, this device could provide adequate protection for your firm's data and information systems. However, our recommendation has changed.

Today, the bad guys have gotten so good at breaking into law firms that it's becoming increasingly hard to keep them out. When they do get in, most law firms don't realize that they've been compromised for months.

For this reason, there is no longer an entry-level routing solution that we can recommend with confidence. Your firm's data is just too valuable.

Given the types of data that your firm stores, such as Social Security numbers, credit card numbers, patient/medical records, and other sensitive client information, the only way to combat hackers and have a chance of keeping them out is through the implementation of a defense-in-depth security strategy. This type of information protection strategy provides security at all levels of your computer network, including the point at which your local network interfaces with the public Internet. For this reason, we recommend the Cisco Small Business RV Series line of routers, even for a solo lawyer.

The Cisco Small Business RV Series routers provide high-performance connectivity for small businesses and have built-in threat defense, including a proven stateful packet inspection firewall, an intrusion detection system, and an optional content filtering subscription package to restrict a user's access to undesirable websites that may contain malware and phishing attacks. The Cisco RV130W router offers a wireless option for those firms that require it. The Cisco Small Business RV Series routers start at around $150.

A Cisco device is a little more complicated to configure from the command line, although a graphical user interface (GUI) is available to assist those less familiar with the Cisco configuration syntax. Unless you are comfortable with the syntax of Cisco's IOS (yes, Apple used the iOS term after Cisco), we recommend that you not attempt to configure the device. Seek out the expertise of your IT professional or another resource that "speaks" Cisco's IOS language.

It's becoming harder to find a router for a small to medium-sized business that doesn't include wireless 802.11 capabilities. Be careful when purchasing these devices for your firm's computer network, as you may unintentionally open up your network to unwanted guests if your system is not configured properly. The majority of these devices come preconfigured with open, unsecured wireless networks—which may be OK for your guest network, but even most wireless devices now have an option to set up a separate guest network to keep your visitor's computer network separate from the firm's. You can never be too safe. Remember, you also have the ability to disable the wireless capability if you don't need it.

Make sure you consult with your IT vendor on best practices when implementing a wireless network for your law firm. And for heaven's sake, make sure all the default settings are changed. Even "script kiddies" know all the default settings.

## Firewalls/IDS/IPS Devices

An intrusion detection system (IDS) is used to detect many types of malicious network traffic and computer usage that can't be detected by a conventional firewall or router. These malicious activities include network attacks against vulnerable services (web hosting, e-mail, databases, etc.), data-driven attacks on applications, host-based attacks, such as privilege escalation, unauthorized logins, and access to sensitive files. Privilege escalation is the act of exploiting a known vulnerability in an application to gain access to resources that would have otherwise been protected. When an IDS and an Intrusion Prevention System (IPS) are used in combination, they also can detect and prevent malware such as viruses, Trojan horses, and worms from entering the network.

An IDS/IPS device is commonly placed at the gateway of the computer network so that all incoming and outgoing network traffic passes through it. This allows the device to scan all incoming/outgoing traffic before it is passed on to the destination located on the local computer network, denying the entry of any malicious traffic and prohibiting the exit of any malicious traffic. A firewall has the ability to permit or deny data traffic based on port number, originating or receiving Internet Protocol (IP) address, and protocol type, to name just a few, and it is usually based on rules that are set up and configured by an administrator. An IP address is a unique address or identifier assigned to a networked device, such as a computer, that allows the device to communicate with other networked devices. Just think of an IP address as being the same as a home address, which is a unique way to identify your home's physical location.

A firewall device with these described capabilities is critical for the protection and security of your firm's computer equipment and information systems. For those users who have a broadband Internet connection at home, a router with firewall should also be used to protect your home-based computer network from outside attacks. This is especially important for those lawyers who work remotely, because you do not want your clients' data to become compromised while working offsite. According to the Internet Storm Center, which is part of the SANS Institute, it takes only twenty minutes or less for an unprotected and unpatched computer connected to the Internet to become compromised. Imagine that the computer is yours and it contains confidential client data. This is the stuff of which nightmares are made.

For this reason, we recommend the Cisco ASA 5500-X Series Adaptive-Security Appliance, which provides a good solution for solo and small firms looking to secure their local computer network from outside attacks. This appliance integrates a world-class firewall, unified communications (voice/video) security, SSL (Secure Sockets Layer) and IPSec (Internet protocol security) VPN, intrusion prevention, and content security services into a single piece of hardware. These devices offer advanced security features such as granular control of applications and micro-applications with behavior-based controls, highly secure remote access, and near real-time protection against Internet threats. Combining all of the functionality into one piece of network hardware eliminates the need to purchase a single device for each function. Using a single piece of hardware saves time in setup and configuration, eliminates complexity, and tremendously reduces the cost to adequately secure your business computer network.

The Cisco ASA 5500-X Series provides intelligent threat defense and secure communications services that stop attacks before they affect your firm's business continuity. The firewall technology is built on the proven capabilities of the Cisco PIX family of security appliances, allowing valid traffic to flow in and out of the local network while keeping out unwelcome visitors. The URL and content-filtering technologies implemented by the device protect the business as well as the employees from theft of confidential and proprietary information and help the business comply with federal regulations such as HIPAA and Gramm-Leach-Bliley. The application control capabilities can limit peer-to-peer and instant messaging traffic, which often leads to security vulnerabilities and can introduce viruses and threats to the network. The implementation of a Cisco ASA 5000-X Series device will deliver comprehensive, multilayer security to your computer network and will help you to sleep better at night knowing your electronic data and equipment are protected. The Cisco ASA 5500-X Series Adaptive-Security Appliance can be purchased from Cisco Systems online at its website (**www.cisco.com**) or through a distributor.

The cost of the Cisco ASA 5500-X Series device can range in the thousands of dollars, depending on the number of licenses, features, warranty, and support purchased with the product. When purchasing this device, we absolutely recommend that you get SmartNet maintenance. SmartNet allows you access to the excellent technical support personnel of Cisco, hardware replacement for failures, and upgrades to the device operating system.

Make no mistake about it—this is an excellent high-end firewall well worth the investment to protect your network and confidential information.

One other Cisco IDS/IPS that is worth mentioning is the Cisco Meraki MX80. This security device, while not as robust as the ASA 5500 series, is popular among small law firms. The device is configured, is monitored, and receives its updates via the cloud. The device, along with the required Advanced Security License (we recommend the three-year version), costs about $700.

## Racks

A rack unit or enclosure is a piece of hardware that is used to store, organize, and secure your networking and computing equipment. Most often, rack units are used to hold rackmount servers and network communication equipment such as firewalls and switches. Many types of computer and networking hardware are offered in rackmount sizes, due to the need to place and secure equipment within a single physical location. Rack units can be portable units mounted on caster wheels; bolted to the floor; or, if small enough, mounted on the wall. The amount of space that is available for the servers and networking equipment will greatly affect which type of rack to purchase. The leading manufacturers of rack units and enclosures are American Power Conversion (APC) and Chatsworth.

APC NetShelter SX enclosures are rack enclosures with advanced cooling, power distribution, and cable management for server and networking devices. The 19-inch rack is vendor-neutral and is guaranteed to be compatible with all EIA-310–compliant 19-inch equipment, which covers nearly all rack-mountable equipment. The 19 inches refers to the horizontal distance between the mounting screws for the equipment. These enclosures offer large cable access slots in the roof to provide overhead cable egress, which is useful when cable runs come down through the ceiling. The bottom design allows for unobstructed cable access through a raised panel floor, which is common in network data centers. The enclosures are well-ventilated with perforated front and rear doors to provide ample ventilation for servers and other networking hardware that require unobstructed airflow to keep systems cool. The front and rear doors can be arranged to open in either direction, depending on the layout of the room. For physical security protection, both of these doors can be locked.

The enclosure contains rear cable management channels to assist in managing the plethora of cables that servers and network equipment require. The frame design of the NetShelter SX enclosures is made with heavy-gauge mounting rails and casters to provide support for up to 3,000 pounds of equipment. APC's NetShelter SX enclosures are offered in many different sizes (stand-alone, datacenter, colocation, etc.) and can be purchased with accessories, such as UPS battery backups, retractable keyboard, mouse pad, flip-down monitor, cable management arms, additional fans, and power distribution centers. The APC NetShelter SX rack enclosures can be purchased online at APC's website (**www.apc.com**), and the basic enclosures start at around $1,500.

If you're hesitant to spend $1,500 on a piece of equipment just to hold your servers and networking devices, you may be able to find used racks from local businesses that are moving or have been closed, or through your local online classifieds, at only a fraction of the price.

## Cabling

Now that you have all of your computer equipment selected and purchased, you will need to decide how to wire your data and voice network and what type of network patch cables to purchase to connect your computers to the network drops (cables from the wall outlet to the hub/switch location). These patch cables come in various lengths and are primarily offered in two different types.

First, you have the category 5e cable, which is not the same as the generically termed Cat5 specification. Second, you have the category 6 cable, more commonly referred to as Cat6, along with category 7 cables used for networks requiring data transfer speeds of up to 10 Gbps. Each type of cable has a different maximum throughput speed that it's capable of handling. As with computers, as time progresses, newer cable standards are developed that can handle greater data transfer speeds. There is even a category 8 cable that is still going through the standardization process, promising a new copper speedway for data centers in the not-too-distant future, and operating up to speeds of 40 Gbps. This new specification is directed toward cabling that will be used by data centers to transport data up to four times faster than they currently do now, using the same type of cable.

The Cat6 standard cable is now the de facto standard used by businesses, increasing in popularity as more and more networking and computer devices operate and communicate at gigabit speeds. Current data transfer rates and applications operating at speeds of 1 Gbps are starting to push the limits of category 5 cabling; although category 5e cable is rated for gigabit speeds, it should be used with caution. The trends of the past and predictions for the future indicate that data rates have been doubling every eighteen months. The category 6 cables offer double the amount of bandwidth capacity of category 5 cables and a better transmission performance. The category 6 cable provides a higher signal-to-noise ratio, allowing for higher reliability for current applications and higher data rates for the future. Analysts have indicated that the majority of new wiring installations are using Cat6 cabling. This decision is fairly easy because all Cat6 cabling is backward compatible with Cat5e cabling.

Category 7 cabling is only commonly seen in data centers and is not yet widely used in local networks. If your firm is planning on wiring the office for data and voice, it makes all the sense in the world to wire with Cat6 cabling. Remember, once the dust has settled from the construction, it would be extremely costly to have any type of cabling pulled out and replaced. The approximately 10 percent premium that you currently will pay for Cat6 cabling over Cat5e cabling is worth the added cost. As time goes on, the premium is getting smaller and smaller.

## Wireless Networking Devices

A wireless networking device allows for communication between devices without being physically connected by wires or network cables. In a solo or small firm, if the investment cost to wire an office space with data cables is too expensive, a wireless solution may be the answer. Plus, who wants networking cables all over the place? This is particularly true in older properties—and may be aesthetically desirable in historic buildings. A wireless network is extremely convenient for lawyers who use laptops, smartphones, or tablets because they can move from their office to the conference room with these devices and still stay connected to the local network and Internet. However, we do not recommend wireless connections while connecting to a database or database applications such as some case management systems. Wireless connections could cause database corruption, which would require a reload of backup data. The cost to purchase a wireless networking device is extremely low, and the benefits gained are worth the small investment. However, do not implement a wireless network without taking the proper security precautions. By default, most wireless routers and access points are preconfigured not to enable encryption. This means that by default, all communications between computers and the wireless device are unencrypted and therefore insecure. How many people have connected their laptop to an unencrypted wireless network so that they could check their e-mail or perform online banking? We see this all the time—even at legal technology conferences!

Wireless networks should be set up with the proper security. First and foremost, encryption should be enabled on the wireless device. Most wireless devices come preconfigured with either an unencrypted network or a network encrypted using the wired equivalent privacy (WEP) 64- or 128-bit algorithm. Ultimately, neither of these solutions is adequate. WEP is a weak encryption algorithm and can be cracked in a matter of minutes using free open-source software. Do not use WEP! Frankly, the Federal Trade Commission and the Canadian Privacy Commissioner have both found WEP encryption insufficient to secure credit card information, so we suggest it not be used at all. Some time ago, WPA using the TKIP (temporal key integrity protocol) algorithm was cracked by a group of Japanese scientists in about a minute. So avoid WPA as well. This means that you should be encrypting using WPA2 only.

If the wireless network is for the firm only, enable MAC (media access control) filtering on the wireless device. MAC filtering essentially limits the devices that may communicate with the wireless device. If the MAC address of a computer's wireless network card does not match an authorized MAC address, then the wireless device will not communicate with the unauthorized computer. Enabling MAC filtration will also stop employees from connecting their personal smartphones to the wireless cloud without authorization, even if they know the appropriate network name and passphrase. This is an added layer of security. Most commonly, wireless routers and access points ship with default network names such as Linksys or NETGEAR. While in operation, these devices will broadcast their names so that wireless clients can locate the wireless networks. It is strongly recommended, for security reasons, that the default name of the wireless network be changed (not to something identifying who you are—such as TheSmithLawFirm) and that SSID (service set identifier, which is essentially the network name) broadcasting be disabled.

If your router doesn't come equipped with built-in wireless support, there are other wireless solutions available for the solo and small firm that provide reliable and secure network connections.

Linksys continues to be a very popular manufacturer of wireless networking devices for residential users and small to medium-sized businesses. Its products have only gotten better since the company was purchased by Cisco a few years ago. Cisco sold the Linksys line to Belkin, but the products are still rock solid. The Linksys EA3500 N7500 Dual-Band Smart Wi-Fi Wireless Router is an all-in-one Internet sharing router with a four-port switch. Although this router can be used to connect your local computer network to the Internet, it should be implemented as a wireless access point only in coordination with another firewall/IDS/IPS device. The 802.11n wireless standard protocol is used by this device and offers data transmission speeds up to 300 Mbps. This standard is about six times as fast as the 802.11g standard, which offered data transmission speeds up to 54 Mbps. One of the benefits of the 802.11n standard is that it is backward compatible with all 802.11b/g devices. This router supports the latest wireless security encryption standards, such as WPA2, to keep your data communications secure.

The Linksys EA3500 N7500 Dual-Band Smart Wi-Fi Wireless Router can be purchased online from the Linksys website (**store.linksys.com**) or from your local electronics retailer for around $89.99.

Wireless device manufacturers continue their push to get consumers to purchase their 802.11n wireless products. The 802.11n standard has been approved for a few years, so it's fine to purchase 802.11n products. Wireless networks that use the 802.11n standard will see an improvement in connection speeds and range beyond previous 802.11 standard connections. To use the new standard, all wireless devices will have to be 802.11n compatible; otherwise, the wireless network will operate using only the same standard as the "oldest" wireless device on your network. Further, to get transmission speeds as fast as advertised, you'll have to be relatively close to the access point, and only a limited number of devices can be connected and using the wireless network at the same time. You may also see devices that support the latest 802.11ac W-Fi standard. The 802.11ac standard was ratified and approved in January 2014, but is still not widely used at this time. You may see wireless routers that advertise and do, in fact, support the 802.11ac standard—they should be OK to use—since they are backward-compatible with 802.11n products.

If you work out of a large office space, in a building with a lot of brick or mesh metal wiring embedded within the walls, or in a cubicle next to a microwave, you can purchase a piece of hardware to extend or improve the wireless signal strength in your office. These wireless range extenders cost around $100 and can be purchased online.

# CHAPTER TEN

# Miscellaneous Hardware

**A**SIDE FROM ALL OF the computer hardware, software, and networking equipment, many other types of hardware deserve to be discussed. These additional devices can provide mobility, security, or functionality that would benefit a solo or small firm.

## Fire Safe

A fire safe is an important and often overlooked piece of hardware to have in your office to protect your backup media, software licenses, and other valuables from destruction during a fire or other natural disaster. And don't put the items in the safe and leave the door open; it is astonishing how often we see this. Let the safe serve its purpose and don't succumb to the temptation of convenience by leaving it open. Most come with a locking mechanism, so take advantage of the added security to protect your firm's information.

It is strongly recommended that you store backups (if you use external media), software licenses, copies of technical contracts with third parties, insurance policies, emergency contact lists, and other important documents in a fire safe. Purchasing a fire safe is a relatively inexpensive investment; they can be purchased from your local office supply store for a couple of hundred dollars. There are many sizes and shapes of fire safes, so you shouldn't have a problem finding one that suits your needs. The key specification is the rated internal temperature. The safe may be rated to keep the contents from burning, but it also needs to avoid damaging the contents, such as by melting a tape casing, which is why the internal rated temperature is important. If you keep important business records offsite for redundancy, make sure that this information is stored in a fire safe as well. Your ability to recover from a disaster is only as good as the weakest point in the plan.

## Battery Backup Devices

A battery backup device is an electronic device that supplies secondary power in the absence of main power, such as during a power outage. Battery backup devices can also protect electronic hardware from power spikes and dirty electricity. These devices come in all sizes and power capacities, and depending on what devices you are looking to protect, this will affect the size and capacities you choose. APC is the leading manufacturer of battery backup devices used for protecting computers, servers, and other networking hardware and equipment.

It is strongly recommended that every computer within the local network be placed on a battery backup device, such as the APC Back-UPS 350. At our office, we have our computers, printers, routers, switches, phones, and voicemail system all on battery backup devices to protect our hardware investment. This battery backup device will supply your computer system with power for up to five minutes after an outage has occurred. During this time, the battery backup device will communicate with the APC software installed on the computer (bundled with the device) and will instruct the computer to shut down properly and safely. The Back-UPS 350 supports up to 210 watts and has three NEMA 5-15R battery backup outlets and three NEMA 5-15R surge protection outlets. You may elect to have a larger UPS for your computer system in order to achieve a longer run time.

Many computers and servers will experience software or hardware errors after a power outage because they did not have the opportunity to shut down properly—often referred to as a hard shutdown—which is a quick way to lose or corrupt your data. When computers and (horror of horrors) servers go down hard, the result is often not pretty—actually it's more of a catastrophe. There is a great chance for data loss or system failure in the event of an outage. By purchasing battery backup devices for your computers and other electronic equipment, you are protecting your hardware and software investment and avoiding possible IT costs to correct all the problems that might ensue from a hard shutdown. The APC Back-UPS 350 can be purchased from APC's website (**www.apc.com**) for $79.99.

We've discussed battery backup devices for workstations and laptops, but what about servers? Servers require much more power to operate than a desktop or laptop computer. Therefore, they will require more battery capacity to allow them to operate during a power outage and/or the time necessary to properly shut down. On top of that, they take much longer to shut down properly than a workstation due to the greater number of services and processes constantly running on a server. To properly shut down, the average server will take upward of ten minutes or more if it is hosting multiple virtual machines, so supplying the server with enough power to accomplish this task is important. Certainly, you do not want your server to experience a hard shutdown, because the risk is great for data loss or hardware failure. Battery backup devices for servers can be purchased as a tower unit or rack mountable, depending on what your firm needs to support its server configuration.

The APC Smart-UPS 1500VA is an ideal battery backup solution to protect a single server from the power outages, power spikes, or dirty electricity that can damage the server's internal hardware components. The Smart-UPS 1500VA is offered in both tower and rack-mountable forms and can supply a server with enough power to allow the server to shut down properly. Note that this unit has only enough capacity to supply power to one server and its peripheral devices. If there is a need to purchase a battery backup device for multiple servers, there are models with greater capacities that will be able to handle the load.

As with all batteries, someday they will need to be replaced. Happily, the batteries in these devices are hot-swappable, which means they can be replaced without the need to shut down the battery backup device or the devices connected to the unit. It is important to replace batteries as soon as they fail so that the systems connected to the battery backup device continue to be protected in the event of a power failure, and—trust us— you'll know when the battery needs to be replaced, because the beeping alarm is really loud and annoying. Replacement batteries for these devices can be purchased online from APC's website. Because the batteries in these units are replaceable, this is one hardware investment that you will not be replacing every one to two years. In our experience, these devices will always outlast the life of the computers, servers, or equipment connected to them.

The APC Smart-UPS 1500VA comes bundled with software that can be installed on the server itself to enable the battery backup device to communicate with the server. This is necessary so that in the event of a power outage, the battery backup can alert the software installed on the server of the need to begin the shutdown process. The battery backup device connects to the server through a USB or SmartSlot device. The APC Smart-UPS 1500VA can be purchased from APC's website for $559.

You can also purchase an optional network card for many of the larger UPS devices. The network card allows you to connect the communications over your data network and can support multiple servers. You configure the network card with an IP address, and the servers use the APC network shutdown software to "talk" to the UPS for status rather than communicating through the traditional USB or serial connection.

## Fax Machines

Even though the need for fax machines has dwindled, they are still a staple in a law office and do get some use from time to time—we still receive a lot of faxes, and some clients and institutions insist that we receive information via the facsimile machine. Sometimes there just isn't enough time to scan a document and then e-mail it to a recipient, so instead the document will be faxed—or in some cases, although rare, the communicating party doesn't have access to an Internet connection. We still see plenty of solo and small firms where there is no interest in learning how to scan. The fax machine is the devil they know, and they don't want to change. So, even with all of the advancements in technology, the fax machine has a continued role. As previously stated, many digital copiers have fax transmission and receipt capabilities. Check with your vendor representative to see if using the copier is more cost-effective than purchasing a separate device.

If your firm is in the market for a fax machine, the device we recommend is the Brother IntelliFax-2940, which is a high-speed laser fax, phone, and copier. This model was designed for multiple users in a small business to easily share the benefits. Its design incorporates a high-capacity front-loading paper tray that makes replenishing the paper a task that doesn't require a degree in engineering to accomplish.

The IntelliFax-2940 is equipped with 16 MB of memory, allowing multiple faxes to be stored in memory for transmission when it senses the line is free. The 33.6 Kbps SuperG3 fax modem optimizes throughput, transmitting as fast as 2.5 seconds per page. The 250-sheet capacity paper tray is front-loading for easy access, which means less time spent reloading paper. The paper tray can adjust to hold either letter or legal-size paper.

This fax machine also comes with a 30-page auto document feeder. Access to incoming faxes can be protected through the use of a password, ensuring that only the appropriate parties see confidential faxes. Finally, if your needs exceed or grow beyond faxing and copying, this device comes with a USB interface and can serve as a laser printer capable of printing up to 24 pages per minute. This device comes with a standard one-year limited warranty. The Brother IntelliFax-2940 can be purchased online at Brother's website (**www.brother-usa.com**) for around $300.

## Backup Solutions

As hard drive capacities get larger and the volume of electronic data created increases, media with greater capacities is required to store the daily, weekly, and monthly backup files. Luckily, the days of having to purchase expensive tape drives, autoloaders, and media have long passed. The options for media to store backups have increased while the cost continues to decline. Solo and small firms no longer need to purchase or implement an expensive backup system. Usually, a set of inexpensive external hard drives will do the trick. They offer more capacity than most tape media, are portable, have faster transfer rates, and are relatively inexpensive. And don't forget that you should keep at least one complete backup set offsite in the event that your entire office is lost—or inaccessible—during a disaster.

Depending on the backup solution that has been implemented, a lot of storage space may be necessary, especially if your firm has implemented a system where a full backup is run on a nightly basis. The Western Digital My Book adds secure high-capacity storage to your computer system and is compatible with both PCs and Mac computers. It comes preformatted with the NTFS file system, so if you're planning on using this device on an Apple-based network, you will have to format the external hard drive FAT32, depending on your requirements. The USB 3.0 (USB 2.0 backward compatible) interface allows the hard drive to deliver transfer rates up to 5 Gbps and can be connected to any computer or server that supports these types of connections. The Western Digital My Book comes with built-in hardware encryption, keeping your firm's data secure.

The Western Digital My Book is offered with storage capacities ranging from 2 to 6 TB in size, providing enough storage space for the average small to medium-sized firm backups. The unit also comes with a power adapter and cables to connect the device to a computer or server. If you have not yet purchased backup software, you can use the WD SmartWare Pro automatic backup software that comes bundled with the device. The software can be installed and used on both a computer and a server to back up your system and data files. The device comes with a three-year limited warranty. The Western Digital My Book can be purchased online or from your local electronics retailer starting at around $99 for the 2 TB version.

When evaluating backup solutions for your firm, be sure to enlist the rec-ommendations of your IT staff. Cloud-based backup solutions are becom-ing more popular with small businesses and might have a place in your firm. When evaluating cloud backup providers, pay attention to where your data is physically stored (we would never use a provider that stores data outside the United States—although the actions of the National Security Agency may cause us to rethink that statement) and be sure that the data is always stored in an encrypted format, regardless of whether it's in transit or at rest, and that you hold the only decryption key.

Some folks think data is safer in Europe because of its tough data privacy laws, but that is not necessarily true. Besides the obvious headaches that accompany cross-border data issues, some European versions of the Patriot Act make U.S. law look namby-pamby by comparison. Who knows when those laws may be invoked?

# *CHAPTER* ELEVEN

# *Smartphones*

SMARTPHONES REMAIN THE NUMBER one tech accessory among lawyers. We all remember the time (it's getting more distant with each passing year) when a lawyer would carry two separate devices, a cell phone and a PDA (personal digital assistant). The cell phone was used to make phone calls, and the PDA was used to keep your notes and calendar. Some even allowed you to view your e-mail captured during the last synchronization with your work computer. Things have changed radically. Smartphones are like laptops—able to perform almost every function a laptop can, and in some instances, more—but at a fraction of the size. Because smartphones have so many capabilities, lawyers in firms of all sizes tend to view them as a necessity—a device they can no longer live without. Smartphones have become computers in and of themselves, with increasing functionality, and in some cases, they are more important to a lawyer than a computer system.

And sadly, they have become a kind of crack, with many lawyers seriously addicted to them and unable to disengage from technology, risking their health and relationships. That aside . . .

Among business users and especially lawyers, the smartphone debate has evolved into major warfare. Since its introduction and with its growing popularity, the Apple iPhone has grabbed the largest share of the lawyer market, and that is particularly true for solo and small firm lawyers.

According to the American Bar Association's 2015 Legal Technology Survey, Apple's iPhone continues to dominant the usage by attorneys at about

- ◆ Apple iPhone      67.5 percent
- ◆ Google Android     23.9 percent

- ♦ RIM BlackBerry    5.2 percent
- ♦ Windows Mobile    2.5 percent
- ♦ Don't Know    2.2 percent

These numbers have resulted in some major changes over the past few years:

- ♦ There are only two major players in the smart phone market (iPhone and Android), and that should continue for the foreseeable future.
- ♦ iPhone's usage increased from 2014, while Android's fell slightly.
- ♦ Blackberry usage is up slightly from 2014.
- ♦ Windows Mobile device usage continues to be almost non-existent among lawyers.

Both the Android and the iPhone continue to split the market share at an almost 91 percent combined share of the market. The BlackBerry is no longer a player and could become all but nonexistent in the United States a year or two from now, much like the Windows Mobile phone has become. BlackBerry (the name of the device and the company name) may have been lulled into inaction by its success, but the hot new technology clearly belongs to Androids and iPhones. Because BlackBerry is a Canadian company, Canada continues to keep it on life support.

As we write the draft of this book, BlackBerry has announced that it has acquired Good Technologies to leverage Good's capability to manage smartphones in the workplace. It will be interesting to see what, if any, difference that will make to BlackBerry's future. We are not optimistic.

A key functional requirement for any smartphone is the ability to synchronize data with your computer or server. E-mail synchronization is at the top of all lawyers' lists, followed closely by calendar synchronization. The Windows Phone 8 and 8.1, Windows Phone 10, iPhone, and Android phones synchronize with Microsoft Exchange Servers via ActiveSync. This doesn't require any special hardware or software because the function is built into Exchange. However, there are some limitations, such as the inability to synchronize natively with Public Folders over the air. You may have to purchase third-party products to get all of the features you need for over-the-air synchronization of Public Folders, Personal Calendars, or Contacts. Your mailbox will synchronize without any additional software. For those firms that don't host their own e-mail, users can set up their devices to retrieve e-mail directly from their e-mail service provider.

Our continuing recommendation for any lawyer (or anybody wanting to keep his or her data secure) is to not use an iPhone. The iPhone 6 security is better, but there still are some problems. Apple released the next generation of iPhone 6 running iOS 8 in the fall of 2014. The new iPhone comes in two flavors, iPhone 6 and the iPhone 6 Plus. The iPhone 6 Plus is a whopping 5.5 inches long, which is huge for a smartphone. It's almost like you're holding an iPad Mini next to your head—too large if you ask us. Some of the improvements and features that come with the new version include two models varying in size (4.7 inches vs. 5.5 inches), thinner design, higher-resolution Retina screen display, and new video recording features. The features of iOS 8 are discussed later in the book in the More from Apple chapter.

Continuing on the finger print scanner that was introduced with the iPhone 5, the iPhone 6 allows users to unlock their iPhone with a fingerprint as well as approve purchases from iTunes, iBooks, and the App Store without having to enter a password. Apple has released multiple fixes for various vulnerabilities as we go to press, but the fundamental insecurity of the fingerprint scanner cannot be fixed. However, it is unlikely that this will present a problem for most users, as there is some level of sophistication to the compromise. But if you are targeted by a professional, your data is not secure—after all, we leave our fingerprints everywhere we go.

The government has made the same complaints about the release of the Android Lollipop operating system as it has about the encryption of the iPhone 6 models. The encryption of data on these mobile devices is preventing the National Security Agency (and others) from being able to access the encrypted contents of these devices, potentially hampering or slowing down their investigations. Anyone concerned with the privacy of an individual's data should be happy that the government has come out with these criticisms and should be thankful that we just may have a way to keep the data on our devices secure once and for all—whether from hackers or Big Brother!

Apple has made all kinds of marketing claims, yet there are many examples over the years demonstrating why an iPhone should not be trusted. On iPhones running certain older versions of the Apple iOS firmware, the PIN keylock code is easily replaced with a "blank" code. The iPhone also claims to store its data in encrypted form. That is true, but with some older versions of the iOS firmware, you can place the phone in recovery mode and transfer the data to your computer. Apple conveniently decrypts the data as it sends it over the SSH connection, thereby negating the encryption scheme. You can remotely wipe the iPhone, but it needs to be connected to the cellular network to do it.

Not much has changed in the security model, or lack thereof, of Apple's iPhone devices. There still are security problems with the current generation of the devices. Within days of each new firmware version released, a new "jailbreak" method has been discovered. Although iOS 4 held up better than its predecessors, iOS 5, 6, 7, and 8 have all been jailbroken. Even iOS 9 was jailbroken before being released.

Because we know so many lawyers will (and do) ignore our advice, here's what we recommend:

**(A)** Only use the iPhone 6 or 6 Plus. If you're using the 3, 3G, or 4, upgrade immediately.

**(B)** Upgrade to the latest version of iOS 8.

**(C)** Enable a passphrase (not a four-digit PIN) on the device. Enable device wiping upon a set number of unsuccessful logon attempts.

**(D)** Do not enable the Touch ID fingerprint reader. Only use a passphrase to unlock the phone.

As of this writing, the iPhone 6, iPhone 6 Plus, and iOS 8 have been released. Given the insecurity of the fingerprint scanner, make sure you configure a strong lock code and not the default four-digit PIN. There are tools available that can brute-force the four-digit PIN on an iOS 4, 5, or 6 device in ten to forty minutes, even if the device is configured to wipe data after ten invalid attempts. By the time this book is printed, we fully expect that the software also will be updated to brute-force iOS 7 and 8 in a similar fashion. We are well aware that our advice is largely ignored here, as the glamour of the iPhone continues to mesmerize everyone, including lawyers. It is a very slick phone, but remember that the new ABA Model Rules adopted in 2012 require that you balance the risk of the technology you use against the security of client data! As we write this, 14 states have thus far adopted the changes to the rules.

With the introduction of iOS 5, Apple introduced the iCloud service. When enabled and configured, iOS devices use this service to back up information from your local device to the cloud. The iCloud service removes the necessity to connect your iOS device to your computer and either backup or update your device by using iTunes. All of this now takes place wirelessly, over your mobile data connection or your local Wi-Fi network. However, while convenient, there are some serious concerns with data privacy. First, consider that all information from your local device, whether the iPhone or iPad, is being sent to Apple for storage.

The information may be encrypted by Apple, but it holds the decryption key and will turn the decrypted data over to law enforcement when the right paperwork is supplied. The 2014 Celebgate news events have highlighted the insecurity and dangers of iCloud, especially if you want to store your nude selfies on Apple's service.

For any cloud storage provider, whether iCloud, Dropbox, or some other provider, we always recommend that you encrypt the data prior to using and initiating the service. By following this process, the user holds the decryption key—not the service provider.

For iOS devices, using an app like BoxCryptor encrypts the files on your local device before the information is synchronized with the cloud storage provider. BoxCryptor encrypts files on the local device using AES-256-bit and RSA encryption, providing the necessary security to keep your files and information secure. This also allows the user to hold and maintain possession of the decryption key, which is very important. This product used to be free, and still is for personal use, but costs $96 per year for a single-user business license.

During the past few years, many vendors of Android smartphones have continued to release phones designed for business use. They include enhanced security and enterprise management capabilities, like encryption, support for virtual private networks, support for more ActiveSync controls, and remote locking and wiping.

Unveiled in June and made available to the public in November 2014, Google announced the release of version 5.0 of Android, called Lollipop. Google originally intended to enable encryption by default when configured with a lock code. Prior to release, Google changed its mind and did not implement encryption by default due to "performance issues" on some hardware. The new operating system also uses Security Enhanced Linux (SELinux), an enhanced application level security model that was developed by the NSA that enforces application isolation on the device that malware cannot bypass.

Besides the security enhancements, Google also included a refreshed notification system that its users will be sure to love. Notifications can now be grouped by the application that produced them and now can be displayed on the lock screen. As Android matures and continues to increase in popularity, it's very possible that it may become the smartphone of choice, even surpassing the iPhone among lawyers.

For die-hard security enthusiasts, the National Security Agency (NSA) has created and released a hardened version of Google's Android operating system called Security Enhanced (SE) Android. This open-source project was undertaken to limit the damage that can be done to the phone by flawed or malicious apps. It is probably only a matter of time before we see this operating system installed and running on Android phones used by government agencies. The Defense Department has already distributed many of these phones. However, given the previous events surrounding the release of documents by Edward Snowden, we now know that the NSA has its fingers in many sources of electronic information, including encrypted data. We would be very wary of trusting any hardened version of Android at this time, especially one hardened by the NSA, and recommend protecting data with methods that you, the user, control and configure.

For those users looking for a smartphone recommendation, we strongly recommend investing in Android phones. We officially made the jump three years ago to the Samsung Galaxy S3 and are not looking back. We have fallen in love with the Samsung Galaxy S5 device that has recently replaced our S3s. The Samsung Galaxy S5 is only available currently with 16 GB of internal memory in the United States. Our older Galaxy S3 was the 32 GB model, and we were worried that 16 GB wouldn't be enough space. The operating system for the S5 appears to take less space since we have installed all of our applications and still have over 8 GB of memory available. Of course, we configured as many applications as possible to use the expansion micro SD card if the application allowed it.

The Samsung Galaxy S6 and S6 edge+ have been released as the latest version of the Galaxy model lines, but for now, we're sticking with the S5.

There are many Android devices to choose from. It may help to select your cellular provider first and then see what options it has. We've been to many Sprint, Verizon, and AT&T stores—nowadays, they all pretty much have the same models in stock with many more options available online. For an Android, the Samsung Galaxy S5 is our current recommendation.

Over-the-air synchronization with Exchange Public Folders is a requested feature by many solo and small firm lawyers. You may require a third-party server implementation such as Goodlink to perform these functions. Good Technologies, Inc., makers of Good Mobile Messaging products, provided enterprise-level messaging and control for iPhone, Android, Windows Phone 7/8/8.1, Symbian, and PalmOS phones. Good Technologies, Inc., was just purchased by BlackBerry, so we remain cautious as to the future of this product.

Hosted versions of Good for Enterprise are no longer available through any major cell carriers. In fact, Good had priced the software so high that it is no longer an alternative for solo or small firm lawyers. Because of the licensing costs and minimum device requirements, a Good solution would cost several thousand dollars (not counting the server cost) just to get started. Mobile Iron used to be another alternative to manage a small population of smartphones. Like Good, Mobile Iron has increased its licensing cost to a point that only makes sense for larger firms. Believe it or not, BlackBerry's Enterprise Service 12 Server Software may be the only cost-effective solution to manage solo and small firm smartphones. This free software can be downloaded from Blackberry's website at no cost and can be used to manage iOS and Android devices from a single console. However, there is an added cost if you want to manage non-BlackBerry devices.

Another alternative may be to install special software on your computer to synchronize with the Public Folders. Your computer must be powered up and logged in to Outlook for the over-the-air synchronization to occur. As you can imagine, this is a potential security vulnerability and must be carefully considered and engineered, and it requires a lot of administration by your IT provider.

On a side note, everyone is familiar with getting spam through e-mail, but how about on the phone? Spam text messages can be costly since most carriers will charge for both text messages sent and received unless you have an unlimited plan. There is no anti-SMS-spam software available to install on cell phones to prevent receiving these messages, but there is a way to block cellular spam, and it's quite simple. The vast majority of spam text messages originates on the Internet and do not come from other cell phones. Why? Because spammers don't have to pay anything when using the Internet to send the text messages. Most carriers, led by AT&T and Verizon Wireless, offer spam SMS-blocking features. To enable this feature, just log in to your online account manager and the options should be available in your account profile. Most cellular providers allow you to block SMS messages only from certain phone numbers and addresses. What are you waiting for? We've signed up. Here are the websites you can use:

> AT&T (**mymessages.wireless.att.com**)
> Verizon Wireless (**www.verizonwireless.com**)
> Sprint (**www.sprint.com**)
> T-Mobile (**www.t-mobile.com**)

Make sure you pay attention to smartphone updates and security notices, as the number of malware threats targeting smartphones have skyrocketed over the past year. Currently, Android devices are the most frequently targeted by malware due to their popularity, open-source operating system, the relatively lawless Android Market, and the availability of apps from multiple sources.

For Android phones, we recommend a security product called Lookout Mobile Security (**www.lookout.com**). This product used to be free, but now is free only for personal use. The Enterprise version of this software provides many advanced features and an interface to manage all of your firm's devices from one console. This utility will scan all of your applications for malware and spyware and has a built-in "find my phone" feature, allowing you to locate your device using the GPS if it goes missing.

This edition also includes a backup feature, which is helpful if you haven't integrated your Android phone with your Google account. Some of the other features include protecting your device from malware, blocking malicious websites, seeing which apps access your private information, and preventing encounters with phishing scams. Some of the advanced features in the Enterprise edition include the abilities to manage company data located on personal devices (BYOD), automate application approval, and investigate suspicious activity on mobile devices. Lookout also has a version for iOS devices, which alerts owners if their device may have been exposed to security vulnerabilities because of outdated software or if the device has been jailbroken. It also offers device location and backup functionality. Lookout now makes you contact its sales team for Enterprise Level pricing, which can be done from the website at **www.lookout.com**.

Even with the rising threat of malware, there are some basic steps you can take to protect yourself. First, make sure that when you're downloading an application, you do so only from Google Play or the App Store. When choosing an application to try or to purchase, be sure to read carefully through the reviews. Also, pay attention to the access permissions that an app requests when you install it, especially on an Android device. Finally, vendors of security software are now offering antivirus and anti-malware products for smartphones. This is software that you should seriously consider purchasing to protect your mobile devices, especially if they contain confidential information.

Basic security measures for any smartphone should include strong passwords, passphrases or PINs, automatic logoff after a set time, encryption of the phone and storage cards, and remote wiping capability.

# CHAPTER TWELVE

# *Productivity Software*

**H**AVING WORKED WITH SO many solos and small law firms through the years, we know that lawyers are constantly striving to be more productive and thereby increase their billable time. We see a few lawyers (fewer than the number of digits on one hand) who still prefer to use Corel WordPerfect over Microsoft Word, but that number is continuing to approach zero as Corel is becoming more and more of a nonfactor in the productivity software market.

Microsoft Word is what the business world uses and will continue to use for the foreseeable future. There are alternatives, but they all come with some degree of pain and a large learning curve. There are adherents of WordPerfect who are religious in their fervor and others who are evangelical in their admiration for open-source solutions. Whether you are a fan of Microsoft or not, the reality is that Word is the preferred application of the business world, and your clients will expect you to use it. They will not appreciate any conversion problems that may occur if you are using something else. In this section, we detail the latest and greatest releases of productivity software that can help lawyers be more productive.

## *Microsoft Office*

Microsoft's latest version of Office, Office 2013, was released about two years ago and has been thoroughly vetted at this point. The software was redesigned to make the most of the Windows 8 operating system, work with mobile devices, and strongly push Microsoft's cloud services. It works and runs just fine on Microsoft Windows 10, and it is our current choice and recommendation for a productivity suite. At the time of this writing, Microsoft is in development of Office 2016. It has already released the 2016 version of Office on the Mac, and the Windows version was released last fall.

To compete with Google's cloud storage options, Microsoft designed the new version of Office as a service in which applications and files are primarily stored in the cloud and not on your local computer system. This may come as a shock to most traditional Microsoft users, and lawyers should be aware that this type of service may pose ethical issues depending on how and where their information is actually being stored. However, users also have the ability to store documents on their local computer system.

Each of the three editions of Office 2013 includes Word, Excel, PowerPoint, and OneNote:

♦ Office Home & Student 2013, designed for families and consumers; retails for $139.99

♦ Office Home & Business 2013, designed for the small business market; provides e-mail, shared calendars, and web conferencing tools; retails for $219.99

♦ Office Professional 2013, designed for enterprise customers; provides advanced business and cloud deployment features; retails for $399.99

If your firm is using Microsoft Office 2007 or older, we would highly recommend that you upgrade to Office 2013 at this time. It is a closer call for Office 2010 users as there is little more Office 2013 has to offer unless you want to take advantage of the cloud capabilities.

Microsoft, like a lot of companies, is making a very strong push to get users to the cloud and away from local applications. To accomplish this goal, Microsoft has introduced a Software as a Service (SaaS) called Office365, which gives users and companies the option to purchase a subscription (monthly or annually) to use the Microsoft Office applications in the cloud, and in some instances, also includes the ability to install and use the stand-alone versions.

The subscription-based Office365 may not be for everyone, but for a solo or small firm, it at least presents another licensing option—rather than having to shovel out hundreds of dollars for the stand-alone versions of the Office 2013 suite. The Business Essentials subscription is entirely cloud-based and costs $5 per user per month ($60 per year), but doesn't include the ability to run Office on a mobile device, such as an iPad, or to install Office on your local computer. This requires you to be connected to the Internet in order to use Microsoft Office, which is a major downside. The Business subscription costs $8.25 per user per month ($99 per year), but doesn't include e-mail. This subscription plan does allow you to install the full version of Office on your local computer and use the Office apps on your tablet or mobile device. Finally, the Business Premium sub-scription costs $12.50 per month per user ($150 per year), includes Office for tablets, and allows for the installation of Microsoft Office 2013 on up to five computer systems per user. For a small firm just starting up that is looking to be mobile, shelling out $12.50 per month for your employees to use Office may be easier to swallow than paying up to $400 per copy of Microsoft Office 2013. It's just another option to consider.

In addition to the Business subscription plans, Microsoft offers several Enterprise plans. The top level Enterprise plan costs $20 per user per month (annual commitment) and includes features that attorneys will love. As an example, Enterprise E3 includes Compliance and Information Protection, including Legal Hold, Rights Management, and Data Loss Prevention for e-mail and files. There are also eDiscovery tools to support compliance. The Enterprise plans can get expensive for some solo and small firm attorneys, but some may feel it's worth the extra money just to get Data Loss Prevention for their e-mail. You can see the features for each edition of Office 365 at **https://products.office.com/en-us/business/compare-more-office-365-for-business-plans**.

We are seeing a lot of solo and small firms migrating to Office365, and in general, we hear that lawyers are very satisfied with the cost and perform-ance.

It should be noted that Microsoft Office 365 now includes support for Office 2016 for Macs, which is available for those subscriptions with the ability to install a full version of the Office suite locally on a computer system.

Editing Office documents on tablets (and other mobile devices) has long been a major headache, which could only be overcome by using third-party applications to perform the simplest tasks of opening, editing, and saving documents on the mobile device. Microsoft has finally released Office for mobile devices, including Office for iPad and Office Mobile for the iPhone, Windows Phone, and Android devices.

Office for iPad has been an app that the legal community has been anxiously awaiting. Now it is here. This app allows users to edit and create documents, including spreadsheets and presentations. Office for iPad requires a subscription to Office365; however, Office Mobile is free to download on your Android, iPhone, or Windows Phone. Just remember that an Office365 subscription is required if you want to edit Office files and not just view them.

For those attorneys who require e-mail encryption (most of you should be using e-mail encryption by now), Microsoft has released a service called Office 365 Message Encryption. This service lets users send encrypted e-mails to people outside your firm, regardless of the destination (Yahoo, Gmail, Outlook, etc.). Encryption is critical when sending messages that contain Personally Identifiable Information (PII), credit card numbers, medical records, and Social Security numbers, to just name a few types of sensitive information. Office 365 Message Encryption requires Microsoft Azure Rights Management, which costs $2 per user per month. If you have the E3 or E4 subscription of Office 365 Enterprise, Azure Rights Management is included in the cost, so you automatically get e-mail encryption without having to pay the extra $2 per user per month.

## Corel Suite

WordPerfect Office X7 is the latest version of Corel's Office Suite, and it is available in Standard, Professional, and Legal editions for the business user. WordPerfect Office X7, the successor to WordPerfect Office X6, was released in April 2014. New features of Corel WordPerfect Office X7 include a new PDF Form Feature, allowing users to create their own PDF forms; Macro Manager; and Roxio Secure Burn. The components of WordPerfect Office X7 Standard Edition include:

### *Main Applications*
WordPerfect® word processor

Quattro Pro® spreadsheet program

Presentations™ slideshow creator

WordPerfect® Lightning™ digital notebook

Enhanced! eBook Publisher

Roxio Secure Burn disc burning software

### Also included

900+ TrueType fonts

10,000+ clipart images

300+ templates

175+ digital photos

BrainStorm training videos*

The Pocket Oxford English Dictionary

WordPerfect® Address Book

Presentations™ Graphics—bitmap editor and drawing application

WordPerfect XML Project Designer

Batch Conversion Utility to convert Microsoft Word documents to WordPerfect documents

Corel X7 is offered in Standard, Professional, and Legal Editions, but the Standard Edition is best suited for serving solo or small firm needs. Unless a solo or small firm needs a database application, there is no reason for it to invest in the Professional Edition.

One of the touted advantages of WordPerfect over Microsoft Word is the Reveal Codes option, which allows users to manage document formatting with a fine-tooth comb. We are constantly amazed when lawyers mention the reveal code "excuse." Perhaps they are unaware that Word 2013 actually has a reveal code type display (and Office has since 2007), where the user can see formatting codes.

Even with the new features included with WordPerfect Office X7, we still prefer the more seamless, although imperfect, Microsoft Office 2013. Another concern is the integration of WordPerfect with other software in your practice such as case management and document management. You can see a listing of products that work with WordPerfect at **http://www.wordperfect.com/us/pages/4500028**.html?storeKey=us. Corel used to price the software suite at a much reduced cost when compared to Microsoft Office, particularly for business-friendly packages, but that is no longer the case with the latest X7 version. Users who don't need the extensive features of WordPerfect or Microsoft Office might opt to use a product such as OpenOffice.org (described in the next section), which is free. Full license and upgrade costs for the three editions are below.

| Edition | Full license cost | Upgrade cost |
|---|---|---|
| Standard Edition | $179.00 | $129.99 |
| Professional Edition | 399.00 | 259.99 |
| Legal Edition | 349.99 | 224.99 |

## OpenOffice.org

Apache OpenOffice.org (formerly just OpenOffice) is a free open-source software office suite that is available for many different operating systems, including Linux, Windows, and Mac OS X. The latest release of OpenOffice.org (version 4.1.1) was in August 2014, and it contains many features and functions that are present in Microsoft Office and Corel WordPerfect Office. This suite was developed to reduce Microsoft Office's dominating market share by providing a free, open, and high-quality alternative. Some of the new features in version 4.1 include comments on text ranges, support for IAccessible2, in-place editing of Input Fields, interactive cropping, and the ability to import pictures from files. The micro release, version 4.1.1, was released to fix a number of errors and critical issues, only in terms of features, only added support to run on Windows Server 2012 and updated a few of the word dictionaries that the program uses for spell-checking. This release was more for program stability than feature enhancement.

OpenOffice.org can read and write most of the file formats found in Microsoft Office, including Office 2007/2010/2013 file formats, which is important if you are going to choose to use a free utility for your productivity software. It also natively supports the standard OpenDocument Format (ODF) and has the capability to read WordPerfect Office, Rich Text Format (RTF), Lotus, and other common productivity file types.

The components of OpenOffice.org work together to provide the features expected from a modern office suite and include:

Writer—word processor

Calc—spreadsheet application

Impress—presentation program

Base—database program

Draw—an editor used for drawing

Math—allows for creating and editing mathematical formulas

All of the components of the OpenOffice.org suite look and feel like the corresponding components in Microsoft Office and Corel WordPerfect Office. Microsoft, seeing the need for and popularity of the open-source movement, has sponsored the development of a converter from Office Open XML to OpenDocument format and vice versa. Microsoft and Corel have included add-in support for the ODF file format into their office suite products to allow reading and writing to the format.

However much we all grimace at Microsoft's domination, we do not recommend that you use OpenOffice.org as your primary productivity suite. Because it is developed and maintained by freelance programmers and other companies that make contributions to the project, such as Apache, the software is not very well supported and may not contain all of the features provided by other productivity suites. In addition, most law office staff have never seen OpenOffice.org, so the learning curve would be pretty steep.

The current release of OpenOffice.org can be downloaded from the website free of charge at **www.openoffice.org**.

## Adobe Acrobat

Adobe Acrobat, a family of application software developed by Adobe Systems, uses Portable Document Format (PDF) as its native file format. The PDF specification was originally a proprietary format but is now a published and approved ISO standard. The latest version of Adobe Acrobat (DC) includes Adobe Document Cloud services and is notably different from previous versions. Document Cloud allows users to create, review, approve, and sign documents from any desktop or mobile device. Since the program is integrated with the cloud, a user can begin working on a document on one device and then continue editing it on another. Adobe Acrobat PDF files can easily be created or edited from a mobile device, such as an Apple iPad.

Adobe Acrobat DC allows users to convert, combine, and export PDFs easier than ever. The Export PDF to Word feature has been enhanced, hopefully fixing all of the formatting problems previously experienced when attempting to accomplish this task. The Pro DC version contains all of the features that attorneys love such as Bates numbering and redaction capabilities.

Adobe Acrobat DC is offered in both a subscription model as well as a stand-alone solution, without the cloud-based integration. The Acrobat DC subscriptions cost $14.99 per month per user, which includes the desktop version of the Acrobat DC software as well as the cloud-integration and mobile features. Subscribers will also get 20 GBs of cloud storage with their plan.

Users can still opt for the stand-alone version of the Adobe Acrobat DC software at a cost of $449 for the full version of Acrobat Pro DC or $299 for the full version of Acrobat Standard DC. The upgrade versions of these products are priced much lower than the full versions, allowing for users of Acrobat X and XI to upgrade at a fraction of the cost. The cost to upgrade to Acrobat Pro DC is $199, and the cost to upgrade to Acrobat Standard DC is $139. This product is supported on Windows 10 as well as the latest version of Mac OS X.

## Power PDF

For those users who are looking for an alternative to Adobe Acrobat, our recommendation is to use Power PDF Advanced by Nuance. It is certainly a worthy alternative and is only one-third of the retail cost of Acrobat Pro. Power PDF Advanced has Bates stamping support to create custom profiles for stamping information into headers and footers. There's also an assistant function to convert legal pleadings into PDFs with stamp and line numbering options. Redaction ability is included too. Users may also secure their PDFs with passwords using 128- or 256-bit AES encryption and permission controls to protect document viewing, printing, and modifications. The program also integrates with cloud storage providers, allowing users to save their PDFs directly in the cloud.

There are a lot of other features available with Power PDF Advanced. Suffice it to say that it has the majority of features present in Acrobat Pro that any attorney would find valuable. The cost is attractive as well. Make sure you take advantage of the thirty-day trial to determine if it will meet your needs. It should be noted that this product is Windows 10 compatible.

## OCR Software

Optical character recognition (OCR) software translates graphical images into editable text. This capability is used most commonly to edit a scanned document or image. It's widely used in law firms to convert scanned paper documents in a case file to searchable electronic files. OCR software will translate the image to text, such as a Microsoft Word document, which can be edited.

OmniPage Ultimate, by Nuance Communications, Inc., is an OCR software product enabling the conversion of paper documents and TIFF files to a text-based format for amending as needed with prominent business communications software. OmniPage Ultimate can convert scanned images to Microsoft Word, Excel, PowerPoint, Corel WordPerfect, e-mail, HTML, and even to the Amazon Kindle format. The program generates a formatted text document that preserves the layout and format, character, font, and style of the scanned image. This software boasts a 50 percent greater accuracy rate than its competitors when converting, and the updated recognition dictionaries for financial, legal, and medical specialties allow for legal-specific word recognition, which means that you will spend less time editing your legal documents. This software can also process, edit, and recognize over 120 languages—a great feature for those firms with a global presence.

OmniPage supports data capture from a digital camera. The software can "read" a digital photograph, which may come in handy for lawyers who use photographs as exhibits. This software is the first OCR application designed for the multicore-processor computer, taking advantage of hyperthreading to increase the conversion speed of documents. It was also the first OCR software to support Microsoft Office 2007/2010 native formats. When converting legal documents, OmniPage now has a greater ability to recognize formatting such as line numbers, Bates stamps, signatures, and more.

Other new OmniPage Ultimate features worth mentioning include the ability to convert a scanned document into a readable format and send it to an Amazon Kindle, a "one-click" toolbar in the Microsoft Office Suite that allows for document conversion with a simple click, and a faster load time than previous versions.

Also new in the latest version of OmniPage is the eDiscovery Assistant for searchable PDFs. eDiscovery Assistant provides the ability to safely convert a single PDF or batches of PDFs of all types into searchable documents without having to open PDF files one by one, giving the user greater flexibility when applying an OCR process to an entire group of documents.

As more and more firms look to use the features the Internet cloud provides, so do vendors. OmniPage includes the Nuance Cloud Connector application, which integrates with Evernote, Dropbox, OneDrive, and GoogleDocs, allowing users to scan and/or save their documents to the cloud.

OmniPage Ultimate can be purchased and downloaded online directly from Nuance's website (**www.nuance.com**) for $499.99 for the full version and $199.99 for the upgrade version.

Adobe Acrobat includes an OCR engine too and the ability to batch OCR documents—and not just one at a time. We recommend purchasing Adobe Acrobat first to see if it meets your OCR needs before expending funds on another specialized product like OmniPage.

## Voice Recognition Software

Arguably one of the biggest recent advances in productivity software is the continuing refinement of voice recognition software. Dragon Naturally Speaking 13 by Nuance (**www.nuance.com**) has made voice recognition software a respectable addition to your productivity arsenal. Many solo and small firm lawyers are now using Dragon as their primary composition tool. This is especially valuable for those who are not very accurate or fast typists. It takes only a short time to train Dragon to your voice, and its accuracy is astonishing. Nuance claims that the latest version is 15 percent more accurate than version 12, which is just incredible given how accurate the previous version of this product was.

Dragon can be used to compose e-mail messages, draft documents in your word processor, and even launch software applications without touching the keyboard or mouse. The software now allows users to search the Web and their computers through the use of voice shortcuts.

Along with new formatting and editing commands, the latest version also provides users with the ability to post to Facebook and Twitter by voice and even allows users to use their iPhone or iPad as a wireless microphone, untethering them from their computer.

Some of the new features in version 13 include:

- ◆ Accuracy is improved over the previous version—the new version continues to "learn" your voice and becomes more accurate the more you use the product.

- The software now learns words and phrases you use most.
- Multicore processors provide faster performance.
- Go hands free and headset free—the software now offers multiple microphone options, including those built into the latest laptops, so that you can type even less and not have to use a headset.
- Dictate notes and ideas on the go and transcribe the audio files back at your computer.

This is a great tool and is used by many individuals with disabilities. But make no mistake—this is a mainstream product, and the able-bodied are moving to this technology in hordes!

Dragon Naturally Speaking comes in several versions. We recommend using the Legal or Professional version if you can afford it. The Legal version contains vocabulary specific to the legal profession and carries a price tag of $799.99. The Professional version is a higher-end package that allows for roaming user profiles and allows multiple custom dictionaries. The Professional Individual version costs $300 and may be purchased from many webstores or directly from the Nuance site. The Premium package costs $199.99, and it may be a good, cost-effective alternative for some lawyers as it also supports digital recording devices, smart formatting, and text-to-speech, especially for those just wanting to get started with voice recognition software. At the time of this writing, the Premium version was on sale for $149.99 on Nuance's website. Dragon Naturally Speaking 13 is licensed on a per-user basis. You can install and run it on multiple computers, but you need a license for each user's voice file.

The most important tip about using voice recognition software is to proof any output from Dragon. The speech-to-text is very good, and it "learns" and improves with time, but it's not perfect. Make sure you proofread your documents, especially those that may be submitted to a court.

If you use Dragon on multiple computers, make sure you know how to move your voice files among machines. This will save on the "retraining" time when you use several computers. The process is most appropriate for those lawyers who use a computer at home and one at the office. Moving the voice files between the machines allows you to take advantage of the aggregate training time instead of each machine "learning" on its own.

A key component to the success of voice recognition is the use of a good quality USB microphone headset. We have had great success using a Plantronics 510 headset/microphone system, but they are no longer manufactured. The Plantronics Blackwire 720 Series is available for $149.95

from the Plantronics website (**www.plantronics.com**) and should be an excellent replacement for the older 510 model. The lightweight headphones with noise-cancelling microphone connect to your computer using a standard USB or Bluetooth connection. We would recommend the USB connection as Bluetooth wireless is more susceptible to audio errors. The wideband acoustic echo cancellation feature captures a broad range of voice signals for calls that are clearer and more natural sounding, perfect for use with Skype. The smart sensor technology lets you answer calls simply by putting on the headset or pause mobile device media playback by taking it off. This pair of headphones also allows for dual connectivity between your computer and mobile phone, allowing users to take phone calls while using their computer without the need to take off the headset.

# *CHAPTER* THIRTEEN

# *Security Software*

COMBINED WITH NETWORK FIREWALLS or IDS (Intrusion Detection System) devices, security software provides another line of protection in the defense-in-depth information security strategy against malware, including viruses, Trojan horses, worms, and other external forces. The defense-in-depth approach to securing your network is the best way to keep your systems safe from both internal and external threats. These threats can be extremely harmful to a law firm network and very costly to remove once an infection has occurred, assuming you've been able to identify that a breach or infection has taken place. Even in a solo or small firm network, your client data is of the utmost importance and securing your computers, servers, smartphones, and information should be taken very seriously. The top security protection suites providing antivirus, anti-spyware, and antispam protection for stand-alone computers, networks, and mobile devices are discussed below, with recommendations regarding the setup and configuration of the software.

## *Stand-Alone*

The software selections described in the stand-alone section are primarily for the computers and laptops of solo practitioners.

We do not recommend stand-alone products for targeted protection, such as antivirus protection. This type of software is not sufficient today to keep your systems protected. The Internet security suites are the only way to go, where you get much more functionality and protection and many more features for your computer at a much more affordable price.

Solos and small firms should definitely consider acquiring a single integrated product to deal with spam, viruses, and malware. Norton's security suite is a top seller for the single computer market. It is highly rated and does a credible job in protecting your computer. We don't recommend purchasing Norton for several reasons. It gets average ratings for ease of use and threat blocking is not on par with the top products. We've also found that it may be difficult to uninstall. We continue to find it, along with McAfee, to be a heavier load on computer processing versus its competition, although not as bad as versions from several years ago.

For those users who want to avoid the problems that may be caused by Norton and McAfee, we recommend using Kaspersky Internet Security, especially if you like your security suites to be hassle-free. This product contains firewall, antivirus, antispyware, rootkit detection, antispam protection, and much more. The antivirus engine that Kaspersky uses has been consistently highly ranked by independent testing labs.

The firewall included with this software provides two-way protection, scanning both incoming and outgoing network traffic, effectively blocking any hacker attacks against your system. The automatic exploit protection engine watches program behavior and aims to block zero-day vulnerabilities in the most commonly used software. The anti-phishing engine and URL advisor will keep you safe from drive-by malware while browsing the Internet, and the anti-banner blocks annoying banners and other advertisements on web pages. This product even comes with webcam protection technology that stops criminals from using your own webcam to spy on you. With all the bonus features included in this protection suite, purchasing this product is a very good deal. Kaspersky is available directly from **www.kaspersky.com** and costs $79.95 for one-year protection on up to three computers. This is an excellent choice for the small firm environment, and it is Windows 10 compatible.

## Enterprise Versions

Enterprise versions of integrated security solutions are designed for small, medium, and large computer networks, and the software administration is performed from the server rather than on each individual computer system. The client software is installed or pushed from the central server to the local workstations with little or no effort. The server supplies the clients with program and definition updates and provides an interface to centrally manage all clients from a single console. Of course, enterprise licenses are a little bit more costly than purchasing a single license, but not by much. Even with the slight increase in cost for an enterprise license, you'll more than make up for it on the money you will not have to pay your IT consultant to manage and support the product.

## Integrated Security Solutions

Kaspersky Endpoint Security for Business protects Windows and Linux-based servers (including 64-bit versions) and even Mac computers from all types of malicious programs and threats. The product provides protection from threats such as viruses, Trojans, worms, keyloggers, malware, rootkits, bots, and so on. This is now the standard that we are seeing in the security product market. Former providers of antivirus software are providing protection from spyware and other malware, offering a more complete security solution to their business customers and all but eliminating the need for multiple applications to protect your systems from viruses and malware. This software provides real-time protection by scanning all files that are opened and quarantining infected files. The application can scan specified areas of the file system based on preconfigured, scheduled scans or on demand from the administrator. The scanning of critical system areas, such as running processes and startup objects, helps prevent malicious code from launching, and the ability to scan inside compound files provides an extra layer of protection.

Another great feature of this product is the inclusion of encryption. Administrators may select from full-disk or file-level encryption, protected through the implementation of the AES 256-bit encryption standard. This feature is even supported for removable devices.

Kaspersky Endpoint Security for Business is a scalable security solution, allowing administrators to define the number of instances of the program they would like to run simultaneously to accelerate the processing of server requests. The software offers flexible administration through centralized installation and control. The administration tool can be used centrally to install and manage client applications and, once they are downloaded and installed, to push updates to the clients for rapid deployment of critical security updates.

Endpoint Security for Business, similar to other integrated security solutions, scans not only for viruses but also for other threats and malicious programs, such as spyware and keyloggers. In most instances, this solution can serve multiple functions. We use a Kaspersky security solution on our network systems to provide us with complete malware protection.

By using an integrated solution that is capable of handling both antivirus and antispyware protection, we have one less product to purchase and renew on a yearly basis. The product also allows for different configuration settings depending on the type of network to which the computer system is currently connected, similar to the way Microsoft Windows 7 and 8 handle the different firewall settings.

As the security of smartphones is brought to the public's attention, more vendors are integrating smartphone security with their products. Kaspersky is no different. Endpoint Security for Business protects smartphones from data leaks, malware, and viruses, and it also allows an administrator to lock and wipe the device remotely should it be misplaced, stolen, or lost. Some of the additional key features include GPS tracking, SIM card monitoring, privacy protection, and folder or device encryption. The antispam protection feature works to block both unwanted calls and text messages. For those firms that allow employees to bring their own devices (BYOD) and connect them to the firm's network and data, administrators can use this product to separate corporate and personal data on these devices. Through the creation of "containers," this software can store all of your firm's data within the encrypted work "container" fully separate and apart from your employee's personal information on the device. If a problem were to occur, such as a lost device or unexpected termination, you could wipe the firm's data off of the device without harming the personal information. Integrating security for mobile devices can save you money by not having to deploy a separate Mobile Device Management (MDM) solution, which could cost thousands of dollars.

Kaspersky Security for Mobile runs on Android, iPhones, Windows Mobile, Symbian OS, and BlackBerry devices.

There is a ten-license minimum purchase for Kaspersky Endpoint Security for Business Select. Cost for the product begins at $44.99 per license and includes technical support and upgrades for a year. This product is Windows 10 compatible. Kaspersky is priced much lower per license than its competition and is an affordable, complete security solution that is rapidly taking over the market. This software product is offered for purchase with one-, two-, and three-year subscriptions. Licenses can be obtained directly from Kaspersky's website (**www.kaspersky.com**) or from any authorized reseller.

Besides Kaspersky, we also recommend the enterprise product Trend Micro Worry-Free Business Security. It is highly regarded and available in three editions: Advanced, Standard, and Services. We don't recommend the Services solution, as the entire configuration is set up and maintained by Trend Micro as a hosted solution.

All of the editions include antivirus and antispyware capabilities, as well as advanced security features such as the ability to limit or prohibit the insertion and usage of USB devices attached to company computer systems. The software will protect both servers and computers from malicious threats and will automatically change settings on laptops to protect employees when they are out of the office. The software will monitor active processes and applications to prevent unauthorized and harmful changes to your computers. Unlike the Standard Edition, the Advanced Edition includes antispam filtering for Microsoft Exchange Server as well as multilayered spam protection, and it offers protection for Mac clients and servers. The Advanced Edition also protects mobile devices using Microsoft Exchange ActiveSync. Cost for the product starts at around $38 per license for the Standard Edition and $62 per license for the Advanced Edition, which includes technical support and upgrades for a year. This software product is offered in one-, two-, and three-year subscriptions, and licenses can be purchased directly from Trend Micro's website (**www.trendmicro.com**).

We see fewer and fewer installations of Symantec's enterprise products. There's a lot of "bad blood" out there since Symantec introduced its Endpoint Protection product. Independent testing has shown that Symantec is improving this product with each new version. It is getting better at detection, is less problematic with software conflicts, is more stable, and is not nearly the processor load that prior versions experienced. Even with these improvements, we are reluctant to suggest Symantec, especially since we've been burned in the past.

## Antispam Protection

For antispam protection in an enterprise environment, we use and recommend McAfee's SaaS Email Protection & Continuity service and love it. If you are not using enterprise products and have implemented a stand-alone solution, there is probably antispam capability contained within your stand-alone product.

McAfee's antispam solution provides a lower-cost alternative service for e-mail antispam and antivirus without any of the headaches that come with other products, including the products you actually need to install and run on your e-mail server. Note that your e-mail flow will be rerouted so that it goes through McAfee's servers before being delivered to your mail server or e-mail client. You can purchase the McAfee service directly from the vendor or through a reseller. McAfee's SaaS Email Protection & Continuity solution provides a web-based interface to manage the quarantine, where spam messages are held. Users receive a quarantine message in which they are provided with a summary of the e-mail messages quarantined throughout the day. From this message, a user can choose to release a quarantined message with just a simple click of the mouse.

That's all you need to do to release a captured false positive. As the administrator of the account, you can choose when and how frequently you'd like your quarantined summary delivered, whether at the close of business or sometime overnight and whether just once a day or a couple of times throughout the day. We recommend that you set the delivery of the quarantine summary for at least once near the end of the work day so that any false positive quarantined messages that need to be released can be released the same day without the need to wait overnight until you get back into the office the following morning.

McAfee also has a "mail bag" feature included with this recommended solution. This feature spools your e-mail in the event you lose your Internet connection or your e-mail server goes down. Once your connection or server comes back up, McAfee will feed you the e-mail that it held during the outage, which means you won't lose any e-mail even if your server goes down for a period of time. Even while your server is down, you can access your e-mail from the McAfee portal. In other words, you will not be without e-mail even when your server goes down. Some may think that is a curse rather than a benefit, so we'll let you choose.

McAfee has a very good reputation for quality service, and clients seem to be very happy with it. Since we started using this product three years ago, all of our clients have switched as well (now that Postini is defunct), and the feedback continues to be excellent. You may need to tweak the default rules a bit upon initial installation since McAfee is pretty aggressive in blocking messages. As an example, by default, any message with the word *webinar* in it is blocked. That doesn't work for us since we attend (and give) a lot of webinars. Modifying the spam rules is easy, but your administrator should take on this task if needed.

McAfee provides 24/7 technical support; automatic maintenance and upgrades; and a monthly, annual, or multiyear subscription. This product can be purchased directly from McAfee's website (**www.mcafee.com**), and costs start at $23.71 per license for a one-year subscription.

## Ransomeware Protection

Over the past year, we have seen many law firms affected by a new type of malware called ransomware. Some of the most recent variants that we have come across include CyrptoLocker and CryptoWall. Ransomware is a type of malware that restricts access to a computer system and demands that the user pay a ransom to the operators of the malware to remove that restriction—in short, the malware encrypts the user files on a computer system, making them inaccessible. For a fee, the files can be decrypted. It should be noted that we do not recommend paying any ransom, as there is no guarantee that the decryption key will be turned over upon receipt of payment. Rather, to protect against ransomware, we recommend the use of security software and a well-configured backup solution.

Ransomware has been successful in bypassing some security solutions, such as those listed above. One of the reasons for this is the malware's ability to change, and in most instances, it is actually installed by a user with administrative privileges over his local computer. This software has been documented primarily to infect a user's computer through the inadvertent clicking of links embedded within a spam/phishing e-mail or in attachments to such an e-mail.

However, there are steps a firm can take to protect its systems from ransomware. First, make sure your security software is up to date and configured properly for doing regular scans and actively monitoring your users' computers. Many security solutions have definitions to catch and prevent older versions or variants of ransomware, so it's important to keep these programs running as recommended. Second, we recommend a product called CryptoPrevent to assist in the blocking and prevention of this malware. CryptoPrevent was designed to protect systems from CryptoLocker and has grown to protect computers against other malware that utilizes the same infection tactics and launch point locations. CryptoPrevent can be downloaded and purchased from the vendor's website at **www.foolishit.com/cryptoprevent-malware-prevention/** for $15 per license. This program updates itself automatically as new definitions and signatures are released by the vendor, and it is a product that we have recommended and installed on our clients' computer systems.

Finally, you must have a proper backup solution designed to mitigate the effects of a ransomware infection. Ransomware has the capability to infect or run against any volume accessible from the infected computer, including any directly attached USB drives. To combat this, we recommend that users disconnect USB drives directly attached to their computer systems or servers when not in use. Further, we recommend firms utilize an offsite backup solution in addition to having locally stored backups of your data. Backups, whether local or offsite, should always be encrypted. This way, if you were to become infected with a variant of ransomware, you would have the ability to restore the infected data from a recent backup.

# CHAPTER FOURTEEN

# Case Management

IF YOU STILL LIVE in the paper world, you may not know that a case management application provides all of the functions that you are probably currently performing. You use a Rolodex or some other type of method to aggregate your contact information. We still see address books at the office supply store, but more and more contact information is collected in an electronic form and synchronized to mobile devices. You have a calendar to schedule events, which may be written in a Day Planner. You have a file for each client or each client matter. We hope you use a word processor—or at least your administrative assistant does—to generate documents. You track everything you do for each client matter or keep some sort of diary. You probably even generate some sort of status concerning each matter. These are all functions of a case management system.

Even in a world full of smartphones and wireless devices, it amazes us that most solo and small firm lawyers still don't use a computerized case management software application. We've been making that statement for more than ten years. Case management is a must-have for today's modern law office. You may have heard other terms that describe the same type of software. Vendors attempt to differentiate themselves by describing their products with different names. You may hear descriptions such as practice management, contact management, litigation management, and so forth. Bottom line: They are all case management products, although they vary greatly in functionality. Arguably, the term *practice management* is more inclusive and encompasses what is termed "front office" (case/client information) and "back office" (accounting and billing).

There are several choices for case management, some of which we will cover here. The features vary by manufacturer, so make sure you understand what you're buying. Probably the feature we are asked about most is the integration of e-mail and contacts with case management. Make sure that the product will work with your e-mail system and that you understand how it needs to be configured. The synchronization is getting better, but most of our clients are less than impressed with many of the implementations of synchronization support. For example:

♦ How does the software deal with a common firm-wide Public Folder Calendar?

♦ Will the product synchronize with your iPad or smartphone?

♦ What if you don't have an Exchange server and use hosted Exchange services?

♦ What e-mail clients are supported?

♦ Can you access your e-mail using other devices and software, or are you restricted to using only the e-mail interface of the case management software?

♦ Can you synchronize data with your Google account?

♦ Will synchronization occur wirelessly, or do you have to connect a cable and manually sync your data?

♦ Are IMAP connections supported or only POP3?

♦ Can you sync everything in your personal mailbox, or are you limited to a subset, such as contacts and calendar only and not the tasks?

There are two mistakes that we consistently see when firms decide to implement a case management system. The first mistake is the failure to require everyone in the firm to use the system. You will not realize the full return on your investment if only a few employees use it. In fact, it tends to cause a whole new set of problems, because sometimes there is crossover between lawyers and cases and some operate within the case management system and some don't. The second most common mistake is the failure to invest in training. Training will allow all employees to use the features of the case management system fully, thereby becoming more efficient and properly organizing all data for a client matter. Simply dumping a case management system into a firm is worse than useless. When you price the software, price the training as well.

As with other sections of this book, we cannot mention or address every case management package or every feature of every product. We mention the most popular and widely used case management packages that we see being used by solos and small firms.

## Amicus Attorney

Amicus Attorney (**www.amicusattorney.com**) from Gavel & Gown Software is a good small firm package that provides a fairly simple approach to case management. The technical requirements are very reasonable and don't require a huge and expensive computer to run. There are essentially two desktop versions available, or you can choose to select the cloud version. The Amicus Attorney Small Firm Edition should work for most solo and small law firms. It is an on-premise solution that can be installed for a single user or on a server for multiple users. The pricing has not changed in the last seven years (highly unusual, but welcome) and remains at $499 for the first user license and $399 for each additional license. The same pricing applies even if you are upgrading from a previous version of Small Firm. As of this writing, the current version is Amicus Attorney Small Firm 2014.

The 2015 Premium Edition uses SQL Server to achieve unlimited user and unlimited data access. The good news is that the Premium Edition comes with an embedded SQL Server Standard Edition Restricted Runtime for use with the Amicus Application Server. This mean you don't have to make a separate SQL purchase unless you want a more robust environment.

For very large-scale installations, a separate SQL server is recommended. SQL Server 2014, 2012, 2008 R2, and 2008 (Standard or Enterprise) are supported. Certainly a consideration is the cost of the SQL Server software and the hardware to run it on, which can add a hefty price to the implementation costs, especially if you need a lot of CALs (Client Access Licenses). An improvement over prior years' versions is the support for 64-bit versions of the operating system and SQL server. This means that more memory can be supported if you implement the 64-bit versions instead of the 32-bit versions.

The first user license for the Premium Edition costs $999, and each additional user is $699. The first user cost is the same as the last five years, and the additional user cost is the same as last year's price.

Mobility is a real focus for the majority of vendors these days. Amicus is no exception. Amicus TimeTracker is an available add-on that is used to connect your mobile phone to the features of Amicus Attorney. You can record your time, edit previous entries, see your list, and much more. The data is securely transmitted over the Internet between your firm's Amicus Server and your device. The data stays on your server and is not stored on your mobile device. TimeTracker works with most mobile devices with a modern browser. That would include iPhones, iPads, Android and BlackBerry and Windows phones and tablets, and Windows and Mac desktops and laptops. Amicus TimeTracker is available during the thirty-day evaluation period and will always be available if you run Amicus Attorney (Premium or Small Firm) that has a valid maintenance plan.

If you have the Premium Edition, you can synchronize contacts, tasks, and calendar entries by using Google or Outlook as a conduit without any additional purchase. If you need more than just contact and calendar synchronization, the Amicus Anywhere product is available to provide a secure remote connection to your Amicus Premium environment using a browser. Amicus Anywhere provides you with a remote access solution and keeps your data under your control on your server and not in the cloud. Amicus Anywhere also includes TimeTracker, which was mentioned above. Amicus Anywhere is only available for the Premium Edition and not the Small Firm version. There is no additional cost for Amicus Anywhere, but you will have to have a maintenance plan in place. In other words, as long as you pay for maintenance (a touchy subject among a lot of users) you'll be able to take advantage of Amicus Anywhere.

The Premium Edition includes a client portal to facilitate collaboration with your clients. Client portal access is an often requested feature from both attorneys and clients. We are beginning to see more and more case management systems include client portal access. The Amicus Client Portal access gives clients real-time access to selected matter information securely. You can grant specific clients access to particular matter files, specific documents, notes, and events on those files. Clients can upload new documents to their matter files and even add notes to the documents. The Amicus Client Portal is available as an opt-in when you sign up for a maintenance plan. Notice the push for you to purchase maintenance just to get additional features.

In addition to the on-premise solutions (Amicus Small Firm and Amicus Premium), there is also an option for a cloud-based implementation of Amicus. Amicus Cloud is a full-featured solution that includes matter management, calendaring, task management, contacts, phone call management, global full-text searching, billing, time entries, expense tracking, reporting, document management, and trust accounting. There are also additional features such as a date calendar, collections assistant, and conflict checker. Amicus Cloud uses the cloud services of Microsoft Azure. It is accessible from any device using a modern browser. Supported browsers are Internet Explorer 9 or above, Firefox 9 or above, Safari 5 or above, and Chrome 16 or above. The cost for Amicus Cloud is $45 per user per month (billed annually), which is $540 per user per year. In addition, hosted Exchange services are available for an additional $10 per user per month. That means $660 per user per year if you opt to include Exchange. These dollars are going to add up quickly, especially if you have more than one or two users. As with any other cloud service, make sure you understand the terms of service when placing client confidential data on a third-party server.

A trial version of Amicus Attorney (both on-premise and cloud) is available and highly recommended if you are considering purchase. Try the product first to make sure that it meets your needs and will work in your computing environment. Amicus Attorney is often mentioned in reviews as being the most user-friendly product, probably because of the graphic representation it uses as the interface.

## Time Matters

LexisNexis has a couple of offerings suitable for the solo and small firm market. Time Matters (**www.timematters.com**) used to be the most popular case management package for solo and small firms (before being purchased by LexisNexis), but we have yet to do a single new installation in over fifteen years. Time Matters is a very powerful case management application, but it can also be fairly complicated for many small firm lawyers. It is an absolute necessity to purchase training if you are considering implementing Time Matters in your firm. The learning curve is steep but well worth it because Time Matters is truly a feature-rich program.

The current version is Time Matters 14, which includes a Mobility service to keep you connected via your smartphone. Time Matters requires the installation of a dedicated server, which can significantly increase implementation costs for the solo and small firm lawyer, but we agree that Time Matters needs a dedicated server for adequate performance of the application. Also, Time Matters is only supported in a local, directly connected environment. This means that the use of any wireless connections or WAN technologies for the application, which prevents most data center implementations, is not supported. The workstations and server need to be connected to the same local network. Peer-to-peer networks are not supported, hence the requirement for a dedicated server. You can use some versions of Windows (e.g., Windows 7, 8, or 8.1) as a server with five or fewer connected workstations. There is limited support for virtual servers, but that shouldn't be a problem if it is properly sized. Perhaps the installation requirements are why we haven't seen any new Time Matters installations for a long time.

Version 14 includes the Time Matters Client Portal feature. This feature is designed to allow you to share your Time Matters documents with clients, experts, and other third parties. The portal provides Fortune 100–level security using WatchDox, previously available only to Fortune 100 companies. WatchDox is now integrated into Time Matters, you don't need to pay more for online document sharing. However, you will have to maintain an annual maintenance plan in order to take advantage of the portal features.

With the Time Matters Client Portal your firm will have:

- Easy file sharing capabilities across desktop, laptop, and mobile devices
- Complete control over shared confidential documents, including the ability to
  - ◇ Restrict which viewers can copy, print, or forward documents
  - ◇ Add visual watermarks unique to each user
  - ◇ Set an expiration date for access according to your schedule
  - ◇ Revoke previously granted access to block the opening of documents
  - ◇ Prevent screen capture with Spotlight
    - Obscures all but small areas of a document at one time
    - Scrolls with the viewer to allow access to every section of content, but never all at one time
- Encrypted and secure cloud storage to allow access to content at any time, on any device
- System administrator power to wipe access to your firm's documents at any time

Licensing for Time Matters is based on concurrent users. Time Matters 14 starts at $985 for the first user, which is the same price as last year and includes a maintenance plan for the first year. Additional users are $640 each. The ordering process for Time Matters has improved over the last several years, and you can complete the transaction online without contacting a sales representative as was required previously. We highly recommend that you register for the free thirty-day trial if you are considering purchase. Time Matters can be a very large investment for your firm, so you should try it before you buy it.

## PracticeMaster

A highly rated case management application (and our personal favorite) is PracticeMaster by STI (**www.practicemaster.com**), which is the choice of most solo and small firms in our area. By the time this book is published, version 18 should be the shipping version of PracticeMaster. PracticeMaster comes in three versions: PracticeMaster, Platinum, and SQL. The first license for PracticeMaster Basic Edition is already included if you have the Tabs3 billing software. The regular version of PracticeMaster contains a number of useful features that most lawyers would desire. You can view a comparison chart for PracticeMaster at **http://practicemaster. com/products/practicemaster/pm_comparison.html**.

PracticeMaster introduced workflows with version 16. Workflows are essentially triggers that automate tasks within the software. In addition, PracticeMaster has one of the best e-mail integration schemes that we've seen. Smartphone support is excellent as well, especially with Tabs3 Connect.

PracticeMaster and Tabs3 licenses include the first twelve months of maintenance—the same as the distribution plan used by Time Matters. Perhaps it is a new trend to include maintenance automatically as a way to ensure that users pay for support. The cost of the regular PracticeMaster version is $600 (including twelve months of maintenance) for the first active user license, and each additional license will set you back another $280. The pricing hasn't changed for the last three years.

In addition to the regular PracticeMaster version, STI offers PracticeMaster in a client server version, which scales to larger implementations. The Platinum version costs $1,320 (including twelve months of maintenance) for the first user license and $365 for each additional user. Don't forget to add the cost of the client server environment when calculating the total cost of the project. As an example, the Platinum Server Software is required for any client server implementation of Tabs3 or PracticeMaster. This Server Software could cost from $965 for 8 connections up to $7,475 for 1,024 server connections. An even more robust implementation would be using Platinum SQL Server Software. Cost for the SQL version is $1,320 for 8 connections and up to $39,340 for 1,024 server connections.

The good news is that STI has updated its website to calculate the software cost quickly. Just go to the price estimator page (**http://practicemaster. com/products/pricing_info.aspx**) and select which products you are interested in, the number of concurrent users, and the number of billable entities if selecting any of the financial packages.

Version 18 of PracticeMaster is the current shipping version and it includes several new features. The Fee and Cost Entry has been modified to be more like Tabs3. The Rate Code and Sales Tax values from Tabs3 are now displayed and can be modified. In addition, "Budget exceeded" now displays when entering fees and costs in PracticeMaster. There is a new Fee Recap icon that has been added to the main toolbar and provides a quick summary of fees entered for a timekeeper on a specified date. There is a new Outlook Synchronization Settings Report, which will aid your IT support personnel in troubleshooting any Outlook synchronization problems. The Form Designer has two new buttons in the toolbar. Magnetic Snaps and Snap to Grid will help with alignment of fields. There are additional enhancements as well. Improvements to Calendar Conflict, Graphical Calendar, and WorkFlows round out the upgrades included in version 18.

In a move to enhance security, the version 18 SQL edition of PracticeMaster has an option to enable encryption to protect your data with an extra layer of security. When you enable encryption, there is no place to enter a user-defined passphrase, which would indicate that STI could technically access the data since they presumably have access and knowledge of the encryption keys. To be fair, someone with knowledge of the encryption key would have to connect to the law firm network or be given physical access to the database. We are beginning to see vendors offering some form of encryption as a way to protect access to the user's data. This is especially important for attorneys who have an ethical duty to protect the confidentiality of their clients' data. It is unfortunate that only the SQL version has the encryption option, which will put it out of reach for the majority of solo and small firm lawyers.

Mobile access requires the Platinum versions of PracticeMaster and Tabs3. There is no additional cost for Tabs3 Connect if you are enrolled in a maintenance plan. With Tabs3 Connect, you have access to Tabs3 and PracticeMaster anywhere you can connect to the Internet. This means you can get to your data from your smartphone or other mobile device. You have access to your client and contact information, fee and cost entry, personal and firm-wide calendar, and more. The connection is secured using SSL, and the data resides in your Tabs3/PracticeMaster environment in your office. Because you must have the Platinum Editions of Tabs3 and PracticeMaster to take advantage of Tabs3 Connect, however, the mobile access feature will be out of the reach of many solo and small firm lawyers, which is very unfortunate, especially since Tabs3 Connect is the best remote access solution to practice management data we have ever seen. After the original introduction of Tabs3 Connect, STI changed its offering, and you can now purchase a subscription instead of requiring all products to be on a maintenance plan. The subscription cost is $5 per user per month. You can learn more about Tabs3 Connect by visiting **http://www.tabs3.com/products/tabs3_connect/tabs3_connect.html.**

Finally, it is highly recommended that you obtain the trial version of PracticeMaster. This will help you determine whether the product is right for your practice and your installed infrastructure. We don't think you can go wrong with this product. It is constantly being improved, and the support is among the best in the industry.

## Clio

Clio (**www.goclio.com**) is a SaaS (Software as a Service) solution that is used by solo, small, and midsized firms. Access is via an Internet browser, which means it will work just fine on an Apple computer. The maker of Clio is Themis Solutions, which is headquartered in Vancouver, British Columbia. Themis Solutions has the excellent reputation of listening to its customers and constantly enhancing Clio based on users' suggestions. The company also has remote offices in Toronto, Canada and Dublin, Ireland.

Clio is a full-featured practice management platform. Features such as document management, time tracking, calendaring, tasks, billing, and so on, provide a complete solution. The billing component works well for hourly and flat-fee billing. Users have control over billing rates at the activity or matter level. Clio is highly customizable: Custom fields can be inserted into any matter file. These custom fields have many different formats, so lawyers can enter dates, dollar amounts, website addresses, and even full-text paragraphs.

Clio can also be configured to synchronize with Outlook and Gmail to provide bidirectional syncing of calendar, contact, and task entries. Clio integrates with many online service providers like Box, Dropbox, Google Drive, Chrometa, NetDocuments, Fastcase, Law Pay, QuickBooks online, and many others. You can see all the apps that integrate with Clio at **https://www.goclio.com/features/integrations/**. Like many other practice management products, Clio is constantly being improved, as can be seen by the increased integration with third-party products.

Clio Connect is a feature that enables firm members to share resources and collaborate with clients, contacts, or co-counsels easily through a secure web-based portal. This grants clients, contacts, or co-counsels the latitude to review and contribute to relevant matter developments and helps to mitigate associated inefficiencies related to time-consuming communications.

Clio's dedicated iOS application makes it easy to manage your law firm from your mobile Apple device. There's also an Android app for Clio. With the mobile app, you can track your time and expenses, add tasks, check appointments and deadlines, and anything else you need to manage your practice from the road. If you don't have an Android or iOS device, not a problem. There's also a mobile web version of its service, making Clio accessible on BlackBerry and Windows mobile phones as well as other types of mobile devices.

Another key feature is the ability to use the Amazon S3 cloud for data storage, giving you complete control over your data. Your data is automatically backed up to Amazon S3 on a weekly basis. Once the data is replicated to the Amazon cloud, you have the option of downloading the data to your own computer. It is available to subscribers of the Boutique and Elite plans. There is no additional cost to use this feature other than the cost from Amazon, which is pennies per gigabyte. Clio calls this the Data Escrow feature. Just search the help forum on the website for complete instructions on how to activate Data Escrow.

Finally, Clio provides extensive support to customers free of charge. In-house telephone support is available seventeen hours a day. The same service is also available by e-mail and live online chat. Training webinars are available online, typically three days a week. Clio also offers a library of training articles and videos.

Take advantage of the free thirty-day trial to make sure Clio will work for you. Clio has changed its pricing and moved from a flat cost to a tiered pricing model that adds additional features as you move up the tiers. The Starter level costs $39 per user per month (billed annually) and includes the performance dashboard, custom invoices and templates, time tracking, support, and the secure client portal: Clio Connect. The next level is the Boutique offering, which costs $59 per user per month (billed annually). It includes everything in the Starter version and adds accounting integrations, custom fields, UTBMS coding, Zapier integration, API access, and data escrow. The top tier is the Elite plan, which costs $99 per user per month (billed annually). It includes all the Boutique features plus priority support, originating attorney revenue report, and court calendaring rules.

There are no longer reduced costs for support staff, which drives the cost up compared to prior years. Discounts are available as a member benefit from more than thirty state and municipal bar associations and the American Bar Association. Be sure to ask your bar association if a discount is available.

Clio is one of our favorite SaaS practice management systems, and we highly recommend it. Several of our clients have converted to Clio and never looked back.

## Rocket Matter

Rocket Matter, around since 2007, is another SaaS practice management system, but it is web-based and designed specifically for the legal industry. It also contains a time and billing function, which provides almost all you need for your law practice. Rocket Matter is very popular among Macintosh users, as it is web-based. There really isn't any case management application that is specifically geared toward the Apple user community, so Rocket Matter meets that need through web browser access. You can still use Rocket Matter if you are a Windows shop, since all you need is an Internet connection and a web browser.

Many practice management providers offer specific apps for the mobile market. Rocket Matter is no exception. There are specific apps for iOS and Android devices. As we become more and more mobile in our practice, we need mobile access to the firm's data. You can access Rocket Matter using the dedicated apps, but you can also use any mobile device capable of running a full browser. Rocket Matter has been optimized to work with the iPhone, iPad, and Android devices.

Rocket Matter has released an app specifically designed for the iPad. As CEO Larry Port said, "This is not just a companion app to our Web version. It is a full-featured practice management platform." You have the full ability to edit and access contacts, tasks, matters, notes, etc. Probably one of the most valuable features is that you can operate the app with or without an Internet connection. This means that you can have your full practice management environment with you at the courthouse even if there is no Wi-Fi access to the Internet, which many locations ban or prevent. Any information that you modify or add while you are offline will synchronize with your Rocket Matter environment once you reconnect to the Internet.

Two years ago, Rocket Matter introduced a client portal offering, which allows users to create branded portals. You have the ability to share calendar information, documents, and invoices with clients or anybody else. The portal integrates with LawPay, allowing clients to pay their invoices online. Another Rocket Matter feature is the integration with Copy2Contact to add new entries to your contacts. Rocket Matter also integrates with other cloud providers such as Gmail, Google Calendar, Box, QuickBooks, Dropbox, and Evernote.

Rocket Matter has maintained the same pricing as last year. Rocket Matter will cost you $65 per month for the first user and then $55 for each additional user. However, Rocket Matter does offer discounts if you make a longer commitment (more than month-to-month) and pay quarterly, annually, or for a two-year term. The discounts—10 percent for quarterly payment, 15 percent for annual payment, or 20 percent for the two-year term—apply to the initial user fee of $65 per month and the $55 per month for additional users. Larger discounts are available, but you have to contact Rocket Matter for details. These dollars can add up quickly when compared to an on-premise solution. As an example, your annual costs will be over $3,400 if you have five users paid on a monthly basis. You could get that cost down to around $2,700 a year for the five users if you commit to a two-year term. There is a fifteen-day free trial period, so you can try it out before making the financial commitment.

Rocket Matter is a SaaS implementation and carries the same issues as other providers. The data is held by a third party even though it is transmitted on an encrypted channel. Like Clio, Rocket Matter is always working on improvements to its product. For example, it now provides offline access to your data. Those who have used Rocket Matter generally give it favorable reviews, and we recommend that solos and small firms that want a SaaS solution take a look at both Clio and Rocket Matter.

## Firm Manager

LexisNexis has its version of a hosted case management system, which is called Firm Manager. It appears that Lexis has Rocket Matter and Clio squarely in its crosshairs as it competes in the SaaS market. Firm Manager is priced at $44.99 per month for the first user and $29.99 per month for each additional user, which is the same as the last two years. New this year is annual pricing. The cost is $400 a year for the first user and $270 a year for additional users. These costs put Firm Manager as a much cheaper alternative to the more robust Clio and Rocket Matter. Some local bar associations may receive additional discounts.

Firm Manager now has many more features than last year's version. There is matter management, document management, calendaring, billing, and mobility. The Money Finder function searches through tasks, meetings, and documents to find items that are not associated with time and expense entries. You are asked if you want to bill for these unassociated entries, therefore capturing more income. Trust accounting is also included in Firm Manager. With Firm Manager, you get unlimited online storage for case exhibits, documents, client lists, and more.

We have yet to hear of any attorney using Firm Manager. We're very impressed with the improvements to Firm Manager. LexisNexis really wants your business and will import all the matters from your existing matter management system for free. It depends on what your current practice management product is as to what data will transfer. Firm Manager isn't nearly as robust and full-featured as something like Time Matters or ProLaw, so we are pretty sure there won't be a home for some of the data in Firm Manager. The other concern is potential price increases over time, which LexisNexis is known for historically. Firm Manager finally looks like a good candidate for the solo and small firm attorney and is worth a test drive. If you are considering Firm Manager, be sure to take advantage of the thirty-day free trial to make sure it will meet your practice needs.

## MyCase

We are seeing a lot great deal of buzz surrounding another web-based case management product. MyCase is similar to the other products and provides similar functions, such as shared firm calendars and reminders, tasks, contact management, document organization, document assembly, time and billing, and so on. It even has iOS and Android apps to facilitate mobile access. MyCase is also jumping into the lawyer marketing game by providing a MyCase website. Actually, the value of the website is working as a portal for clients to get information about their case, pay their invoices, and securely communicate with the firm. Besides the portal aspects, MyCase looks to be getting into the website provisioning business by building lawyer websites that integrate with MyCase (that's where the client portal feature comes in) and include a blog, social media integration, Google analytics, a responsive code for mobile device access, and basic Search Engine Optimization. The website feature is a one-time fee of $500 and then $50 a month.

MyCase uses Amazon services to deliver its product to the end user. It runs on Amazon EC2 cloud servers and is backed up using Amazon S3 storage. Data is transferred using SSL encryption and encrypted before being written to disk. Originally, the client access portal differentiated MyCase from the other case management products, but today, the client portals of many of the others function similarly to MyCase.

MyCase now has a one-way integration with QuickBooks. There is a one-time fee of $99 to add this feature. Essentially, it takes the accounting data from MyCase and pushes it into QuickBooks. The integration offers transmission of detailed invoice data, recording of payments on invoices, trust account transactions, new customer data, and cash and accrual accounting. Frankly, we're not sure why you would want to implement this feature since it really isn't a synchronization but a one-way push. Typically, integrations with QuickBooks are problematic since you have to make sure the QuickBooks accounts are always mapped properly to the data coming from and to the case management system.

MyCase costs $39 per month for each lawyer and $29 per month for each paralegal or staff member. There is a free thirty-day trial, which we recommend you take advantage of. In late 2012, MyCase was acquired by AppFolio, a provider of web-based software for vertical markets. Time will tell if MyCase will survive the acquisition or migrate more to a marketing application rather than dealing with the daily needs of the solo and small firm attorney. We still don't have any clients using MyCase, but the feedback on the listservs has been positive.

## HoudiniEsq

HoudiniEsq is an interesting product in that it offers an on-premise and cloud-based version. The feature set is comparable to the other case management offerings. Document management, workflows, contacts, matters, notes, calendars, invoicing, document automation, and much more are all functions contained within HoudiniEsq. There are free plugins to work with Outlook, Word, Acrobat, SoftFile, Excel, QuickBooks, Evernote, QuickBooks, and so on. There's even a plugin for WordPerfect X7, which doesn't exist for any other case management platform that we are aware of.

HoudiniEsq has no user software application; everything is accessed via a web browser. Even the on-premise solution uses a browser to run HoudiniEsq. The on-premise solution does require a dedicated computer to host HoudiniEsq, and the technical requirements suggest that you could get an inexpensive ($300–$400) computer from Best Buy to run HoudiniEsq. Sorry, but we certainly don't agree that a cheap consumer-grade machine should be used to house your critical firm data and the core of your practice. Perhaps spending a couple hundred bucks is acceptable to run the trial and to accomodate one user. The reality is that most firms (even solos) have at least one support person in addition to the attorney. Speaking of a trial, there isn't one. At least not in the traditional sense. The on-premise single-user version is given away for free. It's a full-blown version of HoudiniEsq, but only supports one person.

The cloud version costs $64 per user per month and requires a minimum of three users. The on-premise solution is sized for 2 to 1,200 users. You are required to purchase an annual subscription for each user. There are two on-premise plans. If you have thirty users or less, the cost is $192 per user per year and a one-time server fee of $1,280 for every ten users. That means you will pay a minimum of $1,664 for the first year ($1,280 for the server and $192 × 2 users) for the minimum two-user requirement. The annual cost would then drop to $384 ($192 × 2 users). The maximum thirty users would cost $9,600 [($1,280 × 3) + ($192 × 30 users)] for the first year. Subsequent years would cost $5,760 ($192 × 30 users). If you are at thirty users or more, you are required to move to the HoudiniEsq Elite package. That cost is a one-time fee of $8,160 and an annual subscription cost of $240 per user per year.

The annual subscription cost makes it much more attractive from a cost perspective than the other case management options. Besides the ridiculous notion that you can run your practice on a Best Buy computer, the user interface is based on Flash technology. HoudiniEsq will have to change that very quickly since Flash will no longer be supported (actually blocked) by many of the popular browsers because of security issues.

## *Others*

Additional products are available, but some of the vendors aren't public with the cost or system requirements. We are less than impressed with companies that aren't open about their pricing and technical requirements. Products like ProLaw (Thomson Elite) and AbacusLaw (Abacus Data Systems, Inc.) require you to fill out a contact form so that a representative can contact you about pricing. We are not fond of this practice and recommend a relationship with more open vendors, especially when you are entering this arena and want to make an apples-to-apples comparison.

# CHAPTER FIFTEEN

# Time and
# Billing Software

PROBABLY THE SECOND MOST important function of your law practice is billing your clients for services rendered. Practicing law is clearly the most important, but getting paid is second, thereby ensuring the continued success and sustainability of your practice. Lawyers tend to hate the billing process and are not much fonder of the software that helps them generate invoices. Some solos and small firms still generate invoices manually, although their numbers are diminishing. We'll look at both options and try to give you some guidance.

You have a lot of options for generating your bills, from a completely manual system to the fully automatic capture and assembly of invoices. Two components make up the items in your bills. One is time. This component is calculated by taking the hourly rate and applying it to the amount of time spent on a task. You can capture this time manually or automatically while the task is being accomplished. Flat fees are also considered time components, where the dollar amount is applied irrespective of the time spent. The second component is the fixed-cost items of the invoice. This would include such expenses as postage, copier costs, filing fees, courier charges, and any other fixed fees. As with the time components, you can track these expenses manually or automatically (to some level or another) through the use of technology.

We are seeing more and more firms adopting some sort of alternative fee arrangements (AFAs) for their practice. It may be flat fee only or a hybrid type of billing with a flat fee portion and an hourly portion. AFAs are more complicated to automate because of the various customized rules that may apply. The good news is that many of the software packages are sophisticated enough to handle customized rules and they are getting better and better as time goes by. You may have to deal with some manual override techniques if the billing software can't accommodate a particular AFA scenario.

As in other sections of this book, we'll try to cover a lot of the billing methods and applications that we see being used by the solo and small firm attorneys. This will not be an all-inclusive list, so if your favorite product isn't mentioned, it probably means that we've never seen (or heard of) it being used by solo or small firms.

## Manual Generation

Pencil and paper are the simplest way to capture time and expense. With manual generation, however, you must remember to log your time and the number of copies or whatever other chargeable component needs to be tracked. Make no mistake about it, studies have shown over and over again that this manual tracking results in a lot of lost time and expense. Because a lawyer's time equals money, many lawyers are shortchanging themselves by not moving to a technology-based solution.

Nevertheless, if this is what you do, on a periodic basis (daily, monthly, the end of the case, and so forth), you total the charges and generate the bill. Many solo practitioners start by using a word processing package to generate their bills to save some money. These bills are professional enough in appearance but still require manually adding up numbers and multiplying other numbers. In addition, another method is needed to keep track of payments made by the client and/or transfers of funds from other sources, such as the trust account. As the practice becomes more complicated, the billing process becomes more susceptible to mistakes.

If you must start with a manual method for generating your invoices, invest in billing software as soon as possible to improve your accuracy, maximize your income, and minimize your losses.

## Accounting Software—QuickBooks

Some lawyers are actually using a financial accounting package to generate their bills. Certainly the most popular software application we see is QuickBooks by Intuit (quickbooks.intuit.com). Using QuickBooks to generate invoices allows the firm to have a total financial package, where all sorts of financial reports are available. However, productivity reports are not available. You won't be able to determine easily how many billable hours are attributed to a specific individual or how much money you lost due to write-offs. One advantage of using QuickBooks is the ability to generate payroll. This may not be a compelling reason for many lawyers, especially given the added cost, complexity, and reporting requirements. In general, it is more cost-effective to use a third-party service provider, such as ADP or Paychex to handle solo and small firm payrolls. QuickBooks can also handle processing of credit card payments, thereby integrating another piece of the financials into a single product. We hear that most lawyers began using QuickBooks because their accountant told them to. Make sure your accountant sets up your chart of accounts in QuickBooks so you know where certain charges and fees should go. Your CPA should be familiar with financials for a law firm. If not, it's probably time to look for a new accountant.

QuickBooks comes in several different versions—even an online version that allows access from any computer and does not require installation of any software. We don't recommend using the online version, as it requires that your data be stored at Intuit. Your financial data is highly sensitive, and we recommend that you control your own data and not risk compromise by holding it at a third-party site. Consider, too, the possibly severe consequences if the third party is "down" and you can't manage the financial part of your law practice. In fact, QuickBooks Online was down for several hours over a couple of days in late March 2011. Services such as QuickBooks Online, Intuit Merchant Services, and Intuit Payroll were unavailable. In the last quarter of 2010, Intuit announced that it was shutting down the Quicken Online service and users could only export their data in CSV (comma separated values) format. While Quicken is a consumer-based product, we certainly wouldn't want to be stuck in the same situation if Intuit decided to shut down QuickBooks Online.

Since QuickBooks is an accounting package, some knowledge of financial principles is helpful. You will need to set up a chart of accounts for your practice. We recommend consulting with your accountant before configuring QuickBooks so that your financial categories are consistent with the accountant's needs and your business needs. If you are new to QuickBooks, you may want to consider purchasing a support plan to help you learn the features of the software and get technical help. Many local community colleges also offer evening classes for QuickBooks, which would be a relatively inexpensive way to get some training in how to use the product.

The QuickBooks versions vary in cost based on the capabilities of the software and number of concurrent licenses that are needed. The Pro version costs $299.95 for a single user, and the Premier version cost $349.95 for a single user. The Enterprise version is now sold on a subscription basis with varying subscription levels. The Silver subscription includes the Enterprise software, a full-service plan and advanced reporting. The Gold subscription adds payroll to the Silver edition. The Platinum subscription adds advanced inventory and advanced pricing to the Gold subscription plan. You can choose to pay the subscription monthly or on an annual basis. Either way, you are required to commit to an annual period for the subscription. The cost for a single user will vary from $75.60 per month for the Silver subscription all the way to $120.60 per month for the Platinum subscription.

Most solo and small firms will find that QuickBooks Pro is more than sufficient for their needs. In previous years, Intuit offered a three-pack license at a reduced rate over the single-user cost directly from its website. The three-pack is no longer a separate product, and you'll need to order three licenses. The good news is that the traditional multiuser discount is applied. The single user price is $299.95. Selecting two users will cost $549.95, or $274.98 per user. Three users will cost $799.95, or $266.65 per user.

To enhance its desktop offering, Intuit has QuickBooks Pro 2016 Plus, which is an annual subscription product that includes support, data backups, and upgrades. The cost is $299.95 per user per year. Phone support is available on a 24/7 basis; up to 100 GB of data can be backed up, and recovered data is available up to forty-five days; and the updates and enhancements happen automatically. You also receive upgrades as they are released. That would save you from spending money to upgrade with each edition (yearly). The $299.99 per-year cost seems rather high to us, especially since you'll be spending money year after year. We would recommend purchasing the standard QuickBooks Pro software and upgrading the version every three years. That will save you several hundred dollars over the life of the software.

The QuickBooks Premier version contains additional features for specific industries and expanded reporting capabilities. As an example, you can track unbilled time and expenses for professional services; set different billing rates by employee, client, and service; and analyze profitability by matter. Intuit has significantly reduced the cost of the Premier version. QuickBooks Premier 2016 is $379.95 per user. Like QuickBooks Pro, there is a QuickBooks Premier Plus 2016 version that includes support, backup, and updates. The cost of QuickBooks Premier Plus 2016 is $299.95 per user per year.

Unlike previous years, there is no upgrade pricing available. In other words, if you owned an older version of QuickBooks, you could get a reduced price for upgrading to the newer version. Not anymore. There is no incentive for being a loyal QuickBooks user. You have to pay the same price as a new user would. Intuit, like many other application providers, is trying to migrate users to a subscription cloud service. That way it gets a constant revenue stream. Microsoft is doing the same thing with Office 365. At some point, vendors will no longer offer local loaded applications and everything will be in the cloud. To that end, there are four versions of QuickBooks Online—Self-Employed, Simple Start, Essentials, and Plus. Each edition adds additional features to the previous edition. As an example, Essentials adds instant sales and profit reports to the Simple Start features. The monthly cost for the QuickBooks Online versions are $10—Self-Employed, $13—Simple Start, $27—Essentials, and $40—Plus.

Besides the Windows version, a version for Macintosh computers is also available. Accountants love it when lawyers use QuickBooks as their billing software. They can take the QuickBooks data file at the end of the year and generate tax returns with relative ease.

However, we don't recommend using QuickBooks for billing for several reasons. First, the invoices are very sterile looking and have very little ability for customization. The data is there and clients can understand the information, but the invoice format lacks any capability for graphics, different fonts, custom text to identify different sections, or rearrangement of how the information appears on the page. Showing remaining balances properly is an issue too—a real problem if you want to show trust account balances and transfers or automatically indicate how much of the evergreen retainer needs to be replenished. As previously mentioned, QuickBooks Pro won't provide you with any productivity reports unless you purchase the Premier version. You're going to have to find a different way to determine how many write-down hours an associate had for a month or the amount of no-charge entries by client. In spite of these limitations, we still see a lot of lawyers using QuickBooks.

## Billing Specific—Timeslips

Arguably the most popular and widely used billing software among solo and small firm lawyers is Timeslips by Sage (**www.timeslips.com**). Timeslips is a billing-specific software package that generates bills, tracks receivables, and manages trust accounting. We see many Timeslips installations in solo and small firm offices, especially those that have no case management system. Even so, we are beginning to see firms implementing invoicing products that are included with the integrated solutions that we describe later on.

Probably one of the reasons for the popularity of Timeslips is that it can be configured specifically for the legal industry right out of the box and supports the LEDES billing format with the optional electronic billing module. When you first install Timeslips, you select the type of business. This configures Timeslips to use the types of tasks and expenses that are specific to the industry. As an example, when you select the legal profession, default tasks are automatically created that deal with those tasks that are performed in the law office. There will be tasks for consultations, document review, and depositions, and so forth. The expense names are also automatically created and would include such costs as copier usage, courier fees, postage, and the like. Trust accounting is also built into Timeslips, which is another reason the software is very popular in solo and small firm offices. You can configure Timeslips to deduct fees earned from the trust account automatically or leave it as a manual transfer process. In addition, Timeslips can automatically create the dollar amount to place on the invoice to bring the retainer amount back to a set level. This is a very popular feature for those attorneys who have evergreen retainer arrangements.

Timeslips is licensed on a per-machine basis. Each computer that needs to access Timeslips will require the purchase of a license. In a small office, it is often the case that only one computer is used to process billing. The timekeepers (typically lawyers) may elect to track their time manually on paper and give the time sheets to the office manager or bookkeeper for entry into Timeslips. This arrangement keeps licensing costs down and allows for growth in the law firm. As the firm grows, additional licenses may be purchased and network access configured for the Timeslips database. Larger firms that may use a terminal server need licenses only for the number of concurrent users. With the expanded interest and implementation of virtual computers, this concurrent license model may be a way to control costs.

The current version is Timeslips 2016. It is the only version of Timeslips that is compatible with Windows 10. Timeslips costs $619 for a single station, which is a huge increase ($99.01) over last year's cost. Additional network stations may be purchased online up to a total of ten stations. The cost per workstation keeps getting lower and lower as the number of workstations goes up. With ten workstations, you will pay $376 per computer. If you only need five workstations, then your cost will be $403 per computer. You'll have to contact Sage if you need eleven or more licenses. Timeslips is also trying to force users into an annual subscription model. There is talk that the perpetual license for Timeslips will be discontinued, leaving only annual subscriptions. Service plans are also available for Timeslips, but they are no longer available online. You will need to initiate a chat session to get the support options and costs. If you have never used Timeslips, we recommend that you consider the purchase of a support plan at least for the first year of operation, although it could be a little pricey. After the first year, we do not recommend that you pre-buy any support. Access to the free online knowledge base is usually sufficient to work through most issues that you are likely to experience.

Sage has totally revamped its maintenance plans. You can no longer just purchase access to the support personnel. The offered plans also include upgrades to the product. Effectively, you are paying for software upgrades as part of the maintenance plan, which significantly increases your total cost of ownership. As an example, maintenance plans for previous years would cost a few hundred dollars a year to get unlimited access to tech support. That same unlimited access (also includes free upgrades) now could cost several thousands of dollars a year. It's pretty obvious that Sage is including the software upgrade cost when they price out maintenance. The three maintenance plans all include software upgrades. The Business Care plan has three levels—Platinum, Gold, and Silver. The Platinum plan gets you unlimited access to technical support, priority calling to the Premium Support Team, the eBilling add-on, unlimited minor data corruption repair, and one major data corruption repair for the year. The Gold plan includes a Timeslips upgrade (2017) and service releases as well as six incidents of technical support and access to Tech Tuesday Courses; it also bumps you up to the Premium Support Team. The Silver plan includes a Timeslips upgrade (2017) and service releases as well as three incidents of technical support. The plans are priced based on the number of licenses you have. You can estimate that maintenance will cost you approximately $210 per seat for Silver up to $285 for the Platinum plan. If you only have one of two licenses, it may make sense to pay a few hundred dollars a year and get a free upgrade to boot. If you only upgrade your Timeslips version only every three years or so, you may elect to forget about maintenance. Without a maintenance plan, it will cost you $180 per incident should you need to contact tech support. Frankly, we think that this change in maintenance will drive a lot of users to other products or to drop any maintenance plan they may have purchased in the past.

Timeslips can also link with QuickBooks. Setting up this integration is a manual process and can be complicated. You have to make sure that the

Timeslips tasks and expenses have a corresponding QuickBooks account. Permissions (Timeslips and QuickBooks) also need to be considered. If you run a networked version of QuickBooks, multiuser versus single user could also cause some complications with the integration. A reader of a previous edition of this book advised us that Timeslips technical support will not help with any of the accounting aspects dealing with the QuickBooks link, as they feel it is giving financial advice and do not want the liability. Perhaps this is one of the reasons why our clients who use Timeslips and QuickBooks don't bother with the integration and manually input data into QuickBooks.

Some of the providers for case management software have also built links to Timeslips. Case management product links are possible for Abacus Law, Amicus Attorney, Legal Files Software, and Time Matters. Contact the provider of the case management software if you are interested in how the link would work and what the limitations are.

## Billing for a Mac

There are not that many legal-specific software applications for Mac computers. Most Mac users will migrate toward web-based products for their firms. There are some native Mac applications, but like the Windows world, more and more users are moving toward the cloud.

### Bill4Time

SaaS offerings are very popular in the Mac community. All you need is an Internet connection and a web browser. Bill4Time (**www.bill4time.com**) is one billing package we see used in law offices with Macs. It is a secure hosted environment that is available from any computer at any time. A free thirty-day trial will allow you to see if it fits your needs. Bill4Time has a legal-specific version, which contains ABA Task Codes, LEDES export for invoices, Litigation Advisor export for invoices, Trust Accounting with Summaries and Reports, and Easily Check for Conflicts of Interest. Most attorneys will want to get the Legal Solo or Legal Pro version. The Legal Solo is limited to 100 clients and 100 matters, whereas the Legal Pro and Legal Enterprise version allow for unlimited clients and unlimited matters. The Legal Solo version limits data storage to 2 GB. The Legal Pro version has a 10 GB storage limit, and the Legal Enterprise version has unlimited data storage. One convenient feature of Bill4Time is the mobile apps. There are apps for iPhones running iOS 5.0+, Android 3.0+, and BlackBerry OS 10.2.1. Supported tablets include iPads running iOS 6.1 or later, Kindle Fire 3.0+, and Android 3.0+. This means you can use your mobile device to enter your time and expenses while out of the office. As we mentioned before, you need to keep track of all your billable activities—otherwise, you are losing money. The mobile app feature is a great way to help maximize your revenue.

Before you commit to spending any money for Bill4Time, take advantage of the free thirty-day trial period. You can try any one of the three legal plans for thirty days for free. After the thirty-day period, you will need to add credit card information to your account; otherwise, the account automatically becomes inactive.

The Legal Solo version of Bill4Time is $30 per month ($10.01 more than last year) and includes one user license. You can only add one additional user at a cost of $20 per month (also $10.01 more than last year). This may be fine for the solo practitioner, but some small firms may need more than two users. The Legal Pro version is $50 per month ($10.01 more than last year) and also includes one user license. However, you can add unlimited users at a cost of $20 per month (also $10.01 more than last year) for each user. Finally, the Legal Enterprise version is $100 per month (only 1 cent more than last year) and also includes one user license. Unlimited users can be added for $25 per month ($15.01 more than last year) per user. We think that $100 per month for unlimited storage and premium support is a bit much for a web-based billing package. At that rate, we would recommend investigating other billing alternatives to include on-premise solutions.

### EasyTime

Many of the practice management implementations also include some sort of billing mechanism, so you may not need a separate software application. We'll mention a few of the billing packages that are available for the Mac, but we certainly can't mention them all. One such stand-alone package for the Mac is EasyTime. EasyTime, by Bright Light Software (**www.brightlightsoftware.com**), runs natively on Mac OS X and does not require any third-party database packages. The current shipping version is 3.0.5, released March 7, 2015. It requires MacOS 10.7 or higher. The cost is $240 (same as last year) for a single user and $320 ($30 more than last year) for a network version. A version 3 upgrade is available for $90 for the single user and $110 for the network version.

Version 4 is under development, but information was not available at the time of publication for this guide.

## Billings Pro

Another popular package is Billings Pro (**www.marketcircle.com/billings pro/**) by Marketcircle. The Billings Pro cost model is one that identifies how many invoices, statements, or estimates you can generate per month. The Freelance plan costs $5 per user per month and limits you to five invoices, five estimates, and five statements per month. This plan doesn't seem to be very practical unless you only have a couple of very large clients and don't invoice all that often. The Professional plan is $10 per user per month and gives you unlimited invoices, estimates, and statements per month. Since there is no contract commitment with Billings Pro, we would recommend starting with the Professional plan. If it looks like Billings Pro is something that works for your firm, then convert to the Professional Yearly plan, which costs $99 for a full year. Additional users are also $99 per user for the year.

A big concern with the Billings Pro cloud offering is that its datacenter is located in Canada. Your data is stored locally and gets synchronized to the servers in Canada. This means that you can continue to work if the network is unavailable or the servers are unreachable. Some attorneys may feel that storing billing information for their clients in another country is not a problem and accept potential cross-border issues. Of course, the Canadian attorneys welcome the fact that the servers are in their own country.

As with most of the products mentioned, be sure to take advantage of the free thirty-day trial before purchase.

## Integrated Packages

Many of the case management products support integration with billing packages. This means that you enter your information into the case management system and the time or expense is automatically captured for the billing process. There are advantages to using the same vendor for your case management and billing needs. The products are designed to work together and share information in a very efficient manner. However, selecting these all-in-one packages may not give you the best features of each package. If you really want a "best of breed" implementation, then make sure you investigate how the case management and billing packages share the data. Many case management applications provide links to billing packages by other vendors. Be careful to understand how to configure these links, especially if it is a manual process. We've seen clients who added tasks to their case management software and forgot to define the linkage to their billing software. This means that you may not bill for the effort when you use these newly defined tasks.

## PCLaw

LexisNexis has a couple of billing options to address the needs of solo and small firm law offices. A very popular package is PCLaw. The current version is PCLaw 14 (**www.lexisnexis.com/law-firm-practice-management/ pclaw/**), which includes a mobility function to keep your mobile devices synchronized with Outlook for access to calendar and contact information. PCLaw includes some features that you would expect from a case management system. You can keep track of contacts, calendar entries, phone calls, notes, tasks, and so on. This choice may be a good alternative for a solo practitioner to keep start-up costs down since it includes basic case management functions along with billing in a single package. PCLaw can also be used as the billing component when integrated with the Time Matters case management software.

PCLaw can handle a lot of different billing methods such as flat-fee, task-based, split, contingency, retainer or LEDES-compliant electronic bills. Trust accounting capabilities are also included to manage disbursements and receipts for those clients requiring trust accounts. PCLaw also includes accounting functions for paying your bills and tracking receivables. You can even send out your bills via e-mail. All of the firm's financials can be managed in a single package. Optional services for payroll integration and credit card processing are available for additional fees.

We are seeing more and more vendors adopting the Lexis model by including the first year of maintenance into the product cost. No more opting out of the annual maintenance for new purchases. You certainly have the option of not renewing your maintenance agreement, although you may not want to let it lapse. The Annual Maintenance Plan (AMP) bundles technical support, software upgrades, support, training, and access to PCLaw Mobility Service. Also, if you let your maintenance lapse, you will be charged a restart fee to get your AMP subscription back on track.

PCLaw 14 costs $935 for the first user and includes a year of maintenance. The cost to add additional users is $695 each and also includes the first year of annual maintenance.

Transparency doesn't seem to be a hallmark of LexisNexis. If you want to know the cost of renewing your maintenance plan or adding additional PCLaw users, you have to already own the product or contact a LexisNexis representative. The pricing is no longer available on the LexisNexis website for the public to view. As we've mentioned before, this is not a practice that we are fond of, and we recommend using products from vendors that are transparent with their pricing.

Juris is another billing software application offered by LexisNexis. It is typically used by larger law firms or in integrating with Time Matters. We have never seen Juris used in a solo or small firm setting. As with some of the other products mentioned, you have to contact Lexis to get pricing information. You can't even get a single license cost as you can with Time Matters or PCLaw.

## Tabs3

Another popular billing package is Tabs3 by STI. Tabs3 is the companion product to PracticeMaster, which is STI's case management software. Tabs3 pricing is based on the number of billable entities. Like so many other vendors, the cost of the software includes the first year of maintenance. The single-user version of Tab3 is $415 for two timekeepers and increases to $675 for five timekeepers. You'll need to purchase the multi-user version if you need more than one person accessing the data at the same time.

The regular multiuser version is available for two, five, nine, and nineteen timekeepers. The cost is $675, $1,340, $1,915, and $3,065, respectively. The Platinum version of Tabs3 costs $950 for 2 timekeepers up to $15,940 for 100+ (maximum of 999) timekeepers. STI defines a timekeeper as someone whose time is tracked in the software.

See the Case Management chapter to learn about the mobility features of Tabs3 Connect, which became available in version 16.2 Platinum Edition. Even though Tabs3 Connect is a "killer" application for mobile access to your data, we don't think many solo or small firms will spend the money to have both Platinum versions of Tabs3 and PracticeMaster along with the requisite maintenance plan to get the feature included for no cost.

Version 18 of Tabs3 is the current shipping version. Most of the enhancements contained in version 18 have to do with reporting. The period-based reports are now date-based reports. The following reports are date-based and can be run for previous periods.

- Timekeeper Productivity Report
- Category Productivity Report
- Timekeeper Profitability Report
- Productivity Report by Category for Each Timekeeper
- Productivity Report by Tcode for Each Timekeeper

Another enhancement is the ability to print a receipt in the Payment Entry and Client Funds programs for any form of payment. Previously, only receipts for credit card payments could be printed. The majority of changes have occurred in the optional General Ledger Software (GLS) add-on for Tabs3. GLS now includes a new Account Information Report that mirrors information from the Balances, Budgets, and Journal Entries tabs. Additional GLS features are a new Bank Account Manager to show all bank accounts and credit card accounts. In addition, you can now import bank account transactions into GLS. The supported file formats are OFX (Open Financial Exchange), QFX (Quicken Financial Exchange), and QBO (QuickBooks Financial Exchange). Finally, you can now Undo Reconciliations in GLS. New features in the optional Trust Accounting Software (TAS) include automatic trust payments from Tabs3; the ability to combine multiple deposit, EFT, or check transaction into a single item for reconciliation purposes; a new Bank Account Manager to see a summary of all accounts in TAS; and the ability to import bank account transactions using OFX, QFX, or QBO file formats.

Unlike other billing packages, Tabs3 has separated out various financial functions and priced them as individual components. As an example, there are additional components such as trust accounting, general ledger, and accounts payable. This means that you can expand Tabs3 from a pure billing package into a complete accounting package. You can find more information about Tabs3 at **www.tabs3.com**. We regard Tabs3 as highly as we do its case management counterpart, PracticeMaster. It also consistently receives high ratings from legal software experts.

## Amicus Premium Billing

A less widely used billing option is provided by Amicus Attorney. A lot of solo and small firms use Amicus Attorney as a practice management package, but few use the billing option. There are two billing packages available, and the version of Amicus you are running determines which is appropriate. You would use the Amicus Premium Billing application if you are running Amicus Attorney Premium Edition. If you are running Amicus Attorney Small Firm Edition, then the Amicus Small Firm Accounting software is for you.

Amicus Premium Billing 2015 adds billing, collections, and trusts to your Amicus Attorney installation. Like most billing packages, it lets you capture time and expenses for hourly, flat-fee, and contingent billing. Each license is priced at $249, which makes it one of the lowest-cost billing packages. This product will not run by itself; it is an add-on to the Amicus Attorney Premium Edition case management software. Maintenance and technical support plans are also available. You can purchase a maintenance plan that includes Amicus Anywhere (Premium Edition Only), Amicus TimeTracker (Premium and Small Firm Edition), Amicus Client Portal (Premium Edition Only), product upgrades, unlimited telephone support, prearranged callbacks, unlimited e-mail support, and remote desktop assistance. The first license will set you back $550 a year but also covers Amicus Attorney Premium software maintenance. Each additional license is $495, so the dollars will add up quickly if you have more than a couple of users. Also, the annual maintenance plan will automatically renew unless you notify Gavel & Gown that you want to cancel the maintenance renewal. You can also commit to maintenance for a three-year period for a lower cost per year. The cost is $420 per year for the first user and includes coverage for Amicus Attorney Premium. Maintenance for additional licenses beyond the initial one would cost $365 per year. You also have the option of purchasing a technical support plan only, without product updates. Unlimited technical support for a year is $295 for the first license (includes the required Amicus Attorney support) and $145 for each additional license.

Amicus Small Firm Accounting combines billing and accounting packages into a single software product. This is a completely standalone application and does not require the base case management software as in the Premium Edition. Although not a requirement, Amicus Small Firm Accounting will integrate with Amicus Small Firm to give you a total practice management solution for your firm. The initial license cost for Amicus Small Firm Accounting is $499, and each additional license is $399. Like the Premium package, the Small Firm version lets you purchase maintenance or technical-support-only plans. The maintenance plan, which includes product updates, mobility, and unlimited technical support is $385 and includes support for the base case management product.

According to the Amicus product pricing page, you must purchase maintenance for the Amicus Small Firm product even if you don't own it when purchasing the billing maintenance. The maintenance cost for each additional license is $305 and includes the Small Firm maintenance. Unlimited technical support only is the same cost as the Premium version. The cost is $295 per year for the first license and $145 per year for each additional license.

## Final Thoughts

One of the higher-level (expensive) billing alternatives is provided by ProLaw, which is a Thomson Elite product. ProLaw is an integrated package, and the billing component is not available as a separate function. Very few solos and small law firms have chosen this route in our experience.

Most of our clients who use stand-alone applications have chosen QuickBooks or Timeslips for billing, and they are generally quite happy with what they have chosen—although everything has a learning curve. All of these vendors are happy to let you sample their product in one manner or another, so don't hesitate to try before you buy. Also, if you aren't keen on accounting, talk to your friends who are equally numbers-challenged and see what has worked for them. In many cases, the choice has been made by someone at the firm who is going to perform the accounting or bookkeeping functions, and that's fine. As long as you stay with one of the "majors," you won't be left scrambling to find someone who knows your obscure time and billing package if that person leaves.

# CHAPTER SIXTEEN

# Litigation Programs

**S**EVERAL PROGRAMS CAN AUTOMATE certain litigation support functions, and while they offer different features, they fall into two general categories: case organization programs and courtroom presentation programs. Case organization programs are databases that are set up to analyze and manage facts and evidence. The common ones include Lexis-Nexis Concordance (**www.lexisnexis.com/en-us/litigation/products/concordance.page**), LexisNexis CaseMap (**http://www.lexisnexis.com/en-us/litigation/products/casemap.page**), Thomson Reuters Case Notebook (**legalsolutions.thomsonreuters.com/law-products/solutions/case-notebook**), and Sanction Solutions Verdical (**www.verdictsystems.com/Software/Verdical**).

Summation (**http://accessdata.com/solutions/e-discovery/summation**) is a case organization program now provided by Access Data. The litigation support products many of you have known, such as iBlaze, are still being offered by Access Data. Access Data has now integrated its forensic products and e-discovery tools in an attempt to provide a total end-to-end solution. The Summation products provide the e-discovery capabilities while Forensic Toolkit (FTK) and MPE+ provide the core forensic capabilities. The newly named offerings are AD eDiscovery, Summation Viewer, and Summation.

These programs help you organize and review the information for your case. You can accomplish various tasks such as tagging for privilege, creating privilege logs, identifying responsive documents, etc. They are typically installed on-premise on your own hardware, but some also offer cloud solutions. More and more companies are now offering cloud-based electronic discovery platforms where you upload electronic files for review and ultimate production. Law firms are embracing these cloud solutions, which can be very cost-effective and don't have the technical headaches of on-premise solutions.

CaseMap from LexisNexis is one of the most popular case organization packages for solo and small firm lawyers, given its lower cost and ease of use.

One of the up-and-coming e-discovery review tools is the cloud-based Logikcull (logikcull.com). You upload your data, and when the system is done processing, you get an e-mail notification. Logikcull handles all sorts of file formats and is completely browser-driven. That means all you need is a browser and an Internet connection. You can use your smartphone, your tablet, your computer, or any other device with a browser. Logikcull can de-dupe, can de-NIST, use OCR, group e-mail threads, and do much more. Security is not a problem either. You define who can access what information down to specific files and permissions (e.g., comment, view only, redact, etc.). Logikcull is priced according to the number of active projects (matters) and not by the user. As an example, $3,000 a month gets you five active projects and 50GB of uploaded data.

Trial presentation programs manage and display electronic evidence, including exhibits, video and text depositions, sound files, and more. They facilitate quick access during trials and hearings and include on-the-fly annotation, such as highlighting and call-outs. Trial presentation programs include Trial Director (**www.indatacorp.com/TrialDirector.html? sc=26**) and Visionary products (**http://www.visionarylegal.com/ products/productslist.aspx?groupId=1**). Sanction (**http://www.lexisnexis. com/litigation/products/hearings-and-trial/sanction**) is a very popular and well-known litigation software application of LexisNexis.

The above-referenced products are full-featured and can give a lot of whiz bang to the presentation of evidence at trial. The reality is that today's jurors want to see trials that seem like they are watching TV. They expect fancy effects, transitions, call-outs, and quick access to exhibits. The day of the document camera is fading, although by no means gone. Annotations similar to the "John Madden marker" are finding their way into courtrooms across the country.

More maturity is now evident in the trial presentation packages for the iPad. Products such as TrialPad (**http://www.litsoftware.com/trialpad/**) by Lit Software turn the iPad into a presentation tool for litigators. Since we are seeing so many litigators equipped with an iPad, we would highly recommend starting with TrialPad for your trial presentation software. For

$129.99 ($40 more than last year), you can't go wrong by giving it a try. Trial Director for the iPad is a free download from the app store, but is a quite limited version of the flagship product for the PC. Free is a good price for the solo and small firm attorney, but reviews indicate that inData Corporation has a long way to go with its iPad application. Try it out, but we'll guess that you will end up using TrialPad instead. There are some other "competitors" to TrialPad, such as ExhibitView. We feel that TrialPad has maintained the beachhead for iPad trial presentation software. Unless you have a compelling, specific reason to use one of the other products, it appears that TrialPad is the product of choice for the majority of litigators.

Most of the above-mentioned products have free downloads for a trial period or online demos. Although we do not review them in detail, they should be considered by lawyers with litigation practices. Be sure to read the iWin: iPad for Litigators chapter by Tom Mighell and Paul Unger, which includes more detail about litigation products that are available for the iPad.

# *CHAPTER* SEVENTEEN

# *Document Management*

**D**OCUMENT MANAGEMENT SOFTWARE SOLUTIONS can be relatively expensive for the solo or small firm operation, although there are some cost-effective alternatives. Several of the better-known document management products tend to be used more for enterprise-size companies because of their cost and complexity. As the industry matures, vendors are merging the functions of document management, content management, and knowledge management. This is especially true as electronic files are becoming a critical component of discovery. You may see applications described as document management systems, content management systems, knowledge management systems, or even enterprise content management systems. Just because a vendor chooses to describe its product using particular words doesn't mean there is anything unique or special about it. In general, all of the terms previously mentioned are used for applications that organize information. The current hot topic is information governance (previously known as records management). It's a very specialized operation of document management. Information governance classifies information and has rules for retention periods according to business requirements and appropriate laws and regulations. We're not going to address products that are used in the specialized world of information governance applications.

The main purpose of a document management system is to organize information into a usable and searchable form. How many times have you looked for a file or document but couldn't remember the name or location? A document management system allows for fast and easy access to the data, whether in paper or electronic form. It also provides access control and enforceability of rules. As an example, perhaps one of your rules is that every document has a specific category (programmed ahead of time) tagged to it. This makes for consistency and removes the human error in typing or misspelling the category tag. In addition, security is another feature of document management systems. Typically, you can set security access to particular matters, specific types of files, or even unique files themselves. One person could have full control over a document, whereas another might be able to view the content but not modify it.

## DocuShare

We will mention just a few of the products that are available, but understand that document management systems are not generally designed for small-scale operations. Xerox's DocuShare (docushare.xerox.com) has been around for many years. Pricing is available directly from Xerox or through partners. An entry-level version of DocuShare (DocuShare Express) is now available for small to midsized office installations, which starts at a couple thousand dollars for ten users. The current version (DocuShare 6.6) requires a 64-bit server, which would significantly increase costs if you didn't have one available. DocuShare Express can run on 32-bit versions of Windows 2003 Server R2 or SP2 and Windows 2008 Server SP2. Unfortunately, Windows Server 2003 is out of support, so we don't recommend running on that. DocuShare may be a viable alternative, especially if you already have a Xerox copier that you could use for scanning documents. Be sure to take advantage of the free thirty-day trial if you are considering acquiring DocuShare.

## iManage

It is really hard to stay current with a product that changes names and companies so many times over its life. Several years ago, we knew it as Interwoven. Then it was known as Autonomy iManage WorkSite. Autonomy then became an HP company, and the product name changed to just WorkSite. Today, a management buyout of the business from HP leaves us with the current name of iManage Work. As with DocuShare, expect to pay thousands of dollars for this system. It is a highly regarded document management environment (if you can remember the name) but is also geared more toward the intermediate to large-scale firms.

## *Worldox*

The most popular and most used document management system for solo and small firm operations is Worldox (**www.worldox.com**). Worldox is licensed on a concurrent user basis and not per seat. The current shipping version of Wordox is GX4. GX4 Professional is the standard network client server installation that has been around for ages. It is the traditional desktop version. The next version is GX4 Enterprise, which is adapted for multi-office, remote access environments. It is typically hosted at a data center and has full communication with local applications, including Microsoft Office, Outlook, and third-party products such as case management. The final version of GX4 is a SaaS hosted solution called GX4 Cloud. With the GX4 Cloud solution, your data is hosted on Worldox servers in its data center. GX4 utilizes Active Profiling technology for ease of use and automation, enabling you to manage, share, and access all your digital content effortlessly.

The cost for Worldox GX4 Professional is $460 ($35 increase from last year) per concurrent user, which makes it very affordable for solo and small firms, especially since there are no minimum seat purchase requirements. Annual maintenance is $97 per license and is mandatory for new orders. No separate server is required, and the indexer can be run on any workstation-class computer. The computer resource requirements for Worldox are very light when compared to other document management systems. The application is very robust and easy to use, hence its popularity within the legal community.

GX4 Enterprise is intended for multiple offices and remote access environments. It looks and acts just like the local desktop (GX4 Professional) version. You must contact Worldox to get pricing information at this time.

Worldox also offers a Web Mobile addition to the Worldox software. The mobile edition gives you access to your documents from multiple devices and locations. It currently supports a wide range of devices, including any web browser notebook or desktop, iPads, BlackBerry smartphones, Android devices, iPhones, Treos, and Windows CE PDAs and cell phones. There are two pricing models for the mobile access. For $30 per user per month, you can implement the SaaS hosted solution, which installs the proxy software on your indexer. You can reduce the cost to $25 per user per month with a one-year prepayment. You can also install it on your own server, but the costs start to climb quickly. You will need a server license ($1,495), a user licenses ($65 per named user), and annual maintenance ($15 per user and $300 per server per year). If you need a proxy server, you may need to expend additional money for a proxy server license ($600) and proxy server maintenance ($120). Doing the math, it will cost you $2,195 for five users in the first year without a proxy server and $2,915 with one proxy server. Years two and beyond would be $375 per year for the maintenance charges for the five-user system without a proxy server. Installing your own Worldox/Web Mobile server makes financial sense if you plan to use it for two or more years.

Worldox also includes a Legal Hold feature. The Legal Hold feature will be a great benefit for firms and companies as part of the litigation process. If you are in litigation or if litigation is reasonably anticipated, you have a requirement not to destroy any potentially relevant evidence. Legal Hold will let you assign rights and restrictions to files. You can even create restricted-access security groups so that only authorized employees can access the designated files. In addition, each action is tracked to create an audit trail showing who did what to which file. The key feature for Legal Hold is the ability to "lock" a file so that it cannot be changed. The best news? The Legal Hold feature is free for all Worldox GX4 Professional users. You can't ask for anything better than that. Well, perhaps you can—it is also very simple to use. Do be forewarned that this is not complex "litigation hold software," which includes many more features. Worldox also has support for Mac computers, which includes many of the same functions as the Windows product. Worldox for Mac is not a stand-alone product. It requires an existing Worldox GX4 installation or the Worldox GX4 Cloud offering.

Worldox also integrates with Sony's Digital Paper device. Worldox will sync documents and notes with the Sony Digital Paper device using the included USB cable or will sync documents and notes wirelessly through a box.com account. Case management systems (see the Case Management chapter) are also used to provide a certain level of document management. Your electronic files are referenced to a client or client matter, making them easily accessible at the click of a mouse. A key point to remember about true document management applications is their stringent enforcement of the classification rules. The user must use the system within the configured rules, which sometimes frustrates people because of the rigid requirements. In contrast, applications that are not specifically document management software aren't restrictive or mandatory. The danger is that data may be lost or misfiled when the rules are not stringently enforced. Worldox is an excellent choice for document management, as it integrates with almost every case management system available. It consistently receives good reviews from legal software experts.

## Matter Center

Microsoft is getting into the practice management game. Matter Center for Office 365 was formally announced at the ILTA annual conference in Las Vegas during August 2015. Matter Center was originally used internally by Microsoft's legal team. Microsoft gave a preview of Matter Center last year at ILTA and spent the past year fine-tuning the offering. Apparently, Matter Center will not be directly available from Microsoft as a delivered product. Microsoft will distribute Matter Center through various IT providers that serve the legal market. Ultimately, Microsoft will make Matter Center available via GitHub, which is an open-source community for software development.

According to our friend and colleague Bob Ambrogi, Matter Center has the following features:

**Access anytime, anywhere**. Just like Office 365, Matter Center is available across PCs, tablets, and phones and across Windows, Apple, and Android devices. You can access matters and documents either online or offline using OneDrive for Business.

**Real-time collaboration**. Using the automatic version control feature of Office 365, you can simultaneously edit documents with multiple people inside or outside your organization.

**Easy search and data visualization**. Search, preview, and find matters and related documents across all cases directly within Outlook and Word. Power BI can be configured to visualize your matter data.

**Pinning and tagging**. Track or pin frequently used matters and documents and connect to Delve to provide personalized experiences about who on your team is working on them.

**Security compliance**. Control who can access, review, or edit a document. Get the same enterprise-grade security, management, and administrative controls as Office 365.

**Flexibility and control**. By offering Matter Center through an open GitHub repository, customers and partners can build or extend the technology to meet specific customer needs faster.

In order to take advantage of Matter Center, you must have a subscription to Office 365 and Azure.

## Acrobat

Many solo and small firm offices are equipped with Adobe's Acrobat product. The latest versions of Acrobat provide the ability to manage documents. The collaboration components within Acrobat are used to organize and reference files in a manner similar to other document management systems.

## Web-Based

Web-based document management systems are becoming very popular. The cost per user is typically more than purchasing a product for use within your firm, but you save on the hardware and internal support costs. The vendor provides the back-end hardware and software for the management of your documents. The nice part about web-based document management systems is that the information is accessible from any computer with an Internet connection. The bad part is that the vendor is holding your data and you are subject to the reliability of the Internet connection. If you elect to use one of the online document management systems, be aware of the security precautions for client data that is being held by a third party. At a minimum, make sure that the connection for accessing the documents is encrypted and that the data is stored in an encrypted form on the provider's equipment. You should also make sure that you have a copy of the data in your hands to avoid being "held hostage" by the third-party provider. And yes, we've seen that happen. More and more vendors now offer cloud solutions in addition to their traditional on-premise solutions.

## NetDocuments

NetDocuments is a popular SaaS provider for document management. Many law firms, small to large, have had great experiences with NetDocuments. We have heard lawyers say that it was very easy to install and configure. In one case, a lawyer converted his firm (tens of thousands of documents) over to NetDocuments in a weekend all by himself.

NetDocuments provides all of the features you would expect in a document management system, in addition to matter-centric work spaces, e-mail management, collaboration, and mobile access.

NetDocuments has cloaked its pricing and capabilities. You can no longer determine the costs or features of its offering. You are forced to contact the company for information or to request a demo. As we've previously stated, we are not fond of this lack of transparency.

## Plain Folders

Finally, a very simple form of document management for solo and small firms is to follow a standard folder and file naming convention along with search software (see the Utilities chapter for search tools). Besides the potential cost for search software, this is a very low-cost solution. Some lawyers will use the search capabilities of Windows or Mac before even investing in supplemental search software. Typically, folders are named on a client or client-matter basis. Files are then given a very descriptive name, such as <client name> followed by the file purpose and sometimes the date. As an example, "Rothburg request for admissions.doc" would be the filename for your request for admissions in the Rothburg matter. This is a very manageable method to organize data when your practice is small. As your practice grows, search software may be needed to assist in finding particular files pertaining to specific issues.

## Searching

Search software such as dtSearch or X1 (see the Utilities chapter) can be used to index the files within your client folders so that you can quickly find the desired document. As an example, you may be looking for the document pertaining to the request for electronic evidence or something concerning a partner's Motorola cell phone.

If you are considering the purchase of a document management system, Worldox is an excellent first choice. We have implemented this software many times, and clients are always happy with it. No matter what product you are considering, see whether there is a trial version available, or at least participate in a demo of the product, to determine if it meets your firm's needs.

# CHAPTER EIGHTEEN

# Document Assembly

Essentially, DOCUMENT ASSEMBLY SOFTWARE automates the creation of legal documents that are used repeatedly. This would include such documents as wills, leases, contracts, and letters. You can think of document assembly as templates that can be used over and over. This shortens the time for document preparation and increases the efficiency of your practice. If you use flat fees, document assembly can be a godsend.

Document assembly software can be specialized for a particular industry or can be generic. As an example, specialized document assembly software is typically used in estate planning and tax preparation. In those situations, the user answers questions in a survey type of form and then the required documents are generated using the answers provided. If you have ever used one of the personal income tax programs (e.g., TurboTax, H&R Block, etc.), you've seen how document assembly works. You may see the term *document automation*, but it means the same thing as document assembly for our discussion.

## HotDocs

In law firms, the top three document assembly packages are HotDocs, ProDoc, and Word according to the ABA's 2015 Legal Technology Survey Report. HotDocs (**www.hotdocs.com**) is the most popular document assembly software by a large margin. HotDocs is a very powerful solution and has significantly matured over the years. HotDocs is composed of many different products, such as those used for template creation, cloud-based access, desktop template distribution, and centralized server-based distribution to the users. HotDocs Developer 11 is one of the most powerful platforms for document automation and allows you to convert word processing documents and PDF forms into document generation process applications, otherwise known as templates. You create a template and determine what text to include or exclude, depending on the answers entered by the user. This is the survey type entry that was described earlier. The presentation walks you through the questions to gather the data needed to generate the document. The current version supports Microsoft Word 2003, 2007, 2010, and 2013 and WordPerfect X3 SP2, X4, X5, X6, and X7. HotDocs User 11 is the other desktop product, and it is used to generate finished documents. With HotDocs User, you complete interviews and generate documents.

As with other application software these days, HotDocs is available in a browser version too. The product, HotDocs Server 11, allows for document assembly using a standard web browser. This is particularly helpful for remote users and means you can deploy templates via the Internet. HotDocs Server 11 must be deployed in conjunction with a web application. It shouldn't surprise you that there are two additional software packages available (HotDocs Workspace and HotDocs Workspace for SharePoint).

HotDocs also has a SaaS (Software as a Service) offering, which extends the browser-based document generation to the small and midsized firm. The HotDocs Document Services are hosted in Microsoft's Azure Cloud. It allows the firm to transition from the desktop to the Internet for document generation. Think of it as the online version of HotDocs User. One of the features of Document Services enables you to e-mail links to your clients that process interviews directly. In other words, your clients can fill in the requisite data for the documents as part of an online interview process. Document Services is available at a monthly subscription rate, but you'll need to contact HotDocs to get a quote.

HotDocs also has a Cloud Services product. Cloud Services could be used by firms that need browser-based document generation, prefer a hosted (subscription-based) solution, and want to integrate HotDocs interviews into existing web applications.

Pricing information is no longer available on the HotDocs website. You must speak with a HotDocs representative to customize you document generation solution. We'll continue to say that we hate the lack of transparency when companies hide pricing information and make you contact them. Besides removing pricing information, it appears that there is no longer a free trial period. It may be that the HotDocs representative will offer a free trial in order to help ensure a sale.

## ProDoc

ProDoc (**www.prodoc.com**) is another document assembly application that is a legal resource from Thomson Reuters. It is the second most popular document assembly product. One of the interesting features of ProDoc is how the licensing works. ProDoc is licensed on a subscription basis. The basic subscription license allows for usage on three computers or by three concurrent users. If you install ProDoc on a network, the licensing enforces the three-concurrent-user limit. You can only install ProDoc on three computers if they are stand-alone and not running in a network installation. You can add additional licenses for a small additional fee. The software is licensed for a single firm at one location. If you share office space with another firm, then each firm needs to purchase its own subscription to ProDoc. Pricing used to be transparent and easily determined from the ProDoc website. Not any longer. When you request pricing, the page is redirected to a page where you are forced to fill out a form so that a Thomson Reuters representative can contact you. When a vendor goes from transparent pricing to "hiding the ball," it makes us wonder how many other things will be surprises.

The ProDoc forms are state-specific and currently only available for California, Florida, Texas, and Texas eFiling. There is also a national package available as a supplement library with links to parent BTS (Business Transactions Solution) forms on Westlaw. There are various document assembly systems available for the supported states. Be sure to check the website to see what modules are contained in each package and that your particular practice area is covered.

## Microsoft Word

We were surprised to see that Microsoft Word is the third most popular document assembly product according to the ABA's 2015 Legal Technology Survey Report. While Word is not technically a document assembly application, you can automate functions to generate documents. You would use macros and form fields as template documents to provide some consistency and automation.

## Final Words

HotDocs is the clear recommendation for solo and small firm lawyers wanting to embark on document assembly. As a generic package, it is very well suited for any type of law practice. HotDocs integrates with many document management and practice management packages. There are many choices for technical support, including HotDocs Wiki, HotDocs Forum, HotDocs Resource Center, and HotDocs Documentation. HotDocs resellers are the primary method for consulting and product acquisition.

# CHAPTER NINETEEN

# Cloud Computing

Everybody is talking about the cloud—in the legal profession and elsewhere. You can't go a single week without there being some mention of a new cloud service offering. The really scary part is that many users don't know what it means to use cloud computing and believe that the weather impacts the "cloud." That's not a joke—more than half of Americans believe that.

For our discussion purposes, the cloud is generally viewed as an external computing resource that is typically accessed via the Internet. You can participate in cloud computing by putting your own equipment in a secure data center and accessing your data (and perhaps applications) via the Internet. If you don't use your own equipment and software but elect to purchase applications through third parties, then you are using a SaaS (Software as a Service) solution. To make it easy to understand, imagine that you don't own a copy of Microsoft Office; you simply go to a site on the Internet where you are, by subscription, allowed to use Office. The resulting data is held by the provider, not you. This is exactly the environment that Microsoft is pushing with its Office 365 product.

Stats from the ABA Legal Technology Research Center's 2015 survey of ABA lawyers:

- ◆ A web-based software or solution was used by 31 percent (compared to 30 percent in 2014, 31 percent in 2013, 21 percent in 2012, and 16 percent in 2011).
- ◆ Solo practitioners were the most likely to respond affirmatively at 37.2 percent.

- Among those who had not used cloud computing, 45.9 percent said they did not intend to use the cloud in the future.
- Of those who had not used cloud computing, the top concerns they cited were:
  - 59 percent: confidentiality and security concerns
  - 48 percent: unfamiliarity with the technology
  - 47 percent: less control of data because it's hosted by the provider
  - 36 percent: losing access to and ownership of data
  - 28 percent: non-Web-based software programs are sufficient for current needs
  - 25 percent: cost or effort of switching from their current solution

The traditional client/server model puts total control in the hands of the law firm. The data is held internally, and access is controlled by the firm. You can choose to encrypt the data locally, which we recommend, or leave it in plain text. Either way, it is within the technology walls of the law firm and not directly accessible by any third party.

In contrast, the SaaS model puts your data in the hands of a third party. This is not necessarily a bad thing, but do you really know if the information is safe? Your contract with the provider may specify that the data be stored in encrypted form, but what if a disgruntled employee has access to tools that allow him or her to decrypt the data and sell it to the other side in a major lawsuit? An ongoing concern for lawyers, in light of the Edward Snowden revelations, is whether there is a government "back door" that allows it access to your data.

When you contract with a SaaS provider, you are required to accept the service as it is delivered to you. This means any upgrades or bug fixes will be implemented by the provider. Sound like a good thing? Just ask Ben Schorr, CEO of Roland Schorr, an information technology consulting firm with offices in Hawaii, Arizona, and Oregon and author of *The Lawyer's Guide to Microsoft Word 2013*, *Microsoft OneNote in One Hour for Lawyers*, *The Lawyer's Guide to Microsoft Outlook 2013*, and *Microsoft 365 for Lawyers*, all published by the American Bar Association:

> *"One of my concerns about SaaS is the double-edged sword called 'upgrades.'
> A selling point of SaaS products is that the vendor just transparently updates it
> in the background, and you don't have to worry about it. Monday morning
> you log in and . . . 'Oh, look, new features!' But what if you don't like those
> new features?*

*"What if you're on a tight deadline and Google decides to do a massive upgrade to Google Docs? Do you have time to get yourself and your staff up to speed on how the new version works? With Microsoft Office, you upgrade when you're good and ready. We do quite a bit of work with firms all over the country, in fact, helping them plan and approach that migration. Training their staff, preparing for the various consequences of the rollout, making sure their ancillary apps and add-ins are ready to support the new version. (Want some fun? Tell a managing partner that the new version of her e-mail app is NOT compatible with her case management system . . . the day AFTER she upgrades.)*

*"With SaaS, you don't generally get that. You may get no warning at all that features, user interface (UI), behaviors are about to change. You certainly aren't going to get a chance to use it before your staff does so that you can get up to speed on it and be ready to answer questions when the 9:15 messenger run is waiting to go and the documents still aren't printed (unless you want to sign into the SaaS app at 3 A.M., I guess).*

*"Hey, it's great that somebody else manages your upgrades and updates. That's usually a good thing. But it's not always a good thing. Unpredictability is not a quality I value in my mission-critical apps."*

Enough said. Besides the data security and access concerns for the SaaS model, the financial stability of the provider may be a consideration, but it is becoming less of an issue as more and more vendors are providing cloud solutions. Even if you have adequate notice that the vendor will stop providing a contracted service, the cost to migrate your data to another provider or bring it back in-house can be significant. This brings us to the topic of exit strategy. At some point, you will likely want to bring the function back within your IT control or move to another provider.

The contract should provide for specific costs and timetables to facilitate the move. It should also specify what file format you will get your data in. Will you get a copy of the complete SQL database along with the schema or just a comma delimited text file?

Another issue is the stability of the communications network. By design, you are dependent on the speed and quality of your Internet connection. Smart firms will have dual network connections to the Internet, although this will mean an increase in cost over what is normally installed at the firm. The Internet connection must be available at all times; otherwise, you will not have access to your data. There aren't many judges who are sympathetic to your problems if you miss a filing date because your

Internet connection went down. And Internet connections, as we've all miserably learned, do sometimes go down—and always without notice.

To be fair, let's look at the upsides of using the cloud . . . and yes, there are some compelling upsides.

There can be some financial advantages to contracting service to a third-party provider. Your investment in hardware and software is minimized, since you are really only passing keyboard, mouse, and screen data over the communications link or accessing the application via a web browser. The actual processing occurs at the cloud provider. All configuration and data hosting are external to your firm's infrastructure. Costs for the SaaS model can be based on the number of users or the amount of data storage volume. Either way, it is fairly easy to identify and budget for the cost of the service, which is a big selling point for a lot of firms. However, to get these "stable" price points, the contract terms are typically three to five years. This means that the firm must make a pretty long commitment to using the SaaS model and the specific provider.

The alternative to the long contract term is a much shorter subscription model. Many cloud service providers are now providing solutions where you have to commit to an annual subscription. Some are even offering month-to-month subscriptions. Typically, the shorter the commitment period, the higher the cost. As an example, many cloud-based case management applications won't make you commit to more than a year.

Another advantage to the SaaS model is the rapid reaction time to changes. It is very fast to add new users or to increase the amount of space for data storage. By the same measure, it is very fast to decrease the number of users or amount of storage space. This means that you are more flexible in controlling your costs. If your firm is in contraction mode, you can reduce expenses, assuming that the contract doesn't tie you to a minimum amount. Many firms like the mobility aspect of the cloud model, since they can access the applications from any machine with an Internet browser. Typically, there isn't anything special that needs to be installed on the client computer. The user needs only a browser and perhaps some type of plug-in to access the application. This means that it is easy to gain access to the firm's data from the office, the home, or an Internet café in the Bahamas.

Too often, all costs and all risks are not considered when analyzing a cloud solution. The cloud ballyhoo has drowned out all reasonable objections. We originally moved slowly and carefully in moving clients to cloud solutions, but we do understand that some cloud services make sense for the solo and small firm attorney. More on that later. Client/server solutions can be clearly defined from implementation through the life of the solution. You control the implementation, configuration, and ongoing costs. While you can contractually specify some costs with a cloud provider, future upgrades and exit conversions may tip the financial decision.

You may also hear of two other cloud solutions. Platform as a Service (PaaS) and Infrastructure as a Service (IaaS) are two additional cloud computing services. With PaaS, the client creates software using features and capabilities as available from the provider. Most law firms will not entertain the PaaS model. With IaaS, the necessary infrastructure is supplied by the solution provider. It owns and controls the equipment, operating system, network, and so on, and you load your applications onto the services. Think of it as having your data and applications running on "rented" hardware.

## Contract Considerations

Now for a show of hands. How many readers have actually read the Terms of Service (ToS) or Terms and Conditions (TaC) for a cloud provider service? When we ask that question at CLEs, you could count the number of raised hands with the fingers on one hand. Shame, shame, shame. As lawyers, you should be reading the contracts and the terms that you are agreeing to. Fear not. We'll point out some of the items and considerations you should be looking for in contracts with service providers.

Where will the data reside? Will it be in the United States or in some foreign country? Can you specify where the data will reside? Certainly, we would recommend that the data remain in the United States, which would avoid any cross-border issues and having to deal with international laws. And yes, even with the Snowden revelations, we don't want data in privacy-focused Europe where we don't know the laws and would potentially need a European lawyer to help in the event of a problem. "Better the devil you know," as we say ruefully.

 ♦ **Is the data encrypted in storage and in transmission?**
   Encryption will help protect the confidentiality of the information. The majority of cloud providers will encrypt the data in transit (e.g., SSL connections), but not necessarily at rest while it sits on their servers.

♦ **Who controls the encryption keys, and is there a master decryption key?** Just because the data is encrypted doesn't mean it is accessible only to you. Services like Dropbox encrypt the data in transit and while it is stored on their servers; however, they hold a master decryption key and have the ability to decrypt your data. Services like Spider Oak allow you to define the encryption passphrase, and they have no master decryption key.

♦ **Who can access your data?** This may not matter if you control the encryption, but it is worth knowing your exposure.

♦ **What is the exit strategy?** This was referenced above. Is there a cost? What form will the data be in? How long will it take to get your data? You certainly don't want to be held hostage by the vendor when trying to leave its service.

♦ **Who owns the data?** It seems like it should be a silly question, but is the data really yours or can the provider access it and redistribute it?

♦ **What about data breaches?** Make sure you understand who is responsible should there be a data breach. Who makes and pays for the data breach notifications? Will the cloud provider pay for any identity theft monitoring if required? Does the provider have adequate cyberinsurance coverage?

♦ **Is your data stored on separate physical devices, or are you comingled with other cloud customers?** Comingled storage puts you at risk should the authorities want to seize equipment for a cloud customer that you share storage with. Think of the Megaupload situation, in which many businesses went bankrupt when the authorities seized servers in a criminal investigation and their data was commingled with the company being investigated.

## Private Cloud Solution

We think that moving your data and applications to a secure data center is a much better solution for most solo and small firm lawyers. Think of it as the best of both worlds. It's your data and software running on equipment that you own and control. If you don't like the data center, you can always move or bring it back in-house. The costs are even more predictable because you control any upgrades. We have purchased rack space at data centers over the last several years and moved our clients' equipment into the secured racks. Not long ago, weather conditions in our area (a massive snowfall and a drenching storm that had folks without power for weeks) made more firms cognizant of business continuity solutions. Data centers have redundant power (generators too) and Internet connections. This means that weather conditions will not impact your ability to access your data and applications. Data centers generally guarantee at least 99.999 percent (called the five nines) uptime. Our data center guarantees 99.99999 percent (the six nines) uptime. Remember, though, that your own equipment could fail and you are still dependent on your local Internet connection. However, if your power in the office and at home is down, you can drive (as one of our clients did) to a Starbucks a few miles away and be back in business using a VPN.

As you engineer the architecture to implement a private cloud (some may call it a hybrid solution), be particularly aware of any software applications that contain databases such as your case management software. Database access using the Internet as the network is extremely risky and will typically result in corrupted data. You may have to implement a Terminal Server–type connection so that you run the client software from equipment at the data center instead of "dragging" all the data between your computer and the server over the Internet. Your IT consultant can help you determine the right connection scheme for each of your applications to achieve the greatest stability for your needs.

Bottom line: Although we don't regret our initial caution with moving law firms to the cloud, we feel we have now solved most potential problems and that the law firms can feel comfortable that they are complying with ethical requirements when storing confidential data in the cloud. We are now actively moving more and more clients to the cloud, though using the client's hardware rather than the cloud provider's. If you feel that you need to investigate and research SaaS vendors, we describe a few in this book. We just ask that you do it carefully and ask the right questions before making your decision.

We believe that many cloud providers actually offer better security than law firms themselves. There's some truth in that, and we are therefore moving in the direction of recommending cloud solutions from proven providers with good track records. Finally, be sure to check with your bar, as a number of states now have ethics opinions regarding cloud computing. If you're wondering how states are dealing with the cloud from an ethical perspective, the general view is that it is acceptable to use the cloud as long as you investigate the provider, particularly making sure that confidential client data will be adequately protected. An excellent resource is provided (free of charge) by the Legal Technology Resource Center (LTRC) of the American Bar Association available at **http://www .americanbar.org/groups/departments_offices/legal_technology_ resources/resources/charts_fyis/cloud-ethics-chart.html**, where you will find a list of cloud ethics opinions for the various states. Remember that, ethically, you are outsourcing when you contract with a cloud provider, so the ethical rules relating to outsourcing also apply.

# CHAPTER TWENTY

## Collaboration

COLLABORATION MAY OR MAY not be at the top of your list, especially if you are a solo lawyer. However, we're sure you will have occasion to deal with other lawyers or even have a need to collaborate with your clients on a case. There are some great technology solutions that allow for collaboration—and solutions are multiplying week by week. These are just a few of the primary tools available for sharing information and working in a collaborative mode.

Social networking is a collaboration area that is gaining in popularity. Facebook has won the social networking war and is now being used extensively for business purposes. Twitter and LinkedIn are also very popular, with many lawyers preferring LinkedIn as a network for professionals. So what are the top social networking sites? If you consider popularity as number of unique monthly visitors instead of registered users, Facebook is still the "800-pound gorilla." After Facebook is Twitter, LinkedIn, Pinterest, Google+, Tumblr, and Instagram—although the order changes a bit from year to year. While Google+ has not died, it seems pretty moribund to us from a business point of view.

Some lawyers are getting business through social media sites, and others are raising their visibility with potential clients or colleagues who might provide referrals. Still others have obtained opportunities to write or speak on their area of expertise. See the social media chapter for more information on how lawyers are using these new applications.

We're also seeing an increase is collaboration with clients by using client portals with cloud service providers. More and more of the case management vendors have client portals so that clients can collaborate with their attorneys and even gain access to documents and other information for their matter.

## Google Drive

Probably one of the most well-known of the collaboration tools is Google Docs, which is now an offering within Google Drive. Most users know Google Docs as a web-based office suite that can create documents, spreadsheets, presentations, forms, and drawings. Not so fast. Google has repackaged its offering, and what used to be considered a suite is now separate applications known as Docs, Sheets, and Slides, all accessible within Google Drive. Actually, you can bounce around to a bunch of the Google offerings from each of the applications. As an example, from Drive, you can get to Docs, which can access Slides and Sheets. Docs also has a return path to Drive. Other Google offerings are also accessible, such as YouTube, Maps, Photos, and Gmail, etc. The popularity of this cloud product is no doubt due to the fact that it carries the favorite price tag of all lawyers—it is completely free. The applications allow you to work on a document, spreadsheet, or presentation with others and see the modifications in real time. You just use the web browser on your computer with your Internet connection. There are even enhanced features that you may not be aware of.

You do need to have a Google ID to use Google Drive and Google Docs. Just go to **https://drive.google.com** and enter your login information. You can also create an account from the main entry page. Besides creating your files from scratch, the Google apps allow you to upload files you've already created on your computer. Documents can be downloaded to your computer as .DOCX, .ODT (OpenDocument format), RTF, PDF, TXT, or HTML (zipped). Spreadsheets can be downloaded as .XLSX, .ODS (OpenDocument format), .PDF, .CSV (current sheet), .TSV (tab separated value—current sheet), and HTML (zipped) files. Presentations can be downloaded as .PPTX, .PDF, .SVG (Scalable Vector Graphic), .PNG, .JPG, or .TXT files.

If you are used to the way Dropbox operates, you will not have any trouble with Google Drive. The easiest way to synchronize files and work on your spreadsheets, documents, etc., is to install the Google Drive application to your computer. Once it is installed, you will have a folder to drag and drop files into. They will then automatically get synchronized with your Google Drive storage. Google gives you 15 GB of free storage when you create your account. If you need more than that, you can get up to 100 GB of space at a cost of $1.99 per month or up to 1 TB for $9.99 per month.

You can upload files to your Google Drive. The Google Drive viewer currently supports many different file types:

- Image files (.JPEG, .PNG, .GIF, .TIFF, .BMP)
- Video files (WebM, .MPEG4, .3GPP, .MOV, .AVI, .MPEGPS, .WMV, .FLV, .ogg)
- Text files (.TXT)
- Markup/Code (.CSS, .HTML, .PHP, .C, .CPP, .H, .HPP, .JS)
- Microsoft Word (.DOC and .DOCX)
- Microsoft Excel (.XLS and .XLSX)
- Microsoft PowerPoint (.PPT and .PPTX)
- Adobe Portable Document Format (.PDF)
- Adobe Illustrator (.AI)
- Adobe Photoshop (.PSD)
- Tagged Image File Format (.TIFF)—best with RGB .TIFF images
- Autodesk AutoCad (.DXF)
- Scalable Vector Graphics (.SVG)
- PostScript (.EPS, .PS)
- TrueType (.TTF)
- XML Paper Specification (.XPS)
- Archive file types (.ZIP, .RAR, tar, gzip)
- Audio formats (MP3, MPEG, WAV, .ogg)
- .MTS files
- Raw Image formats

By default, files are not shared until you make them shareable. This is certainly the preferred security policy and keeps your data private unless you make a conscious decision to share the information. Once you've created or uploaded a file to your Google Drive, you configure how the file is shared. Your first option is to set what access is allowed via the link. The default is "Private—Only you can access." Selecting the "Change . . ." option lets you modify the access. Selecting "On—Public on the web" means anyone can access the file or folder on the Internet through search results or the web address without logging in. Selecting "On—Anyone with the link" means anyone who is given the link to the file or folder can access it without logging in.

Besides determining how the link is shared, you can also change what a user can do with the data. The creator of the document is tagged as the owner and can obviously do anything. Once you share the file via a link, you can define what the user can do with the file. The choices for access are "Can edit," "Can comment," and "Can view." This gives you some level of granularity in the access and visibility options. The default access is "Can edit."

As a practical point, multiple people can collaborate on a file and everyone doesn't need to have the same software or version. You can go online and create a file to start the process. Once completed, perhaps you download the file as a .docx file, since you use Word as your word processor. Another person downloads the .rtf version that he reads in an old version of WordPerfect and a third person downloads the .odt version because she uses OpenOffice. Each person downloads the same information but in a different file format to match what's used on each computer.

Rather than downloading the file, users can directly manipulate the file contents within the browser. Changes are immediately seen by all users in real time. This means everyone is working from the same information and you won't get out of sync by people downloading and uploading different versions at different times. Certainly the preferred method of collaboration is to edit using the browser.

The current version of Google Drive now supports mobile access. As smartphones become the computing platform of choice, Google has developed additional methods for you to get to your information. Currently, Google Drive is accessible from an Android phone or tablet running Android 4.0 or higher. For an Apple device, you need to be running iOS 7.0 or above. The Google Drive app is what facilitates access to the Google files from your mobile device. You will need to install the Google Drive app to your Android or Apple mobile device. Just access the files from your Google Drive app and the changes are synchronized across all devices connected to your Google Drive. You can access Google Drive from other mobile devices by using a browser and going to the mobile web at **https://drive.google.com**.

The caution with Google Drive is that the data is being held by a third party. Obviously, you would not want to use it to work on highly proprietary information such as a patent application. Even though you can control who has access to the files and what they can do, Google still holds the "keys" to all of the data. Google has had some highly publicized security issues over a period of years, so it is wise to consider what data you store there.

There have also been some recent stirrings over Google's privacy policy and what data Google accesses. We remind readers to review the terms of service and privacy policies for any third-party provided service, including Google. Apparently, there were a ton of folks that never read the terms and got all upset when they heard that Google scans the data you create and deposit on its servers. This is true for the free services that Google provides, such as Gmail and Google Drive. However, Google Apps for Work (previously known as Google Business Apps) does not have the same terms of service. In fact, the terms of service for the Apps for Work have specific confidentiality provisions, where Google will protect the data. They will also notify you if they are required by law to disclose confidential information so that you have an opportunity to challenge the disclosure. You should note that Google Apps is also HIPAA-compliant, but you must first sign a Business Associate Agreement (BAA) with Google.

There are now two offerings for Google Apps for Business. The Base version is $5 per user per month or $50 per user per year if you commit to twelve months of service. You get the following features with the Base version:

- 30 GB of storage
- Business e-mail hosted at your own domain (e.g., email@yourcompany.com)
- Calendar, Docs, Sheets, and Slides
- HD video meetings
- 24/7 phone, chat, and e-mail support

There is also a Premium offering. The Premium version costs $10 per user per month or $120 per user per year. It is interesting that Google will discount the Base version if you commit to a year, but the annual cost for the Premium version is nothing more twelve times the monthly charge. Why would you lock yourself in to an entire year? Just go with the monthly charge if you opt for the Premium version. The features you get with the Premium version include:

- Unlimited storage and Vault (1 TB per user if there are fewer than five users)

♦ Advanced admin and audit controls

♦ Business e-mail hosted at your own domain (e.g., email@yourcompany.com)

♦ Calendar, Docs, Sheets, and Slides

♦ HD video meetings

♦ 24/7 phone, chat, and e-mail support

Google Apps Vault is an add-on for Google Apps that lets you retain, archive, search, and export your organization's e-mail and chat messages for your eDiscovery and compliance needs. You can also search and export your organization's files in Google Drive. Vault is included with the Premium offering and can be added to the Base version for $5 a month. Since Vault is a $5-a-month add-on, why not just go with the Premium version and get additional administrative controls?

## Acrobat

Today, more and more lawyers have Acrobat (**www.adobe.com/products/ acrobat**), especially if they do e-filing of court documents. Acrobat allows for collaboration with PDF documents, so you can conduct shared document reviews that allow the participants to view one another's comments. Adobe has radically changed the Acrobat product with the release of Acrobat DC. It is much more cloud-driven and part of the larger offering called Adobe Document Cloud. Document Cloud will let you create and edit documents from any mobile or desktop device. The intent is to have documents available in the cloud so that you can have anytime access.

Acrobat DC is sold on a subscription basis, as is Document Cloud. You can also get Acrobat DC as a stand-alone product, but it has fewer features than the cloud option. All of this can be very confusing. Just remember that the version lawyers should be using is the Pro version. Lawyers should opt for the Pro version primarily for the enhanced security, Bates stamping, and redaction ability. Acrobat DC Pro allows you to create a document that your clients may find useful. It allows Adobe Reader (the free reader version) users to participate in reviews with complete commenting and markup tools, including sticky notes, highlighter, lines, shapes, and stamps. This means your clients (or other lawyers, for that matter) don't have to purchase Acrobat to collaborate with you. Sharing of documents can occur via e-mail transmission or through Adobe Document Cloud.

Acrobat DC Standard desktop version is currently $299, and Pro is $449. Adobe Document Cloud (includes Acrobat DC) is available in two subscription plans. You can purchase a month-to-month subscription for $22.99 per month or an annual subscription for $19.99 per month. The subscription for the Standard version is $24.99 per month or $12.99 per month for the annual commitment to the Document Cloud Standard product. As we've mentioned, lawyers should be using the Pro version. A Document Cloud Pro subscription costs $24.99 per month or $14.99 per month for the annual commitment. The extra $2 a month for the Pro version is well worth the cost, especially considering all the advanced features you'll get. Adobe also offers a free trial download from its website. Like the other products we recommend, use the trial first if you are unsure of your purchase commitment.

## Microsoft Word

Another collaboration tool is the Track Changes feature of Microsoft Word. With this tool, you can see the modifications made by each user who modifies the document. The caveat is that the software must be configured to identify the user properly. Some preloaded Office installations have the user configured as something generic, like "Owner" or "Satisfied Customer," and not the user's name. You can see how your Office (2003 and prior) installation is configured by going to Tools > Options and selecting the User Information tab. Word 2007 users would click the Office button in the upper left, select the Word Options button at the bottom, and see the user information in the Popular menu choice. Word 2010 and 2013 users select File and then the Options menu choice. Once this option is properly configured, the user information will show properly with the tracked changes. The user also has the ability to insert comments in addition to modifying the document contents. Do not strip the metadata (as you might normally do for confidentiality reasons) from the document if you are sending it to another party for collaboration. Removing the metadata also removes the tracked changes, so the recipient will not see the intended modifications. When you have the document ready and want to send it to a client, scrub the metadata at that point.

## SharePoint

SharePoint is Microsoft's solution for collaboration. Basically, SharePoint is a web-based server environment that allows the end user to collaborate on data that is managed through a SharePoint server. There is no special client software needed, as access is accomplished via a browser.

SharePoint 2013 is considered to be expensive for most solo and small firm operations, especially for new installations. Besides the cost of the server hardware, you will need the server software and Client Access Licenses (CALs). Microsoft has attempted to simplify the previously confusing licensing model for SharePoint. The on-premise solution is licensed using the server/CAL model. SharePoint Server 2013 is required for each running instance of the software, and CALs are required for each person or device accessing a SharePoint Server. There is even an option for enterprise CALs if you need a very robust and flexible SharePoint environment to take advantage of Microsoft's Business Solutions or Business Intelligence for Everyone features not available with the standard CALs. Suffice it to say that it is all very complicated and can get rather expensive. If you need the services of a full-blown SharePoint server, you may want to consider some of the hosted solutions, which should be a lot more affordable for a solo or small firm office. Microsoft offers SharePoint Online, which is licensed on a per-user basis and starts at $5 per user per month (Plan 1) for the basic set of features and $8 per user per month (Plan 2) for more advanced features such as enterprise search, E-Discovery, ACM, Compliance, etc. Another alternative is to investigate Microsoft's Small Business Server 2011 Standard, which includes SharePoint in addition to Server, Exchange, and Server Update Services.

Microsoft is continuing to push SharePoint in a major way. It keeps threatening to remove the Public Folders function of Exchange with each new release and force users to go with a SharePoint installation to get the same features you currently get with a base Exchange installation. We thought this was going to happen with the release of Exchange 2010 and then Exchange 2013, but we are happy to say that the Public Folders function is still there. Since Microsoft has been making this threat for many years, we have no reason to suspect that Public Folders will be removed from future Exchange versions.

We've written about SharePoint in the last several editions of this book. Microsoft continues to hype it, but we don't see much traction in the real world, especially for solo and small firm attorneys. Surveys show that 78 percent of the Fortune 500 companies are using SharePoint, but only one of our clients has it installed and we don't see that SharePoint is worth the expense, especially for an on-premise solution. Many solo and small firm practitioners use cloud solutions instead of investing in a complex SharePoint environment. We agree with that direction and don't think SharePoint is going to change the world, as Microsoft has often predicted.

## Office 365

Microsoft has finally introduced a product that may give Google a run for its money. Office 365 is really a web-based productivity suite that also contains some collaboration capabilities. The solution is a subscription-based service, so the out-of-pocket cash flow is very reasonable. There are several subscription plans available, depending on the number of users and any advanced features that may be needed. The company is trying to steer users toward a subscription model and away from the traditional retail software packages. As we've mentioned elsewhere, it seems as though a lot of vendors are following Microsoft's lead and traditional locally loaded applications are slowly being phased out in favor of cloud subscription offerings.

Solo and small firms will probably opt for Office 365 Business Premium, which is geared toward small businesses and can handle up to 300 users. The cost is $15 per month per user (billed monthly) or $12.50 per month per user (annual payment of $150), which is very affordable. It includes access to business class e-mail, shared calendars, 1 TB of OneDrive for Business storage space per user, the ability to use your own domain name, web conferencing, and document sharing. You also have the ability to have Office on your desktop on up to five PCs or Macs. The Office applications include Word, PowerPoint, Excel, Outlook, OneNote, and Publisher. With the desktop version, you can work on your files while offline. Once you are connected to the Internet, all of your work will automatically sync. For you e-mail junkies, each user gets a 50 GB mailbox with the ability to send attachments of up to 25 MB in size. We would recommend starting with the month-to-month plan, which can be cancelled at any time without penalty.

## Skype

Many users are familiar with the VoIP solution called Skype. Skype is now owned by Microsoft, and things seem to be going along fairly well. Telephone calls are free between Skype users. You can opt for pay plans if you need to call mobile or landline numbers, and the cost is very reasonable. Skype for Business is even included in your Office 365 subscription for no additional charge.

Unlimited calling to United States and Canadian landline and mobile phone numbers is only $2.99 per month. New features with Skype make it an excellent tool for collaboration. Video conferencing is now supported within Skype. You can create a low-cost or no-cost video conference call in just a few seconds. Many laptops now have a video camera built into the screen case, and there are Skype apps for mobile devices such as iPhones, iPads, Windows Phone, and Android smartphones. Finally, you can share files through Skype as well. File sharing, video conferencing, and free teleconference calls via the Internet make Skype a great low-cost collaboration tool.

Beware of security issues though. We learned in 2013 that Microsoft was now routing Skype calls through its servers, contrary to previous practice. Also, researchers have proven that Microsoft accesses users' content within Skype. Finally, documents revealed by Edward Snowden state that Microsoft has cooperated with the NSA and actually decrypted data at the behest of the NSA. We would not recommend using Skype for confidential conversations or file sharing.

## Dropbox

Dropbox is not just for file synchronization between your computer and mobile devices. We have seen a tremendous increase in Dropbox being used to share files among multiple parties and even as a vehicle to deliver evidence for discovery. You can create a custom folder within Dropbox and share that folder with multiple people. Only those that you authorize can have access to the folder contents. This means you can collaborate with co-counsel, consultants, experts, and even opposing counsel.

Dropbox is free for the initial 2 GB of storage. You can purchase additional storage starting at $9.99 per month for 1 TB (1,000 GB). New this year is an offering called Dropbox for Business. At a cost of $15 per month per user, you get unlimited storage and file recovery. You also get enterprise file sharing controls with central administration. Dropbox transmits the data in a secure fashion using SSL and also stores it in encrypted form on its servers. However, Dropbox holds the encryption key and can decrypt the data should it receive a valid court order or law enforcement request. Therefore, you should consider Dropbox to be an insecure service and not use it for transmitting any confidential or sensitive information. That doesn't mean you can't use Dropbox to share confidential information. Your data is safe if you encrypt it BEFORE you deposit it in Dropbox. That way you control the encryption key and not Dropbox.

## Desktop Sharing

Several products enable you to share your desktop with other people, and sharing your desktop may be a good way to collaborate on a document or share pictures of an accident scene. Products like Webex, Teamviewer, join.me, and GoToMeeting allow for desktop sharing. If you elect to use desktop sharing products, be advised that you may not be able to determine if the remote party is recording the session. You may want to get agreement and confirmation from all parties that they are not recording the session, especially if you don't want it recorded or you want to be the only one with a record of the session. In addition, be wary if you give control over to a remote user, as they may be able to transfer data from your computer without your knowledge. We would recommend that you "push" your desktop to the remote parties and not let them take control.

# CHAPTER TWENTY-ONE

# Remote Access

**M**OST LAWYERS ARE ROAD warriors today. If their entire office is not on a laptop or smartphone, a good chunk of it is—and the rest is accessible through remote access. Whether in court, on vacation, on the road, or in a meeting, lawyers need access to their e-mail, calendar, appointments, and files—and they need access fast.

Many lawyers have discarded workstations entirely, using only their laptop and a docking station at work and tablets and smartphones while on the move. Others have both a workstation and a laptop. The popularity of laptops and other mobile devices has zoomed in the last decade, to the point where the lawyer without a laptop or smartphone is a rarity. Our new mobile lawyers are now equipped with technologies that allow them to be as productive on the road as they are in the office, minimizing downtime and keeping those billable hours (or productivity hours, in the case of the alternative billers) up. Many clients and colleagues have a strong expectation that lawyers will be constantly accessible via e-mail—even, sadly, while on vacation. We privately joke (and lament) that vacations are times when our mobile devices get a nice view of the beach. Many clients will disregard your out-of-office message and will expect a quick response. So how do we stay in touch with the office when on the road?

## Virtual Private Networking

A virtual private network (VPN) connection is a secure communications network tunneled through another network such as the Internet. The

VPN connection allows a user to connect to the office when working remotely. The communications tunnel encrypts the data traffic between the remote user and the office network, maintaining the security of the information as it is passed back and forth. This is extremely important for law firms whose lawyers work on client files while traveling or while away from the office and have to download a local copy of a client file to work on. Best of all, the VPN service software is included with Microsoft's server operating systems and the VPN client software is included with Microsoft operating systems at no additional cost to the user.

The average lawyer is likely to be dumbfounded when confronted with setting up a VPN, especially if third-party software and a certificate are required, so this is best left to your IT consultant. However, it is not terribly expensive, and it offers terrific security for your data. The greatest advantage of VPNs is that they are multiuser, whereas other methods are one-on-one solutions.

## GoToMyPC

GoToMyPC is a remote connection service that allows you to connect to your work computer when you are away from the office. This service is a great alternative if you're a solo practitioner or if your law firm does not have the ability to set up a VPN-type connection for remote users (for example, if you don't have a server). Like a VPN connection, data communications between the client and the host are encrypted and secured. To connect to your work computer, software must be installed and running on the host machine (the computer you wish to connect to), and both the client and the host computers must have Internet access. The GoToMyPC website maintains contact with the host computer, so the IP address of the host is always known. This is critical: This solution works even if the host has a dynamic Internet connection (constantly changing IP address) instead of a static one, which remains constant. No modifications to the configuration of your firm firewall will need to be made to get GoToMyPC up and running.

Users can even connect to their work computers (Mac or Windows) from a tablet or smartphone. Apps are available for Android, iOS, and Kindle Fire devices.

GoToMyPC costs as little as $120 per year for one computer license and will need to be renewed yearly. There is a monthly plan, but the cost jumps to $12 a month. There is no limitation on how often you may connect to your host computer, and you are allowed to connect to your host computer from any device. For each additional computer to which you wish to connect, there is an additional $10 charge per computer. The software requires little setup and configuration and can be purchased online from GoToMyPC's website at **www.gotomypc.com**. This software is more costly than its competitors, so be sure to check out all of your available options before selecting which remote access solution to purchase. GoToMyPC also has a thirty-day free trial, so take advantage as you experiment to find which remote access solution works best for you!

## LogMeIn

LogMeIn Pro is a remote access solution that is very similar to GoToMyPC. The software works the exact same way, with the service provider maintaining the IP addresses of host computers. This is another good solution for those firms with dynamic (constantly changing) IP addresses. With this service and very little effort, you can gain seamless and total access to your office PC (Mac or Windows) from any computer with an Internet connection. To connect, a user logs in to the LogMeIn website (or uses the app downloaded to her mobile device) and the connection to the host computer is made automatically. Some of the features include remote printing, the ability to transfer and share files between the connected computers, and the ability to map network drives to your local computer. Just like GoToMyPC, this service is extremely secure, using 128- to 256-bit SSL end-to-end encryption. When compared to GoToMyPC, this remote access solution is currently priced the same ($99 per year) but allows a user to access up to two different computers, instead of just one with GoToMyPC.

This service also supports connecting to your work computer from your iOS or Android device. We've used the iPad app, and it works as advertised—easy to use, great with the touchscreen, and very convenient.

A LogMeIn Pro subscription costs $99 per year for two computer licenses and will need to be renewed annually. There is no longer a monthly plan to choose from. This service can be purchased online from LogMeIn's website at **https://secure.logmein.com**. We strongly recommend the use of this product for remote accessibility because of its ease of use and ability to access two computers instead of just one. Like GoToMyPC, LogMeIn offers a free trial, so we recommend taking the product for a test drive before purchasing it.

## TeamViewer

TeamViewer Business Edition is a remote access solution on steroids. It contains a number of features that are not available with LogMeIn or GoToMyPC. Although it's a one-time purchase, it comes with a hefty price. Just like the two remote access solutions described above, TeamViewer works flawlessly behind network firewalls and is a good solution for firms that use dynamic IP addresses. While TeamViewer is not difficult to install and run, the connecting computer will need to download, install, and run the client application, which, in our experience, may be a bit more confusing and cumbersome for lawyers to perform rather than just logging in to the service with the web browser. However, once the local application is installed, it's very easy to use.

Some of the additional features include:

♦ Multiplatform support, including Mac OS X, Windows 10, and Linux computers

♦ iOS, Android, and Windows Phone 8, 8/RT, Blackberry (Preview) support

♦ Communication tools that allow users to connect with each other through video chat or VoIP

♦ One-time charge for a lifetime license; no recurring yearly costs

♦ The ability to transfer files securely

♦ File box for common file sharing

♦ Microsoft Outlook calendar integration

♦ The ability to record meetings

♦ Space for up to twenty-five meeting participants

Mobile device support is offered for iOS, Android, and Windows Phone 8, but users will need to purchase a separate add-on license for this feature, unlike the included mobile support offered in both of the LogMeIn and GoToMyPC alternatives to this product. TeamViewer can be purchased online from **www.teamviewer.com**, and a single lifetime business license for one computer costs $749. The cost to add additional computers to control remotely is $139 per system.

## Mobility Tips

Besides providing remote access solutions for the legal road warrior, we wanted to include some useful tips to think about before heading out on the road:

—Pack a surge protector. It doesn't matter what brand. You never know when you will need more than two outlets to power all of your devices and to protect your electronic devices from power surges and dirty electricity.

—Purchase a lock for your laptop. Ninety-nine percent of laptops have a Kensington security slot, and it's prudent to use it. Kensington locks, such as the MicroSaver DS Notebook Lock, can be purchased online from Kensington's website (**www.kensington.com**) for around $50—a small price to pay to keep your laptop secure.

—If you use a wireless Bluetooth mouse, be sure to pack extra AA or AAA batteries.

—Pack a spare cell phone charger and tablet charger with an extra sync cable. You shouldn't travel without either one.

—Pack an AC extension cable. This will come in handy when you are far away from a power outlet.

—Keep an AC power adapter for your laptop in your bag. You never know when you might need one.

—If you're traveling internationally, be sure to pack multiple converters so that you can connect your devices. In the United States, we operate on a system that runs at 120 volts. Be sure to check the voltage of the country you're visiting before leaving and find out whether your power supplies will auto-convert. You may not need voltage convertors if the power supplies auto-adjust, but you will need the plug adapters to match the outlet connections.

—It is always a good idea to have a hard copy printout of your hotel reservation and itinerary, in the event your mobile device stops working or isn't accessible when you need it. If you are using your mobile device to keep track of your itinerary, try using an app like TripIt, which can track all your travel arrangements, including your flights, hotel, and rental car information, and will eliminate the searching of your e-mail for your travel plans. How nice is it to have all of the information in a single place? Plus, another great feature is that this app allows you to share your itinerary with family and friends.

—Another tip for international travelers: Leave your cell phone at home. Roaming charges can be staggering and can be initiated even if you're not actively using your phone. Do you really trust putting your phone in airplane mode?

—Keep appropriate video adapters with your laptop in your laptop bag. You never know when you might need to connect your laptop or tablet to a TV or projector for a presentation.

—Pack headphones to keep the noise out. Have you ever tried to be productive on an airplane? It's hard when the person next to you can't stop talking. Just plug in your headphones and your problem is solved. You can even listen to relaxing music while you work. For those who want wireless Bluetooth headphones, check out the Jabra Revo Wireless, costing about $200, which can be found on Jabra's website at **www.jabra.com**; however, you may not be able to use these on an airplane because they are transmitting devices. For music aficionados, the Bose QuietComfort 25 Acoustic Noise Cancelling headphones offer top-of-the-line headphone technology and include the noise-cancelling circuitry that you hear everyone talking about. The downside, though, is the price—very, very expensive at around $300. The authors are particularly fond of the Bose QuietComfort 20 earbuds. They are small and lightweight and have amazingly effective noise-cancelling capability. However, they are also pricey at $300.

—Back up your data to an external hard drive or the network server. If your laptop crashes or is stolen, you will want a recent backup of your most important files.

—Encrypt your hard drive and data. There are many software tools available to do this, such as PGP, TrueCrypt (version 7.1a and not the compromised version 7.2), and PC Guardian. In the event your laptop is lost or stolen, your data is protected. Configure a power on or BIOS password on your computer, if available. Again, this adds another layer of data protection. One point to note, however, is that if you're traveling internationally, encryption is illegal in some countries, which could lead to the confiscation of your encrypted devices—so be prepared and know the local laws. In some cases, it may make more sense to leave your data at home and connect remotely to your system to access your information, rather than to take it with you.

—If you have a tablet, be sure to password-protect your device with a passphrase. PINs aren't as secure and can be easily cracked. On an iPad, a passphrase requirement on the Lock Screen will enable encryption of your data. On Android devices, you can encrypt your data as well through the configuration settings.

—If you have a smartphone with a data plan that allows device tethering or a mobile hot spot, take advantage of the data service you have already paid for and tether your laptop or tablet with your smartphone for Internet service. Avoid paying daily hotel fees for an Internet connection if it's not provided free during the course of your stay. However, data overage charges from your wireless carrier can be expensive, so it's best not to stream the movie at the top of your Netflix queue while tethered unless you truly have an unlimited data plan.

—Encrypt your USB flash drives and external hard drives.

—Disable your wireless auto-connection feature within the Windows operating system. Most laptops with wireless cards will automatically connect to any unencrypted, open wireless network when your default connection is unavailable. If by chance your device does connect to an open wireless network, never log in to any e-mail or bank account when using an unsecure connection.

—Before leaving the office, make sure that your security software has the latest updates and definitions to protect your devices while you're away. The same applies to Windows updates.

—Download and install an app to track your club membership cards so that you don't have to carry all that plastic around with you. The one that we like the most for iOS and Android mobile devices is the Key Ring Rewards Cards app. It not only allows you to enter and store your club card or membership numbers but also generates a bar code that can be scanned should one be required. You might as well get miles points and hotel rewards while on the go.

—Another great app to download and use on your mobile device is GateGuru. This app comes in handy when your flight has been cancelled or delayed, and you're looking for a few hours to kill. This app provides maps of all major airport terminals, including restaurants and stores, along with reviews allowing you to find a bar or restaurant in which to relax and unwind until your flight.

These are just a few of the recommendations we have for the legal road warriors, all based on our own experiences traveling. We hope you find them useful.

# CHAPTER TWENTY-TWO

# Mobile Security

TECHNOLOGY ADVANCES IN THIS area have come at warp speed. Gone are the days when you carried around a 50-foot phone cord, looking for an analog phone jack that could be used with the modem in your laptop and America Online. Being übergeeks, we then carried along a splitter, a coupler, and additional phone cords so we could work comfortably on the bed or desk while we traveled around the nation. No more. It's even difficult to purchase a modern-day laptop with a modem these days. We can't remember the last time we even saw a modem as an option when configuring a laptop purchase. Wireless, whether using Wi-Fi or a 3G/4G data connection with your cellular carrier, is the preferred method of connectivity in the modern age. More and more hotels, motels, conference centers, coffee shops, bookstores, cafés, and so on, are offering wireless access solutions, many without charge. The question is . . . should you use the free Wi-Fi?

## Software

Before we jump into the boring details, let's cover some solutions that should be on your laptop no matter what other technology you use for remote connectivity. It goes without saying that you should have some sort of all-in-one security solution installed on your laptop. It should be configured to check for automatic updates and to perform a periodic full scan (we do weekly scans) to catch anything that may have "landed" before the signatures were updated. It would be just your luck to catch a virus or other malware on day one and be the first kid on the block to suffer the effects. Most of the current Internet suites also analyze the computer operation and identify activity that could be virus-like or some process trying to access something it shouldn't. This type of real-time monitoring provides added protection beyond mere signature files. Normally, the all-in-one security product will contain security features like antivirus, anti-malware, firewalls, spam control, and anti-phishing. Don't leave home without it. Software solutions for your smartphone and tablet are also available, but we'll discuss those later.

## Encryption

Secure mobile computing must contain some method of encryption to protect valuable personal and client data. We prefer whole disk encryption. This means everything on the hard drive is encrypted and kept secure: We don't have to remember to put files into special folders or on the encrypted virtual drive. All too often, people are in a big hurry and may not save their data in the special protected encrypted areas, leaving the information vulnerable.

In addition, without whole disk encryption, artifacts of the decryption passphrase could be present in various places [e.g., master file table (MFT), Page File, temp files, unallocated space]. Forensics can extract these artifacts and make it probable that the passphrase can be determined. Many of the newer laptops have built-in whole disk encryption. To state the obvious, make sure you enable the encryption; otherwise, your data won't be protected. Also, encryption may be used in conjunction with biometric access. As an example, our laptops require a fingerprint swipe when powered on. Failure at that point leaves the computer hard drive fully encrypted. A very comforting thought if laptop thieves, who constitute a large club these days, make off with your laptop.

If you think we are being too cautious, bear in mind that a laptop goes missing every fifty seconds in the United States. In 2011, PCWorld.com reported that about 12,000 laptops were lost or stolen at U.S. airports per week. Where does it happen most? In Chicago, fitting for a city whose history is so steeped in criminal lore. The fact that one of ten corporate laptops will be lost or stolen over their three-year life is enough reason to take steps to protect the data. We mean it when we say, "Be careful out there." Also, don't forget to encrypt your USB flash drives. Unfortunately for us good guys, these devices are easily lost and almost always contain our valuable data.

## *Wireless*

What's next? We won't cover modem access in the traditional sense, since dial-up isn't desirable, effective, or even available these days for most travelers. Wireless is the norm for all the road warriors. There are two basic types of wireless access you'll encounter. The first type is generically termed a "wireless hot spot" and is what you find at your local Starbucks, fast-food establishment, hotel, or airport. You may or may not have to pay for these wireless connection services. Many businesses are offering free wireless as a way to attract customers—heck, even McDonald's offers a free wireless hot spot. Most of these hot spots are unsecured and wide open. This means it is possible for your confidential data to be viewed by the customer at the next table or the person sitting on the park bench outside the café if you are not encrypting the traffic.

Does this mean you shouldn't use any of these wireless clouds? If you have a choice, we would say these clouds are best avoided by those who are technology averse and don't understand how to operate securely in an unsecured cloud. Read on and determine whether you can safely be trusted to do what follows.

See if there is an option to have a secure connection to the cloud. This would be indicated if you use https:// (note the *s*, denoting "secure") as part of the URL. Typically, website connections are unsecure and do not provide an encrypted session like the https:// connections do. Be especially careful if you have to pay for the wireless connection. Be wary when you are at the screens that have you input your credit card and billing information. Do not enter any of this sensitive information without an https:// connection. Once you've established a connection to the wireless cloud, be sure to use your VPN or other secure (https://) access to protect your transmissions. Also, when connecting to a secure website, if you're presented with an error message referencing a SSL certificate error or invalid certificate, proceed with extreme caution or, better yet, don't proceed at all.

Some hotels may give you a wireless cloud that is already secured. Typically, these wireless implementations use WPA (Wi-Fi protected access) or WPA2 to secure your connection and data. The cloud will be visible to your computer, but you will be required to provide a password before your computer connects. Once connected, the data you transmit will be encrypted and secure.

One scheme we see all the time: You are in a hotel that requires you to pay for Internet access. But when you ask your computer to show "all available wireless networks," it will display something like "free public wireless" as a network name—or something else that sounds innocuous, usually using the word *free* to entice you. Beware—these are often data thieves offering up an insecure cloud for the sole purpose of making off with your data. You can get the "free Internet"—but at a terrible price. Never be tempted by these clouds.

## AirCard

Another wireless connection method is commonly called an AirCard. These are cards that are used to connect to the high-speed wireless networks of cellular phone providers. We're pretty sure you've seen the cellular providers advertising their 3G/4G networks. You may see terms like EDGE or EV-DO to describe the older 3G networks and WiMAX or LTE to describe the latest 4G networks. Don't be swayed by vendors' claims for speed and availability. Make sure that you will be able to have service in those areas you travel to the most. Reliability is another consideration, as is whether you already have a cellular plan.

The AirCard itself is a hardware device that you can externally connect to your laptop or select as a built-in option when configuring a new computer system. External AirCards come in both USB and PC card formats. These cards can be used on any laptop with USB ports or PC card slots. Some laptops and netbooks have the electrical circuitry built in, so no additional hardware is required. The built-in capability means you have nothing to lose, but it is "married" to the laptop and can't be transferred between machines. Further, you would also be stuck with a single cellular vendor, as each vendor's radio is different. The external AirCards can cost several hundred dollars, but most providers offer significant discounts. Or course, you will also need a data plan from your cellular provider.

Also, it should be noted that if you have multiple devices that need Internet access, rather than purchasing a subscription for each device, which can be very costly, invest in something like the Verizon Ellipsis Jetpack or another mobile hot spot. These devices create a local wireless network that can provide Internet access (over the cellular network) to up to ten devices. Verizon offers the Ellipsis Jetpack for 99 cents with a two-year commitment.

Frankly, you should be using the "hot spot" capability that is built into your smartphone. That means you don't have to carry around or pay for another piece of equipment. Like the dedicated AirCards, the data connection is encrypted between the smartphone and the cellular carrier. We haven't seen an AirCard in some years as more and more lawyers use their smartphone as a Wi-Fi hot spot.

## Public Computer Usage

A word of warning here. Be very careful about using a public computer, such as those in a library, an Internet café, or the business center of a hotel. Even if you are only accessing your web-based e-mail account, the data is temporarily written to the local hard disk. There is also the risk that some keystroke logging software is installed on the computer, thereby capturing everything that you do on the machine. Studies have shown an average of seven pieces of malware on these public computers.

Does that mean all public computers are off limits? Not at all. We are big fans of the IronKey hardware encrypted USB flash drive. Besides the drive encryption and secure management of passwords, the IronKey has portable applications intended for use with public computers. As an example, there is a specially modified version of the Firefox browser that doesn't write any data to the computer. All data stays on the IronKey, thereby making it secure and keeping it with you when you leave. Of course, this does mean that the computer has to accept the insertion of USB devices. Some business center machines are locked down and do not allow USB devices to be inserted, because it is a security risk to the business—USB devices can be used to introduce malware to the machine or network. Although we have tipped our hat to those who secure their computers this way (it's absolutely the right thing to do), it has prevented us from using our IronKey several times. Another reason to travel with your own equipment.

## Smartphones

Want to know what the most secure smartphone on the market is? That really isn't the right question. The question should be . . . what smartphone can be made the most secure? The answer is an Android phone. Because of its design architecture, Android can be configured with enhanced security settings as well as installing security software to protect the OS. You can't do that with an iPhone. It's pretty clear that the iPhone was designed as a consumer phone first, with security an afterthought. However, the latest versions of iOS on the newer iPhones have improved security to the point where it more closely approaches the other smart-phones in protecting data. It still doesn't change the fact that the iPhone holds a tremendous amount of data, unbeknownst to the user that is orders of magnitudes more than any other smartphone. In other words, the iPhone is very evidence-rich. One day, we'll have to record a video of the "happy dance" we do when iPhones come into our forensics lab. While the latest models are encrypted by default, remember that a court (at least in a civil case) may order you to turn over "the keys" to your device.

At a minimum, everybody should have a PIN code programmed into her phone to prevent unauthorized access, along with a fairly short time-out period. It doesn't do much good to have an unlocking PIN and then have thirty minutes pass before the phone relocks. We know it's a pain to constantly punch in the unlock code, but that will keep your data from being accessed by prying eyes. Better yet, it will stop someone from installing spyware on your phone that can effectively trap all of your communications (voice calls, e-mail, text messages, etc.). For those devices that offer a passphrase alternative to the PIN, such as the iPad or iPhone, this would be the preferred choice to secure your device. Why, you might ask?

A passphrase can be longer than a PIN and can contain non-numeric values, vastly increasing the strength of the protection. In fact, we do not recommend that any iPhone or iPad be configured with the very weak default four-digit PIN lock code. There are tools available to brute-force a four-digit PIN on an iPhone or iPad in less than fifteen minutes, even if it is set to wipe the data after ten attempts.

Encrypt the phone! This is easier to do than you think. Enabling a lock code on the iPhone or iPad automatically encrypts the device. To encrypt a BlackBerry device, all you have to do is enable the "Content Protection." The last several versions of the Android operating system have built-in encryption. Just check the box to encrypt the device within the Security settings. You may need a third-party application if you are running an older version of the Android OS. Actually, if you are running an older version of Android that doesn't have built-in encryption, it's time for you to replace the phone. There are significant security vulnerabilities in the older versions of Android and iOS.

Besides PIN-protecting your phone, make sure you encrypt any memory cards or just don't store any sensitive data on them. We're talking about the SD, micro SD, etc., cards that you can insert into the smartphone to increase storage capacity. There are programs available for some models that allow you to encrypt the card contents if the feature is not already built into the phone. The point is, you don't want any confidential information to be accessible on the card if you lose your phone. The PIN will protect the phone access, but the "bad guy" will pop out the memory card and read it from his computer if it is not encrypted.

Finally, investigate the ability to wipe the data from the smartphone remotely if it is lost. You should have the phone configured to wipe automatically after a set number of invalid unlock attempts. This will clear the data even if you are not connected to a cellular network. Remotely wiping the device on demand requires that it be in communication with the cellular data network. Configure the "Find my iPhone" function within the iCloud settings on an iPhone or iPad. The remote wipe capability is built into the BlackBerry devices and can be invoked through the BES (BlackBerry Enterprise Server) console. Android devices can use the free Lookout application for the remote wipe function. Google has a new app called Android Device Manager that will help users locate or remotely wipe their phone. You must enable Android Device Manager from the Google settings on your phone and associate the phone with your Google account. Remember that the remote wipe feature is for the memory within the phone itself and may not wipe the memory cards we spoke about earlier.

## Flash Drives

USB flash drives are those small portable devices that attorneys (and others too) use to transfer data between computers. They are also known as thumb drives. They are inexpensive and vary in capacity from several GB up to several hundred GB of storage space. Since they are portable and small, it is very easy to lose them. This is where encryption is your friend. If you intend to store client confidential information on a flash drive, make sure that the device is encrypted. Some encryption software for your computer can also be used to encrypt the flash drive. There are also flash drives that have built-in encryption capabilities. Our favorite is the IronKey by Imation, which has hardware encryption. The DataTraveler series from Kingston is another good choice for an encrypted flash drive.

## Final Words

The options and requirements for mobile security have certainly changed quickly over the years. Talk to us next year and we're sure the world will have changed again. For now, make sure that you are aware of all the issues related to secure data transfer and that you are not relying on antiquated knowledge. You must assume that there is absolutely no protection of the communication stream between your laptop and your remote device. We've seen hotel networks that didn't have a firewall, so all traffic was allowed to flow through. We immediately saw probing attacks on our computers, which were stopped by the firewalls on our laptops. It's the wild, wild West out there, and you're the only marshal in town. Good luck, Wyatt.

# CHAPTER TWENTY-THREE

# More from Apple

**A**PART FROM THE INFORMATION conveyed previously about Mac laptops and desktops, we want to offer you additional Apple recommendations in light of the continued interest lawyers have shown in potentially switching to Mac computers. Many lawyers may have never used a Mac, either in their personal life or for their job, but most have used one Apple product or another. Most are only familiar with the iPod or the very popular iPhone and iPad. Many people argue that Macs are ready for "prime time," to take on Windows-based PCs in the business setting. From a hardware standpoint, Macs are just as good as, if not better than, PCs. You can't really tell them apart since Macs made the switch to using Intel-based processors. The major difference now is the operating system, which is still the main obstacle preventing Macs from gaining a greater piece of the pie in the business marketplace.

Frankly, the problem lies with software compatibility with Macs. Most law firms, no matter the size, use legal-specific software on a daily basis to do their jobs. Whether you're looking at case management, billing, or trial-related or field-specific software, most vendors still do not make versions for Macs. However, this argument is becoming more of a nonissue as vendors move their applications to the cloud. But for lawyers who use a computer just for word processing, Internet research, filing of motions, billing, and accounting, a Mac could suit these functions perfectly.

However, centralized management is much more difficult, if not impossible, in a Mac environment. Group policies and multiple third-party tools enable a very cost-effective way to distribute updates and restrict abilities in a Windows environment. The lack of centralized control and restrictions of Macs makes them less desirable (and much more costly) to deploy in an enterprise setting. Macs are more expensive to maintain because you have to touch each individual Mac to make changes or install updates. The lack of centralized control is a large reason you see Macs in solo and small law firms and not uniformly implemented in larger firms. Below, we discuss some Mac-specific hardware and software solutions that may come in handy if you are or want to become a Mac user.

## Hardware

### Apple iPad

Year after year, Apple continues to provide its fanboys with more and more enthusiasm about the next version of the iPad, and it has continued to find ways to improve this great device.

In September 2015, Apple announced the release of the iPad Pro. This behemoth device, larger than any previously released iPad by almost 3 inches, is targeted toward businesses, with its sights set directly on the Surface Pro market share.

This device comes with a 12.9-inch Retina display and nearly double the CPU performance of the iPad Air 2. This device is powered by the A9X, a 64-bit, third-generation chip. The 12.9-inch LED-backlit widescreen Multi-Touch display boasts a resolution of 2732 × 2049. The refined Multi-Touch technology adds another dimension to the user experience. The camera has been upgraded to 8 MP and can record 1080p HD video at thirty frames per second. This device also contains four speakers.

The iPad Pro comes with a built-in Wi-Fi network card with two antennas supporting the 802.11ac protocol, enabling the device to connect to wireless networks, and the 4G model comes with a broadband AirCard and GPS locator. The device also includes Bluetooth 4.2 capability and a 38.5 watt-hour battery lasting up to ten hours, even when continually surfing the Internet. This version of the iPad is available with 32 or 128 GB of Internet memory at a starting cost of $799.

Along with the introduction of the iPad Pro, Apple released the next version of its iOS software, version 9.

Some of the new features of iOS 9 include:

   —Updated and improved Siri
   —Improved multitasking with Slide Over, Split View, and Picture in Picture

—All new News app

—Updated Maps and Notes app

—Apple Pay using the Wallet app

—iCloud Drive app allows access to any file you save to iCloud from just one place

—Increased responsive performance and better battery life

—Increased security through requirements of six-digit passcodes, upped from the previous four, and built-in support for two-factor authentication

In our opinion, the last revolutionary change to the iOS software was iOS 5, when Apple introduced its iCloud service. The iCloud service allows users to synchronize their music, photos, apps, documents, bookmarks, calendar, contacts, e-mail, and other data between multiple iOS devices. As a cloud service, Apple will actually store this data for you in an online account associated with your Apple ID. As with many Apple products, we have determined there are a number of security and privacy concerns with using this service. If you don't believe us, just read the Terms of Service—we did, and we will not use this service for anything business related. If you have enabled iCloud, be careful with what information you choose to synchronize with Apple. A lot of celebrities now understand that after the Celebgate debacle of 2014, when naked photos of them flooded the Internet. That's all we will say. We only have the Find My iPad feature configured in iCloud so that we can locate the device if lost. Unfortunately, that also means Apple knows where our iPad is at all times.

Today, lawyers frequently use the iPad for court or meetings, rather than lugging around a laptop. Originally thought to compete against e-book devices such as the Kindle and Nook, the iPad has actually established a new class of devices that compete against smartphones, netbooks, smaller laptops, and ultrabooks. Lawyers are drawn to the functionality and portability of the device, and we believe their interest will only increase as future generations are released.

Tom Mighell, lawyer and iPad expert, has three wonderful books available to assist lawyers who need help in understanding how to best use the iPad in their practice of law. The three books—*iPad in One Hour for Lawyers* (make sure you get the third edition), *iPad Apps in One Hour for Lawyers*, and *iPad in One Hour for Litigators* (make sure you get the second edition), can be purchased directly from the ABA's webstore and should be considered an invaluable resource for lawyers who are looking to test-drive their iPads at work. You can get all three for less than $150, which is quite a deal!

Having given many lectures on the use of the iPad, we can tell you that this was the largest CLE magnet for the past several years. Although things have slowed a bit, it is clear that the iPad is the tablet of choice for most lawyers. As one of our attendees said while proudly brandishing his iPad, "This is a game-changer."

## Apple Watch

Released early in 2015, Apple has entered itself into the field of wearable technology with the release of the Apple Watch.

This device, available in three distinct flavors—Watch, Watch Sport, and Watch Edition—will suit everyone from young adults to working professionals. The watch features a Retina display, a multifunctional input device that will let you zoom, scroll, and select without covering the screen through the use of the Digital Crown. The Digital Crown will allow you to zoom and scroll nimbly to the app of your choosing or press the button to return to the Home screen. Users can even tap or deep-press the display to access a range of contextually specific controls such as an action menu in Messages. Incoming notifications will add a physical dimension to alerts and notifications, providing users with a gentle tap when they receive an incoming message. The device runs on an internal battery, which is charged using a combination of MagSafe technology with inductive charging. Like the iPhone, the Apple Watch tends to be a battery killer. Several sources say that the watch must be plugged in each evening to stay operational, as the battery will not last more than a day, especially if actively used.

The price of the Apple Watch starts at $349 (ouch!) and will need to be paired with an iOS device (iPhone, iPad, or iPod Touch) in order to function fully. At that price, John will keep his Citizen Eco-Drive dual time zone watch that is charged by solar energy and avoid searching for an outlet before going to bed. Why do we include a watch in this book? Because other smartwatches are starting to be used by lawyers to read and respond to texts and e-mails. How useful these watches will be to lawyers is as yet unknown, but wearable tech is a trend worth watching.

## Touchfire Keyboard

Some have labeled this keyboard the accessory that turns the iPad into a true laptop "killer." We won't go that far just yet, as we will have to see how much businesses adopt the usage of the iPad Pro, but we are still impressed with this piece of hardware.

This lightweight Bluetooth keyboard is actually a super-thin keyboard overlay and not a separate external device like other Bluetooth keyboards. It attaches to the bottom half of your iPad with built-in magnets. This device provides tactile feedback when pressing the patented 3-D keys, enabling users to type much more quickly than on the flat keyboards often used with the iPad.

If you don't use a keyboard often, you can store it in the included carrying case; otherwise, you can keep it attached to your iPad. It is compatible with and fits into the Smart Case. The downside . . . it only works in landscape mode.

In terms of compatibility, this device works with all generations of the iPad. If you want to try out this device, you can purchase one from Touchfire's website (**https://touchfire.com**) for $40. Touchfire has also paired its signature keyboard with a Touchfire case, and the pair retail for $69.99 on the vendor's website, offered in a number of different colors.

### AirPort Extreme

Apple's AirPort Extreme is its wireless solution for home, school, and business. The wireless router plugs directly into your cable or DSL modem and connects you wirelessly to the Internet. This new version of router supports the 802.11a/b/g/n protocols, including the new 802.11ac standard, which provides data rates of up to 1.3 Gbps—triple the previous 802.11n standard. The wireless router supports NAT, DHCP, and VPN passthrough, allowing users the capability of connecting to their office network from home. The AirPort Extreme comes with built-in security features such as a NAT firewall, Wi-Fi Protected Access, WPA/WPA2 and WEP encryption, and MAC address filtering. The router contains one GB Ethernet WAN port for connecting to a cable or DSL modem and three GB Ethernet LAN ports for connecting computers or networking devices.

The built-in USB port is provided to connect a printer or hard drive that is shared with other users on the local network. The AirPort Extreme is both Mac and Windows compatible; is 64 percent smaller than its predecessor; is only 6.6 inches from top to bottom; and comes bundled with software, a power cord, and documentation. The AirPort Extreme can be purchased directly online from the Apple Store (**store.apple.com**) for $199.

### AirPort Express

The AirPort Express is a portable wireless router, perfect for taking with you while on the road. However, this device has limited functionality in a business setting, allowing only fifty devices to connect to it at a time. The small wireless router is extremely portable, about the size of a postcard, and weighs less than 8.5 ounces. The router supports the 802.11a/b/g/n protocols and offers simultaneous dual-band 802.11n, transmitting at both the 2.4 GHz and 5 GHz frequencies at the same time. This provides 802.11n support no matter which band your wireless devices use. This wireless device is great for hotels, supplying your laptop with wireless Internet so you can surf from any location in the room.

The device has a built-in USB port for connecting a shared printer and an Ethernet port for connecting to your DSL and cable modem or your local network. The built-in wireless security supports WPA/WPA2, WEP, NAT, MAC address filtering, and time-based access control. The AirPort Express is both Mac and Windows compatible and comes bundled with the necessary software to get your computer connected to the wireless network. The device even allows the option for a Guest Network that provides users with access to the Internet, but not other parts of your local network such as your computers, printers and network-attached drives. The AirPort Express can be purchased directly online from the Apple Store (**store.apple.com**) for $99.

### AirPort Time Capsule

Looking for a solution to back up your files automatically? Time Capsule works seamlessly with Time Machine, backup software included with the Mac OS X operating system. Time Capsule is simply a wireless router with a built-in hard drive used for storing backups of your files. Using the Time Machine backup software, the application will back up your files and folders automatically, without user intervention. The data is backed up over the local wireless network to the Time Capsule hardware device.

Time Capsule can be purchased and used solely as a backup solution, or it can also provide wireless Internet connectivity to your local network. It has the same built-in features and functionality as AirPort Extreme. Time Capsule is offered in two models, with storage capacities of 2 and 3 TB. Time Capsule, like the AirPort Express, supports the new 802.11ac protocol, offering data rates of up to 1.3 Gbps. This device can be purchased directly online from the Apple Store (**store.apple.com**) starting at $299 for the 2 TB model.

### Apple Thunderbolt Display

The Apple Thunderbolt Display is a high-definition (HD) flat-panel LCD monitor offering 27 inches of diagonal viewing area. Its wide-screen format makes this monitor a perfect display for legal professionals, providing enough real estate to display two or more documents side by side. The display is compatible with any Thunderbolt-enabled Mac notebook or desktop and supports resolutions up to 2560 × 1440 pixels.

The monitor has a 1,000:1 contrast ratio, 12-millisecond response time, and screen with an antiglare coating. The monitor has three USB 2.0 ports and can be purchased with an optional VESA wall mount. It also includes a built-in FaceTime HD camera with microphone and a 2.1 speaker system. The monitor even has an ambient light sensor that can automatically adjust the brightness of the LCD display. It also includes one GB Ethernet port, one Thunderbolt port, and one FireWire 800 port.

The Apple Thunderbolt Display comes with a one-year limited warranty and can be purchased directly online from the Apple Store (**store.apple .com**) for $999.

### Apple Wireless Keyboard

The Apple wireless keyboard uses Bluetooth wireless technology, eliminating the need for obstructive and unfriendly wires to connect your keyboard to your computer. The wireless keyboard comes in a low-profile anodized aluminum frame that matches the Apple theme and takes up 24 percent less space on your desktop than full-size keyboards. The keyboard contains function keys for one-touch access to Mac features and has power management features to conserve the batteries when not in use.

The Apple wireless keyboard requires Mac OS X version 10.6.8 or higher, takes two AA batteries, and can also be used with the iPad. It can be purchased directly online from the Apple Store (store.apple.com) for $99.

### Apple Magic Mouse

Like the Apple wireless keyboard, the Magic Mouse uses Bluetooth wireless technology to connect the mouse to your computer. Laser tracking allows you to use the mouse on a number of surfaces while maintaining the precision and accuracy of tracking movement. The mouse uses multi-touch sensitive technology to detect both right and left clicks, and the innovative scrolling ball allows for 360-degree scrolling capabilities. The mouse is powered with two AA batteries and, when paired with the Apple wireless keyboard, allows you to work wire-free at your desk. This wireless device requires Mac OS X version 10.5.8 or later to operate. Sorry, folks, but there is no mouse support for the iPad, so this is limited to working with Apple computers only. The Apple Magic Mouse can be purchased directly online from the Apple Store (**store.apple.com**) for $79.

## Apple iPod

Formerly Apple's most successful hardware device, the iPod has sold over 350 million units since its creation in 2001, and this number released by Apple hasn't been updated since 2012. It has only been supplanted by the iPhone in total sales within the past few years.

The portable digital-file-playing devices are the most popular handheld multimedia devices in use today, and some models can be used to play and shoot video, take pictures, play podcasts, and even play games. All models are capable of playing music. The iPod is available in three models: Shuffle, Nano, and Touch. The iPod Shuffle is the smallest, with no display screen, and is available in a 2 GB size. The Shuffle allows you to shake the device in certain positions to change the song, play the songs in order, or shuffle the order. The newest version also includes a new VoiceOver function that will tell you the song or artist you're listening to. The iPod Shuffle costs $49 and is available in six different colors.

The iPod Nano is one of Apple's more popular devices and has just recently had a makeover. The current version of the Nano includes a radio tuner with live pause functionality, VoiceOver, and even a pedometer. Some of the new features include a 2.5-inch multi-touch display, the ability to play video, Bluetooth 4.0, Nike+ support, and all-new EarPods. This device has been updated with Apple's new Lightning connector pin. The iPod Nano is offered in six bright colors, and it is available only with 16 GB of storage capacity. The cost is just $149. Flash memory is used in the Nano, making it ideal for workouts at the gym.

The iPod Touch is probably the most versatile iPod, providing users with a way to listen to music, watch videos, and play games, as well as surf the Internet and check their e-mail. Like the Nano, the iPod Touch just went through its own refresh. The latest version is much thinner and lighter than the previous models, weighing just 3.1 ounces. It comes with a 4-inch Retina display, upgraded iSight 8-megapixel camera, upgraded A8 chip with 64-bit architecture, and the all-new EarPods. The iPod Touch has a 4-inch diagonal color display and a touchscreen interface, and it is available in 16, 32, 64, and 128 GB sizes. The iPod Touch even has a built-in Wi-Fi network adapter supporting 802.11ac network connections. The device also includes Bluetooth 4.1 and Nike+ support. The iPod Touch costs anywhere from $199 to $399, depending on the model capacity.

All of the iPod devices can be purchased online from the Apple Store or at your local electronics retailer. The devices are both Windows and Mac compatible, and they connect to your computer using a USB connection.

## *Software*

### Microsoft Office 2016 for Mac

Microsoft Office for Mac 2016 is the latest version of Office for Macs and includes better compatibility across platforms, improved collaboration tools, and an improved user interface. Microsoft Office for Mac includes Word, PowerPoint, Excel, Outlook, and OneNote. Some of the new features include new Online Template files; a redesigned interface and sharper graphics to take advantage of the Retina display; the ability to navigate documents and files using Multi-Touch gestures; and the integration with OneDrive, OneDrive for Business, and SharePoint. One of the improved features in this version that lawyers may find useful is the coauthoring feature, which enables several people to work simultaneously in the same Word document at the same time.

Like the Windows-based counterpart, users are able to opt to subscribe to Office365 instead of purchasing the stand-alone version of Office for Mac. Depending on the subscription level, users may be able to install Office for Mac on up to five computers.

The stand-alone version of Office for Mac 2016 requires Mac OS X v. 10.10 or later and will be available for purchase by the time this book is published. At the time of this writing, the stand-alone version wasn't available on Microsoft's webstore, but was "coming soon."

### Toast 14 Titanium by Roxio

Toast 14 Titanium is the latest version of Roxio's long-running disc-burning software for the Mac. With this software, you can burn video or data to CDs or DVDs. This version gives users the ability to burn high-definition video to Blu-ray discs and record content directly from their screen with Live Screen Capture. Toast even allows a user to capture streaming audio from any website and then transfer the audio to an iPod or any other iOS-based device. The software has built-in basic features, such as the ability to compress, convert, and compile video in most formats, along with backup software that can be scheduled to back up your data. Features new to this version include the ability to extract clips from any DVD video and convert them to a format of your choice, to convert audiobook CDs for playback on iPod devices, and to build your MP3 library with the automatic capture and tagging of Internet audio. New to this version is the capability for users to convert video recorded on their TiVo DVRs, EyeTV tuners, and Flip Video camcorders to play on their iPad, iPhone, or video game consoles. Users can even share their video compilations directly to YouTube, Twitter, Google+, and Facebook.

This latest version added support to convert video from the Apple iPhone 6 and Samsung Galaxy S6 devices.

The software can be purchased online from Roxio's website (**www.roxio.com**) for $99.99.

## Norton Security for Mac

Every Mac user needs to protect his or her computer from viruses and other threats. Using antivirus protection on a Mac is no longer an option; it's a necessity. Norton Security has an edition specifically for Mac computers that offers protection from the latest viruses, spyware, rootkits, and other web-based attacks. Norton Security is compatible with OS X v. 10.9 or higher.

The antivirus protection can automatically scan and clean downloaded e-mail files and attachments and provide real-time protection and removal of viruses and other threats.

Some users still believe there are no viruses or threats for a Mac. Not so. Just look at how many systems were infected with the MacDefender or Flashback Trojan over the past few years. These were such a problem that Apple released security patches just to address these specific threats. There are many other documented viruses and vulnerabilities that are specific to Macs and many more that are operating system–independent. The message here is to get and install a full-blown (not just antivirus) security solution. You should never use a computer on your business or home network without the proper security protection, even if it's a Mac. Apple itself removed from its website (rather late, in 2012) language suggesting that it was impervious to malware. Norton Security can be purchased online directly from Symantec's website (**www.symantec.com**) for $44.99 for a one-year subscription.

## Kaspersky Internet Security for Mac

For users looking for an alternative to Norton Internet Security, Kaspersky has a great product called Kaspersky Internet Security for Mac. We use Kaspersky's security software on our networks and have tried this product on our Mac laptop, and it works as advertised. This software offers real-time protection against malware, phishing, and malicious websites, as well as antivirus protection and parental controls. This product requires Mac OS X 10.7 or higher to run. This product can be purchased online from Kaspersky's website (**www.kaspersky.com**) for $59.95 for a one-year subscription.

## Intuit Quicken 2015 for Mac

Intuit Quicken for Mac offers a complete personal financial management package, providing immediate access to your accounts from a single location. By using Quicken, you can better organize your financial information and easily track your finances. Quicken provides a simple way to track and enter expenses without launching the entire application through the QuickEntry Dashboard Widget. Some of the new features allow you to check your account balances and budget on the go using the free mobile app, which syncs the data between your phone and your computer. This product also allows you to see all of your accounts in one place. The software will run only on Intel-based Macs using 10.7.5 or higher.

Quicken users can export their basic tax information to TurboTax and other applications that can read a TXF or QXF file.

If you need to switch your data files from Quicken Windows to Quicken Mac, there is a walk-through guide on Intuit's website to help you out. You can find the instructions to complete this procedure at **https://quicken.intuit.com/support/help/what-quicken-data-can-be-converted-from-windows-to-mac-/GEN82214.html**.

Quicken 2015 for Mac is the latest version of the software from Intuit that is available for purchase and download on its website (**www.intuit.com**) for $64.99.

## QuickBooks 2015 Desktop for Macs

QuickBooks, another financial and accounting package from Intuit, has an edition for Macs. QuickBooks 2015 Desktop for Macs can be used to organize your business finances. This software package will also track and manage your business expenses, invoicing, and payroll from a single financial application. QuickBooks for Macs can synchronize your contacts directly with the Mac OS X Address Book and set reminders in iCal. This software is compatible with Mac OS X v. 10.9 or higher.

Some of the new features added in this edition include:

- ◆ Improved budget creator
- ◆ Improved batch invoicing, payments, and bills
- ◆ Ability to see an overview of your orders, what you own, and what you've paid in one place with Expense Tracker

QuickBooks 2015 Desktop for Macs can be purchased online from Intuit's QuickBooks website (**www.quickbooks.intuit.com**) for $199.95 for a new license. Two- and three-user versions are also available for purchase on the website.

## Symantec Drive Encryption for Mac OS X

PGP Corporation (now owned by Symantec), a leading vendor of hard disk encryption software, has released an updated version of its hard disk encryption suite compatible with Mac computers (previously called Symantec Full Disk Encryption for Macs). Symantec Drive Encryption software provides comprehensive, nonstop disk encryption for Macs, securing data on desktops, laptops, and removable devices. A user name and passphrase are required to decrypt the contents of the hard disk, protecting the data from unauthorized access. Symantec Drive Encryption requires Mac OS X version 10.8.4 or higher and only runs on Intel-based Macs. Symantec Drive Encryption can be used to provide quick, cost-effective data protection for information on hard drives and removable media. Any lawyer using a Mac laptop should definitely have this software installed to protect sensitive and confidential information. An alternative is to enable File Vault or File Vault 2, which is included as part of the Mac operating system.

Symantec Drive Encryption software can be purchased online directly from Symantec's website (**www.symantec.com**) for $85 for a single license with one-year upgrade assurance.

## Apple iTunes

If you've ever owned an iPod or older version of the iPhone or iPad, then you're certainly familiar with Apple iTunes. It is Apple Software's most popular product, mainly because it used to be necessary to manage your digital music library on your iPod, iPhone, iPad, or other Apple iOS device. The newest version of iTunes allows users to download more content with their purchased songs, such as the album cover, band pictures, and even song lyrics. Using the Home Sharing feature, users can share their digital libraries with up to five authorized computers in their home, allowing them to share purchased music files across multiple computer systems. Apple now allows you to follow your favorite artists and view what music your friends are downloading and listening to. A new feature called iTunes Match lets you store all of your music in iCloud—even songs you've imported from CDs—synchronizing your music across all of your iOS devices. iCloud provides users with the ability to access their music,

TV shows, apps, and books from multiple devices without the need to synchronize files manually using iTunes across multiple iOS devices.

Using the iTunes Store, users can download apps, music, videos, podcasts, and more and then synchronize them to their devices, such as an iPad or iPhone. Users can subscribe to podcasts, and without any user input, the iTunes application can download the latest shows as they're made available. We use this feature a lot when it comes to managing the legal technology podcasts to which we subscribe and constantly monitor.

Apple's new Music service, which was released this past year, allows users to subscribe to and stream any track within Apple's music library. Currently, Apple is offering a three-month trial membership for the service. Once the trial period ends, membership is currently priced at $9.99 per user per month or $14.99 for a family membership per month.

Apple iTunes is available as a free download for Mac OS X and Windows 10 from Apple's website.

### Apple Pay

Apple Pay is a mobile payment and digital wallet service provided by Apple that lets users make payments using the iPhone, iPad, or Apple Watch devices. This service doesn't require Apple-specific terminals and is compatible with Visa's PayWave, MasterCard's PayPass, and American Express's ExpressPay terminals. To use this service, users must register a credit card with Apple Pay. This service uses near field communication (NFC) to communicate with the payment terminals and is increasing in popularity as users move to paying with their mobile devices rather than fumbling for their wallets. As more and more retailers begin to accept this form of payment, the usage of this payment method will only increase.

# CHAPTER TWENTY-FOUR

# iWin:
# iPad for Litigators

## by Tom Mighell, Esq., and
## Paul J. Unger, Esq.

### Introduction and Tour of iPad

In the five years since Apple released the iPad, it has firmly established itself as a very useful tool for lawyers and one of the biggest innovations in legal technology to come along in some time. The iPad's design is ingenious and handsome. Its functionality is equally as nice and continues to improve as legal software developers create new and innovative apps for lawyers. Indeed, the iPad remains the tablet of choice for legal app developers, far outpacing Android and Windows tablets in the number of legal apps available.

Tablets are now integrating themselves into the workflow of lawyers, irrespective of firm size or practice area, and nowhere has this been more apparent than for litigators. Whether you need to take notes, mark and handle exhibits, or manage deposition transcripts, these little computers can supercharge your trial practice. But the iPad can make any lawyer more productive, regardless of practice; while we primarily discuss how litigators can use tablet computers to enhance their day in court, we will also provide a general overview for anyone interested in using the iPad (see Figure 24.1) in her practice.

### Why Use an iPad in Your Practice?

We like to describe the iPad as an "instant-on" computer that you can control with your finger. There's no booting-up process, and no keyboard

**Figure 24.1** An iPad

is needed (but as we discuss below, you'll still want to have one). It provides instant access to information traditionally accessed from your desktop computer or laptop.

Although the iPad's initial purpose was thought to be as a "consumption" device—a tablet used primarily for reading and accessing information and very light typing—its ease of use and big screen is so addictive that it evolved into a tool that can do so much more, especially for lawyers.

Trial presentation apps available for the iPad make it easy to display those exhibits on projectors or monitors (wired or wireless) in the courtroom.

If you carry around a legal pad and a lot of paper in a legal file or Redweld, the iPad can become your legal pad and digital folder. It is truly redefining the idea of the "paperless law office," allowing you to carry most of your office around with you, all in a very small, light device. For courtroom work, the iPad can be used to access exhibits, pleadings, legal research, depositions, and just about any document you might need in hearings or at trial (see Figure 24.2).

Trial presentation apps are available for the iPad that make it easy to display those exhibits on projectors or monitors (wired or wireless) in the courtroom.

### Overview
If you want to learn more about using the iPad, check out Tom's books *iPad in One Hour for Lawyers* (3rd edition) and *iPad in One Hour for Litigators* (2nd edition), both published by the ABA and available in the ABA webstore.

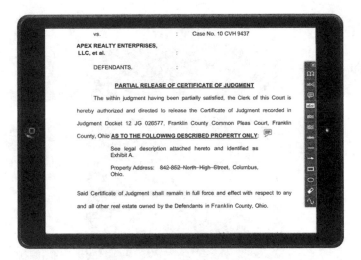

**Figure 24.2** Viewing Documents

## Why Use an iPad in the Courtroom?

Certainly, most of you have seen an iPad at this point (see Figures 24.3 and 24.4). The iPad has some drawbacks as a computing tool that make it unsuitable as a complete replacement for your desktop or laptop; however, we believe it is ideal for courtroom use because it is so light and easy to hold and operate. It is very easy to understand and use, with little training required. (In fact, if you already use an iPhone, you'll be able to start working with an iPad right away.)

Among the often-cited negatives of the iPad are (1) that it has no USB port for plugging the tablet into other devices and (2) that the battery is not removable or replaceable. One of the reasons that the lack of a USB port is not troubling is that the iPad comes with Bluetooth capability, so keyboards, printers, and other devices can be connected wirelessly to the device. Also, a number of cloud providers (Dropbox, Box, and SpiderOak, among others) make it easy for you to access all of your documents online, without needing to connect your iPad to anything.

The iPad Air 2 has a 10.1-inch display, while the iPad Mini features the smaller 7-inch screen and has become very popular for its compact design and ease of use. Because lawyers need to work with documents during trial, however, we believe that the larger 10-inch display is far preferable and will make working with documents, legal research, and notes in court much easier.

## iPad Air

Status bar

FaceTime HD camera

App icons

Multi-Touch display

Home

**Figure 24.3** Front View

Sleep/Wake button

Microphones

iSight camera

Side Switch

Headset jack

Volume buttons

Nano-SIM tray (cellular models)

Speakers

Lightning connector

**Figure 24.4** Back View

In our opinion, it is this ease of use that explains why iPads are rapidly catching on with trial lawyers. A laptop, netbook, or even the "traditional" convertible tablet PCs, which are useful at counsel table, cannot be carried around the courtroom easily when the lawyer is standing at the podium or addressing the jury. We firmly believe the iPad is the preferred mobile device for trial lawyers, because the apps designed for use in the courtroom are not only very powerful but also simple enough that they will not distract from actually trying a case.

Essentially, the iPad is just a little heavier than a paper legal pad and not nearly as heavy as the lightest netbook or laptop.

When selecting a jury, it doesn't make sense to question a jury pool while keyboarding your responses into a traditional computer; there's probably no better way to get jurors to clam up and give them the impression that you are transcribing their personal information. (This is true even though the court reporter may be quietly transcribing it in many cases.) The iPad, however, is ideally configured for you to use in taking notes on your jury panel, either within a jury selection app or your favorite note-taking application.

Let's take a look at some of the ways a litigator would benefit by using an iPad, from initial receipt of a lawsuit all the way through jury verdict.

## iPad Apps for Lawyers

### Court Days Pro
**($2.99, bit.ly/yT171w)**

Court Days Pro is a rules-based legal calendaring app for the iPhone and iPad. It provides legal professionals with the ability to calculate dates and deadlines based on a customizable database of court rules and statutes. Once the rules are set up in the application, you can perform date calculations using a customizable list of court holidays. It comes with California's Superior Court rules preinstalled; however, if you do not live in California, you will need to add your own local court rules for the jurisdiction in which you practice. Unfortunately, Court Days Pro has not been updated in some time, which typically means the developers have lost interest in supporting it. We still believe it is a worthwhile app because it will allow you to input your own deadlines and reuse them over again, which is unique for a calendaring app.

Once you choose a triggering event (e.g., a motion hearing date or receipt of a complaint), the application will display a list of all events and corresponding dates and deadlines based on the triggering event (e.g., last day to file moving papers, opposition, reply briefs). Icons on the screen show the number of calendar days and court days from the current date for all resulting events (see Figure 24.5).

Date results can be added to the device's native calendar app, and all results can be e-mailed to your client or others straight from the application.

The app is preprogrammed with a list of all federal holidays but is fully customizable to allow the addition or removal of any court holiday to the list.

Other calendaring apps are DocketLaw (Free, bit.ly/PmiBlW) and Smart Dockets (Free, bit.ly/URZGmj). Both apps are free to download, but DocketLaw charges a subscription to access court deadlines. Like Court Days Pro, neither of these apps has been updated in some time, which suggests that there is not much demand for calendaring and docketing functionality on the iPad.

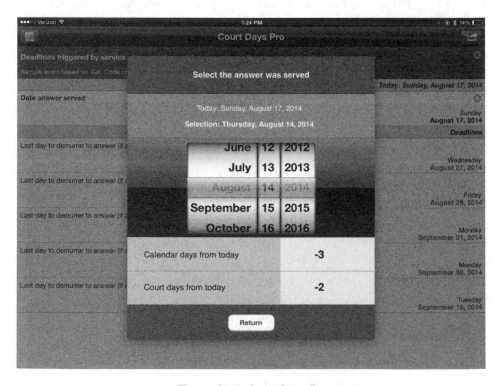

**Figure 24.5** Court Days Pro

### Lawyer's Professional Assistant
### ($4.99, bit.ly/x5j7Fq)

The Wolfram Lawyer's Professional Assistant (see Figure 24.6) is a reference tool that takes advantage of the company's "Computational Knowledge Engine" to help lawyers with calculations that may be relevant to their practice. Some of the features include:

+ Calendar computations
+ Legal dictionary
+ Statutes of limitations for each U.S. state (see Figure 24.7)
+ Visa types, including basic requirements, common issues, and extensions and limits
+ Financial computations, including fee calculator, settlement calculator, current interest rates, historical value of money, and federal U.S. tax rates
+ Crime rates and history for specific crimes, as well as state and national average comparisons
+ Demographics of population and economy for a specific city
+ Investigative information, including weather, company information, IP lookup, and blood-alcohol calculator
+ Damages and estate planning computations for occupational salaries, cost of living, life expectancy, and present or future value

## Depositions and Documents

### TranscriptPad
### ($89.99, bit.ly/w7JGHt)

For reviewing and annotating depositions, it is hard to beat an app like TranscriptPad. Once you have taken your depositions, you can load all of the transcripts into TranscriptPad to review them and create designations. The app only accepts text transcripts, so be sure to ask your court reporter for the deposition in TXT format. Once it's loaded, you can easily highlight testimony and code the designations with the issues you want to include (see Figure 24.8).

When you complete your designations, it's simple to e-mail them to co-counsel, the judge, your client, or others (see Figure 24.9). If you use

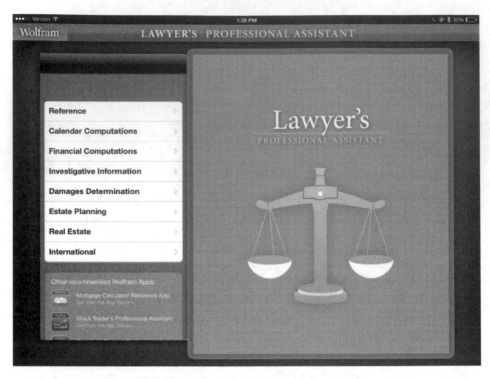

**Figure 24.6** Lawyer's Professional Assistant

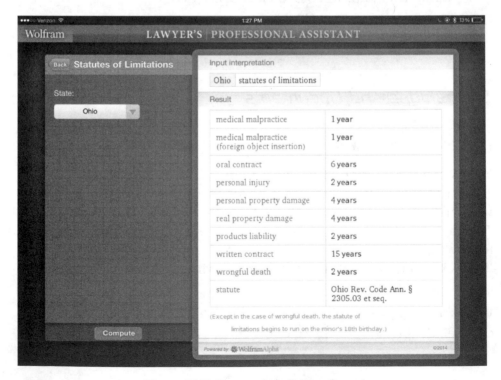

**Figure 24.7** Statute of Limitations Screen

**Figure 24.8** The Deponent

**Figure 24.9** TranscriptPad

TrialDirector or Sanction for evidence presentation, you can also import your designations directly into those tools from TranscriptPad.

### DocReviewPad
### ($89.99, apple.co/KPm8qz)

There aren't many apps that allow you to review large volumes of documents, annotate or otherwise code them, and then Bates stamp all of them with the touch of a button. DocReviewPad is a relatively new app that makes it easy to import, review, code, and then export your documents into TrialPad or some other format for use at trial (see Figure 24.10).

## Jury Selection/Tracking

### iJuror
### ($19.99, bit.ly/xJFlOT)

iJuror is an app developed to assist with jury selection (see Figure 24.11). Features include:

**Figure 24.10**  DocReviewPad

**Figure 24.11** iJuror

♦ Tap the seats to add juror information.

♦ Track patterns.

♦ E-mail the jury information to any e-mail address.

♦ Configure seating arrangements for up to ninety-six prospective jurors.

♦ Get easy access to popular social networks to conduct quick research on potential jury members.

♦ Add notes as the trial goes along, and score jurors based on their answers to voir dire questions.

♦ Name view provides quick access to names and notes.

♦ Drag and drop to choose jurors.

♦ Drag and drop to choose alternates.

♦ Drag and drop to dismiss jurors.

## Honorable Mentions

♦ **JuryStar** ($39.99, **bit.ly/S38DSJ**) Similar to iJuror, but it requires that you manually enter a lot more information.

♦ **iJury** ($14.99, **bit.ly/ymg87i**) This nice jury selection tool has pre-populated questions and a system for ranking jurors based on their answers. However, you can only enter twelve people, which is not very helpful if you have a larger voir dire panel.

♦ **JuryTracker** ($4.99, **bit.ly/xpvyuO**) This app goes to work after you have selected your jury; it works as your "personal jury consultant" to help track the reactions of jury members throughout the trial (see Figure 24.12).

## Evidence Presentation

### TrialPad
### ($89.99, bit.ly/ApMDjM)

TrialPad is a legal document and exhibit management and presentation tool originally developed for lawyers to use in the courtroom. Lawyers and other legal professionals also are finding other great ways to use the app, including client presentations and law school lectures. With TrialPad, you can organize, manage, annotate, and store your documents and video while leveraging the portability of your iPad. It is designed to work like full-featured tools such as Sanction and Trial Director; however,

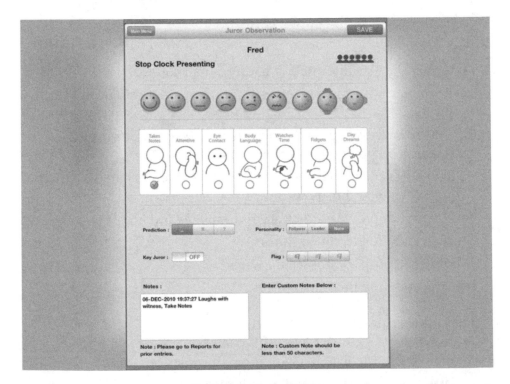

**Figure 24.12** JuryTracker

because the iPad is not as powerful as your laptop, TrialPad does not offer all the functionality of traditional trial presentation software. But for many types of trials and hearings, TrialPad is the ideal presentation tool.

TrialPad differs from programs like PowerPoint and Keynote in that the presenter can present documents, images, and video in any order. It's possible to jump around, zoom, magnify, and annotate an exhibit on the fly. TrialPad is not really a competitor to PowerPoint or Keynote because it was designed to handle different situations; PowerPoint and Keynote are designed for more rehearsed linear presentations (opening and closing), whereas TrialPad works in more spontaneous situations like witness examination. Unlike PDF readers, it lets you create separate case folders, organize and sort important documents, and dynamically annotate and present documents via its flexible output options.

TrialPad cannot handle huge amounts of data as well as Sanction or Trial Director, and its video editing tool is not as powerful, but it works very well for hearings and most cases with manageable volumes of records. Features include:

- ◆ Organize and present evidence electronically (see Figure 24.13).
- ◆ Import process via Dropbox, Box, Citrix ShareFile, Transporter, WebDav server, e-mail, or iTunes.
- ◆ No Internet connection is needed once files are loaded.
- ◆ Present wirelessly with Apple TV or AirServer (requires iPad 2 and above).
- ◆ Highlight, annotate, redact, and zoom in on your documents (see Figure 24.14).
- ◆ Make multiple callouts from documents or depositions.
- ◆ View documents side by side, comparing pages.
- ◆ Edit video clips or take snapshots of frames of surveillance video.
- ◆ Create Key Docs with saved annotations and then print or e-mail them with the annotations.
- ◆ Have your expert mark up an exhibit and save it as a Key Doc for closing.
- ◆ Use the whiteboard tool to draw freehand.
- ◆ Create separate case and witness folders.
- ◆ File formats supported: Adobe Acrobat PDF, JPG, PNG, TIFF, multipage TIFF, and TXT. (Also imports DOC, DOCX, XLS, XLSX, PPT, PPTX, Keynote, Pages, and Numbers. Please note: Our best prac-

**Figure 24.13** Presenting Evidence with TrialPad

**Figure 24.14** TrialPad Photo

tices recommendation is to convert these files to Adobe Acrobat to maintain the formatting and look of the original document.)

♦ Video formats supported: All formats supported by iPad, such as .m4v, .mp4, and .mov.

### Honorable Mentions

♦ **ExhibitView** ($49.99, **bit.ly/zUwFnq**) This app is a worthy competitor to TrialPad. It offers a "Witness View," where you can hand the witness your iPad to view an exhibit without showing any of your other case files.

## Legal Research

When you go to court, how many rulebooks do you bring with you? During trial or a hearing, it's important to have access to the case law, codes, and rules that are applicable to your case. Tools like the iPad now make it easy to have access to your entire law library, no matter where you happen to be. Here are a few of the tools we like:

♦ **Fastcase** (Free, **bit.ly/ysOcTY**) It's the companion to the legal research service.

♦ **WestlawNext** (Free, **bit.ly/z5pKRs**; requires Westlaw subscription) A great tool for the courtroom, it allows you to conduct legal research, annotate the results, and e-mail case law to the judge or others.

♦ **Lexis Advance HD** (Free, **bit.ly/vo7wzp**; requires Lexis subscription) Similar to WestlawNext, LexisAdvance provides most of the same features for accessing your Lexis account.

♦ **RuleBook** (Free with in-app purchases, **bit.ly/1tgxNXf**) Offers access to court rules and selected statutes of 21 states, which are available on an à la carte basis.

♦ **FedCtRecords** ($9.99, **bit.ly/yb7gav**) This is an iPhone app, but completely worth the purchase for your iPad. The app provides access to your PACER account, so you have anywhere access to records on just about any federal case.

♦ **ProView** (Free, **bit.ly/wVrUZc**; requires purchase of rulebooks) If you practice in a jurisdiction that has rules published by Thomson Reuters, you can access the full version of those rulebooks on your iPad with this app.

## Courtroom Chatting

### BT Chat HD
**(Free, [bit.ly/xE16tG](bit.ly/xE16tG))**

If you have ever had the need to pass a note discreetly in the courtroom, you will completely understand the need for this app (see Figure 24.15). With BT Chat HD, you can chat with other iPad users via Bluetooth or Wi-Fi (Wi-Fi is better if sitting at a distance).

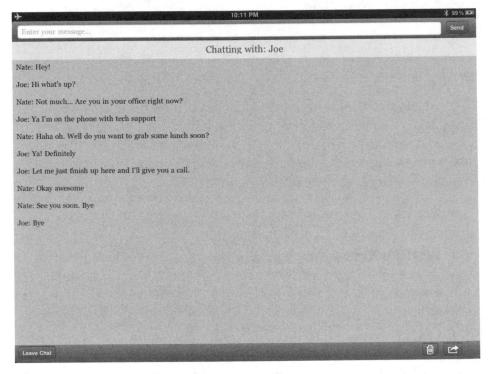

**Figure 24.15**  BT Chat HD

## Other Must-Have iPad Apps

### So Many Apps . . . Which One Is Best?

There are many incredible apps for the iPad. In fact, there are so many that you will probably be overwhelmed about which ones to select, especially if you are new to the iPad.

We have listed our picks below, and we also have some honorable mentions. Some of our honorable mentions may end up being your top picks.

Don't let this overwhelm you. With so many fantastic apps out there, it is hard to go wrong. In deciding which apps are best for you, follow these guiding principles:

♦ There are probably a dozen apps that accomplish the same thing. Review legal app blogs, read consumer reviews, and ask trusted people what they recommend.

♦ Your workplace may prefer one app over another. Consistency and uniformity at the office is typically a good thing.

♦ If your coworkers or friends use the app, they can provide you with a support network to better learn and use the app.

♦ If a new app is released from a competing software company, don't be too quick to switch! Your app will probably catch up fast and may have features the other app doesn't have yet. Remember your time invested in the app you already own.

♦ Apps are cheap; if you are curious, just buy it. Most apps are less than $10. The most expensive app cited in these materials is $129.99.

♦ If you want more recommendations, check out Tom's book *iPad Apps in One Hour for Lawyers*—he lists 200+ of his choices for the best productivity; document creation and management; and legal, travel, and leisure time apps in the App Store. It's available from the ABA webstore.

## 1. Dropbox
**(Free app, <u>bit.ly/z54Tpv</u>; Free Dropbox account up to 2 GB at <u>www.dropbox.com</u>)**

**Paul and Tom's Top Pick**

If you have an iPad, Dropbox is almost mandatory. Setting aside debates about security, Dropbox has become the gold standard for storing files and getting them to the iPad. Most software developers build their apps to integrate with Dropbox because it has become so widely used.

Dropbox sets up a local folder on your computer that allows you to create any subfolder structure. These subfolders synchronize into the cloud and can be shared with other people (clients, co-counsel, coworkers, etc.), if desired. The iPad can also connect to your Dropbox account so that it can see and access everything that you can see on your PC (see Figure 24.16).

**Figure 24.16** The iPad's View of a Dropbox Account

If you can create a folder, copy and paste, and drag and drop, you can use Dropbox.

## 2. Dictate + Connect
## ($16.99, bit.ly/wuv1Mq)

**Paul's Top Pick**

Dictate + Connect is a dictation application for your iPhone or iPad (see Figure 24.17). Like a traditional digital recorder, it allows you to rewind,

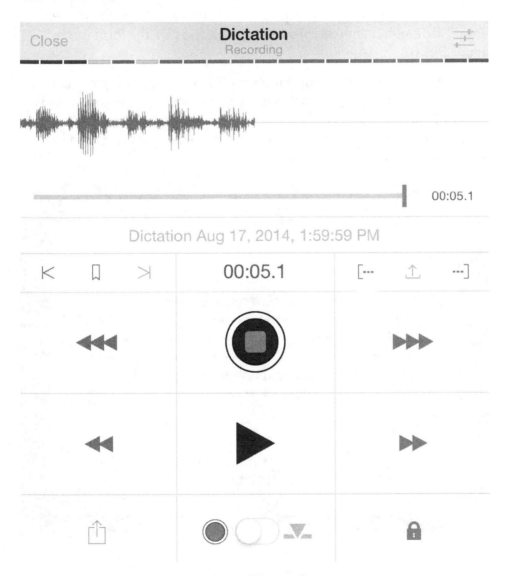

**Figure 24.17** Dictate + Connect

overwrite, and insert anywhere. Download recordings; send as e-mails; and upload to Dropbox, iCloud, FTP, or WebDAV.

## 3. GoodReader
## ($4.99, bit.ly/xb99kc)

### Paul and Tom's Top Pick

Since documents are the lifeblood of the legal profession, it makes sense that one of the best uses of the iPad in a law practice is to read and annotate documents. GoodReader is best described as a universal document viewer, although it arguably works best with the PDF file format (see Figure 24.18).

It provides excellent annotation tools for PDF files, including the ability to highlight text; insert text boxes; post sticky note comments; compose freehand drawings; and add lines, arrows, rectangles, and so on (see Figure 24.19). These tools are extremely useful when you're reading a court opinion or law review article.

**Figure 24.18** GoodReader

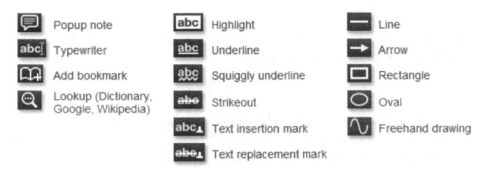

**Figure 24.19** GoodReader Annotations

GoodReader also has a robust file manager and has the ability to sync directly with your accounts from Dropbox, Box.com, Google Drive, OneDrive, or even your own web-connected server (see Figure 24.20).

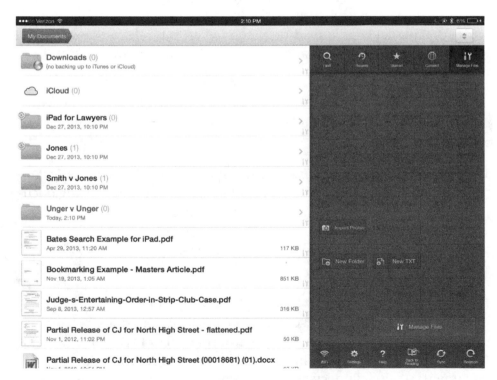

**Figure 24.20** GoodReader File Management

## 4. Microsoft Office for iPad
(Free, http://bit.ly/1e17n4j (Word), http://bit.ly/1g8csnl (Excel), http://bit.ly/1jApmPu (PowerPoint))

**Paul and Tom's Top Pick**

Microsoft has finally brought its Office suite to the iPad, and for Office users, this is the recommended set of apps to use. Working in these apps is almost like working in the desktop versions of Word, Excel, and PowerPoint, although Microsoft modified the layout to better accommodate the tablet interface. The experience using these apps is the closest you'll get on the iPad to working with the real thing.

Even better, the apps are free to download for basic review and editing. For more advanced editing or creation of documents, however, you'll have to purchase a subscription to Microsoft's Office 365 product; this can range between $69 and $150 per year, depending on the version you purchase. This is actually a good deal—for this price, you get five licenses to Microsoft Office. Further, there's no need to wait for the next version to come out, then use CDs to install it on your computer; the Office 365 model is download-only, so as Microsoft releases new versions of the software, it is downloaded and your computer is automatically updated.

The Office apps also allow you to save documents to cloud storage, with connections available to OneDrive, OneDrive for Business, Dropbox, and SharePoint.

We highly recommend the use of Office apps on the iPad, especially if you plan to spend a lot of time on your tablet creating and revising documents or presenting slideshows (see Figure 24.21).

## Honorable Mention: Documents To Go Premium
($16.99, bit.ly/A5LPMq)

If you don't want to pay for Microsoft Office, Documents To Go is currently your best low-cost option. While it does not come close to the functionality of Microsoft Word or Excel for iPad, Docs To Go provides basic editing tools for Word, Excel, and PowerPoint documents. It also connects to most major cloud services for easy sharing and syncing.

**Figure 24.21** PowerPoint for iPad

## 5. Notability
**($5.99, bit.ly/wZT4wD)**

### Paul and Tom's Top Pick

Very few note-taking apps perform all three functions of handwriting, typing, and audio. We have found that Notability provides a great writing experience. You can change the thickness of the pen and the width of lines and add lines and gridlines—all important to simulate an experience similar to writing on a piece of paper (see Figure 24.22).

You can use your finger to write notes on the iPad, but we recommend investing in a stylus so that the writing experience is as similar as possible to writing on paper with a pen.

The audio feature not only records your meetings, conferences, and other gatherings but also synchronizes the recording to your notes so that you can simply tap a word or picture and hear what was being said at that moment.

**Figure 24.22** Notability

Paul finds the ability to record a meeting, lecture, and so on, to be immensely helpful in certain situations. He absolutely loves this feature and does not want to have a separate notes program to do this (like Auditorium), a separate typing program, and a separate audio recorder. Notability provides all three functions.

## 6. Noteshelf
**($7.99, bit.ly/y73OZd)**

**Tom's Top Pick**

For pure handwritten note-taking, Noteshelf is one of the highest-ranking and most popular apps (see Figure 24.23). You can create notebooks for your clients, cases, or projects and see them at a glance on your Noteshelf bookshelf (see Figure 24.24). You can e-mail notebooks to yourself or others, or you can export notebooks to a PDF file and save them in Dropbox, Box, Google Drive, or Evernote. Tom recommends this app because it has just enough features that lawyers need to take notes without being overwhelming. It just works and works well.

**Figure 24.23** Noteshelf

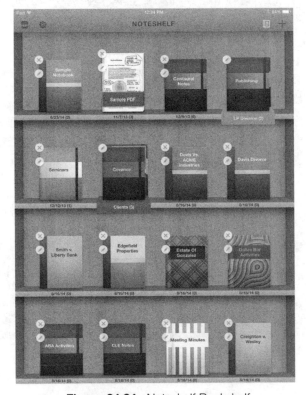

**Figure 24.24** Noteshelf Bookshelf

## 7. Keynote for iOS
**($9.99, bit.ly/z6C1R9)**

**Paul's Top Pick**

Keynote for the iPad or Mac is the equivalent of PowerPoint in the PC world (see Figure 24.25). Keynote truly is an excellent presentation tool, and Apple has ported the software to the iPad iOS.

Keynote on the iPad can certainly be used to give presentations on a large screen with a projector. But many lawyers also use Keynote as a way to share a set of images and information with a small group, such as at a client meeting. Keynote is a beautiful app on the iPad, and you can easily manipulate the slides and images.

If you have an iPhone, you might want to enable the Keynote Remote feature, which turns your phone into a remote for the iPad's Keynote app. You can control your slides from the phone or another iOS device and even view any notes you might have included as part of the presentation.

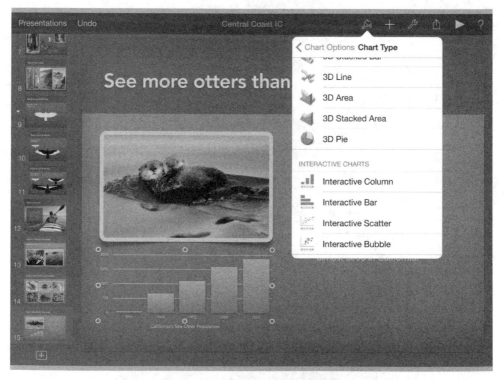

**Figure 24.25** Keynote for iOS

## 8. Scanning Apps
**Scanner Pro ($2.99, http://bit.ly/1q9B3fT) and PDFPen Scan+ ($6.99, http://bit.ly/1vJyBEN)**

**Paul and Tom's Top Picks**

We believe that lawyers should be trying to reduce the amount of paper they create and use in their practice. To that end, these scanning apps are great for scanning paper files to PDF format, when you receive documents from a client, from opposing counsel, or in discovery. We like Scanner Pro because it is so simple to use and does a great job of capturing and saving paper scans as PDF files. Just take a picture of the document; adjust the image to your preference; and e-mail the document or save the PDF to your Dropbox, Google Drive, or Evernote account (see Scanner Pro in Figure 24.26).

If you need to make your PDF files searchable, then you'll need an app that can perform Optical Character Recognition (OCR). That's where

**Figure 24.26** Scanner Pro

PDFPen Scan+ comes in handy. This app will scan your document and identify the text on a page—you can then save the file as a searchable PDF or even copy the text from the PDF to paste it into an e-mail or another document.

## Honorable Mention: Scannable
**(Free, apple.co/1DcxhuT)**

**Tom's Picks**

Tom loves the simplicity of Scannable, an app published by the makers of Evernote. The best part of Scannable is that it works automatically. Just hold your iPad over a document, and the app finds the corners and imme-diately scans it, without you having to do a thing. The images are good quality and can be exported via e-mail or saved in other apps—including Evernote, of course.

## 9. PDF Expert
**($4.99, http://bit.ly/1ra1wjz)**

**Paul and Tom's Top Pick**

Many lawyers use PDF Expert because (1) clients can sign documents that can then be e-mailed back to the office and (2) form-fillable PDFs can now be "mobile" and filled out on the go (see Figure 24.27).

Similar to GoodReader, PDF Expert will let you read and annotate PDF files and has just the right amount of annotation tools a lawyer would need. But PDF Expert offers a few additional features that appeal to legal professionals and are hard to find in other apps.

PDF Expert supports PDF forms and allows you to fill them in using text fields, check boxes, radio buttons, and other form elements. You can cre-ate a PDF form on your computer and transfer it to your iPad when you need to complete the form away from the office.

## 10. LogMeIn/LogMeIn
**(Free, bit.ly/ws9m3y)**

**Paul's Top Pick**

As much as the iPad can do, there will inevitably be a time when you need to work on your office computer or need to access a file that is only locat-ed on your home computer.

**Figure 24.27** PDF Expert

To access a computer from your iPad, you'll need to install the LogMeIn software client on the computer you want to access and that computer will need to be running. When you need to access the computer from the iPad, you'll simply launch the LogMeIn app and put in your credentials (see Figure 24.28). Controlling and manipulating your computer from the iPad can be a little tricky due to the small(er) size of the iPad's screen. But when you need access to your office computer from the road, the LogMeIn app can be your saving grace.

To use LogMeIn on your computer, you'll need to purchase a subscription, which currently starts at $99 per year for two computers.

### 11. Find My iPhone (for the iPad)
**(Free, bit.ly/xbwDkm)**

**Paul and Tom's Top Pick**

The Find My iPhone/Find My iPad service is part of the free iCloud service. Because there is so much personal information and confidential client data stored on iOS devices today, we urge every legal professional with an iPad to sign up for a free iCloud account and enable the Find My iPad service. When you misplace or lose your iPad, you can use the Find My iPhone app installed on another iPhone or iPad or log on to any computer at icloud.com/find to locate the iPad geographically (see Figure 24.29). From there, you can lock your iPad, send a message to the person who might have it, or erase the data that's on it.

**Figure 24.28** LogMeIn Ignition

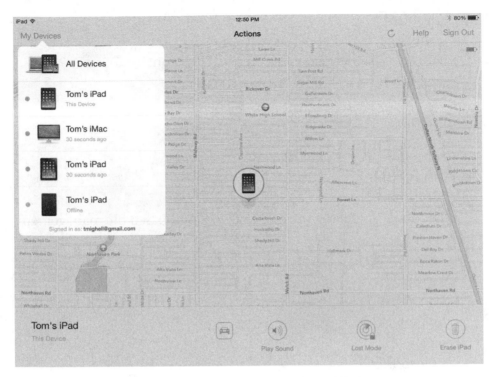

**Figure 24.29** Find My iPhone Desktop Display

Since this service is free and the risk of losing so much information on an iPad is so high, many leading experts, like Brett Burney, argue that setting it up should be mandatory for any legal professional. See "Free Security for Your iPhone & iPad That Should Be Mandatory" at **www.macsinlaw. com/find-my-iphone-free-security/**.

## Library of Other Favorite Apps

We couldn't mention all of the apps we like in detail here, so we've listed the names of some of our favorite apps in several categories. To find out more about them, go to the App Store in iTunes or on your iPad or simply type "[app name] iPad app" into your favorite search engine.

### Browsers—Alternatives to the iPad's Safari Browser
- Atomic Web
- Google Chrome
- Skyfire—allows you to view Flash-based content

## Entertainment

+ Fandango—great app for buying movie tickets
+ HBO Go—subscribers can watch all HBO content for free
+ Hulu+—for watching television shows
+ IMDb
+ Netflix
+ YouTube

## File Management

+ Box.com
+ Dropbox—probably the best-known cloud-based file management tool
+ GoodReader
+ Google Drive
+ OneDrive
+ SpiderOak
+ SugarSync
+ Transporter

## Finance

+ Bank of America
+ Chase Mobile

## Food

+ Food Truck Fiesta
+ OpenTable—make reservations online
+ Yelp

## Games

+ Angry Birds
+ Crosswords
+ Plants vs. Zombies (1 and 2)
+ QuizUp!
+ Scrabble
+ Words with Friends

## Legal-Specific

+ All Law
+ Black's Law Dictionary

- CFR Live Lite—access to all CFR regulations
- Court Days Pro—deadline calculator
- Deponent—conduct an entire deposition from your iPad
- DocReviewPad
- Fastcase
- FedCtRecords—Access your PACER account on your iPad
- iJuror
- iTimekeep—timekeeping app that works with most major time and billing software products
- Jury Tracker
- TranscriptPad
- TrialPad

## Meetings and Calendars

- Calvetica Calendar
- Fantastical
- Fuze Meeting
- GoToMeeting
- Join.me—easy-to-use screen-sharing app
- WebEx
- Zoom Web and Video Conferencing

## News

- AP News
- CNN
- LinkedIn Pulse
- News 360
- NPR
- USA Today

## Photos

- Google Photos
- Photogene—photo editor
- PhotoSync—transfer photos from iPhone to iPad
- Pro HDR—improved HDR photography
- Snapseed

## Productivity

- Documents To Go—document creation and editing
- DocuSign—sign documents on the iPad
- Dragon Dictation—fantastic voice recognition/transcription tool
- Elements—note-taking
- Evernote—a fantastic repository for notes
- iThoughts HD—mind-mapping app
- iType2Go Pro—text editor and camera viewer
- JotNot Scanner Pro—document scanner
- Keynote
- Microsoft Excel for iPad
- Microsoft PowerPoint for iPad
- Microsoft Word for iPad
- MindMeister—mind mapping
- Note Taker HD—note-taking
- Noted—note-taking
- Notes Plus—note-taking
- Office2 HD—document creation/editing
- Outliner—organize your thoughts
- Pages—document creation/editing
- PDF Expert—document editor
- Penultimate—note-taking
- PlainText—text editor
- Prezi—great alternative app for conducting presentations
- Prizmo—scanning and OCR
- SignMyPad—have clients sign documents on your iPad
- SmartNote—note-taking
- UPAD—note-taking
- WritePad—note-taking

## Reading

- Feedly—probably the best news reader/RSS feed reader currently available
- Flipboard—creates magazine-style layout of Facebook/Twitter feeds

- GoodReader—best file reader, period
- iAnnotate PDF
- Instapaper—save articles to read later
- Kindle for iPad
- Mr. Reader—imports RSS feeds from just about anywhere
- NextIssue—"Netflix for Magazines"—for a low monthly price, subscribe to over 100 magazines
- Pocket—save articles to read later
- Reeder—another great choice for reading newsfeeds/RSS feeds
- Text'n Drive Pro—read text messages and e-mails
- Zinio—read magazines on your iPad
- Zite—creates magazine-style layout of latest news on many topics

## Social Networking and Communications

- Facebook
- HootSuite—social media aggregator
- IM+—multi-platform instant messaging client—Skype, Google Talk, and so on
- Imo.im—another good multi-platform instant messaging client
- Skype—VoIP calls and video
- TextNow—send texts for free from your iPad
- Tweetbot—the best Twitter client for iOS
- TweetDeck—a Twitter client
- Twitter

## Travel

- FlightBoard
- FlightTrack
- GateGuru—airport information
- Google Maps
- Google Translate
- Kayak—fantastic travel search engine
- Orbitz
- Taxi Magic

♦ TripAdvisor

♦ TripIt

♦ xe Currency

## Utilities

♦ Air Display—create a second monitor with your iPad

♦ Appzilla—over 100 utility-type apps

♦ Citrix Receiver—remote access

♦ Digits Calculator

♦ Eye Glass—magnifying glass

♦ Google Voice—phone service

♦ GoToMyPC—remote access

♦ IFTTT—Create "recipes" to make the services you use work better with each other

♦ Jibbigo—voice translation

♦ Text Expander—macro utility

♦ Word Lens—translation

## Navigation Tips & Settings

***Add apps and folders to the iPad's dock.*** Out of the box, the iPad features four apps on the Dock, which is the always-visible bar at the bottom of the screen (see Figure 24.30). You can add up to six apps in the Dock, and you can also add folders containing multiple apps in the Dock.

***Launch apps from the Spotlight Search screen.*** While the Spotlight Search bar (accessed by swiping downward on any screen) can be used to search Notes, E-mail, Calendar Appointments, and more, you can also search for an app and tap to launch it (see Figure 24.31).

***Double-tap space bar to add a period and a space.*** You can quickly add a period and a space to the end of a sentence by double-tapping the spacebar. You can turn this option off in the Settings menu if you prefer.

***Use the side switch to lock rotation.*** The side switch on the right side of the iPad (above the volume rocker) can be used to mute the sound on the iPad or to "lock" the rotation of the screen. You can change the setting in the Settings menu of the iPad.

**Figure 24.30** iPad Dock

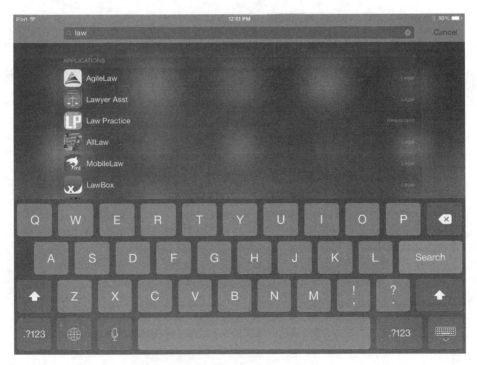

**Figure 24.31** Spotlight Search Screen

***Turn on battery percentage indicator.*** While the iPad by default shows you a graphical representation of the battery level, you can also turn on the percentage indicator under Settings > General > Usage > Battery Usage (see Figure 24.32).

***Undo typing.*** Many people aren't aware that there is an Undo option for the iPad. When you want to undo your most recent typing, you simply (and carefully!!) shake the iPad back and forth. A small window will appear, allowing you to undo your most recent typing.

***Disable the clicking sound for typing and other sounds.*** You can turn off the clicking sound for typing by going to **Settings > Sounds**.

***Take a screenshot.*** You can take a screenshot from your iPad by simply holding down the **Home** button (front-center of device) and **Wake/Sleep** button (top of the device) at the same time. You'll see the screen flash once, and the image will be saved in your iPad's Photos app.

***Use your iPad as a second monitor.*** You can use apps such as Duet (Mac or PC), Air Display (Mac), and MaxiVista (Windows) to turn your iPad into a second monitor. This probably won't be your standard setup, but it can be helpful when you're traveling and need the convenience of a

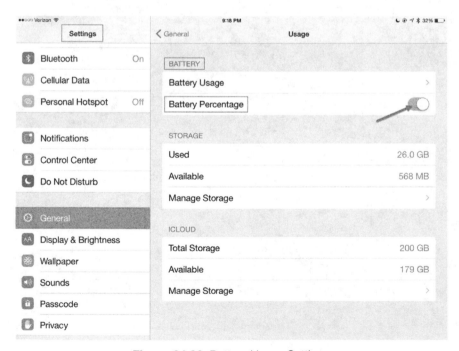

**Figure 24.32** Battery Usage Settings

second monitor (see Figure 24.33). Our favorite is Duet. It uses the Lighting or 30-pin cable to plug directly into your Mac or PC, eliminating latency that you may experience using Wi-Fi with Air Display or MaxiVista.

***Save an image while browsing the Web.*** If you see a picture you want to save while browsing the Web on your iPad, simply tap and hold your finger on the image, and you'll be prompted to save the image into your iPad's Photo app (see Figure 24.34).

**Figure 24.33** iPad as Second Monitor

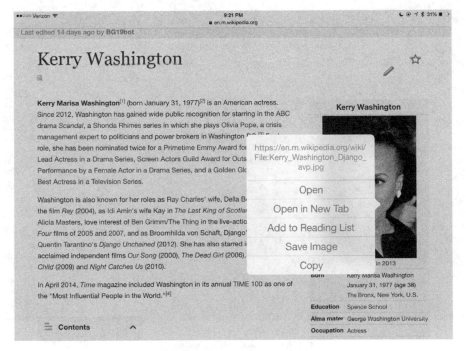

**Figure 24.34** Save Web Image

## Passcode Lock

It is very important to become familiar with the security settings of the iPad so that you can keep information stored on your tablet safe.

You can access the security settings through **Settings > Passcode**. At a minimum, lawyers and their agents should assign a passcode lock in conjunction with the auto-lock function. This will auto-lock your iPad after a set number of minutes and requires a passcode to regain access to the iPad (see Figure 24.35).

The iPad defaults to a "Simple Passcode," which is a four-digit number similar to your ATM PIN. We recommend that you turn "Simple Passcode" off and set a longer passcode—at least ten to twelve numbers, letters, and characters. You should also set a time for the iPad to be idle after which the iPad will then require the passcode. Finally, you should enable the option that erases data after ten failed passcode attempts.

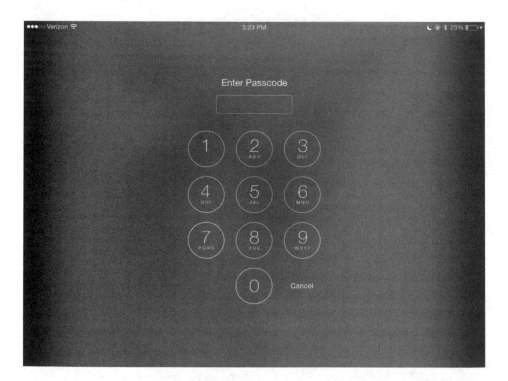

**Figure 24.35** Passcode Lock

## Resources

There are a number of good resources for lawyers using an iPad.

- *iPad 4 Lawyers* by Tom Mighell (**ipad4lawyers.squarespace.com**)
- *iPhone J.D.* by Jeff Richardson (**www.iphonejd.com**)
- *iPad Notebook* by Justin Kahn (**ipadnotebook.wordpress.com**)
- *Macs in Law* by Brett Burney (**www.macsinlaw.com**)
- *The Mac Lawyer* by Ben Stevens (**www.themaclawyer.com**)

Another fantastic website to use for app recommendations and information is App Advice. It provides access to hundreds of articles and reviews of new iPad apps.

## About the Authors

### Tom Mighell, Esq.
Contoural, Inc.
**tmighell@gmail.com**

Tom Mighell is Vice President of Delivery Services at Contoural, Inc., where he helps companies deal with their information governance, privacy, and litigation readiness issues. Before becoming a consultant, Tom was a litigator for eighteen years in Dallas, Texas. He is a frequent speaker and writer on the Internet and legal technology and is the author of several books: *iPad in One Hour for Lawyers* (3rd edition), *iPad in One Hour for Litigators* (2nd Edition), *iPad Apps in One Hour for Lawyers*, and *The Lawyers' Guide to Collaboration Tools and Technologies: Smart Ways to Work Together* (with Dennis Kennedy). He has published Inter Alia (**www.inter-alia.net**), a legal technology blog, since 2002. He and Dennis Kennedy are the cohosts of The Kennedy-Mighell Report, a legal technology podcast. Tom is Past Chair of ABA TECHSHOW 2008, as well as past Chair of the ABA Law Practice Division.

### Paul J. Unger, Esq.
Affinity Consulting Group
**punger@affinityconsulting.com**

Paul J. Unger is a national speaker, writer, and thought-leader in the legal technology industry. He is an attorney and founding principal of Affinity

Consulting Group, a nationwide consulting company providing legal technology consulting, continuing legal education, and training.

He was the Chair of the ABA Legal Technology Resource Center (2013–14, 2014–15) (**www.lawtechnology.org**); former Chair of ABA TECHSHOW (2011) (**www.techshow.com**); and a member of the American Bar Association, Columbus Bar Association, Ohio State Bar Association, Ohio Association for Justice, and Central Ohio Association for Justice. He is also the author of *PowerPoint in One Hour for Lawyers*. He specializes in trial presentation and litigation technology, document and case management, paperless office strategies, and legal-specific software training for law firms and legal departments throughout the Midwest. Mr. Unger has provided trial presentation consultation for over 400 cases. He is an adjunct professor for Capital University Law School's Paralegal Program. In his spare time, he likes to run and restore historic homes.

# CHAPTER TWENTY-FIVE

# Voice and Data Communications

**T**HE ABILITY TO MAKE and receive phone calls is an absolute necessity for a law firm. In addition, some sort of data access is critical to the success of a firm these days. We are a very connected society, and any potential client expects to be able to contact you with relative ease, whether via voice or data transmission such as e-mail. We'll cover some of your technology options for voice and data communications.

## Unified Messaging

Unified messaging is the delivery of traditional voice communications into your e-mail box, including the delivery of facsimile transmissions. Unified messaging systems began to appear around 2001 and were fairly unsuccessful for the first couple of years, but now they are stable. As a result, you can monitor your communications constantly from (potentially) one location—a blessing and a curse, but it is becoming a service that many clients expect you to have.

The simplest way to implement unified messaging is to have it integrated with your phone system. Some small firms may not even have a phone system, and we'll address that issue in a moment. Many of the modern PBX (private branch exchange) systems can incorporate a voicemail card directly into the telephone system chassis. Stand-alone voicemail systems are also an alternative for larger office environments. You can even integrate unified messaging with your Exchange server or your VoIP implementation. The latest versions of Exchange Server (2007, 2010, and 2013) include unified messaging capability at no additional charge. Some outsourced providers of VoIP solutions will provide unified messaging capabilities too, which means you don't have to have any physical equipment to gain the benefits of integrating all your communication streams.

For budget purposes, plan on spending around $3,000 for a voicemail system with unified messaging. As is true for most technology solutions, your mileage may vary. Vendors implement unified messaging in many different ways. Some are better than others, and frankly, some are nothing more than kludge workarounds to make their systems sound more robust than they really are. Our recommendation is to stick with well-known vendors of communication equipment. You really can't go wrong with suppliers such as Avaya, Cisco, NEC, Toshiba, and so on.

Some companies resell complete unified messaging solutions, thereby saving you the investment in hardware and software. These solutions are typically available for a monthly fee, and you may have to commit to a multiyear contract to obtain the service. Also, you are stuck with whatever features and methods the vendor provides. As an example, you may not like the file format for a fax delivery into your inbox, but you'll have no choice but to accept what the vendor gives you. Another concern is that all of your communications may be going through a third party if it is not an on-premise solution. This means your phone calls actually route through the vendor's system before being delivered to your location. In that way, it can capture a voicemail message or fax and repackage it for delivery to your e-mail address. We are generally not fans of having client data move through third-party providers and would recommend that you first investigate systems you own and can control. While a price tag of $3,000 isn't cheap, the value is so great that a good number of solos and small firms have made the leap, and the numbers grow monthly. We are beginning to see on-premise solutions for the SMB market, which may reduce your cost and provide a more stable environment versus hosted solutions.

We'll attempt to cover some of the concerns and questions you should have when considering whether to implement a unified messaging solution. These issues are related to equipment that is provided as part of your telephone communication system. The first issue is what communications the system handles. Can it manage both voice messages and fax transmissions or just one? Even though most systems will handle both voicemail and fax, generally firms use only the voice capability and route the faxes to a dedicated fax machine or printer rather than to a specific person's inbox.

How do you want the voice messages delivered? Most firms will elect to send only an e-mail notification that a voicemail message has been received. This configuration saves bandwidth because the message itself is not transmitted to the e-mail client. It stays on the voicemail server until you retrieve it—hardly convenient if you are traveling. In fact, as a security measure, some telephone systems are configured not to allow remote connections, even for voicemail retrieval. A lot of lawyers use some type of smartphone, and sending a notification-only message saves on their data usage, but what hoops do they have to jump through to listen to the message? The other alternative is to deliver the actual message to your inbox. Obviously, this method uses much more bandwidth, especially if you are delivering it to a cell phone that also receives your e-mail. If you elect this configuration, you'd better have a data plan that can cover your traffic load. Make sure your portable device can play back the file format for your voicemail if you elect to deliver the message to your inbox. As an example, the iPad doesn't natively play back WAV files, which is the format of our unified message system. This means you'll have to purchase an app just to play attached voicemail files.

Another question for your PBX provider is how it handles the message delivery itself. Is the message forwarded to your inbox and then deleted from the voicemail system? If so, there is only one copy of it and you'll never know you received a message if it gets trapped or trashed by your spam filter. If the original stays on the voicemail system and a copy gets delivered to your inbox, does the message light stay lit on your phone? You may not want this, but then again you may want a visual indication that a voice message was delivered.

How does the vendor identify the voice message in your inbox? Is the "From: address" something that is easily recognizable as the phone system, or does it come from you? What does the subject line contain? Showing the caller ID in the subject line is particularly helpful, but not all vendors package messages that way. How is the voice message delivered to your e-mail system? Do you have to have a user ID and password configured on your voicemail box that is consistent with your network credentials? If so, you have the issue of constantly synchronizing your logon credentials with the telephone system, assuming that your network passwords must be changed after a set number of days (shame on you if your password never expires). Many phone systems only accept numbers as a password, so you can't even use letters (forget capitals). This restriction may render your integration unacceptable.

Finally, how do you retrieve your messages? Are they delivered as standard audio attachments to e-mail messages? This is certainly preferred, since you don't need any special software to listen to the messages. Some of the lower-cost (and kludge) solutions require that you install a software add-on to your e-mail client to listen to the voice message. This solution won't work if you are trying to deliver the voicemail to your cell phone. Another problem deals with specific software versions. You must make sure that any potential voicemail system is compatible with your firm's e-mail solution. If you have questions regarding what versions of Microsoft Exchange and Outlook the voicemail system is compatible with, make sure you ask your vendor before you make the investment. As you can see, having specialized software is not a recommended solution. Better to have the voice message packaged as a standard (not proprietary) audio file attachment. That way you can even retrieve your voicemail using a web browser from an Internet café while on vacation in Rio.

If all of this has given you a headache, don't worry. Make sure your IT consultant reads this chapter—he or she can answer all the questions for you. But make no mistake about it: No one who has successfully implemented unified messaging has ever discarded it. The value of unified messaging is phenomenal—being able to access your voicemail on your cell phone is a remarkable enhancement. You need never worry again about being out of touch. If you prefer not to give clients your home or cell phone number, you'll still get their messages. We cannot count the number of times that having voicemail sent to our cell phones has been worth its weight in diamonds.

## Google Voice

For those lawyers constantly on the road, a free service they might find useful is Google Voice. If you'd rather not give your personal cell phone number to your pesky clients, who always have emergencies regardless of the time, then this service might be for you. Google Voice allows you to select a phone number local to your area that forwards inbound phone calls to your other personal phone numbers. This service allows you to provide your clients with a phone number (not your personal number), screen incoming phone calls, and receive voicemails left on the Google Voice phone number in your e-mail inbox. You can specify which e-mail address you would like the voicemails forwarded to. By default, the notification is sent to the address linked to your Google account, but you can add additional e-mail addresses. Google Voice will even transcribe your voicemails to text and provide them in the body of the e-mail, allowing users to read the content before they choose to listen to the messages. The voicemail itself can be downloaded and is delivered as an MP3 file, not a WAV file as in most other voicemail systems. Google Voice also allows users to receive and record phone conversations (be mindful of the laws in your state if you do this), index and search voicemails, and set up conference calls.

If you are currently a Sprint customer, you can take advantage of the Google Voice features without changing your phone number. Be sure to review the Google Voice help section (**support.google.com/voice/**) to see exactly what features you get by integrating your Sprint account with Google Voice.

## Voice over Internet Protocol (VoIP)

In its most basic definition, VoIP is a family of technologies for delivery of voice communications over Internet protocol networks such as the Internet. VoIP systems are digital and can run voice and data systems over the same network, reducing investment in infrastructure. Corporate usage of VoIP phone systems has increased dramatically over the past decade, replacing the traditional copper wire telephone systems that we all used in the past.

VoIP systems are primarily aimed at providing users with unified communications, delivering all services (voice, fax, voicemail, and e-mail) to a single location. VoIP systems are generally more flexible and less costly to implement than your standard dedicated copper wire systems, and they can integrate easily with most existing data network infrastructures.

Security used to be a major concern for VoIP systems. That concern has been greatly reduced. It appears that vendors have finally overcome the performance hit associated with encrypting the voice traffic. You would be hard-pressed to find a current vendor that sends voice traffic in an unencrypted stream. This means that you'll sleep a little better knowing that your voice traffic travels in secure encrypted channels. That doesn't mean your VoIP traffic isn't subject to hacking. In fact, security guru Bruce Schneier has published several blog posts describing how to hack a VoIP data stream. One past post discusses how it is possible even to "identify the phrases spoken within encrypted VoIP calls when the audio is encoded using variable bit rate codecs." Sound scary? Given the recent news of the capabilities and actions of the National Security Agency, VoIP systems carry just as much risk of interception as traditional phone networks.

Because the underlying IP network that a VoIP system uses is unreliable, it's not uncommon to experience latency or jitteriness when making a call using a VoIP phone system, especially to off-site destinations. Once your voice packet hits the already congested Internet, you are no longer in control of how fast your data gets to where it's going, and that's what causes the delays. Using a VoIP system on the same data network as your computer system might tremendously slow down how fast you can access your server and case management applications because of all the data traffic on your local network. Be sure your existing data network and Internet connection are capable of handling the increase in load before implementing a VoIP system. If you have to upgrade existing hardware or the speed of your Internet connection, those are hidden costs that you might not be aware of and that you will have to plan for.

Implementing an MPLS (Multiprotocol Label Switching) network gives you the option of configuring QoS (Quality of Service), where you can give the voice traffic a higher priority. MPLS networks are not cheap and tend to be used in larger firms with multiple office locations. Frankly, we think MPLS is overkill and too expensive for a solo or small firm considering VoIP. As an alternative, a large number of VoIP installations use the IP network on the local premises. They then route the external calls to the Internet and may even have some traditional phone circuits connected too. The reality is that the telephone carriers themselves are using VoIP between two IP gateways in order to reduce the long-haul bandwidth.

Finally, VoIP systems are susceptible to power failures and outages. Unlike analog phones that get their power directly from the copper phone lines, VoIP systems need electricity to operate, just like your computer system. You better have an analog phone line as a backup, or at least a cell phone. We're still hanging on to our traditional copper wire analog lines, despite the telcos trying to force fiber and VoIP down our throats.

VoIP phone systems have their pros and cons when compared to other digital phone systems. Be sure to ask your vendor the right questions to determine which type of system is right for you. And be wary of those vendors and definitely check their references. We have seen a lot of VoIP installations that caused major-league heartburn for the law firms that undertook them.

Besides hidden costs pushing budgets far beyond the original numbers, vendors tend not to plan for redundancy or to warn of the potential downsides of VoIP. We have had both happy and unhappy VoIP clients, so we're not saying, "Don't do it," but be aware that VoIP may not be the right choice for everyone. As a side note, we have yet to hear of a client who wasn't happy with his Cisco VoIP installation. That has to tell you something about the quality and stability of Cisco products.

## High-Speed Internet

None of our lawyers or other clients ever complain that their Internet connection is too fast. We have collectively almost forgotten how slow the Internet used to be and how patiently we had to wait for our screens to load. High-speed Internet is now a requirement for solo and small law firms. High-speed Internet has all but replaced dial-up Internet connections because of the low cost and fast connection speeds, although there are still some parts of the country where dial-up is the only option. Why continue to wait for web pages to load and attachments to open if you don't have to? Few creatures are more impatient than lawyers, so virtually all of them have jumped to high-speed Internet installations.

High-speed Internet connections are available from your local Internet service provider (ISP and usually are provided over a cable, DSL, or fiber-optic connection. These high-speed connections offer download speeds in excess of 25 Mbps (some can reach 75 Mbps) and varying upload speeds, depending on the provider and the service tier to which you've subscribed. If your firm hosts its own services, such as e-mail or a website, you can obtain static IP addresses from your local provider for these types of connections. The ISP may charge more to issue your business a static IP address than if you just require a dynamically leased IP address. High-speed Internet access connectivity generally will cost $75 to $200 per month.

If your firm requires a larger amount of bandwidth due to the number of users sharing the Internet connection or to run web-based applications, your local ISP may be able to provide a connection type that meets your requirements. Historically, the ISPs and telco providers classified upgraded service connections as T1 or fractional T1 connections. While they may call them upgrades, they are much slower than alternative technologies and will cost hundreds of dollars more per month. These types of connections also require longer service agreements and usually include a large setup cost. They do have the advantage of a service level agreement (SLA), which means the connection must be repaired within a particular time and must be available a high percentage of the time. DSL or cable modem connections do not carry an SLA, so repair times could be several days during an outage. T1 circuits are becoming less and less popular, even though they are very reliable and guarantee bandwidth. A full T1 provides only 1.544 Mbps up and down and typically will cost $300–$500 per month. Compare this to other broadband services (cable or DSL), where you can get 30 Mbps download and 5 Mbps upload for less than $200 a month. Do the math: 30 is a MUCH bigger number than 1.544.

If available in your area, a speedy alternative to a T1 is fiber optics. Fiber to the curb, such as Verizon FiOS, can offer business subscribers increasingly faster Internet connections at a much lower cost. Check with your local service providers to see if such a connection is currently available. In general, solo and small firms are well served by cable and DSL to meet their Internet connection needs.

Another option for Internet access is from your cellular provider. Mobile broadband Internet access has gained steam lately and is becoming a growing trend with mobile lawyers. Plus, it's a good way to avoid having to pay those outrageous prices for Internet access that hotels commonly charge. You may have heard the terms 3G, 4G, and so on, used to identify mobile broadband. Carriers are now charging for wireless broadband based on the amount of data consumed. The cost is approximately $20 a month for 2 GB up to $60 a month for 10GB. Some will even sell you 100 GB for over $700 a month. If you've purchased a laptop recently, you might already have a broadband card installed. For everyone else, most providers will throw in the broadband card for no cost when you sign up for their service. We have found that it is cheaper to activate the mobile hotspot feature on our smartphones instead of acquiring a separate mobile data plan. That way we use the data plan from our phone to create the Wi-Fi "cloud" for other devices to share. We can then use the Wi-Fi-only iPad (a lot cheaper) instead of one with the built-in 3G/4G capability.

# CHAPTER TWENTY-SIX

## Utilities

**W**HAT WE ALL NEED is Batman's belt, with a full repository of tricks that we can draw upon at any moment to perform the myriad tasks associated with the practice of law. Failing that, we must acknowledge that it is impossible to list all of the utilities that a solo or small firm might find useful. There are many great selections and just as many opinions as to what makes one utility more valuable than another.

The threshold question is, what constitutes a utility? For our purposes, we will consider a utility to be a software application that takes data and manipulates it for a specific purpose. That definition allows us a lot of latitude.

The challenge is to list utilities that offer a unique purpose for the solo and small firm lawyer. We have used many of these utilities ourselves and have had some great suggestions from our friends and colleagues. If you don't see your favorite utility here, just drop us a line and perhaps it will be listed in the next edition of the book.

### X1

How often do you find yourself frantically searching your computer for a file only to discover that you have no clue where you saved it? It's happened to all of us, and the problem is compounded when you have copies of the same file saved in multiple locations. Which file is the right one? What a headache!

To relieve some of the stress, we recommend that lawyers use X1 Search 8, which is a piece of software that enables users to search for and instantly find information while keeping the resulting file in its native format. The product is marketed as a premium alternative to Windows Desktop and Outlook Search. No more messy conversions. X1 allows users to search for any file, whether located within their e-mail on the local computer, a network share, removable storage drive, or even within virtual desktops. This software currently supports more than 500 file types in their native format and layout, and it can even search for data within multiple Microsoft Outlook PST files and Lotus Notes without having to mount the files.

The X1 program displays the search results as you type, similar to the Google Instant Search, which allows users to modify their search query in real time. The advanced searching options allow users to search multiple e-mail metadata fields such as From, To, and Subject and then sort the resulting files by any of the file properties.

The X1 program is a powerful search tool that includes a number of advanced features, such as support for searching inside compressed ZIP files and RSS feeds, as well as a number of export options, such as exporting the search results to a folder or Microsoft Outlook PST file. The product is even administrator-friendly, supporting integration with Active Directory and Group Policy, for ease of deployment and flexibility in its configuration.

Before installing, you will need to make sure that you have enough storage space for the search index this program will create, which is roughly 20 percent of the total volume of files indexed. X1 supports Microsoft Windows (32- or 64-bit) operating systems, Microsoft Outlook XP/2003/2007/2010 (32- or 64-bit), and SharePoint 2007/2010/2013 and 365, as well as al IMAP-based e-mail accounts. Support for Lotus Notes, Eudora, and Thunderbird e-mail clients has been dropped in the latest version of X1 Search 8 and can only be found in prior versions of the X1 Search Professional Client.

The X1 Search 8 software costs $49.95 per license and can be purchased with varying levels of support. If you want to try before you buy, a fourteen-day trial is available as well. To view or purchase this product, visit **www.x1.com**.

## dtSearch

dtSearch is another powerful search tool that has been used by lawyers for many years, dating back to the early MS-DOS days. This product has come a long way and remains one of our favorite and most popular searching tools—and honestly, it doesn't change much from year to year. That's how solid this product is. The dtSearch program is offered in a number of different versions, but solo and small firms should consider only the following versions:

- ♦ Desktop with Spider
- ♦ Network with Spider

The Desktop with Spider version is perfect for solo lawyers who need to be able to search their client files instantly on a single computer, although this version can also be configured to index network drives. The Network with Spider version allows multiple users to search the same search index, which is a must when working in a multiuser networking environment.

The dtSearch products include Unicode support, support for full-text searching, the ability to search a number of common metadata fields, and even the ability to search within nested ZIP files. The product highlights search hits in most web-based file formats, such as XML and HTML, while maintaining the format and layout of the page, including graphics and embedded hyperlinks. dtSearch also displays search hits in other popular file types, such as documents, spreadsheets, database files, and e-mails. The built-in spider can add website content to the searchable database, including secure password-protected websites. The ability to index and search website content is a great feature for those lawyers involved in cases or matters involving e-discovery.

Like other full-text search applications, dtSearch uses a large volume of disk space to store its search index, requiring approximately one-third of the total volume of files indexed. The software states that a single index file can handle more than a terabyte of indexed text, which is a lot of files. When creating the index, the default operation is to ignore "noise" words (e.g., *the*, *a*, and, *etc.*). If you need to search phrases that include those words, make sure you override the defaults and index the "noise" words too.

dtSearch supports Windows 10 operating systems and even has a version for Linux, with a version for Mac OS X currently in development. dtSearch also supports the latest Microsoft Outlook/Exchange and Thunderbird formats. Also new in the latest version is the ability to highlight search hits within PDF files retrieved after a search using Adobe Reader X or XI. dtSearch Desktop with Spider can be purchased on dtSearch's website (**www.dtsearch.com**) for $199 per license. dtSearch

Network with Spider can also be purchased at a cost of $160 per license for five to twenty-four users or $140 per license for twenty-five to ninety-nine users. Further discounts are offered for purchases of more than 100 licenses.

## *Credenza*

Are you looking for a way to enhance your ability to run and manage your law firm using just a single piece of software? It can be done, believe it or not, with Microsoft Outlook and a small add-in named Credenza. Surprisingly, many lawyers use Microsoft Outlook for their case management solution rather than purchasing a separate application for the job. While we don't recommend this, we have to bow to the inevitable and help those who choose to do this, even though Outlook is not a case management product. If you are one of those lawyers who uses Outlook for case management, you should consider Credenza.

Credenza is a legal-practice management tool that integrates with Microsoft Outlook and allows legal professionals to manage their firms more effectively. Credenza allows you to:

- Create and open a file for each client matter or case.
- Track time spent on individual e-mails (it even flags messages that may have been missed or forgotten).
- Keep and make notes regarding phone calls, voicemails, and other messages.
- View a complete chronology of a file.
- Check for conflicts, automate inbox controls, and share information with other users.

Previously, Credenza offered only a free trial version to its potential users. Now it offers a Basic version of the program that is free to download and use. The Pro version can be purchased and downloaded from the Credenza Software website at **www.credenzasoft.com**. It costs $24.95 per user per month.

The Basic version includes all of the basic practice management features, while the Pro version is multiuser and includes collaboration tools, cloud integration, incorporated billing, and full text searching, along with many other more powerful features.

To determine which version of the software is right for you, you can view a comparison chart of the Basic and Pro version features at **http://www.credenzasoft.com/comparison.html**.

## Outlook Send Assistant

Concerned about inadvertently sending an e-mail message to an unintended recipient? If so, we have the tool for you. This add-in warns or prevents accidental disclosure and sending of e-mails to unintended recipients. It is a must-have utility for every Microsoft Outlook user. Outlook Send Assistant (**http://www.thepaynegroup.com/products/outlooksend/**) is a small tool that packs a big punch.

Here are some of the features of this simple and elegant tool:

—Integrates with Microsoft Outlook 2013, 2010, and 2007

—Is compatible with Windows 10, Windows 8.x, Windows 7, and Windows Server platforms

—Available in both 32- and 64-bit versions

—Supports HTML and Plain Text formats

—Alerts users when the Reply All button is selected

—Warns users that the message has a blank Subject line

—Prompts the user when external recipients are detected

—Confirms with e-mail senders if they'd like to continue sending the message

—Prompts when the e-mail is addressed to a Distribution List

—Alerts users when recipient(s) are detected in the BCC field

—Inserts BCC disclosure text into the recipients' message, thus notifying them of the BCC status

—Customizes warnings when specific recipient addresses are detected

—Automatically adds Marketing, Circular 230 Disclosure, SEC, SPAM warnings, and security disclaimers to e-mail messages

—Warns for missing attachments

—Alerts for specific e-mail attachment types, including document links attached to the e-mail from a document management system

—Warns when specific text is detected in the subject line

Outlook Send Assistant v3 can be purchased from the PayneGroup web-site (**www.thepaynegroup.com**) at a cost of $45 per license. There is also a free trial should users wish to take the product for a "test-drive" first, and discounts are available if you need twenty or more licenses.

## GreenPrint

GreenPrint Technologies (**www.printgreener.com**) has a software prod-uct, GreenPrint, that eliminates unwanted pages from your printing jobs, saving you ink, toner, paper, money, and trees. The software intercepts your print jobs and highlights unnecessary pages, such as blanks, that can be removed. How many times have you printed a web page that prints on two pages of paper, with only a single line of text on the second page? Usually the second page contains only a URL, logo, or banner ad. No longer will these wasted pages need to be printed. The Enterprise Edition includes such additional features as the GreenPrint Advisor, a tool to help your firm select low-cost printers; GreenPrint Analytics, a powerful reporting tool documenting your firm's true savings; and GreenPrint Preview+, an interactive preview of your print job that helps to eliminate print waste and reduce volume. If you don't already have Adobe Acrobat or another third-party PDF printer, you can also get a PDF printer from GreenPrint.

GreenPrint makes recommendations about pages that should be removed from the print job and prompts the user for approval before the job is sent to the printer. There is an edition for the Home User, Small Office, and Enterprise Edition for businesses. The Home User edition costs $19 per computer. A thirty-day free trial of the software is available.

If you're firm is interested in the Small Office version of the product, you have to contact the vendor at **sales@printgreener.com** to get pricing. The product works with Windows XP/Vista/7. Support for Windows 8 or Windows 10 isn't currently listed on the website at the time of writing.

## Winscribe for the Legal Profession

Winscribe, a leading developer of dictation software, has made a product specifically for the legal profession that allows dictations to be transcribed automatically, converting recorded words to text. Automating the process saves both time and money, increasing the efficiency of your employees. It marks the end of the "listen . . . type" era. Now your employees can spend their time doing something more productive and billable. Winscribe can even integrate with existing applications, such as your document management system, streamlining your workflow process.

As the creator of the dictations, you can manage and monitor the status of your work as well as retrieve jobs for review and editing. Another innovative feature of this software is that it supports a wide range of input from recordings made on telephones, PCs and laptops, digital handheld devices, BlackBerrys, Windows Phones, iPhones, and Androids. With the Winscribe Mobility Suite, the days of carrying around a digital recorder may be over. Now you can install mobile software on your smartphone to record dictations and transfer the files wirelessly to your firm's network. As always, client confidentiality is an extremely important issue. Winscribe protects dictations through the encryption of the files and through the implementation of a secure file transfer process. Winscribe has been vetted by the experts and found worthy. This product is available on Winscribe's website at **www.winscribe.com** and can be purchased as an in-house package or an on-demand Software as a Service (SaaS) over the Web.

## Eyejot

What a slogan: "Video mail in a blink." Is video the future of e-mail? If so, Eyejot has got it right. Eyejot is a comprehensive, client-free, online video-messaging platform ideal for both personal and business communications. Eyejot is currently supported on Apple's iOS platform, with Android support expected soon—but it's not yet here. The vendor has been promising an Android app now for the past few years but still hasn't released one. We're getting skeptical as to whether this will actually come to fruition.

Users can sign up for the service by creating a free account, which allows an unlimited number of five-minute video e-mail messages and provides support for both RSS feeds and iTunes. If you can send an e-mail, then you can send an Eyejot.

The Free account keeps your video messages for up to one month; allows you to send a video message to any e-mail address (not just an Eyejot account); and, if needed, provides code for you to embed the Eyejot widget on your website. However, the free account is ad-supported.

To send a video message, once an account has been created, a user must log in to his or her account, upload the video, and then click the Send button. That's it, plain and simple. The software requires no client installation and works with all major web browsers. For those users who require more, there is a Pro account for $29.95 per year that allows you to upload videos, provides an enhanced mobile inbox, and is advertising-free— plus your messages never expire.

There is also a Pro+ account subscription for $99.95 per year that is advertising-free and allows you to attach other documents to your video messages as well as customize your own message templates. Users can purchase and create an Eyejot account online at **www.corp.eyejot.com**.

## Hightail (formerly YouSendIt)

What a wonderful resource to transmit large file attachments without charge. There are several service packages, one of which is free. The free offering, called Lite, can transmit an attachment that is up to 250 MB in size. The Lite package also provides a user with 2 GB of online storage space, mobile access, data encryption, and a Desktop Sync application. Since many ISPs limit the size of attachments, Hightail is a great alternative to "push" the occasional large attachment. The service works by creating an account at **hightail.com** and actually uploading the file to the Hightail service. You provide the e-mail addresses for the recipient(s), and an e-mail message is sent with a hyperlink that allows for downloading the file from the Hightail website.

If you regularly need to transmit very large attachments, especially those larger than 250 MB, or need more than 2 GB of storage space, Hightail provides several pay services to accomplish this. These services provide enhancements such as e-mail support, longer availability for file downloads, reports, advanced security options, custom branding, and more bandwidth for downloads. The Professional plan costs $15.99 per month or $159.99 per year, while the Teams and Enterprise plans cost much more. We have found this resource to be invaluable for sending conference attendees copies of our PowerPoint presentations, which tend to be quite large because of the graphics. Don't forget to encrypt your data before uploading it to Hightail's servers if it is confidential. This terrific utility can be found at **www.hightail.com**.

## *Copy2Contact*

Copy2Contact, formerly Anagram, is a piece of software that allows you to "sweep" text from an e-mail message and create a record within Outlook. You can sweep contact information the sender has added in his or her message footer and instantly create an Outlook contact. The software is not limited just to creating of contacts. You can "grab" text and create calendar entries, to-do items, and even tasks. The text can originate anywhere. Copy2Contact will create the contact, calendar entry, task, and so on, in your personal folder area, which is fine for most solos. If you have a Microsoft Exchange Server with Public Folders, you will have to move the data from your personal folder if the intended destination is a Public Folder. Copy2Contact is currently available for Gmail/Calendar, Salesforce.com, Microsoft Outlook, Netsuite, iPhone, and BlackBerry. Copy2Contact is compatible with all Windows-based systems, including Windows 8. The program also has a version available for BlackBerry and iPhone devices.

The base Copy2Contact for Outlook product costs $34.95 for a single user. The Pro version is $49.95 and includes features like smart capitalization, formatting, address book selection, and extended hotkeys. There is a fourteen-day trial version to make sure that Copy2Contact will work on your computer and perform according to your expectations. Make sure you download and try the trial before you spend the money; however, we're sure (especially you solo lawyers) that you'll be typing in your credit card number shortly after your first use of Copy2Contact. This product can be purchased and downloaded from its website at **www.copy2 contact.com**.

## *TwInbox*

Are you a Twitter junkie? Here's a program that integrates with Microsoft Outlook that allows you to update your Twitter status directly from Outlook. TwInbox (**http://www.techhit.com/TwInbox/twitter_plugin_out- look.html**), a free add-on for Microsoft Outlook, allows you to receive your follower updates and archive, manage, group, and search your tweets in the same way that you manage your e-mail. Some of the additional features of this tiny program include allowing users to search and track keywords, group tweets by sender or topic, and upload and post picture files and Outlook e-mail attachments. A newly added feature also allows users to manage multiple Twitter accounts directly from within Microsoft Outlook. This product is free—why not give it a try?

## TweetDeck

If you're a Twitter user and prefer not to tweet from within Microsoft Outlook or from the Twitter website, then this program might be for you. TweetDeck, another free utility, helps you organize Twitter and those you are following. You can group people so that you can concentrate on "special" individuals whose tweets are more important to you. This helps you reduce the noise level of Twitter and focuses attention on specific tweets. It also includes a URL shortener. TweetDeck used to require the installation of Adobe Air, which needs full administrative access to your hard disk, but since it was purchased by Twitter, the service is now offered as a web app within your Internet browser or as a desktop application that no longer requires Adobe Air. This is a wonderful dashboard for managing Twitter—we know because we use it. You can sign in to TweetDeck or download the desktop application at tweetdeck.twitter.com.

## TinyURL

Have you ever wanted to give somebody a reference link only to discover that it is about 400 characters long and contains all kinds of goofy characters and nonword representations? Probably the biggest problem is the breaking up of the URL link, especially when the e-mail is viewed as formatted text. The last thing you want to do is have the recipient cut and paste the various parts of the URL back together. TinyURL stores the complete URL on its servers and provides a very small URL instead. The user selects the smaller TinyURL, which translates and redirects to the much larger one. This is a free service to make the posting of long URLs easier—especially handy for Twitter. If you're a frequent user of TinyURL, there's even a toolbar for your browser that you can install to make the service more accessible. It is available at tinyurl.com.

Security issues arise when dealing with any shortened URL. The "bad guys" are sending malware links disguised as shortened URLs in phishing e-mails appearing to come from someone you know. As the recipient of the shortened URL, you have no idea where the URL will actually send you unless you decode it first. If you want to use any URL shortening service, make sure you trust the originator of the URL or use a service to decode it before you click on the link.

TinyURL has a preview feature to show you a preview of the URL before directly going directly to TinyURL. You can then get an idea of where the shortened URL is going to send you. It requires that cookies be enabled for your browser.

## CheckShortURL

Since we're talking about the security risk of shortened URLs, CheckShortURL is a free service to expose the real URL destination. Just go to checkshorturl.com and enter the shortened URL. Besides determining the actual URL, a thumbnail image will help you determine the web page contents.

## IrfanView

Do you have some graphic files for a construction case that you can't seem to view? Or a video or sound file for a wrongful termination case and don't know how to play it? IrfanView (**www.irfanview.com**) is a wonderful software application that can view a very large number of different graphic file formats and can play several audio and video formats. IrfanView is compatible with all Windows-based systems but not Mac or Linux. IrfanView is free only for home use, so you can't legally use it for your law practice unless you pay money. You will have to send an e-mail to irfanview@gmx.net to get the cost and payment method if you need to use IrfanView in a commercial setting. They now offer a 64-bit version of this program.

Some of the common file types and formats that IrfanView supports include:

—JPG
—TIFF
—GIF
—MPG

—MP3

—AVI

—WMA

You can view all of the file formats displayed by IrfanView by visiting **www.irfanview.net/main_formats.htm**.

## DBAN

Darik's Boot and Nuke (DBAN) is a free program that can be used to securely wipe the contents of your hard drive. DBAN is an open-source project that can be downloaded from **www.dban.org**. DBAN will automatically and permanently delete the contents of any hard disk it can detect. DBAN also allows the wiping of multiple hard disks at the same time. We all love "free," and this program is the perfect complement to any lawyer's software tool chest. You use DBAN to wipe the data contents from your hard drives and USB flash drives so that your confidential client information cannot be recovered. We have all read stories of customer data being found on hard drives purchased on eBay. Make sure that you wipe any media that may contain information you don't want someone else to recover. Could the National Security Agency recover something wiped with DBAN? Frankly, we think that's another urban legend, and we've never—ever—seen evidence of it, even with the documents released by Edward Snowden. However, we continue to monitor the capabilities of the federal government in particular. DBAN is free, it's safe, and it helps you comply with your ethical duty to keep your client data confidential. When you're getting ready to donate or ditch your old computers, this is an invaluable tool. DBAN is downloaded as an ISO file that can be burned to a CD or DVD, which would then be booted from to load the DBAN program.

Note one of this wiping program's limitations: DBAN does not detect or erase data securely from solid-state hard drives, which are becoming increasingly common on new laptops. For those systems with a solid-state hard drive, you can purchase a piece of software called Blancco (the same company that now owns the DBAN product also has this tool) for $14.95 for a single license (only one erasure per system) that will securely wipe data from solid-state hard drives. This product can also be found on DBAN's website.

## SimplyFile

Long ago, we realized how much time we were losing each day carefully dragging and dropping e-mail into the correct Outlook folder, often accidentally filing messages in a folder below or a folder above the intended destination. Maddening.

With the SimplyFile software, each e-mail will display the name of the folder SimplyFile believes it belongs in. After it initially indexes and "learns" your filing system, it is correct more than 90 percent of the time. If it has guessed incorrectly, there is a QuickPick feature. Open it, and you'll likely find that the correct folder is near the top of the list of possibilities presented. If not, you can just type in the first few letters of the folder and it will appear. Most of the time, you'll just be clicking "file" and it's done. It can also turn e-mail into a calendar or a task. Marvelous. Authors Nelson and Simek regarded this product as their "find of the year" from 2009 and don't know how they functioned without it. They remain passionately devoted to it today. The current version is compatible with Outlook 2013 (32- and 64-bit versions) and Windows 10. This product does not work with Outlook Express.

The latest version, SimplyFile 4 may be purchased (or there's a thirty-day free trial) at **www.techhit.com/SimplyFile/**. The cost for a single license is $49.95.

## File Shredder

Every lawyer should have a utility to delete files securely. One of those tools is the free file wiping utility called File Shredder, available at **http://www.fileshredder.org**. The user interface is simple enough to understand, but the software author is a little lax with the consistency of the website. As an example, when you click the update menu option in the application, it sends you to a web page announcing a new version; however, the version being distributed is not the one announced. Even with the inconsistencies though, the product works as advertised. We've tested the product using our forensic tools, and it does securely delete the targeted files. We have not tested it on Windows 10, but since it works on Windows 7 we don't expect that there will be any issues. You can select a file to "shred" or "wipe" by right-clicking on the filename. You can also drag and drop files into the application interface. There are several wiping methods available from the simple single pass (good enough to prevent recovery) to the totally paranoid 35 pass overwrites. Even though the product is free, you should donate (via PayPal) to the software developer if you use the software and find value in its use.

## SnagIt

No lawyer should be without a screen-capture program. SnagIt 12 is a screen-capture utility that can capture anything on your desktop. You can capture a specific window, a defined area, a specific object (e.g., the title bar), or a multitude of other things. There are more than forty ways to capture the information you want to preserve. A screen-capture application is a great tool to "grab" images to place in a motion or brief that show exactly what is shown on the computer screen. This is particularly handy when you want only a specific area of the screen. SnagIt can output the "snagged" image to a multitude of formats as well. The latest version includes additional video capture options, new stamps, more zoom options, including features that make it easier to edit and resize captured images. SnagIt costs $49.95 for a single license version, with discounts for multiple copies. A thirty-day trial version is available, so you can see whether it fits your needs before purchase. It is available from **www.tech smith.com/download/snagit/default.asp** and now works on all Windows 32- and 64-bit operating systems, including Windows 10. A Mac version is available as well.

If you are using Windows, you should try the Snipping Tool before deciding to purchase a third-party application for your screen-grabbing needs. The Snipping Tool, Microsoft's version of a screen-grabbing utility, is included by default and allows you to save the captured data to a file or copy it to the Clipboard, which is handy when creating PowerPoint slides. On a Mac, you should try the Grab app, which is Apple's equivalent screen-grabbing utility.

## QuickView Plus

If you're willing to spend a little money, you can get a utility that can view more than 300 file formats, including Microsoft Office 2013 and Corel WordPerfect Office X5. That's what you get when you purchase

QuickView Plus 13 Standard. The file support comes without the need for the native application, potentially saving you the costs of having to purchase a license for a product just to view a file. QuickView Plus maintains the formatting of the files you view, so you can view and print files as they were originally created and meant to be seen. This is a great application to view file formats, especially from your electronic discovery cases. You can handle e-mail attachments and various obscure software packages that you've probably never heard of. QuickView Plus is compatible with Microsoft Windows computer systems, including Windows 8. As of the time of writing, compatibility with Windows 10 wasn't listed on its website.

At $49 for a single download license of the standard edition, it is a perfect complement to IrfanView. QuickView Plus is available for purchase and download at **www.avantstar.com**, and a fully functional evaluation copy of the product is offered for thirty days. The professional edition adds advanced viewing, searching, etc., and you must contact sales@avantstar.com for pricing for this version.

## Sam Spade

The name of this utility, obviously, is meant to evoke Humphrey Bogart in *The Maltese Falcon*. Indeed, this utility can perform some gumshoe functions, such as troubleshooting and dealing with Internet communications. However, the most useful function of this free utility is the ability to decode e-mail headers so that anyone can decipher the cryptic entries in a readable English form. Unfortunately, the original site for Sam Spade is down and no longer active. The good news is that there are several websites that have the latest version (1.14) available for download. Just do an online search for "Sam Spade spam," you will find several download locations on the first page of the results, including one from PCWorld. This product hasn't been updated since 2002 and most likely never will be again.

As we move forward into the world of electronic evidence, having the ability to decode e-mail headers is an invaluable asset to help ascertain where an e-mail really came from. Mind you, there are still ways for the world's miscreants to hide, but Sam Spade can provide you with a lot of helpful information. For instructions on how to use the application, the SANS Institute has a great white paper on the matter that can be downloaded here: **www.sans.org/reading_room/whitepapers/tools/ sam-spade_934**.

## Metadata Assistant

One of our favorite metadata analysis and removal tools is Metadata Assistant by Payne Group (**www.thepaynegroup.com/products/ metadata/**). Metadata Assistant integrates with your Microsoft Office installation and is particularly valuable when sending file attachments. The product will display a dialog box asking if you want to clean the attachment or just send it as is. As we mentioned previously, don't clean the metadata if you are collaborating on a document with another person, as it will remove the tracked changes. Metadata Assistant can also convert the attachment to PDF on the fly. The product is available in both 32- and 64-bit versions. Metadata Assistant 5 offers more file type handling than earlier versions and has also accelerated the cleaning process.

Metadata Assistant is extremely flexible and works with Word, Excel, and PowerPoint versions 2007, 2010, and 2013. It has e-mail integration with Outlook 2007, 2010, and 2013 and Lotus Notes 8.5 and 9.0; OpenText eDocs DM 10, 5.3 and 5.2; Worldox GX/GX2/GX3; iManage 8.5/9.0; and NetDocuments 14.1. This product is also compatible with Windows 10. Users may purchase this product directly from Payne Group for $98 per license. Discounts are available for Enterprise-level installations involving twenty or more licenses.

No lawyer should be without some sort of metadata scrubber to ensure removal of potentially confidential data. Some states are even addressing the removal of metadata in their ethics opinions. Whether you are required to scrub metadata or not, Metadata Assistant is a possible solution for your practice.

You can also remove metadata by converting the file to PDF. This does not remove all of the metadata, but it does remove a large portion of it and leaves only what are typically considered innocuous values. Microsoft also provides the ability to analyze and remove ("clean") a document's properties in Microsoft Office 2010 and 2013. However, some values that it leaves behind are still viewable by third-party products like Metadata Assistant.

## Litera Metadact and Metadact-e

If you're looking for another possible solution for metadata analysis and scrubbing, we have become very fond of Litera's Metadact-e and Metadact programs. Metadact installs to the user's computer just like Metadata Assistant. Metadact identifies and removes all of the commonly known types of metadata, such as author and creation date, as well as many of the hidden metadata fields that are behind the scenes. This product's features include:

—Clean and convert files

—Choose which types of metadata to clean

—View detailed reports

—Batch clean

—Clean metadata from within Microsoft Outlook

—Create custom policies and settings

—Specify safe e-mail domains

—Utilize an exclusion list

—Take advantage of Seamless integration with Windows Explorer and document management systems

—Utilize intelligent content clean, such as identifying and removing credit card/Social Security numbers from within Microsoft Word documents

—Assess risk

This product integrates with iManage, DM5, DocsOpen, PowerDocs, Worldox, NetDocuments, and Microsoft SharePoint.

The Metadact-e program, which is a server-based product, adds profile management to the list of features mentioned above. It has the ability to scrub metadata from documents in Outlook and Outlook Web Access on tablet, smartphone, and desktop-based documents. Whether it's a Microsoft Office, PDF, image, or ZIP file, this product will ensure that all metadata has been removed. We are not aware of any other product on the market that has the ability to enforce metadata policies on mobile devices such as smartphones. We are huge fans of Metadact-e.

Unlike stand-alone versions, this product is centrally managed and administered, and it's suggested that this application be installed on its own server, so your practice can enforce its metadata policies on employees without giving them the option to bypass your written policies and procedures. The benefits of a server-based solution include the ability to prevent the disclosure of client-confidential and other sensitive information, transparency for the users (no more waiting for a locally installed product to do the cleaning—you are immediately released to go to your next task while the server does the scrubbing), and compliance control through enforcement of your practice's policies and procedures.

Metadact can be purchased from Litera's website at **www.litera.com** for $54 per license per user and must be renewed on a yearly basis. Users must contact Litera directly for Metadact-e pricing. Even though this product is licensed with an annual subscription model, we would highly recommend investigating its purchase. It is a very cost-effective tool that is extremely flexible to meet the specific needs of your firm. We'll also add that from personal experience, Litera's support staff is top-notch and totally committed to solving a user's problems.

## Livescribe Echo Smartpen

The Livescribe Echo Smartpen is a device that can record a user's written notes along with the accompanying audio. The Echo Smartpen can transmit the data to a computer via USB cable, allowing a user to view digitalized notes and hear recorded audio. The pen has an infrared camera that records seventy-five images per second to track the spatial movement of the device on the provided sheets of dot paper, the required use of which is one of the few downsides of the product. Users can now purchase their own dot paper, notebooks, and lined and unlined journals compatible with the Smartpen.

Using the bundled Livescribe Desktop software, users can manage written notes and recordings but cannot convert notes to text because the software lacks OCR capabilities. However, using the software's PDF export capabilities, you could always OCR the exported PDF files using Adobe Acrobat.

The Echo Smartpen, just like a computer, can be updated with new firmware and software and is currently offered with 2 GB of storage capacity. The Smartpen is compatible with Microsoft Windows 7, 8, or later as well as Mac OS X 10.5.5 or newer.

Livescribe also has a Sky Wifi Smartpen, which features an embedded Wi-Fi adapter that sends recorded notes and audio directly to your Evernote account. The wireless connection removes the need for access to a computer or USB cable to transfer the data.

## *YouMail*

Tired of the standard voicemail options provided by your cellular carrier? Looking for more advanced features? YouMail (**www.youmail.com**) is like Google Voice, without the extra phone number. YouMail provides your smartphone with a visual voicemail client that offers personalization of voicemail greetings based on the caller, as well as voicemail sharing, caller blocking, and voicemail alerts by e-mail and text. You can even organize your voicemails into folders and download them to MP3 format. YouMail is compatible with iPhone and Android, but it has dropped support for new BlackBerry devices.

When a call doesn't get answered, the forwarded call is transferred to your YouMail voicemail box rather than to your cellular provider's voicemail box. The Personal Edition, which allows a user to store up to 100 voicemail messages, is free but ad-supported. The Premium Edition, starting at $5 per month, allows a user to store up to 500 voicemail messages and has no advertisements. The Business Edition, starting at $10 per month, allows up to 10,000 voicemail messages and provides a host of other advanced features.

To view a comparison of these plans, visit YouMail's pricing page at **https://store.youmail.com**.

## *SmartDraw Business*

SmartDraw Legal Edition has been merged with the VP version of the software, now called SmartDraw Business, which is a powerful software tool that allows lawyers to create sharp, professional-looking diagrams and trial exhibits with relative ease. It's a must-have for your software arsenal. The tool, more robust than Microsoft PowerPoint, can be used to create timelines, estate planning diagrams, accident reconstruction, crime scene layouts, and more. The look and feel of the software is similar to Microsoft Office, and creating diagrams from the provided templates is simple. The Business Edition provides specialized templates for the legal profession—more than 1,000—and if you can't find one to use, you can create your own. SmartDraw comes with more than 20,000 symbols and shapes to choose from, giving you the power to re-create that crucial event in your case dynamically. SmartDraw provides a number of export options, allowing users to save their work in a variety of formats, such as PDF, DOC, XLS, WPD, or JPG. SmartDraw does a good job as an alternative product to Microsoft Visio or Project at a fraction of the cost.

The latest update to SmartDraw Business includes automatic formatting of charts and diagrams, more diagram templates, MS Office integration, automatic backup of your diagrams and presentations, and new features related to mobile access and viewing of SmartDraw files on your iPhone or iPad.

SmartDraw Business can be purchased directly from the website (**www.smartdraw.com**) for $297 (regularly $397) for a single-user license. A trial edition is also available for download for those users who wish to test-drive the software before purchasing it.

## CaseSoft TimeMap 5

Another great timeline-generating utility is CaseSoft's TimeMap, which was acquired by LexisNexis several years ago. TimeMap is a timeline-graphing tool that can be used to create polished timeline graphs for trial exhibits, presentations, and professional documents. TimeMap can be integrated with CaseMap or used on its own. Data can be directly imported into the application from Microsoft Excel, Summation, Concordance, Microsoft Access, or almost any other spreadsheet or database programs, eliminating the need to enter data manually.

As data is entered into the program, TimeMap will automatically generate a proportional time scale and allow you to adjust it if necessary. Once your timeline graph has been generated, you can present the timeline using TimeMap's Presentation Mode, or you can embed the timeline directly into your PowerPoint or Sanction presentation. TimeMap 5 includes new features such as vertical timelines, additional timeline templates, a new PDF writer, and enhanced integration with presentation software. The latest version also includes a new Spreadsheet view, a global find-and-replace option, expanded images, and improved date display tools. TimeMap 5 supports Microsoft Windows 2000/XP/Vista and Windows 7 and can be purchased directly from Casesoft's website at **www.casesoft.com**. Currently, Windows 8 or 10 support isn't listed on the product's website.

Like the other LexisNexis products, you must register on the website before you can see product costs. This is a change from previous years, where the pricing was prominently displayed. A full-featured thirty-day trial edition is also available for download for those users who wish to give the software a test run before purchasing it.

## Evernote

Have trouble remembering everything? We sure do. That's why we use Evernote (**www.evernote.com**). This program makes it easy to remember things big and small, allowing you to capture everything you see when using your computer, cell phone, or mobile device. Using the program, you can clip a web page, snap a photo, or grab a screenshot and upload it to Evernote. Once uploaded, everything you capture is automatically processed, indexed, and made searchable. Of course, you can add your own tags and labels to your notes. Evernote will even scan handwritten notes and make the content searchable. There are a limitless number of ways to use this program, whether for play or work. Since all of the data you capture and tag is uploaded to your Evernote account, these files are accessible from all of your devices. Evernote is available for free, but the Plus ($24.99 per year), Premium ($49.99 per year) and Business ($12 per month per user) subscription levels offer the same features as Evernote Free, with the addition of enhanced search features and collaboration.

Evernote can integrate with your web browser, or you can install a small application on both Mac OS X and Windows-based computers or your iPhone, iPod Touch, iPad, BlackBerry, Android, Android tablet, or Windows Phone 7/8 smartphone. To sign up for a free account, visit Evernote's website at **www.evernote.com**.

## WinRAR/7-ZIP

WinRAR is an application for compressing data. WinZip is a very popular program as well, but WinRAR has some distinct advantages. WinRAR is faster than WinZip and supports more archive file types. It can also create compressed archives that are much smaller than WinZip, so we see WinRAR used for transmitting large amounts of data. Data production as part of a discovery request would be one place to use WinRAR. This program supports all popular compression formats (RAR, ZIP, CAB, ARJ, LZH, ACE, TAR, GZip, UUE, ISO, BZIP2, Z, and 7-Zip). This is a valuable tool for sending data via the Web as well.

WinRAR is available in 32- and 64-bit versions and is compatible with Windows 10. The cost is $29 per license, and it is available directly from the website at **www.win-rar.com**.

An alternative to WinRAR that we often use is 7-Zip (**www.7-zip.org**), which is an open-source archive utility program. You can use 7-Zip to create password-protected ZIP files in which the contents are encrypted to protect your data securely. We use this program almost daily and don't know how we'd get by without it.

## Chrometa

Track your time and bill for it without any notes or timers. Chrometa is a piece of software that plugs into Outlook, into Gmail, or into an app offered for your mobile device (Android and iOS) to help you keep track of time so that it can be billed to your clients. Think of it as a personal timekeeper, silently sitting in the background, recording how long you worked in a particular application, and specifically noting what file or e-mail you were working on. You can have these entries categorized in a time sheet or use the keyword-based rules feature to invoice clients automatically.

There are several price plans available. The individual plans range from $12 per month for the Startup plan to $29 per month for the Plus plan.

The Plus plan holds twelve months' worth of data, allows usage on up to three devices, creates invoices, and will export data to accounting packages or legal software such as Clio and QuickBooks. You may want to consider the Basic package ($19 per month), even though it only handles two devices and three months' worth of data, especially if you are exporting data to Excel. Chrometa is an excellent add-on, especially if you are using a web-based practice management application like Clio or Rocket Matter, but you will need the Plus version for that. Chrometa also has mobile apps for Android and iOS devices.

## eWallet

Do you have a hard time remembering all of your different passwords to your web-based accounts? We certainly do—especially since we should all be using a different password for each of our accounts. Whatever you do, do not use the same password over and over for your different accounts. This is basic security 101.

To help you remember your passwords without having to write them down, we recommend a product called eWallet. eWallet is an app that is available for iOS, Android, BlackBerry (OS 7 or OS 10.2.1 or higher), Windows Mobile 6.5, and both Windows-based (including Windows 7, 8, RT, 8.1, and 10) and Mac OS X 10.7 or higher. It keeps your passwords safe by remembering them so you don't have to. The app stores the passwords in a vault using 256-bit AES encryption and allows you to synchronize your data across all of your devices on which the application is installed. eWallet can store website passwords, frequent flyer numbers, credit card information, membership data, and much more. This product can be purchased from your device's app store or eWallet's website at **www.iliumsoft.com**. The price varies, depending on the device for which you're purchasing the software, but runs between $9.99 and $19.99.

## LastPass

Like eWallet, LastPass is another secure password management tool. LastPass allows you to save your passwords and form data in a secure database and access it when needed. You no longer have to remember another password, and filling out forms and password fields is as easy as a single click. This software works on Mac, Windows, and Linux-based computer systems, as well as all of the major smartphones.

There is a new security feature called LastPass Sentry that will alert you if your logon credentials are compromised. LastPass checks the PwnedList database (database of compromised accounts) to see if your e-mail address is on the list. If so, you receive an e-mail notifying you that your ID has been compromised. The new feature is available for all versions of LastPass.

LastPass does offer a free version available for download, as well as a paid premium version that offers a few additional features. We recommend trying the free version to see if the software meets your needs before making any purchases. You can download and take this software for a test run from its website at **www.lastpass.com**.

## WordRake for Microsoft Word

WordRake fundamentally consists of a set of rules designed to cut flabby verbiage from your writing. Even good authors (and we have a club ring!) clearly can use some editing. Even our editors missed most of what WordRake found. There is now also a version for Microsoft Outlook, which is sold separately from the Microsoft Word version.

To be sure, it's not perfect. The founders purposely do not include an "Accept All" button because they know we can never tame the infinite variety and positioning of words. You have to approve each edit. Because of that, we wouldn't use it for casual writing. But for articles or any other writing that is significant, we sure would.

WordRake's creator, Gary Kinder, is a lawyer himself, and he's taught over 1,000 writing programs to firms like Sidley and Jones Day. He's also a New York Times best-selling author. He must use his own program!

WordRake is a Word add-on that inserts itself into Word's ribbon. It works with the 32-bit versions of Word 2007, 2010, and 2013 running on Windows Vista, 7, and 8. Support for Word 64-bit versions includes 2010 and 2013. Support for Windows 10 isn't currently listed on the vendor's website. The program is licensed on a subscription basis. The one-year cost is $129, two years is $229, and three years will cost $259. All of them can be purchased from the website at **www.wordrake.com**. We recommend that you try the free thirty-day trial before committing.

Users may opt to bundle the purchase of WordRake for Microsoft Word along with WordRake for Microsoft Outlook, saving you some money off the two subscriptions should you be in the market for both products.

## Redact Assistant

Redact Assistant, another wonderful piece of software from Payne Group, provides an invaluable tool to assist users with removing sensitive content from documents. This product can be run against a single file or multiple files at the same time.

Some of the features of the redaction tool include:

—Redact multiple terms in a single process

—Search and Replace multiple terms in a single process

—Create lists of terms for specific redaction and search/replace criteria

—Use Word's and Excel's native search options as well as Regular Expression to create your list of terms

—Save and share your lists with colleagues on projects for collaboration

—Process multiple files at once using the stand-alone component

—Manually select words for quick redaction using Word and add-ins

—View and save reports instantly

This product is compatible with Windows 10 and can be used to redact information present within Microsoft Word (2010/2013) and Microsoft Excel (2010/2013). Please note that it is only compatible with the 32-bit versions of these Office products, and it doesn't currently support Adobe Acrobat PDF files.

There is a free thirty-day trial, which users should take advantage of. This product is sold on the vendor's website for $45 per license (**www.the paynegroup.com**).

## *Redact-It*

Redact-IT Desktop version is another redaction tool that we wanted to inform our readers about. This product supports multiple file formats to redact sensitive content from. Unlike Redact Assistant, this product can remove sensitive content from Adobe Acrobat PDF files, but cannot be run against multiple files at the same time (their Enterprise version does this).

This product does not output redacted documents in their native formats. Instead, users may select the output file format as PDF, TIFF, or CSF (Content Sealed Format) files.

Finally, this redaction tool is a stand-alone product and doesn't integrate with the native applications. This requires the user to launch this software in order to redact sensitive content from a file the user selects. This software also provides the ability to redact Social Security numbers, telephone numbers, e-mail addresses, and dates of birth automatically.

The Redact-IT desktop version starts at $295 per license (Premier version), but you are also required to purchase maintenance at a cost of $59. That makes the total cost $354 for the first year. Redact-IT is available for purchase from the vendor's website at **www.redact.com**.

# CHAPTER TWENTY-SEVEN

# Social Media
# for Law Firms—
# An Overview

### by Jennifer Ellis

SOCIAL MEDIA HAS BECOME a crucial part of the average American's life. As a result, whether they want to or not, attorneys must, at the very least, appreciate the impact of social media on their clients. Failure to understand how social media can impact clients' cases could lead to serious damage to a case, which might result in a malpractice complaint. Further, wise attorneys will take advantage of social media to develop their practices through the networking and marketing opportunities provided by both their own websites and the various social media sites and applications.

The best way to appreciate how important social media has become in people's day-to-day lives is to look at some statistics for popular sites:

- Facebook—1.49 billion monthly active users[1]
- 161 million daily active users in North America[2]
- 169.2 million users in the United States by 2018[3]
- LinkedIn—380 million users[4]

---

[1] As of July 28, 2015. **expandedramblings.com/index.php/by-the-numbers-17-amazing-facebook-stats/**.

[2] April 22, 2015. **expandedramblings.com/index.php/by-the-numbers-17-amazing-facebook-stats/2/**.

[3] March 4, 2015. **expandedramblings.com/index.php/by-the-numbers-17-amazing-facebook-stats/2**

[4] July 30, 2015. **expandedramblings.com/index.php/by-the-numbers-a-few-important-linkedin-stats/**.

- 107 million users in the United States[5]
- Snapchat—almost 100 million daily active users
- The majority of users are between the ages of 18 and 24.[6]
- YouTube—Over 1 billion users[7]
- Instagram—300 million users[8]
- Twitter—316 million monthly active users[9]

Seventy-four percent of all Internet users use social media.[10] Mobile use of cell phones is high as well. "40% of cell phone owners use a social networking site on their phone and 27% do so on a typical day."[11] This ease of access means people use social media on the go as a method to locate businesses they plan to hire. It also means people have a tendency to use social media to share intimate details about their lives and activities quickly. The former shows the value of social media as a marketing tool. The latter shows the amount of information people are sharing, which can be harmful to their cases.

Attorneys who seek to begin using social media should keep in mind that the ethical risks involved with social media, in terms of both evidence collection and marketing, are very real. Therefore a proper understanding of appropriate and ethical behavior is extremely important.

It is also important to understand that in certain areas of practice, use of social media is now verging on malpractice, and the author would argue it *is* malpractice to fail to communicate with clients about whether and how they use social media. Failing to warn the client to halt or at least limit social media use could result in that client posting materials that will harm his case. Failure to warn a client about evidence preservation could result in substantial sanctions for spoliation.[12] In addition, it is quite conceivable that the opposing party will post information harmful to his case, and failure on the part of the attorney to seek out possible harmful posts can result in loss of a substantially better bargaining position or even loss of a case that might have been won.

---

[5]November 9, 2014. **expandedramblings.com/index.php/by-the-numbers-a-few-important-linkedin-stats**

[6]**www.snapchat.com/ads/**.

[7]**www.youtube.com/yt/press/statistics.html**.

[8]**https://instagram.com/press/**.

[9]**https://about.twitter.com/company**.

[10]**www.pewinternet.org/fact-sheets/social-networking-fact-sheet/**.

[11]*Id.*

[12]See *Lester v. Allied Concrete Co., et al.*; order dated September 1, 2011.

## Specific Sites and Applications

Social media essentially includes sites and applications that enable people to share information, pictures, videos, and the like at a rapid rate and in return allows other people to respond to the shared content. In some cases, social media is referred to as Web 2.0. Web 1.0 refers to sites that serve to provide one-way communication, much like a newsletter or a book. Traditional websites are Web 1.0.

Currently, the most popular social media sites and applications in the United States include Facebook, Twitter, LinkedIn, Google+, Pinterest, YouTube, and Instagram. Further, blogs are sometimes considered part of social media and so will be included in this discussion. At this point, there are over 150 million blogs on the Web and almost 50 percent of Internet users read blogs.

## Marketing and Networking

It is not always easy to understand how social media can increase the potential for bringing in new clients. It is therefore important to think of social media as having uses for practice building.

### Advertising

Social media includes straightforward advertising. Sites such as Facebook, YouTube, LinkedIn, and others provide the opportunity to purchase small ads that appear on the top or side of the page. These ads are controlled through varying means, demographics, keywords, areas of interest, and so on. Generally, the cost of the ads is controlled through a bidding process known as pay-per-click. The site provides a suggested fee that its algorithm suggests will be successful. The purchaser identifies the amount he is willing to pay and competes against those who are seeking to advertise to the same individuals. Normally, the purchaser only pays when someone clicks on an ad.

### Networking

Social media provides substantial opportunities for networking. It simply moves the networking from the bar association or educational program, to networking online. Providing information about interests, sharing day-to-day activities, responding to the posts of others—each of these behaviors is simply a way to connect with other people. Those people, in turn, may need an attorney or may need to refer someone else to an attorney, just as in the offline world. Further, people tend to recommend individuals they know, or feel they know, and social media allows the formation of that kind of relationship.

### Content

Sharing useful content is a crucial part of social media for attorneys. Providing high-quality content that informs users about the areas of law in which an attorney practices is an excellent way to bring attention to that attorney. The content can be as simple as commenting on a case on Facebook, sharing a useful link on Twitter, or providing a detailed analysis of a specific issue on a blog. This content shows potential clients that the attorney is knowledgeable in her area(s) of practice. Further, well-written content provides a substantial boost to search engine optimization and online reputation.

### Specific Sites

Different social media sites provide different tools. Further, some sites are better utilized by attorneys who tend to represent businesses, while others are better utilized by attorneys who represent individuals. It is important to target the correct site or mixture of sites for the best return on investment of time and/or money.

### Content of Posts

When you post on social media, you need to consider whether you are causing any ethical problems for yourself. Given the open nature of social media, a number of issues can arise when lawyers post. Two important issues to focus on include (1) whether social media is advertising and (2) whether you forming an attorney/client relationship by answering questions.

#### *Is Social Media Advertising?*

When choosing what to write on social media, it is important to determine whether your post is advertising under model rule 7.2 (or whatever rule applies in your jurisdiction). If your account is completely private and you share only with friends and family, chances are very good that your posts would not be considered advertising. However, the question becomes cloudier when you open up your account to a larger group. My position is that if you are not certain whether your post is advertising, assume it is and act accordingly as far as your jurisdiction's rules. Some jurisdictions define advertising very clearly. Others do not.

As noted previously, Twitter is a site that is problematic for states such as Florida, where any posting might be considered advertising. In its guidelines on social media, Florida's advertising standing committee states about Twitter that "pages of individual lawyers on social networking sites that are used solely for social purposes, to maintain social contact with family and close friends, are not subject to the lawyer advertising rules. Pages appearing on networking sites that are used to promote the lawyer's or law firm's practice are subject to the lawyer advertising rules. These pages must therefore comply with all of the general regulations set forth in Rules 4-7.11 through 4-7.18 and 4-7.21."[13] This language means that many posts on Twitter would be considered advertising simply because most people have their accounts entirely open and it is common for users to discuss a cross section of personal and work-related details of their lives.

Most problematic, given Twitter's 140-character limit, is that in Florida, the Tweet must include geographic information as well as "the name of at least 1 lawyer in the firm." The attorney may use appropriate abbreviations for the geographic requirements, which helps to a degree. However, as soon as the poster puts both the full name of a lawyer and a geographic location, most of the allotted characters are used up, substantially limiting the value of any tweet. Florida is not the only jurisdiction with special Twitter requirements, so be certain to check your state's rules before you Tweet. That said, many jurisdictions have not placed onerous requirements on lawyers' abilities to use Twitter, and a well-written tweet can be an excellent way to drive traffic to your website or to share useful information.

***Pennsylvania's Analysis***   In Formal Opinion 2014-300 (Ethical Obligations for Attorneys Using Social Media), the Pennsylvania Bar Association provides a detailed guidance opinion on social media use by attorneys. This includes analysis of what is acceptable for marketing purposes.

As related to advertising, and connecting with others on social media, the opinion offers the following:

+ Attorneys may advertise using social media.

---

[13]The Florida Bar Standing Committee on Advertising Guidelines for Networking Sites (revised April 16, 2013), **http://www.floridabar.org/TFB/TFBResources.nsf/Attachments/ 18BC39758BB54A5985257B590063EDA8/$FILE/Guidelines%20-%20Social%20Networking% 20Sites.pdf?OpenElement**.

There is nothing in the rules that prevents attorneys from utilizing social media for advertising purposes. In doing so, the attorney must follow all relevant ethical rules.

♦ Attorneys may endorse other attorneys on social media.

It is acceptable to endorse other lawyers; however, the endorsements must be accurate. If you choose to endorse a lawyer, it would be wise to make certain you actually know the lawyer and his or her skillset and abilities. Many attorneys on sites such as Avvo and LinkedIn provide endorsements when they are complete strangers to the lawyer they are endorsing.

♦ Attorneys may respond to endorsements and reviews and may solicit them.

In Pennsylvania, under Rule 7.2, "no advertisement or public communication shall contain an endorsement by a celebrity or public figure." In addition, if an endorsement is paid, this must be revealed. Both of these rules apply to social media use in Pennsylvania. The latter rule, involving paid endorsements, is common in most states.

Regardless of who provides the review or endorsement, it must be honest. It is the job of the attorney to correct the review if it contains improper information, is dishonest or is false or misleading. "If the lawyer is unable to correct or remove the listing, he or she should contact the person posting the information and request that the person remove or correct the item."[14] Attorneys in Pennsylvania may not pay for or offer anything of value in exchange for a review.

It is appropriate for an attorney to respond to a review, but the attorney must be careful in how he responds to a negative review. "[L]awyers may not reveal client confidential information in response to a negative online review."[15] Interpret the concept of confidential client information broadly. In the author's experience, the best way to respond to a negative review is (1) no response at all, (2) a polite response asking for the person to phone or e-mail to see if you can resolve the problem, (3) a general response stating that you are sorry the person was displeased. An attorney in Illinois was reprimanded due to sharing confidential information in response to a negative review. She was suspended when she revealed that the client had engaged in a physical altercation and other confidential information, and that was why the client lost the case.[16]

---

[14]Formal Opinion 2014-300.

[15]Formal Opinion 2014-300, citing Formal Opinion 2014-200.

[16]*In Re Tsamis*, Comm. File No 2013PR00095 (Ill. 2013).

***California's Analysis***   California is a bit unique in the fact that it provides a rather bright-line rule about what is and is not advertising. In California, if something is considered advertising based on the 1-400 RPC and 6157-6159.2 Business and Professional Code, then it is controlled by those rules. If it does not, it is not controlled by the rules of advertising, though it could potentially be controlled by some other rule.

In Opinion 2012-176, the State Bar of California provides an excellent and detailed analysis that helps its attorneys determine whether something constitutes advertising.[17]

In California, a communication is considered to be "any message or offer made by or on behalf of a member concerning the availability for professional employment of a member or a law firm directed to any former, present or prospective client." Under the rules and articles of California, "[a]ny communication or solicitation shall not:

1. Contain any untrue statement; or

2. Contain any matter, or present or arrange any matter in a manner or format which is false, deceptive or which trends to confuse, deceive, or mislead the public; or

3. Omit to state any fact necessary to make the statements made, in the light of circumstances under which they are made, nor misleading to the public; or

4. Fail to indicate clearly, expressly, or by context, that it is a communication or solicitation as the case may be; or

5. Be transmitted in any manner which involves intrusion, coercion, duress, compulsion, intimidation, threats or vexatious or harassing conduct."

The bar, using its Rule and Article as a basis for analysis, next examines several hypothetical posts. They are:

1. "Case finally over. Unanimous verdict! Celebrating tonight."

2. "Another great victory in court today! My client is delighted. Who wants to be next?"

3. "Won another personal injury case. Call me for a free consultation."

4. "Just published an article on wage and hour breaks. Let me know if you would like a copy."

---

[17]California Rule 1-400 (Advertising and Solicitation), California Article 9.5 (Legal Advertising).

In its analysis, the bar found posts 1 and 4 were not communications (i.e., advertising), but 2 and 3 did meet the requirements constituting a communication and therefore needed certain information that they lacked.

Post 1 was not considered a communication because it did not contain an offer concerning the availability for professional employment. Had the post used "Who wants to be next" as in hypothetical 2, the posting would have become advertising based on the attorney stating that he is seeking additional clients. Post 4 was not advertising because, again, it did not state that the attorney was seeking clients; it was simply providing useful information.

Post 2 is a communication because it makes it clear that the lawyer is available for employment. Since the post is advertising, it now has several problems under California's rules. First, it does not contain a disclaimer. Second, it does not state it is an advertisement. Third, it offers a guarantee or prediction of winning. In order to make this particular post appropriate, a lawyer in California would need to add the required language. Such a post would become quite lengthy however, so a question would arise as to whether it would be worth it to share such information in the first place. It also would not be possible to share this particular post on Twitter in California. Post 3 is a communication/advertising for the same reason post 2 is. Asking for readers to call for a free consultation is clearly seeking employment from potential clients.

Remember, the rules in your jurisdiction(s) might be very different from California. However, the broad analysis in the bar opinion is one that you can apply to your posts. The first question is always going to be, is it advertising? The second question will be, if it is, does the post meet the ethical requirements? Be certain to give your posts the appropriate consideration.

### Other States

Many other states have provided opinions on the subject of whether social media is advertising and ethical issues surrounding its use. The states have generally handled the issues in much the same way Pennsylvania has. However, there are some unique opinions. New York, for example, released an opinion to analyze LinkedIn, in particular, in March 2015.[18] In its opinion, the Ethics Committee found that a general

---

[18]New York County Lawyers Association Professional Ethics Committee, Formal Opinion 748, March 10, 2015.

LinkedIn profile listing education and employment experience is not enough to make the profile advertising. But adding "a description of areas of practice or certain skills or endorsement" may make the profile advertising. Regardless, all content on the profile should be accurate.[19]

### Is Blogging Advertising?

If you search "is blogging attorney advertising" online, you will find many different opinions. As with social media, California has established a bright-line test for whether a blog is advertising. In California, a blog is advertising if it addresses the availability of a lawyer for employment.[20] In that state, if a lawyer wants his blog to fall outside attorney advertising, the lawyer would need to have a stand-alone blog, separate from his website, which does not in *any* way, including by implication, express his availability for professional employment. Such a stand-alone blog would need to avoid discussing the qualifications and history of the lawyer as well.

The seminal case on attorney blogs is *Hunter v. Virginia State Bar*. The rather convoluted history of this case involved an attorney who reported the results of cases with favorable results. He also posted about other issues. He did not, however, have a disclaimer on that blog. The Virginia State Bar found ethical violations under rules 1.6, 7.1, and 7.2. 1.6 involving "disclosure of client information," and the latter two rules involved attorney advertising. On appeal, the Circuit Court found no violation of the rules and determined that the blog was protected under the First Amendment. However, it also required that Hunter put a disclaimer on his blog. The Supreme Court of Virginia ruled that a blog is unprotected commercial speech and that Hunter did not violate rule 1.6. The Court felt that the blog was commercial speech for several reasons:

1. Motivation was, at least partly, economic.
2. The majority of posts discussed favorable case results to show the attorney's skills.
3. The blog was part of the firm's website as opposed to a stand-alone website.

---

[19] Opinion 748 references the Social Media Ethics Guidelines of the Commercial and Federal Litigation Section of the New York State Bar Association. As of this writing, the guide, updated in June 2015, provides a solid overview of social media ethics in New York, **http://www.nysba.org/workarea/DownloadAsset.aspx?id=47547**.

[20] The State Bar of California Standing Committee on Professional Responsibility and Conduct Formal Opinion Interim No. 12-006.

4. There was no ability to interact with the blog. This suggests that Hunter's blog did not allow for comments. It is important to note that most blogging software provides the ability to allow communication via a comments feature that may be turned on or off.[21]

### *Are Blogs Advertising?*

So are blogs advertising? The answer is, it depends on how your blog is set up and on what you post. The safest answer is to treat blogging as if it is advertising. For this purpose, it is wise to include an appropriate disclaimer on your blog. The disclaimer should be much the same as the disclaimer you put on the rest of your website.

### *Is a Social Media Post Legal Advice?*

The line for what is and what is not legal advice is a bit blurry. Given this, it is important that you stay on the right side of the line to make certain you are not inadvertently creating an attorney/client relationship. An attorney/client relationship is formed when a client has reason to believe that the attorney is handling her legal interests. The relationship can be formed expressly, or it can be implied. The implied relationship is the one that can cause trouble online. The standard in determining whether an attorney/client relationship has been formed is based on what the objectively reasonable belief on the part of the client is. If you answer questions online, make certain there is an appropriate disclaimer, such as can be found on sites like Avvo and Quora. In addition, limit yourself to providing broad answers that are educational in nature as opposed to providing specific advice that directly answers the asker's question. At this point, there have been no lawsuits involving attempts to claim a lawyer has formed an attorney/client relationship through an ask/answer site. Keep in mind that besides inadvertently forming an attorney/client relationship, if you provide legal advice in a state in which you are not licensed, you might be engaging in the unauthorized practice of law.

### *Recommendations/Testimonials*

The rules around recommendations and testimonials vary greatly across the United States. As a result, it is difficult to provide specific guidelines. Given this, it is crucial that you refer to the state(s) in which you are licensed to make certain you follow the rules. In most states, it is perfectly

---

[21] Renee Choy Ohlendorf, "Attorney Blogger Runs Afoul of Ethics Rules on Advertising," 2013, **https://apps.americanbar.org/litigation/litigationnews/top_stories/053013-blog-ethics-advertising.html**.

acceptable to ask for testimonials. However, those testimonials must follow all relevant rules. When clients write recommendations, those recommendations must not create false expectations and they must be correct. If a client writes a recommendation that violates the rules, it is the attorney's obligation to correct it. In some cases, for example LinkedIn, the attorney will be able to control whether an improper testimonial is posted. In other cases, for example Google+, Avvo, and Facebook, the attorney is not able to approve the testimonial. In such cases, the attorney must ask the client to remove the recommendation or to provide a correction in the comments.

### *Dealing with Negative Reviews*

Negative reviews are a serious problem on social media and on the Web in general. A negative review can be very harmful to a law firm. That said, no matter how negative the review, it is crucial that lawyers respond appropriately if a past client attacks them online. Most importantly, attorneys may not share confidential information about the client in a response to a negative review. For example, a lawyer from Illinois responded to a negative review on Avvo by providing confidential information about her client. The Hearing board found that she engaged in misconduct that included:

1. [R]evealing information relating to the representation of a client without the client's informed consent, in violation of Rule 1.6(a) of the Illinois Rules of Professional Conduct (2010);

2. [U]sing means in representing a client that have no substantial purpose other than to embarrass, delay, or burden a third person, in violation of Rule 4.4 of the Illinois Rules of Professional Conduct (2010); and

3. [C]onduct which is prejudicial to the administration of justice or which tends to defeat the administration of justice or to bring the courts or the legal profession into disrepute.[22]

The complaint against the attorney also involved a bounced check. For both the check and the comment on Avvo, the attorney was reprimanded by the disciplinary commission.[23]

---

[22]*In the Matter of Betty Tsamis*, Commission No. 2013PR00095 (August 26, 2013), **http://www .iardc.org/13PR0095CM.html**.
[23]**http://www.iardc.org/HB_RB_Disp_Html.asp?id=11221**.

### Should You Sue Over a Bad Review?

For the most part, suing over a bad review is a bad idea. There are a number of reasons for this. The first reason it is bad to sue is due to the Streisand Effect. The Streisand Effect is so named because of the efforts on behalf of Barbra Streisand to remove images of the California coastline that included pictures of Streisand's home. Once the lawsuit was filed, the picture that the attorneys had sought to suppress became very popular online. Prior to the suit, the image had been downloaded six times. After the suit, the image went viral and now is used as an example of the unintended consequences of intense publication that can result from trying to remove information from the Web.[24] The second reason it is unwise to sue is because if potential clients learn about the suit, which they might well do because of the Streisand Effect, they may be concerned about retaining a firm that will sue its clients.

### The Best Way to Handle a Negative Review

Unfortunately, in many cases, it is not possible to get a review removed from the Web. On sites such as Avvo, if you believe the review is from someone who was not actually a client, you can ask Avvo to look into the situation. Avvo will ask the reviewer to confirm the review.[25] This, at least, should mean that if the person does not provide a real e-mail address, Avvo will remove the review. The author can confirm that reviews from nonclients have been removed from Avvo.

In the end, the best way to deal with a negative review is to provide a polite response. If you are too angry to give a polite response, the best response is none at all. It is very unlikely that one negative review will have a huge impact on your practice. In fact, the best way to deal with reviews is to consistently ask for them from satisfied clients at the end of representation, assuming, of course, that it is acceptable for you to do so in your jurisdiction(s). Never offer your clients anything in return for the review.

### Specific Rules

**Honest Communication and Integrity**   The first two rules for online behavior should be considered an umbrella under which all behavior is judged. First, attorneys should never be misleading in their communications in relation to their services. No communication should contain a material misrepresentation of either fact or law, nor should any statement omit facts necessary to make the statement appropriate under rule 7.1.

---

[24]Streisand Effect, **http://knowyourmeme.com/memes/streisand-effect**.
[25]**http://www.avvo.com/support/What_if_I_get_a_negative_Client_Review**.

This concept flows throughout all communications by attorneys when discussing their services. The second set of rules, 8.x, involves maintaining the integrity of the profession—in other words, not holding the profession up to ridicule through one's behavior.

***Advertising*** The first rule of which attorneys need to be aware relates directly to advertising, and it is Model Rule 7.2. One of the issues that can be a problem under Rule 7.2 is that various states require attorneys to keep all ads for a certain period of time. In Pennsylvania, for example, attorneys must keep copies of ads for two years. Other states have longer requirements. It is also important to note that a specific attorney must take responsibility for the ad and its placement, so make certain that a specific attorney is responsible for every action, even if performed by a nonattorney. Fortunately, the various accounts are meant to stay intact, so it is easy to keep records. If a post needs to be deleted, grab a screenshot of it and store it where it will be easily located. Make certain to identify the attorney responsible for the item.

Various states have other requirements, so attorneys should check Rule 7.2 in every state in which they are licensed.

***Solicitation of Clients*** Also implicated by use of social media for communication with potential clients is Model Rule 7.3. Attorneys may not solicit potential clients through real-time communication. This aspect of the rule does not apply to family members, current clients, or other attorneys. Real-time communication includes telephone conversations, in-person discussions, and real-time electronic chat. There is disagreement as to whether attorneys may solicit new clients through chat rooms in which a large number of people are present, versus instant messages, which are more personal and direct. Given this, it is safe to assume that starting a chat on Facebook is real-time communication and should be avoided. E-mail is considered written communication. To obey the rule, at a minimum, attorneys must label advertising as such and comply with Rule 7.1.

Attorneys may not solicit a client who has already made it clear that he does not wish to be contacted or if "the solicitation involves coercion, duress or harassment." This means if someone has made it clear through social media that he doesn't want to be contacted, it would be a violation of the rule to contact him. The tone of writing matters as well. If the content is seen as inappropriate, it violates the rule.

In most states, it is also improper to seek to communicate with a potential client who the "lawyer knows or reasonably should know that the physical, emotional or mental state of the person is such that the person could not exercise reasonable judgment in employing a lawyer." Given this, it is inappropriate to seek to communicate directly via social media with someone the lawyer knows or should know is in the midst of a crisis—for example, tweeting at someone who just lost a loved one or sending a direct message to such a person. Also, tagging someone in a Facebook post when you know the person just suffered a loss would be inappropriate in the author's opinion.

**Multi-State Practice**　An area in which it is easy to get in trouble, due to the vast and multijurisdictional nature of the Internet, is multistate practice. Attorneys must comply with their home state rules in relation to:

♦ Where the office is located

♦ Where the attorneys are admitted

♦ How they are seeking clients

♦ How they engage in advertising

♦ All states' rules in which they market

## Additional Ethical Issues

Aside from advertising, communication with potential clients, and inappropriate use of social media in discovery, there are other ways in which legal professionals have gotten themselves in trouble using social media.

**Confidentiality and Honesty**　One potential area of trouble involves confidentiality, Rule 1.6. An attorney got herself in trouble by sharing confidential information about a case in such a way as to make it possible to identify her client. She also provided information that suggested that she knew her client had lied on the stand and did nothing about it. In addition to Rule 1.6, the attorney was accused of violating other rules involving honesty, fraud, and more.[26] In the end, the attorney lost her job of nineteen years[27] and was suspended for ninety days by two different jurisdictions.[28, 29]

---

[26] In the Matter of Kristine Ann Peshek, Commission No. 09 CH 89, Illinois Attorney Registration and Disciplinary Commission (2009).

[27] Debra Cassens Weiss, "Blogging Assistant PD Accused of Revealing Secrets of Little-Disguised Clients," 2009, **http://www.abajournal.com/news/article/blogging_assistant_pd_accused_of_revealing_secrets_of_little-disguised_clie**.

[28] "Illinois Supreme Court Disbars 12, Suspends 26," **http://iln.isba.org/2010/05/18/illinois-supreme-court-disbars-12-suspends-26**.

[29] Office of Lawyer Regulation v. Peshek, 2011 WI 47 (2011).

Another serious consequence the attorney suffered is that when searching her name online, page after page of results show her disciplinary problems. Although she has since opened her own firm, it is difficult to find anything positive about her on the Web.

While it is perfectly acceptable to discuss one's life, and even one's professional activities, it is important to obey the ethical rules while doing so. Discussing a case on a blog while it is going on, outside appropriate public relations, is a bad idea. Failing to protect a client's confidentiality is even worse. And of course, failing to inform the court properly of inappropriate conduct by the client was a serious mistake. Judgment is a critical part of both practicing law and posting online.

***Jokes and Satire***   Jokes can also be a serious problem online. It is impossible to see body language or hear the tone in a person's voice. Something one person might find amusing might not be so funny to another. As a result, joking through social media can be problematic, especially on a politically charged topic. An Indiana deputy attorney general learned this the hard way when he tweeted an unfortunate joke surrounding protests in Wisconsin in 2011. His tweet led to an argument with the editor of *Mother Jones* magazine. In turn, the magazine researched the attorney and found similar comments on his blog. In the end, the price of the attorney's online behavior was his job.[30] The attorney general's office stated that it chose to fire the attorney after a "thorough and expeditious review," noting that it respects First Amendment rights but expects civility from its public servants.

***Seeking Attention for a Client or Friend***   There are rules about how members of the bar may use the press. Similar rules apply to using social media to advocate for a client or even for a friend. As an example, a lawyer in Louisiana was disbarred due to a Twitter and blog campaign in which she created a petition and encouraged the public to contact directly two judges in a custody case involving a friend.[31] To facilitate communication with the judges, she provided their contact information. She also revealed confidential information, including links to an audio recording of the children talking about the alleged sexual abuse they suffered. The disbarred attorney was not admitted in Mississippi, the state where the case

---

[30]"Indiana State Prosecutor Fired over Remarks about Wisconsin Protests," 2011, **http://www.cnn.com/2011/US/02/23/indiana.ammo.tweet/**.

[31]In Re: Joyce Nanine McCool, Attorney Disciplinary Proceeding, **http://www.lasc.org/opinions/2015/15B0284.opn.pdf**.

was located. A judge involved in the custody case filed a complaint with Louisiana. The attorney felt that she was protected by the First Amendment and that she did not engage in any ethical misconduct.

The Hearing Committee determined that the lawyer violated Rules 3.5(a) and (b) as well as 8.4(a), (c), and (d). The Committee determined that, among other violations, the attorney disseminated false, misleading, and inflammatory information about how the judges handled the case and encouraged *ex parte* contact with the judges in an effort to influence rulings. The committee felt that the attorney "acted knowingly, if not intentionally" and "caused actual and potential harm by threatening the independence and integrity of the judicial system and caused the judges concern for their personal safety and well-being." The end result is that the attorney was, as previously noted, disbarred.

Given the opportunity for easy sharing of information on social media, it is critical that attorneys think carefully before using the Web to seek to encourage action on behalf of their clients. They would do well to advise their clients to use the same level of caution.

***Personal Versus Private***    Sometimes attorneys will develop both a private and public persona on the web, believing the two will remain separate. Unfortunately, this is simply not the case. It takes very little effort to perform research on the Web and to connect the public and private behaviors of someone who has written something offensive or upsetting. In an infamous case, an assistant Michigan attorney general was fired due to his online (and perhaps offline) behavior surrounding the student body president of the University of Michigan. The attorney argued that his speech was political and also had nothing to do with his work as an assistant attorney general. But in the end, the public and private became much too intertwined, and the attorney general was left with no choice but to fire him. Recently, the student won a verdict of $4.5 million for invasion of privacy, defamation, abuse of process, and intentional infliction of emotional distress.[32]

The attorney in this case did not hide who he was, but he did try to argue that his actions had nothing to do with his work. However, as a public servant and as an attorney, it was simply impossible to separate the public

---

[32]Kevin Dolak, "Attorney Andrew Shirvell Ordered to Pay 4.5 Million for Attacks on Gay Student, 2012, **http://abcnews.go.com/US/attorney-andrew-shirvell-ordered-pay-45-million-attacks/ story?id=17028621**.

employee from the (not so) private behavior, and that cost him his job. He was fired for "violat[ing] office policies, engag[ing] in borderline stalking behavior," and more. The attorney sometimes posted his online attacks while at work and engaged in behavior that was "not protected by the First Amendment."[33] Much of his behavior was offline, but it was his online behavior that brought an incredible amount of attention to what he was doing, so much so that he ended up on TV shows, including *Anderson Cooper 360* on CNN.[34]

It is unwise to believe that anyone can live two separate lives online. If one engages in controversial behavior, the result will be a magnifying glass of attention. In turn, it is virtually impossible for the individual to keep his private and public online lives from colliding.

## Discovery of Social Media

Given the value of the information contained in social media accounts, it is no surprise that attorneys desire to obtain access to the information. It is not at all uncommon, for example, for an individual to say one thing in person to her attorney or a judge and to post completely contradictory information on Facebook. An individual might claim in court or interrogatories that she cannot leave her home due to emotional harm from an injury, but in turn post a video on Facebook showing her dancing at a party. In the past, it was necessary to hire a private investigator to prove someone was lying about his injury for a workers' compensation claim; now the plaintiff frequently posts a picture of himself chopping wood or carrying a heavy couch, the exact evidence the defense attorney needs to prove her case.

### Privacy Settings Are Important
Privacy settings control what an individual shares on social media sites. However, many users never change their privacy settings or simply find the settings too complicated to alter. Many social media sites barely have

---

[33]David Jesse, Andrew Shirvell Fired from Job at Michigan Attorney General's Office, 2010, **http://www.annarbor.com/news/andrew-shirvell-fired-from-job-at-attorney-generals-office/ #.UFQIPVEQd60**.

[34]"Anderson Cooper: Andrew Shirvell Responsible for His Firing Not 'Liberal Media,'" **http://www.huffingtonpost.com/2010/11/09/anderson-cooper-andrew-sh_n_780874.html**.

any privacy settings at all. Twitter, for example, is open, limited, or pri-vate.[35] Facebook's settings are extremely complicated and confusing.[36] Blogs are meant to be open, and people frequently believe they are private when they are not.[37] Since many people do not change their settings, attorneys should and do look through the social media sites in an ethical manner and view and preserve the information they can find.[38] Keep in mind, if the attorney does the preservation and authentication becomes an issue, the attorney can be forced to become a witness in her own case. It is best to have someone else in the firm do the preservation—or an independent third-party vendor.

## The Client's Social Media

The first step when a new client walks through the door is to ask if he uses any social media. The next step, in some cases, is to inform the client that he must stop posting immediately. Unfortunately, the addiction and use of social media can be so great that the client will be unwilling to stop. As a result, the attorney should also advise the client that if he does post, he should not post anything that deals with the case. The attorney must be clear about what "deals with the case" means, since many clients will sim-ply think it means specifics about how the case is going, as opposed to comments about giving money to his mistress, lifting a heavy couch, attending a party, and so on. Make certain to ask the client not only about his own accounts but also any comments on blogs and websites that might be relevant to the case. Social media and other online surprises can be very harmful. It is also important to remind the client that he may not delete any content from his account, even if it is potentially harmful to the case.

---

[35]**https://support.twitter.com/entries/14016#**.

[36]Approximately 13 million U.S. users never change their Facebook privacy settings. Of those who do, the majority are unaware that their privacy settings can be compromised by allowing additional applications access to their accounts and do not take the steps necessary to further protect their data, **http://www.zdnet.com/blog/facebook/13-million-us-facebook-users-dont-change-privacy-settings/12398**.

[37]Natalie Munroe was a teacher in Pennsylvania who blogged about her students. She believed that her blog was being read by only a few people, apparently unaware that it could be widely read, **http://tinyurl.com/8hx95c6**. Munroe was suspended, brought back, and eventually fired. She claims that she was fired due to the blog. The District claims that she was fired for incompe-tence. Munroe has since brought a lawsuit against the district, **http://www.philly.com/philly/blogs/bucksinq/160413996.html**.

[38]New York State Bar Association, Committee on Professional Ethics, Opinion 843 (September 10, 2010).

The first meeting with a client is also the time to discuss changing privacy settings to make certain that his account is secure. Providing instructions on how to change privacy settings in written form or a video can be very helpful. Most ethics guidance opinions, including the Pennsylvania Bar Association social media opinion, make it clear that it is acceptable to alter privacy settings.[39] It might well be wise to encourage clients to adjust their privacy settings if you are concerned about the content. However, it is similarly appropriate to ask opposing parties whether they altered their settings.

It is also a good idea to have the client sign a document making it clear that he was told not to delete any content without having the attorney preserve it first.[40] This will protect you from accusations of spoliation later on. In some cases, it might be wise to ask for access to the account(s). Asking to friend the client is not enough; the password is necessary for a complete review of the client's online conduct. You must make a decision as to whether connecting with the client and reviewing his account is wise. Remember, if you become aware of any content that shows the client is lying or will lie before the court, you will be in an ethical quandary.

Also, if the client has a personal relationship with the opposing party, ask about whether he is connected to the other side's social media, for example as a friend on Facebook. In addition, ask the client if any potential witnesses are using social media. Find out if the client is connected to those witnesses and therefore has access to private areas of the accounts.

Finally, it is important that attorneys speak not only with their clients but also with other relevant individuals about their online conduct. In a recent case, the daughter of the plaintiff caused an $80,000 settlement to be overturned because she posted about the result on Facebook.[41] In the end, what matters is proper communication with the client in order to protect both the client's case and your ethical obligations.

## Opposing Party and Witnesses

Immediately view the opposing party's accounts and witness accounts if they are freely accessible. It is permissible to view the accounts if the

---

[39]Pennsylvania Bar Association Opinion 2014-300.

[40]Most ethics opinions allow for deletion of content, as long as the content is properly preserved and provided as appropriate during discovery. PBA Opinion 2014-300; Florida Professional Ethics Committee, Proposed Advisory Opinion 14-1 (2015).

[41]Matthew Stucker, "Girl Costs Father $80,000 with 'SUCK IT' Facebook Post," March 2014, **http://www.cnn.com/2014/03/02/us/facebook-post-costs-father/**.

client has access. It is also permissible to ask witnesses to provide access to their accounts, although the attorney or another individual asking for access must be honest about her relationship to the case.

Also send a Notice of Preservation to opposing counsel. Fortunately, the amendments to the federal discovery rules from 2006 allow for discovery of electronic data to begin very early in the litigation process. Make it clear to opposing counsel that all data must be preserved. Do not just name specific social media sites, but be clear in the preservation that it means all sites and all accounts. Unfortunately, exactly what preservation is required is not yet clear. Does preservation mean keeping the privacy settings as is so that if an account was open, it would remain open? Does it simply mean that data may not be deleted? Be clear about expectations and do not be surprised if the matter ends up before a judge.[42]

Send out the Interrogatories relating to social media as quickly as possible and ask the right questions. Again, do not give the opposing client a chance to wiggle out by asking simply for Facebook data when the client might have a Plaxo account. Ask for everything. Ask for all e-mail addresses as well, because the opposing party might have several accounts under various e-mail addresses. Further, keep in mind that with strict privacy settings, the opposing party can all but hide the existence of his account(s).

## Trouble for Failure to Preserve

In the past, some have believed that it is acceptable to delete posts from social media accounts. A Virginia decision from 2011 puts the debate to rest. It is spoliation to delete relevant posts without preserving them and providing them when properly requested through discovery. In the case, the attorney instructed his client to "clean up his Facebook because we don't want blowups of this stuff at trial." The attorney further instructed the client to delete or deactivate the account and then responded to discovery requests by informing opposing counsel that his client had no Facebook account. The client deactivated the account instead of deleting it. Upon reactivating the account, the client deleted sixteen photographs, following his attorney's instructions. Based on the spoliation, the court

---

[42]In a recent opinion, the Philadelphia Bar Association made it clear that it is acceptable not only to change privacy settings but also to delete content, as long as that content is properly preserved prior to deletion. In addition, the lawyer must "make reasonable efforts to obtain a photograph, link or other content about which the lawyer is aware if the lawyer knows or reasonably believes it has not been produced by the client." The Philadelphia Bar Association Professional Guidance Committee, Opinion 2014-5, July 2014. A Pennsylvania Bar Association Formal Opinion provides the same advice, 2014-300.

held that sanctions should be granted against both the attorney and the client. The sanctions amounted to $722,000 in legal fees, over $500,000 of which was payable by the attorney. In addition, the judge in the case reported the attorney to the Virginia State Bar.[43] In the end, the attorney agreed to a five-year suspension of his license and ultimately left the practice of law.[44]

A New Jersey case shows the serious consequences of deleting (without preserving) content from Facebook. In that case, the plaintiff claimed that he deactivated his Facebook account and did not restore it quickly enough, resulting in deletion of his account. Leaving aside that this is not how Facebook's deactivations and deletions actually work,[45] the end result was that the court found that deletion of the account was spoliation of evidence and granted an adverse inference instruction.[46] Given the cases and the trend, it seems to be straightforward that deleting posts, pictures, or videos without preservation is unacceptable and likely to lead to serious sanctions.

## Ethical Pitfalls in Research, Discovery, and Communications

There are a number of relevant guidance opinions from the New York City and State Bar Assocations,[47] the Pennsylvania Bar Association,[48] the Philadelphia Bar Association,[49] and the San Diego County Bar Association[50] surrounding issues related to performing research utilizing social media.

### General Research

First, as already noted, it is perfectly acceptable to search and access social media sites that are freely accessible. The New York Guidance Opinion states, "[an attorney] may access the public pages of another party's social networking website (such as Facebook or MySpace) for the purpose of

---

[43]See *Lester v. Allied Concrete Co., et al.*; order dated September 1, 2011.

[44]"On July 17, 2013, the Virginia State Bar Disciplinary Board suspended Matthew B. Murray's license to practice law for five years for violating professional rules that govern candor toward the tribunal, fairness to opposing party and counsel, and misconduct. This was an agreed disposition of misconduct charges." VSB Docket Nos. 11-070-088405,11-070-0884222.

[45]In the author's experience, when a Facebook account is deactivated, it is not deleted. When the owner logs into his account again, it is restored. For a Facebook account to be deleted, specific actions requesting deletion must be taken on the part of the account owner.

[46]*Gatto v. United Air Lines, Inc., et al.*, Case No. 10-cv-1090-ES-SCM (D.N.J. Mar. 25, 2013).

[47]New York State Bar Association Guidance Opinion 843 (2010).

[48]Pennsylvania Bar Association Formal Opinion 2014-300 (2014).

[49]Philadelphia Bar Association Guidance Opinion 2009-02 (2009).

[50]SDCBA Ethics Opinion 2011-2 (May 24, 2011).

obtaining possible impeachment material for use in the litigation."[51] On the other hand, the 2009 Philadelphia Opinion makes it clear that an effort to obtain access to the account through deceptive or illegal means is unacceptable.[52]

### Friending a Witness

In the 2009 Philadelphia opinion, the attorney asked whether it would be acceptable for the attorney to have a third party request a witness to "friend"[53] the opposing client. The third party did not intend to lie, but neither did he intend to reveal his relationship to the attorney.

The opinion noted that such behavior would violate several rules of ethical conduct. The lawyer would be "procuring conduct [and be] responsible for [that] conduct" in violation of Pennsylvania Rule 5.3 (Responsibilities Regarding Nonlawyer Assistants). Also, the lawyer would be violating rule 8.4 (Misconduct) by engaging in "deceptive" conduct. In addition, the attorney would be encouraging a third party to violate Rule 4.1 (Truthfulness in Statements to Others) by having the third party "omit a highly material fact."[54] Based upon the Philadelphia Bar Association's 2009 Guidance Opinion, it is very clear that having a third party (or the attorney herself) friend a witness without revealing her relationship to the case would be highly inappropriate.

A real-world example of what can happen when an attorney lies to potential witnesses comes from a lawyer who is learning a hard lesson in negative publicity. This attorney, a prosecutor in Ohio, posed as the ex-girlfriend of a murder defendant on Facebook. The attorney's stated goal was to convince the two female alibi witnesses to change their stories. In the end, the prosecutor was fired and has seen numerous stories written about this conduct online.[55] The lesson from this case is that lawyers may

---

[51] New York State Bar Association Guidance Opinion 843.

[52] Philadelphia Bar Association Guidance Opinion 2009-02.

[53] *Friend* is Facebook's term for two people who are connected to each other on the service. Different social media providers use different terms. For example, LinkedIn uses "contact" and "connection." Friending someone requires the affirmative action of a request on the part of the individual seeking the connection and an affirmative action on the part of the individual accepting the connection. See Facebook, "How Do I Add a Friend?" **http://www.facebook.com/help/?faq=12062**.

[54] Philadelphia Bar Association Guidance Opinion 2009-02 (2009) and Pennsylvania Bar Association Formal Opinion 2014-300.

[55] Martha Neil, "Prosecutor Fired after Posing as Ex-girlfriend in Facebook Chat with Defendant's Alibi Witnesses, June 2013, **http://www.abajournal.com/news/article/prosecutor_is_fired_after_posing_as_woman_in_facebook_chat_with_murder_defe/**.

not lie when communicating with anyone through social media, including witnesses.

### Communicating with a Represented Party

The San Diego County Bar Association took on the issue of communicating with a represented party. In short, as is the case offline, it is inappropriate to communicate with a represented party online. In the instant case, the attorney did not identify himself as the attorney, which made the effort to communicate all the more grievous. An additional issue, of concern for those involved in employee cases, includes an analysis of whether the contacted employees were represented parties.[56]

In 2012, the issue of friending represented parties came up in New Jersey where two attorneys are likely to face sanctions due to their paralegal friending the opposing party in a case.[57] The issue came to light during a deposition when it became clear that the attorneys had access to the private areas of the plaintiff's Facebook account. The attorneys denied responsibility because they asked the paralegal simply to perform a general search of the Web. The issue with this defense is that attorneys are responsible for the behavior of their staff. The attorneys are charged with violating New Jersey rules 4.2 (communications with represented parties); 5.3(a), (b), and (c) (failure to supervise a nonlawyer assistant); 8.4(c) (conduct involving dishonesty and violation of ethics rules through someone else's actions or inducing those violations); and 8.4(d) (conduct prejudicial to the administration of justice). In addition, the more senior of the two attorneys is charged with violating RPC 5.1(b) and (c) (ethical obligation in relation to supervising another attorney). These are all very serious charges, and regardless of the outcome, the publicity, which will spread rapidly through social media, will no doubt be very harmful to the two attorneys in question.

At this point it seems well-settled that the action of friending someone or seeking to access her account through some form of communication is contact. Therefore, attorneys should never seek to friend or obtain access to the account of an opposing party through any form of communication with a represented party. If seeking to friend a witness, the attorney or

---

[56]SDCBA Ethics Opinion 2011-2, May 24, 2011.
[57]Eric Meyer, "Ethics Charges for Two Lawyers over Facebook Friending a Litigant," 2012, http://www.lexisnexis.com/community/labor-employment-law/blogs/labor-employment-commentary/archive/2012/09/13/ethics-charges-for-two-lawyers-over-facebook-friending-a-litigant.aspx.

individual assisting the attorney must make clear her relationship to the case.

## How to Obtain Access

If an attorney believes that there is useful information contained within a social media account, she should seek to obtain access to the information hidden therein. There are a number of ethical ways to do so, aside from just looking to see what is freely available.

### See if the Client or a Friendly Witness Has Access

In family law cases especially, the parties or witnesses might have access to each other's accounts. It is perfectly acceptable to view and use any information that is freely available through this method. Be cautious though where it looks as though a witness might be sharing the information under duress. For example, in an employer/employee case, if another employee is friends with a plaintiff on Facebook, that person might feel as though he has no choice but to share the information. If that employee complains later and says that he was forced to share the access, it is uncertain how a court will look upon it.

### Ask for Access to the Account

During the discovery process, unless there is a reason not to do so, ask for access to any and all social media accounts. In terms of Facebook, it is possible to download an entire account, so request that the opposing party do so and provide a copy.[58] Be sure to ask for continuing access as well. The opposing party will likely refuse this request, and wisely so. Social media postings can provide a plethora of private information, some of which may be harmful to a case. It is possible simply to ask the opposing party to adjust privacy settings so that the account is viewable, but again, it is likely this request will be refused. It is always best to ask though because during the discovery process, the judge will certainly ask if the request was made.

### Send a Subpoena to the Site

Although generally the social media sites will not cooperate with a civil subpoena, from time to time, they will be surprisingly helpful.[59] As a result, it never hurts to send the subpoena. Even if the site won't provide content, citing the Stored Communications Act, it will normally provide

---

[58]Facebook's "Download your information" tool is located under Account Settings.
[59]See "Won't the Social Media Provider Help," *infra.*

assistance in connecting an account with an e-mail address. This can be helpful if ownership of the account is in issue. For example, in a criminal case, the prosecution's verdict was overturned when it was shown that prosecution had failed to tie the account in question to the defendant's girlfriend.[60] Proof of ownership could have been shown with MySpace's assistance.

### Compel Discovery

This is where things get tricky. Different judges tend to have different responses to the request to compel discovery of a social media account. The best approach, and the one that has shown the most results, is to capture what is already viewable (through appropriate ethical means) and to show it to the judge. If the judge can see that the account has relevant and contradictory information, she is likely to provide access to the account. If the judge has concerns about the privacy of those other than the account holder, request that the court review the data first to help resolve the issue. Some judges do not feel that there are any privacy rights in social media content.[61]

### Case Law

There are a number of opinions related to discovery of social media when the account itself is not a part of the case—in other words, when opposing counsel believes that she might find useful data in the account but the online behavior is not at the center of the dispute. At this point, the trend in such cases is to provide access to social media accounts only when the opposing party can show that there is relevant and/or contradictory information contained therein. For example, in *McMillen v. Hummingbird Speedway, Inc.*,[62] a review of the public areas of McMillen's Facebook page revealed information contradictory to what he was claiming in terms of his injuries. The judge provided access, noting specifically that the Facebook information was not privileged.

Another case is simply the paragraph-long *Piccolo v. Paterson.*[63] The judge denied access to the Facebook pages the defense desired. The judge noted

---

[60]Kashmir Hill, "Bad MySpace Detective Work Results in Overturned Murder Conviction," 2011, **http://blogs.forbes.com/kashmirhill/2011/05/10/bad-myspace-detective-work-results-in-overturned-murder-conviction**

[61]*NY v. Harris*, 2012 NY Slip Op 22175, June 30, 2012.

[62]*McMillen v. Hummingbird Speedway, Inc.*, No. 113-2010 CD (C.P. Jefferson, Sept. 9, 2010).

[63]Gina Passerella, "Facebook Postings Barred from Discovery in Accident Case," 2013, **http://www.thelegalintelligencer.com/id=1202493920630/Facebook-Postings-Barred-From-Discovery-in-Accident-Case#ixzz3COUstMur**.

that the defense already had many pictures and that no pictures or other data were freely available that showed contradictory information to what the plaintiff was claiming. It is interesting to note that the plaintiff actually changed her privacy settings early in the case to preclude anyone other than a friend from viewing her pictures.

In *Zimmerman v. Weis Markets Inc.*,[64] the judge granted discovery due to the public availability of pictures that contradicted the plaintiff's claim that he did not wear shorts due to his embarrassment about a scar. The plaintiff posted pictures on his MySpace profile that clearly showed him wearing shorts after his injury (the scar was visible.) Due to the public availability of this contradictory information, the judge found that there was clearly relevant data to be found within the MySpace account and therefore access to the account was properly compelled.

Another important case comes from Judge R. Stanton Wettick. Judge Wettick is known as a discovery judge in Pennsylvania, so his view on the discovery of social media was quite welcome. Judge Wettick denied mutual requests for access to Facebook accounts in the case of *Trail v. Lesko* because he was not going to allow a fishing expedition when there was no evidence that contradictory or useful information could be found in either Facebook account.[65] Therefore, Judge Wettick used the same reasoning as in many of the other cases on this issue.

In a Florida case, the judge granted in part and denied in part the request by the defense in a personal injury case for complete access to the plaintiff's social media network. He held that the plaintiff must provide copies of all pictures depicting her since her injury, rather than provide access to the entire social media account in question. He further held that in requesting that the plaintiff provide every device on which she accessed her social media accounts, the defense had overreached.[66] In reaching his decision, the judge noted that social media sites are "neither privileged nor protected by any right of privacy." He also noted that the discovery request must be properly tailored, and to support both assertions, he cited the decision in *Tompkins v. Detroit Metropolitan Airport*.

---

[64] *Zimmerman v. Weis Markets, Inc.*, No. CV-09-1535 (2011).
[65] *Trail v. Lesko*, No. GD-10-017249.
[66] *Davenport v. State Farm Mutual Automobile Insurance Co.*, Case No. 3:110-cv-632-J-JBT (M.D. FL, 2012).

In *Tompkins,*[67] the court found that while social media is discoverable, and "generally not privileged," the opposing party still may not "have a generalized right to rummage through information that Plaintiff has limited from public view." The court required a "threshold showing that the requested information is reasonably calculated to lead to the discovery of admissible evidence." As in the other cited cases, the court wanted to see some evidence that justified the defendant "delving into the non-public section of [plaintiff's] account." The court noted specifically that if the public segment of plaintiff's account had "contained pictures of her playing golf or riding horseback," that the defendant would have had a better case to access the private portions of her account.

The conclusion to be drawn thus far about the majority of social media discovery decisions is that while courts are willing to provide access to private sections of social media accounts, they are not willing to allow fishing expeditions simply based on the view that the accounts *might* have useful information. Some evidence showing that relevant information can be found in the account must be offered before discovery will be granted.

### Won't the Social Media Provider Help?
Social media providers will not provide content from a social media account in civil cases. As recently as 2007, some providers did respond to civil subpoenas with content, but now the providers state unequivocally that due to the Stored Communications Act, 18 U.S.C. § 2701 et seq., they may not provide content.[68] The providers will respond to a subpoena only with information about who owns the account, perhaps dates and times of connections, IP addresses, etc.[69] This means the only way to get the data is to have the owner of the account cooperate. In criminal cases, most social media providers will assist when provided with an appropriate subpoena or warrant. On occasion, a social media site will be surprising, go against its stated rules, and provide the evidence. Therefore, it never hurts to ask with a subpoena in a civil case. Just be prepared for a no,

---

[67] *Tompkins v. Detroit Metropolitan Airport,* Case No. 10-10413, 2012 WL 179320 (E.D. MI. 2012).
[68] Facebook states, "Federal law prohibits Facebook from disclosing user content (such as messages, wall posts, and photos) in response to a civil subpoena," **http://www.facebook.com/help/ ?faq=17158**.
[69] For Facebook this requires the e-mail address that the attorney desires to connect to the account, **https://www.facebook.com/help/?page=211462112226850**.

which is the general response, and be sure your client is advised of that and wants you to spend the time and the client's money.[70]

The various social media sites generally have details on the subpoena process and what they will provide. Review each site to learn the appropriate steps.

### What Happens if the Owner of the Account Deletes the Data?

Most social media providers claim that when a user deletes information from his account, it is gone forever. Facebook, for example, explains that its deletion system works much like a recycling bin. In essence, when a user deletes data, that data is stored on Facebook's server briefly until the system writes over it; this means, unfortunately, if someone is savvy and starts deleting harmful data, there is nothing that can be done to bring it back once it is overwritten. Facebook does state, "[i]f a user cannot access content because he or she disables or deleted his or her account, Facebook will, to the extent possible, restore access to allow the user to collect and produce the account's content. Facebook preserves user content only in response to a valid law enforcement request."[71] Of course, if there is nothing to find because it has been deleted and destroyed, the site cannot restore the data. And outside of criminal cases, it must be the account's owner who requests the data be restored.

### Responding to Social Media Requests

It is important to be prepared to respond appropriately to requests for social media content. All businesses (including law firms) should have a social media policy that controls who may (and may not) speak on behalf of the company. The policy should also consider addressing whether supervisors may be connected to employees on the more social sites (as opposed to professional sites such as LinkedIn) and remind employees about the fact that policies online are the same as policies offline, specifically in relation to sexual harassment and other such issues. Employees should also be reminded not to discuss private information and/or litigation on their social media accounts. Employers should train employees on social media privacy settings to assist in security. As already explained, individuals should be warned not to post anything that can be harmful to their cases on social media.

---

[70]See Send a Subpoena to the Site *supra*.
[71]See Information on a Civil Summons, **https://www.facebook.com/help/?page= 211462112226850**.

Social media evidence needs to be preserved appropriately. For a business with a great deal of social media evidence to preserve, it is wise to involve a company that can help in the preservation process during litigation. An individual can simply print out the pages (less desirable for reasons of authenticity) or download the account. If the account is large (and is not on Facebook where it can be downloaded) and it is likely the history of the account will enter into the lawsuit, it might be wise to arrange for preservation of the account through a third party, to avoid any accusations of spoliation later on.

In the end, it is crucial for clients, indeed for everyone, to remember that any content posted on a social media site, even back in 2004 when Facebook was first created and the client might have been in college, could come up later during litigation. Therefore, everyone needs to be careful to think before she posts. This does not mean that people should go back and clean up their accounts just because some day they might, by chance, be sued. But it does mean they might want to give some thought to their online reputations due to their past and current postings.

### Admissibility of Social Media Evidence

The standard for admissibility of social media content, in most jurisdictions, is the same as the standard for other types of documents. The lawyer must be able to show relevance and must be able to authenticate. Frequently, due to the unwillingness of social media accounts to cooperate in civil cases, authentication is extremely difficult. As a result, it is critical that lawyers be able to connect the person to ownership of both the account and the specific post(s) she wishes to enter into evidence.

There is not a large amount of case law related to admissibility of social media. As a result, it is necessary to examine both cases on social media and cases on similarly situated content, i.e., text messages, instant messages, and e-mail.

### Traditional Standards

The first step in determining admissibility of social media content is a traditional analysis.

- Is the evidence relevant and not unduly prejudicial?
- Is the evidence hearsay, and if so, does it fall under an exception?

With social media, authentication is an especially difficult problem.

### Relevance and Admissibility

In Pennsylvania, the major case surrounding admissibility and relevance comes from a federal opinion in the Western District, *Newell v. Campbell Transportation Co., Inc.*, No. 2:12-cv-1344 (W.D. Pa. Jan. 14, 2015). In that case, Plaintiff desired to prevent Defendant from introducing Facebook posts, claiming they were irrelevant and unfairly prejudicial. Plaintiff claimed he was physically injured; Defendant desired to show, through the posts, that Plaintiff was engaged in "physically taxing activities."

In determining relevance, the Court noted that content "that reflect[s] physical capabilities inconsistent with plaintiff's claimed injury are relevant" [citing *Giacchetto v. Patchogue-Medfor Union Free Sch. Dist.*, 293 F.R.D. 112, 116 (2013)]. Further, the court noted that while Plaintiff might be "embarrassed by the content of some of his posts, that alone is not a sufficient basis for excluding the posts."

### Authentication

It is difficult to prove who actually owns a social media account, never mind who wrote a specific post. The most appropriate comparison to social media is text messages. Some states will look only to determine if the evidence is what it purports to be, based on circumstantial evidence, to determine whether the content is appropriately admitted. Then the jury will be left to decide whether the person in question actually authored the content.

In *Parker v. Delaware*, the court held "[A] trial judge may admit a relevant social media post where the proponent provides evidence sufficient to support a finding by a reasonable juror that the proffered evidence is what the proponent claims it to be."[72] The case involved a fight between two individuals over some Facebook posts. Parker was charged with assault, and Delaware desired to use Facebook posts that she authored to "discredit Parker's self-defense argument." The posts included a picture of the Defendant, her name, and a time stamp for each entry. The victim shared each of the posts on her own Facebook wall and testified about them as part of the authentication process.

In its analysis, the Delaware Court noted that there are two standards involving admission of social media evidence in the United States, one stricter than the other. It held, after reviewing both standards, that the lower standard utilized by Texas was the appropriate one. The Court noted that although it was "mindful of the concern that social media evi-

---

[72]*Parker v Delaware*, 85 A.3d 682 (Del. 2014).

dence could be falsified, the existing Rules of Evidence provide an appropriate framework for determining admissibility." Therefore, when a party desires to "introduce social media evidence, he or she may use any form of verification available under Rule 901 . . . to authenticate a social media post." In other words, the judge is the gatekeeper and the jury makes the final decision on the matter.

The Texas case *Tienda v. State* used the same concept for authentication as Delaware. In that case, photographs with unusual body tattoos, gang references, and other information, including an e-mail address matching the defendant's, were enough to establish that the Defendant had written the posts in question.[73]

Maryland, on the other hand, adopted a considerably more stringent rule in *Griffin v. State*. In that case, the Court of Appeals held that the social media posts must be proved to have been authored by the individual, i.e., not falsified or created by another person.[74] In *Griffin*, the State sought to authenticate the MySpace postings in question through the testimony of the lead investigator in the case instead of through the alleged owner of the account. The Court was concerned about the ease with which an account could be faked and that a picture of the defendant "coupled with her birth date and location were not sufficient 'distinctive characteristics' on a MySpace profile to authenticate its printout." The court felt that the risks necessitated "a greater degree of authentication." It is important to note that Griffin objected to the MySpace printout, denying responsibility for it. The Court specifically stated that it was not refusing the possibility of admitting social networking content in the future. The Court provided a number of suggestions for authenticating the content. This included:

- ♦ Asking the alleged creator if she owns the profile and created the post
- ♦ Searching the computer to analyze the Internet history and hard drive to connect ownership
- ♦ Seeking evidence from the social media network itself

The *Griffin* court created a very high standard for admissibility. Given this standard, if you desire to admit social media evidence in any jurisdiction that follows the Maryland rule, you will find that it is challenging. In such cases, an admission of ownership and responsibility for the specific

---

[73]*Tienda v. State*, 358 S.W.3d 633 (Tex. Crim. App. Ct. 2012).
[74]*Griffin v. State*, 19 A.3d 415 (Md. 2011).

post on the part of the poster is very important. With an uncooperative witness, the correct questioning *may* elicit the necessary evidence to satisfy a court. In initial questioning, it would be wise to determine whether the alleged poster owns the account, ever allows others to access the account, or allows others to access devices she uses to post to the account.

### Questions for Authentication

Whether during discovery or on the stand, there are a number of questions you can ask to show whether the person against whom you seek to use the posts is the owner of the account and the author of the posts.

1. Do you use social media?
2. What social media sites do you use?
3. Have you shared your passwords to any of these accounts with anyone else? Which? Who? When?
4. How do you access your social media accounts (computer, smartphone, tablet, etc.)?
5. Have you saved your password on any of these devices? For which social media accounts? On which devices?
6. Does anyone else have access to any of these devices? Which? Who? When?
7. Do you use devices belonging to anyone else to access your social media accounts? What? Who? When?
8. To your knowledge, has anyone else logged in to any of your social media accounts? Which? Who? When?
9. To your knowledge, has anyone else posted on any of your social media accounts? Who? When? What did he or she post?
10. Do you use anyone else's social media accounts? Who? When?
11. Have you posted using anyone else's social media account? If so, what did you post?
12. Do you have any social media pages? (As opposed to accounts, these are commonly used for businesses, fan clubs, etc.)
13. Who has the ability to post as the administrator on these pages?
14. Has anyone else posted as an administrator on these pages?
15. Have you posted anything on social media related to this case? What? Where?

### Submitting the Evidence

Commonly, attorneys will print the page containing the content they wish to use as evidence. Another better option is to take a screen shot and share it on a tablet or a laptop. Regardless of methodology, it is necessary to show that the content is a true version of the post or posts.

Assuming the author of the content will not stipulate to ownership, the first step in court is to call to the stand the individual who captured the content and have that person testify that she created the exhibit and recognizes it as the item she printed or captured. As noted, one problem is that it is very easy to manipulate screen shots and so the reliability of the evidence could be at question. Proper preservation of the evidence is critical. Preserving a screen shot and capturing a video of the screen as the witness engages in preserving the content is helpful. This will help both the judge and jury feel more comfortable about the reliability of the preserved information. Independent third-party vendors can also capture the content—the costs for this are generally modest unless a huge amount of data is involved.

### Proving Ownership

As noted from the case law, proving ownership is challenging. The lawyer introducing the evidence must make a sufficient showing to convince the judge, for admission, and the jury, for weight of evidence, that the post can be attributed to the appropriate person. In some jurisdictions, if the defendant refuses to cooperate, it may be extremely difficult to satisfy this requirement. Some of these techniques may not be satisfactory to some courts.

### Admitting Ownership

The easiest way to prove the content can be attributed to the party is by asking. If the owner of the content will admit that he wrote it, no more will be necessary for this step of authentication.

### Denial

It is easy for the owner of a social media account to claim he did not write the post in question: Someone broke into the account, the owner left the account open, the owner left his phone on his desk, and so on. It is also easy for the owner of a social media account to completely deny ownership of an account. In the latter case, many social media sites will cooperate in terms of helping you connect ownership, but numerous steps are required.

Those steps include:

1. Obtain the correct link to the account to provide identification to the social media site.
2. Subpoena ownership information—an e-mail address, an IP address, a username, etc.
3. Connect that information to the account holder.
4. IP address information subpoenaed from Internet service providers to connect the person to the account (if possible)
5. Forensic analysis of computer, phone, tablet

### Forensics

Another option for proving ownership is forensics of a computer belonging to the owner and accessed solely by the owner. This is a more expensive option, and the owner might still claim that he did not write the actual post, but rather, someone else used the device.

### Detective Work

Another method for proving ownership of the account is to go through the account itself and connect the content to the owner. This would mean looking for content that exists elsewhere on the Web, finding writings by the owner both on and off the Web, and comparing all content to the content on the social media account.

### Posting Style

An analysis of the posting style of the owner is a way to establish that he did, in fact, write the post. Analysis of posting style means taking other posts and showing that the style of the content in question is the same, taken in the totality of the circumstances.

### Context

As noted, some courts are willing to use context as proof that the person actually wrote the content. For example, Pennsylvania allowed letters to be authenticated by the contents due to the fact that they contained facts known only to the sender and the recipient [citing *Commonwealth v. Brooks*, 352 Pa. Super. 394 (1927)]. One assumes then that if a Facebook post has content known only to the witness, then that is extremely helpful in terms of proving that the witness actually wrote the content.

### *Discovery*

It is best, if possible, to circumvent the authentication problem by addressing it during discovery, at least in civil cases. Lock the other party into identifying his social media account, acknowledging that no one else uses it, and agreeing that he wrote a specific post.

### *Conclusion*

Proving ownership when the witness denies it can be challenging. If the party seeking to admit the evidence cannot obtain an admission and cannot prove that the owner posted the content through circumstantial evidence, it will not be possible to authenticate it. However, the standard in many other states for authentication is low, and circumstantial evidence will be enough for many states.

## *Other Issues: Judges and Juries*

### Judges

Many judges enjoy having an online presence as well. This has led to questions over whether judges should be friends with attorneys and what should happen if a judge is a friend with a defendant.

In attempting to resolve the first issue, the Florida Supreme Court Judicial Ethics Advisory Committee determined that judges may not be friends on Facebook with attorneys who appear before them.[75] In turn, a defendant sought to disqualify a judge based on his Facebook friendship with the prosecutor. The trial judge denied the request, but upon appeal, the motion was granted. The court held that the Facebook friendship "conveys the impression that the lawyer is in a position to influence the judge."[76] Ohio came down on the other side, noting that it is acceptable for judges to friend lawyers who appear before them. However, the judges must comport themselves properly, follow all ethical rules, and be careful to disqualify themselves should the online friendship cause a bias.[77]

Other states have seen issues arise when the judge learns he is Facebook friends with a defendant. Two cases occurred in Pennsylvania. In the first

---

[75]Florida Supreme Court Judicial Ethics Advisory Committee, Opinion Number 2009-20 (November 17, 2009).

[76]*Domville v. State*, No. 4D12-556 (Fla. 4th DCA 2012).

[77]Supreme Court of Ohio Disciplinary Board, Advisory Opinion: Judges May 'Friend' 'Tweet' if Proper Caution Exercised (December 8, 2010).

case, the judge was asked to recuse himself, and eventually did so when it turned out he knew the defendant's father. He was, however, unaware of the Facebook friendship prior to being alerted to it. Like many people, the judge simply friended anyone who asked and thought nothing of it.[78] Another controversy arose when a judge suppressed evidence against a defendant, resulting in dismissal of the case. After the fact, the prosecution realized that the judge was Facebook friends with the defendant, although the defendant and the judge did not know each other. The prosecutor asked the judge to reverse the suppression and recuse himself. The judge decided not to recuse himself due to concern about setting a dangerous precedent.[79] Pennsylvania Bar Association Formal Opinion 2014-300 made it clear that it is acceptable for lawyers to friend judges and vice versa as long as there is no intent to influence the judge improperly.

On February 21, 2013, the American Bar Association released Formal Opinion 462, Judge's Use of Electronic Social Networking Media. It offers a new acronym, ESM, meaning electronic social media. Judges are allowed to participate in ESM so long as they "comply with the relevant provisions of the Code of Judicial Conduct and avoid any conduct that would undermine the judge's independence, integrity or impartiality, or create an appearance of impropriety."

In the end, the best advice for judges is that they be careful and aware of whom they friend. Friending everyone is not a good idea for a judge, since it is easy enough, as shown above, for the judge to end up being friends with a defendant and to be completely unaware of their online relationship. Judges who have many friends on social media sites might want to take a look at who those friends are and determine whether they should remain friends. On the other hand, judges who prefer to have many friends online might find it wise to be certain they know who those friends are and at the least make both sides aware of the Facebook friendship prior to the trial beginning. If necessary, perhaps the judge could have a clerk make a quick check of the judge's account to make certain that the judge is not friends with defendants who appear before him.

---

[78]Sara Ganim, "Cumberland County Judge Thomas A. Placey under Fire for Having Too Many Facebook Friends," 2011, **www.pennlive.com/midstate/index.ssf/2011/09/judges_facebook_ friend_has_som.html**.
[79]"Judge Refuses to Recuse Himself from Parker DUI Case, State Plans an Appeal," 2011, **www.newsworks.org/index.php/neighborhoods/mt-airychestnut-hill-/item/30248-hayden-denial-story-**.

## Jurors

These days it is extremely common to look at the seats behind the prosecution, plaintiff, or defense and see individuals hard at work on their computers during the voir dire process.[80] This is because jurors, like almost everyone else, provide an immense amount of information about themselves online. Some of this information might well disqualify an individual from serving on a jury or simply show a particular side that it would be unwise to seat a potential juror.

While there are currently no conclusive decisions on the issue of researching jurors via social media, there is guidance on the subject.[81] A New York opinion, quite reasonably, makes it clear that it is acceptable to research jurors online, including viewing their social media accounts under several conditions. First, the accounts must be accessed appropriately, i.e., only looking at accounts and information that have been left freely accessible by the jurors. Also, it remains impermissible to communicate with the jurors in any fashion. That means no friending (or having a third-party friend) a juror in order to obtain access to the private sections of an account.[82] However, the American Bar Association does not bar visiting the public portions of a site even if it makes the juror aware that an attorney looked at a profile. Such contact might include using LinkedIn to look at a juror's profile. Unless set properly, LinkedIn will show the name of a person who looks at a profile, under certain circumstances. Pennsylvania's social media guidance opinion supports the opinions of other states related to researching jurors on social media. The Pennsylvania Bar Association deems such conduct acceptable.[83]

Of late, jurors have been engaging in social media or other Internet use that has caused serious trouble for the court system. Judges, prosecutors, and defense attorneys frequently find themselves throwing their hands up in the air due to the frustration caused by jurors who refuse to follow the instructions. While it might seem beyond belief that a juror would choose to engage in social media discussion or Internet research after being specifically told not to do so, the reality is that they do.[84] In

---

[80]Michael Cary, "Lawyers in Murray Trial Using Facebook, Twitter to Screen Jurors," 2011, **www.cnn.com/2011/09/20/tech/social-media/social-media-jurors-murray/**.

[81]NYCLA Committee on Professional Ethics, Formal Opinion 743 (May 18, 2011).

[82]The American Bar Association Standing Committee on Ethics and Professional Responsibility released an opinion, Lawyer Reviewing Jurors' Internet Presence, Formal Opinion 466, 2014, which agrees with previously stated guidelines from other states.

[83]Formal Opinion 2014-300.

[84]Social Media's Clout Worries Legal System, 2012, **http://www.digtriad.com/news/article/245301/175/Social-Medias-Clout-Worries-Legal-System**.

response to juror behavior, many judges and court systems are developing instructions to provide to jurors to warn them against social media use. For example, the Judicial Conference Committee on Court Administration and Case Management recently created "Proposed Model Jury Instructions [on] The Use of Electronic Technology to Conduct Research on or Communicate about a Case."[85] Regardless of the language, it is crucial that judges warn the jury right at the outset of a case of the serious ramifications, and potential punishments, for violating court orders on use of social media during a trial.

## Conclusion

Understanding how the public uses social media is important for attorneys so that they can appreciate the types of evidence they might find online to help their cases and they can appropriately warn their clients about social media use. Knowing the benefits and risks of social media in terms of networking and marketing can help an attorney grow her firm without harming her hard-earned reputation through the use of improper online activities. Being aware of how judges and juries use social media and how that use might affect a case is important, so attorneys can be prepared to respond accordingly.

There is no doubt that social media can be a serious minefield in terms of day-to-day practice and ethical requirements. On the other hand, the substantial benefits available in terms of evidence, research, marketing, and networking cannot be overstated. With the number of people using social media increasing every day, social media will continue to impact the legal profession in every imaginable way, and perhaps some unimaginable ways too. As a result, it is crucial for attorneys to embrace the technology and determine how they can use it both in their practice of law and in their efforts to grow their client base.

---

[85]Proposed Model Jury Instructions: The Use of Electronic Technology to Conduct Research or Communicate about a Case, 2012, **http://www.uscourts.gov/file/3159/download**.

# CHAPTER TWENTY-EIGHT

# Taking Your Firm Paperless

### by David J. Bilinsky, BSc, LLB, MBA

## Introduction

"Tame the wild paper beast and transition to paperless with ease." Well, at least that is the plan. But this lofty and somewhat innocent statement brings back the saying—that it is hard to remember that your objective was to drain the swamp when you are surrounded by snapping alligators or at least lawyers waving around their paper files, saying something about only being able to pull them out from their cold dead hands. . . .

But the transition to paperless does not have to be a troubled and drama-filled exercise either. You can shift to paperless—indeed many law offices already have—with a minimum of fuss and disruption. With most technology projects—moving to paperless being no exception—the greatest hurdles are not technological at all. They are the human-based—getting everyone on board, dealing with the passive-resistors, dealing with those who feel threatened by the introduction of new ways of doing things, and the like. As I say in my presentations, it is the carbon-based units that pose the greatest hurdles, not the silicone-based ones.

This highlights that there are several aspects to going paperless. Certainly part of the process is examining your technology and putting into place a well-thought-out strategic technology plan that will ensure that all parts

---

© 2015 David J. Bilinsky. This chapter was originally based on a paper created for and presented at ABA TECHSHOW 2012 on taming the paper beast. It has been extensively updated, added to, and modified since its original publication.

of the system are robust and can handle the load—and the lofty expectations—that will be placed on them.

So in this chapter, we—you and I—will focus on how best to manage your shift to paperless and ensure you have considered all aspects of your new paperless office before making the jump. I think it is important to put in as much time to planning as you can—as anticipating problems and knowing how to deal with them is much better than having them land on your desk unexpectedly in the midst of the change.

We will also discuss the various procedures you will want to introduce, such as scanning, OCR(Optical Character Recognition), document management, and the emerging mobile and cloud-based practice of law. Security and good off-site backups are essential. Before you start, you need to evaluate your hardware and software and, in so doing, determine what needs upgrading. You need to make all necessary upgrades to your hardware, install all software, and test the systems before starting to go paperless.

Then . . . taking that first deep breath . . . begin with your most receptive lawyer and legal assistant . . . and have them pilot the system. Having done all your homework, planning, upgrading, and piloting, you soon will soon see that flying paperless is not half the challenge you thought it might be . . . and soon the whole office will be there.

So let's take that first step toward your future.

## Transitioning to Paperless: It Isn't (All) about the Technology (Really!)

I have spoken to and consulted with many lawyers and law firms that have called about taking their law firms paperless. Certainly, there is much anxiety exhibited about giving up on paper and practicing in a paper-*less* world (although there will probably never be a situation where we fully abandon paper). Yet lawyers (and staff) express many misapprehensions about going paperless, part of which is rooted in a concern that *somewhere* the regulations of practice *require* firms to keep paper files. There is, of course, no such specific requirement. Information is information, and the medium that it is stored on is largely irrelevant so long as you can meet the requirements of practice. (There are exceptions, such as original wills and such, but even these are changing as new enabling legislation comes into effect.)

The typical concerns that I hear can be summed up as follows:

♦ There is no paper trail.

♦ Computers can go down.

♦ No backup exists.

♦ You can be hacked.

♦ Data obsolescence is a factor.

♦ Media degradation is a factor.

♦ You can lose an e-document.

♦ There is no structure to the documents on the system.

♦ Documents can be sent outside the office easily.

♦ Changes are required to policies, procedures, and work routines.

♦ There will be increased time costs, including costs of running dual systems.

♦ There is a possibility of job elimination or reassignment.

♦ A lack of training could lead to a loss of face in not knowing how to work the new system.

♦ The firm would face increased costs of transferring a file.

♦ What about all the transition issues?

♦ How do we go from here to there?

♦ What about increased hardware and software costs?

♦ What do we do with the original documents?

The requirement in any paperless office would be that the office could produce a full and complete record of the client's file (and render this to paper, CD-ROM, DVD, or flash drive or upload to a cloud service if required). So long as you have a *complete* record of the file (which is organized in a manner that the whole file could be reviewed and produced if necessary), which would necessarily include documenting all transactions and the client instructions in relation thereto, it should not matter on what type of media that file is stored. (Indeed, ethics rulings have been consistent in holding that transferring a file electronically is acceptable in many jurisdictions and in fact may offer greater utility than printing up and transferring a paper file.) The important considerations are that the file be well organized; be in a common format that, if necessary, someone could review; and reflects the level of documentation expected in a well-run law office. If this is met, I submit that it should not matter on what media (paper or electronic) the file is stored or transferred.

Of course, there are also many benefits of going paperless:

♦ You can search the entire network (and file) easily and quickly, particularly compared to paper files.

♦ You can reuse documents easily and thereby craft a precedent library (and build on the knowledge transfer within the firm).

♦ Document management software imposes greater organization as compared to a paper-based office where documents can be left in piles on desks, cabinets, and floors.

♦ The cost of electronic storage is MUCH less compared to paper storage.

♦ Paperless offices enable remote access/telecommuting for full- and part-time lawyers and staff.

♦ Paperless offices are greener.

♦ Paperless systems can integrate and share data, thereby saving time and money.

♦ The cost of handling files can be faster, cheaper, and easier.

♦ Offices are neater.

♦ There is an increased ability to meet new clients' needs (via Share-Point and other extranet portals, for example). At a recent Corporate Counsel meeting, counsel stated that they *preferred* electronic war and closing rooms or portals over e-mailing documents around. You can control access, distribution and versioning, and more importantly, these documents do not travel on (unsecured) e-mail systems.

♦ There is usually a decrease in photocopy/printing costs.

♦ Courts, land title offices, and other organizations and tribunals are increasingly accepting paperless filings in many jurisdictions.

♦ It is harder to forge or alter a properly secured electronic document. Moreover, metadata associated with an e-document records a great deal of information about who created it and when and by whom it was modified that is not typically accessible in a paper file.

♦ Your clients' systems are electronic, and they expect lawyers to be able to accept and use e-discovery documents.

♦ Having a paperless office requires the firm to at least consider a file retention and destruction policy that is consistently applied in accordance with The Sedona Principles (Canada or United States) and current case law and ethics rulings to avoid any suggestion that files were destroyed in order to eliminate evidence.

- The Courts are calling on lawyers to be paperless in court. (See Justices Turnball's and Granger's posts to this effect at **www.slaw.ca**.)

Of course there are many other reasons to go paperless (as well as arguments against it). However, there is no denying that the world is moving in a paperless direction. Barker, Cobb, and Karcher, back in a 2008 publication entitled "The legal implications of electronic document retention: Changing the rules", stated that 99 percent of business documents are currently being produced electronically. At this juncture, it is pointless going against the tide; lawyers need to adjust to the new reality, embrace the possibilities, and examine the risks and benefits in moving to a paperless world. We are headed for a new horizon.

## Assessing Your Office Procedures and People: How Suited Are They to Going Paperless?

Moving to paperless means having to examine the workflows in the office and deciding how they should be changed to maximize the investment that you are making in the paperless world. Your handling of paper must change, as does how you save, store, find, and archive documents. Furthermore, you now must put an increasing amount of attention to security and backup procedures and the like. The one thing that you want to avoid is carrying the costs of dual systems; this provides you with no advantages and only additional costs. Before you embark on going paperless, you should consider your staff (lawyers and others) to determine if you anticipate difficulties with those who will resist the change and cling to the old systems. This aspect of change management will be dealt with in greater depth herein, but being frank in your analysis and being prepared to deal with these difficulties early in the process will be a key consideration in your transition to paperless.

Here are some of the considerations with regard to office policies and procedures.

### Document Naming and Filing

If you go with a DMS—a software document management system (such as Worldox; NetDocuments; DocsOpen; Amicus Cloud with its new document management features; other similar cloud-based legal practice management applications with document management incorporated therein; or even PCLaw, which has a document manager)—the DMS should ensure that no document is saved onto the network without being "profiled." This means the author has told the system the metadata that the DMS needs in order that everyone in the office could find the document if they searched for it (such metadata as author, client, lawyers, file, date created, version, etc.).

Document management software has literally exploded. This web page lists over 387 different applications: **www.capterra.com/document-management-software/**. Most are not legal-specific, and accordingly, selecting the right DMS can be a bit of a challenge when you consider the specific legal, ethical, and business needs of law firms.

However, not all firms elect to acquire DMS software, which then means that they have to implement a file naming and folder convention that, if followed, will allow the document to be stored (and hopefully found) in the correct location. And here is the rub: If you have people or even *just one* person who doesn't follow the convention, the system will fall apart. It is this one factor alone that drives firms to a DMS. They need a "traffic cop" who ensures that everyone acts appropriately and doesn't break the rules. The DMS becomes their "traffic cop."

Common naming and folder conventions use some variation of date (usually year month date in the format of 2015 08 21 for August 21, 2015), nature of the document (LTR for letter, PLD for pleading, etc.), and description of the document (2015 08 21 LTR to john smith on offer to settle, for example).

A common folder structure is used for files that separate electronic documents into subfolders in the same way that a "bucket" folder is separated into pleadings, correspondence, research, etc.

Combining a good folder structure with a good file naming convention can go a long way toward electronic file organization—provided, of course, that everyone plays by the rules.

## Converting Paper Documents to PDF

Paper is not going to go away anytime soon. Accordingly, all paperless firms need a policy on how paper documents are to be converted into electronic files and in what format. The most common format is Adobe Acrobat's PDF (or PDF/A for archive).

I know that many firms like the PDF/A format, as it is an ISO standard, and this should ensure that the files can be opened and read years into the future. However, I dislike how PDF/A removes data from the document, such as images and the like. Personally, I prefer to use the ordinary PDF format and keep all the data in the document—and hope for the best in terms of being able to open and read documents into the foreseeable future.

This raises another issue, and that is whether to use Adobe Acrobat or some other application to convert your documents to the PDF format for storage purposes. TopTenReviews has evaluated the top PDF applications for 2015. Its analysis and suggestions on selecting a PDF application can be found at convert-pdf-software-review.toptenreviews.com.

So typically firms go one of two routes when handling paper in a paperless firm: (1) They have tasked specific people with the job of taking all incoming paper and scanning it (centralized scanning on a large networked scanner/printer). (2) It is left to each person in the firm (distributed scanning on smaller scanners). There are advantages and disadvantages to both.

Centralized scanning ensures that documents are handled in a businesslike and consistent manner and that there is a degree of quality control to ensure that the scans were done correctly (for example, scans should always be dual layer, incorporating the image of the document along with OCR, or Optical Character Recognition of the text in the image, that allows the computer to search the words in the document). Distributed scanning means that you have smaller scanners scattered around the office and that everyone is responsible for ensuring that the scans were done correctly.

## Document Retention

You will also need a policy for how long to keep the original documents before shredding. A story from one firm that went paperless had a legal secretary come to the principal of the firm and confess she had taken home and stored every single document for the last three years as she was convinced the system would fail and she would have to re-create all the files. Her basement became stuffed with documents, and the originals were never needed.

Typically, three to six months should be sufficient time to catch any scanning errors before the documents are shredded.

Of course, you will need a storage policy for documents that should never be shredded, such as original wills and government documents. These can be scanned (of course!) but the originals need to be retained for evidentiary or other purposes.

## Backups and Archives

If you put all your eggs in one electronic basket, there is a consequential rule that says you should watch that basket very, very carefully. Accordingly, you need to ensure that copies of your electronic data are made and that this data is stored in at least two locations—one on a hardened hard drive (such as the ioSafe line of hard drives that are designed to withstand fire, flood, temperatures, immersion, etc., for extended periods of time) and another on a cloud storage system.

Many firms that the writer has spoken to have been hit with the CryptoLocker malware. This application encrypts everything it can find on your network and demands a ransom to be paid; otherwise, it disappears, taking the decryption algorithm with it and leaving your data useless. In one case, fortunately, the firm's cloud backup, which only backed up on a schedule and was not continually connected to the network, was left untouched by the malware, and the firm was able restore its data without paying the ransom. This is perhaps one of the best arguments for backing your data up into a secure cloud backup that can remain isolated from malware attacks such as the CryptoLocker and CryptoWall ransomware and their unending progeny.

It is important that you have a multiple-layer redundant backup system. Don't depend on a sole backup system. If that backup fails, you are left totally vulnerable. It is important to test your backup system and ensure that it is operating properly so that you can restore your data as needed. I have seen situations where the sole backup system *seemed to be functioning fine* until the time came when it was needed. Then the realization hit that the backup was corrupted and useless. In one such case, what had been backed up to Dropbox was recovered, but all other data was lost.

The benefit of having a local hardened hard drive backup is that you can restore your data *quickly* in the event of a loss. Cloud backups, although wonderful for preserving your data in a safe location, will take considerable time to restore onto your network since you are limited by your download speeds. However, if your system is hit with a system-wide problem such as CryptoLocker malware, a flood, fire, or another disaster or a failure of your primary backup, you will be thanking your lucky stars for having a complete cloud backup no matter how long it takes to do the restore. Believe me, I have had to restore data from the cloud after a system-wide failure. A fast Internet connection can never be fast enough when time is money. But ultimately, having a cloud backup made the difference between sheer inconvenience and absolute disaster.

### File Retention and Destruction

You should check with your local bar association and/or insurer to see what requirements and/or recommendations they put forward for file retention and eventual destruction of closed files. Certainly follow their guidelines when setting up your retention and destruction policies. You should also ensure that you follow these policies to be able to demonstrate that you destroyed data pursuant to a written office policy that was consistently and clearly followed to avoid any allegations of spoliation of data.

### Knowledge Management

The ability to start developing a consistent set of precedents, library of research memos, and resources is one of the benefits of a paperless office, particularly if you incorporate a DMS that can search system-wide for work product that you can reuse. Whether you adopt a DMS or not, give some thought to how you can take documents from files and convert them to office precedents or templates (by removing names and other identifying information) and storing them in an organized template (or rescarch) collection. Once you start along this path, you will quickly see how you can add in articles, books, and other resources to create your own library that supports your area(s) of practice. Consider acquiring one of the numerous systems such as Pathagoras, HotDocs, The Form Tool, or another document automation systems to systematize and speed up your ability to convert existing documents into precedents or templates.

## Begin with the End in Mind: Defining the Goal(s)

Stephen Covey, the esteemed author of *The 7 Habits of Highly Effective People*, has stated that you should "Begin with the End in Mind." So how do you build your plan to take yourself paperless? What are the goal(s) of the move to paperless? Here are some of the components to consider:

1. Decide on what your paperless office will look and feel like (the "VISION"). It is important to work out your vision for how the system will look and work before you start building it. Will you

aim to eliminate paper as much as possible? Will everyone be working on workstations with dual monitors, using a central document repository (using a document management system, or DMS) with remote access capability and client portals? By writing down your goals (as many as possible), you can make the transition real and decide how to stage the transition to paperless over time. Moreover, you can visualize your system and thereby make the cost/benefit decisions that are so important in any system design and change management process.

2. Commit to going paperless. Call your staff to a meeting and explain the advantages for each of them individually and as a group. Fully involve them in the process, particularly in drafting the Vision, and invite them to raise their concerns now while you are at a planning stage. Ask for their support and commitment to a successful transition. It will be your job as team leader to communicate the Vision, discuss the benefits of the paperless system, and explain why the cooperation of everyone is central to realizing the benefits of the new paperless system.

3. Call in your IT support as early as possible and involve them in the plan from the get-go. They will have to check your existing computer hardware, including your server, backup, and RAID systems to make sure they can handle the increased load from all paperless applications (hardware and software requirements). They will have to ensure that you have a reliable backup system (including storage off-site). They will need to make sure the software and hardware will run quickly and effectively. For them to do this, there are many things for them to check, such as adequate bandwidth from the Internet connection in order that people are not (frustratingly) waiting for the system and that you have effective security in place, etc. There are many technical issues that will need to be thought about and addressed, and having your IT team think these through in advance will save you countless hours down the road. Listen to them carefully when they raise potential issues.

4. Analyze your needs—now and in the future. Think about what you're likely to need in the future as your business grows as well as your current needs. Think about which documents need to be accessed often or quickly, which may need extra security or encryption, and which could be weeded out after a certain time. After all, you don't want to be storing all documents forever, but

you do have requirements for document storage and retention times from your ethics regulator or insurer (or both). For example, you may need the ability to build an electronic "ethical wall" to isolate lawyers and staff from certain files; you will want that ability before the need for such a wall arises, where the absence of same could potentially jeopardize your ability to keep a client.

5. Develop a paperless transition plan and a timetable. The timetable should be tight enough to keep everyone on line but not so tight so that it doesn't allow for reasonable adjustments and setbacks. Plan to be flexible! Writing down the plan allows for everyone to read and think about it and to provide feedback on the process, the goals, and the methods. You wish to make this as painless for everyone as possible, and listening to their feedback will make everyone feel part of the process and help them feel as though they have a part in the plan.

6. Start small. Use a single lawyer and legal assistant who are both keen on the project to start. Learn from the pilot project so that you can address any problems before broadening your scope. It is easy to correct small things at the pilot stage before they become much bigger things in a firm-wide rollout. Try, listen, and learn from the experience of your most enthusiastic adopters as you expand your scope to remove or reduce any difficulties. Your detractors (and there will be those) will seize on any setbacks as an example that the system is bound to fail, so try to reduce the chances of these happening.

7. Do a thorough investigation of the available tools to help you (document management systems, electronic faxing, scanners, data backup systems, security systems, document conversion companies, process consultants, storage formats, storage devices, remote access devices, etc.). Knowledgeable consultants can help you out a lot here!! Get references of other law firms that have adapted each recommended product and do your due diligence!

8. Develop a budget. This is required! Select your needs in advance (hardware, software, training and installation, consultants) and arrange to incorporate these into your budget and into your business plans. You may have to spread things out a bit to accommodate everything in the budget, perhaps over a couple of years. For software, consider what will fit with your needs, including ease of use and implementation, cost, and integration

with your existing systems. Don't neglect backup needs to keep electronic data from being lost! Also consider both present and forecast needs; you don't want to find yourself constrained as you grow!

9. Do a small test project. Make any needed changes and then move to the transition into the rest of the practice, using your early adopters as change agents. This is most important.

10. Develop a plan for ongoing practice-wide use. Include a document storage plan for employees who have specific guidelines or clients who have specific needs.

11. Consider creating a client portal where clients can view their file documents online without using e-mail. This is one of the benefits of going paperless!

12. Do a celebration followed by a post-mortem. Learn from the experience!

## A Bit about the Hardware That You Will Need

When there was no alternative to paper, the costs of building and maintaining a paper-based filing system were simply taken for granted. Rows of filing cabinets along with physical storage, associated filing clerks, photocopiers, and fax machines all had to be purchased and maintained and took up (expensive) rented floor space. The environmental effects of having to manufacture all that paper had a cost as well—from deforestation to consumption of fossil fuels and electricity to the space in landfill sites used for unwanted documents.

According to IBM ["What Is Big Data?" (**www-01.ibm.com/software/in/ data/bigdata/**)], as of 2012, every day 2.5 exabytes ($2.5 \times 10^{18}$) of data were created. One Exabyte is 1 billion gigabytes. To put this in perspective, according to Wikipedia: "Earlier studies from the University of California, Berkeley, estimated that by the end of 1999, the sum of human-produced information (including all audio, video recordings, and text/books) was about 12 exabytes of data. [Juan Enriquez. (Fall–Winter 2003). "The Data That Defines Us." *CIO* magazine.]

With that volume of information being created electronically, it is apparent that new ways of storing, searching, sharing, annotating, signing, retrieving, and eventually destroying information had to be found. In the context of a law office, we will be increasingly under pressure to deal with all kinds of electronic records (for litigation discovery requirements and the results of forensic audits of hard drives, smartphones, and other devices, for example). This is where the paperless office reaches its potential since we will be building systems and procedures to move us into the paperless world and help us deal with the ever-increasing amount of digital information.

There is another consideration in moving to paperless, at least in a litigation context. Being able to handle digital discovery means that you will have the capacity to examine the metadata that should come with e-discovery. Oftentimes is the metadata about data that is vitally important. For example, in a murder investigation, knowing from what narrow geographic location a text or an e-mail message was sent may be important in being able to tie someone to a specific location at a specific time. Without the metadata associated with that text or e-mail, this bit of evidence would not be available.

So with this as background, what do we need in terms of software and hardware to implement a paperless office?

### Hardware

While it is always fortunate where you find that an office's hardware infrastructure is sufficient to implement a paperless system, in most cases, that is not the case. If you host your own servers and network switches, chances are that they will require an upgrade to handle the increased load that a paperless office will place on them. If you have implemented a hosted office (where you use remote file servers that are on a third party's platform), then you may need to increase your storage and Internet bandwidth capacity to handle the load.

Furthermore, you will have to ensure that the network cards in workstations are sufficiently fast (1000 Base T would be the preferred speed). Switches should be capable of handling gigabyte speeds, as should the cabling connecting all parts of the system. Existing processors may not have the capacity to realistically run the increased load of being paperless or be capable of being upgraded to current standards. For example, there are lawyers who are still running Windows XP machines notwithstanding that Microsoft has withdrawn support for XP and these machines are increasingly vulnerable to malware in addition to being outdated and slow.

Basically, upgrading to paperless should not be undertaken without budgeting for an upgrade of your hardware, particularly if you have not refreshed your computers within the last three years (at a minimum, at least in the writer's experience).

## Servers

You will need, at a minimum, a dedicated server running up-to-date server software (such as a Windows Server operating system or a Mac server if you are in an Apple environment). A server will allow all your files to be kept and indexed in one place and allow your documents to be organized and efficient. A server can manage which users access what resources. Your server setup should be sufficient to handle your DMS (your document management system) as well as host your website, e-mail system, print server software, databases, and accounting software, as well as allow remote access and more. You can see that you are placing a large load on your server infrastructure, and as such, it is essential to check that your server setup will be able to handle the load of going to paperless. This is why you involve your IT support at an early stage as they should be able to advise you on any necessary upgrades to your server infrastructure to support your desired paperless system.

According to *PC Magazine*, the top-rated servers as of August 2015 were as follows:

- HP ProLiant MicroServer Gen8
- HP Proliant DL380p Gen8 Server
- Dell PowerEdge R420
- Dell PowerEdge T620
- Dell PowerEdge T110 II
- Dell PowerEdge R515
- Lenovo ThinkServer TS200v
- Apple Mac mini with Snow Leopard Server
- Asus Server TS500-E6/P4
- HP Proliant ML330 G6
- Apple Xserve
- HP ProLiant DL380 G5
- Silex SecurePrint
- DiskSites FilePort DS-100, DiskSites FileController DS-100
- Aberdeen Stonehaven A261S

Similarly, CRN's Test Center lists its top 10 servers at **www.crn.com/ reviews/crn-test-center-top-10-server-reviews.htm**.

**#1: <u>Dell PowerEdge R720</u>**
**Geekbench high score:** 40250
**Processor:** Intel Xeon E5-2680 (2)
**Frequency (GHz):** 2.70
**Total Cores:** 16
**Memory:** 128 GB
**IOps:** 311,000

**#2: <u>Lenovo ThinkServer RD630</u>**
**Geekbench high score:** 39612
**Processor:** Intel Xeon E5 2690 (2)
**Frequency (GHz):** 2.9
**Total Cores:** 16
**Memory:** 128 GB
**IOps:** 241,000
**MBps:** 740

**#3: <u>HP Proliant DL380p (8th gen)</u>**
**Geekbench high score:** 36295
**Processor:** Intel Xeon E5 2690 (2)
**Frequency (GHz):** 2.90
**Total Cores:** 16

**#4: <u>ION SR-71mach4 SpeedServer</u>**
**Geekbench high score:** 35804
**Processor:** Intel Xeon 2690 v2 (2)
**Frequency (GHz):** 3.0
**Total Cores:** 20
**Memory:** 64 GB
**IOps:** 1,124,172

**#5: <u>HP Proliant DL360p (9th gen)</u>**
**Geekbench high score:** 33336
**Processor:** Intel Xeon E5-2697 v3 (2)
**Frequency (GHz):** 2.60
**Total Cores:** 28
**Memory:** 64 GB
**IOps:** 1891186
**MBps:** 2,640

**#6: <u>Supermicro SYS-2027R-72RFTP+</u>**
**Geekbench high score:** 34298
**Processor:** Intel Xeon E5 2690 v2 (2)
**Frequency (GHz):** 3.0
**Total Cores:** 20
**Memory:** 64 GB

**#7:**  **Dell PowerEdge R730**
**Geekbench high score:** 25161
**Processor:** Intel Xeon E5 2690 v3 (2)
**Frequency (GHz):** 2.60
**Total Cores:** 24
**Memory:** 64 GB
**IOps:** 530,108
**MBps:** 2,014

**#8:**  **Intel EPSD Grizzly Pass**
**Geekbench high score:** 23766

**#9:**  **Dell PowerEdge VRTX M620 Blade Server**
**Geekbench high score:** 22970
**Processor:** Intel Xeon E5-2650 (2)
**Frequency (GHz):** 2.0
**Total Cores:** 24
**Memory:** 96 GB
**IOps:** 151,460
**MBps:** 175

**#10:**  **Dell PowerEdge C6145**
**Geekbench high score:** 22607
**IOps:** 21,606

What should you look for when purchasing a server?

♦ **Scability/Price:** Needless to say, you get what you pay for. A lower-end server may be fine for current needs, but if your needs grow (you add additional people and/or your volume of information grows), then you may exceed the storage capacity of the server (which is supposed to store all the paperless documents on your system). Accordingly, look for a server that can have additional drives installed and has fault tolerance built in (RAID is the measure of fault tolerance—"Redundant Array of Independent Disks"— meaning that if one drive fails, the other drives have copies of the data that was stored on the failed drive and can take over handling the load until you replace the failed drive). If possible, look for a server that has at least a RAID 5 (or even better, 6 level, which has tolerance for up to two failed drives).

♦ **Degree of Use:** Servers typically come in different configurations. Try to anticipate the volume of transactions that you will process on any day and purchase a server that can easily handle that volume. That way, you avoid delays in waiting for information. Your IT person should be able to assist you with deciding which configuration would be best for you.

♦ **Scalability:** Look for the ability to add memory upgrades and hard drive upgrades and a server with a sufficiently fast processor that can handle the increased load.

♦ **Virtualization:** Many organizations have moved to running virtual machines housed in one physical server. There are many advantages to this, not the least of which are energy savings, smaller data centers, almost instant capacity increases, increased uptime, improved disaster recovery, isolated applications, the ability to run legacy applications, and the capacity to prepare your office to move documents to the cloud. If possible, look to build your paperless system in a virtualized server environment.

♦ **IT Support:** If you have an experienced IT person to manage your network, great. But if you largely have to do it yourself, then at least get a server that is easy to administer. Also ensure that you have reliable and competent IT support who can respond to problems quickly in order that you don't end up with down time, which only costs you money (and potentially places you at risks for missing important dates and filing deadlines if your system goes down).

♦ **Server Matched to Your Environment:** If you run Windows machines, then acquire a Windows server and software. While you can marry Macs to Windows networks, you will be increasing the complexity of your system. The same is true with Mac-based networks. Make life easy for yourself!

♦ **Form Factor:** If at all possible, look for a rack-mounted server with a large number of drive bays that is expandable. Consider airflow, temperature, noise level, and fan quality (overheating is a common factor in crashes) in the location that will house your server setup.

♦ **Memory:** Again, the ability to add memory (RAM) is important as needs increase.

♦ **Network Speed:** You will need multiple ports on the server as well as a GigE network switch or switches. The slower your network, the more time spent waiting. Accordingly, have network switches connect all your devices that support GigE speeds.

♦ **Cabling:** Ensure that all devices on your network are connected with Cat 5 or preferably Cat 6 network cabling and that all devices have Gigabyte networking cards installed.

♦ **Operating System:** Is it included in the price of the server? Is it a standard server system? Look for an up-to-date Mac or Windows operating system.

♦ **Power:** You will need a UPS, an uninterruptable power supply, that will allow for the orderly shut-down of your system in the event of a power failure to avoid data loss and corruption.

♦ **Drives:** Your server should have a drive (CD/DVD/Blu-ray) to allow you to install software. Of course, these days, you only really need a USB drive since less and less software is being provided on optical disks.

## Hard Drive Storage

Today, you can have solid-state storage or traditional hard drives. Traditional hard drives have higher capacity but solid-state drives (SSDs) are typically much faster. The downside to SSDs is that they fail without warning, taking your data with them. Whichever media you choose, buy as much as you can afford—you will not regret having large storage capacity! Always ensure that your networked drives and networked devices have a robust backup system to avoid any data loss when, not if, a hard drive crashes.

## Scanners

There are two camps when it comes to scanners. A scanner (or multiple scanners) is necessary to take paper documents and transform them into electronic documents that can be brought into MS Word or converted to PDF formats (preferably both). On one hand, there are firms that have one large networked printer/scanner with a good sheet feeder than can handle large print/scan jobs. Other firms have gone to small individual scanners such as the Fujitsu Scansnap iX1500s or the older S1500s that are scattered around the office. Whichever route you go depends on how big your office is, what volume of paper you will need to scan, whether you will have dedicated staff for scanning, how your office is laid out and con-figured, and whether it will be a trek to find a scanner. The latest iX1500s can work with both Macs and PCs and have some significant improve-ments over prior versions, such as Wi-Fi scanning. They also come bun-dled with software that makes them very cost effective, such as Adobe X Standard for PCs (see **http://solutions.ca.fujitsu.com/products/ scansnap/ix500/**).

Features to look for:

♦ Reliability (the Fujitsu's reputation is awesome), whether there is a sheet feeder, and whether it can take legal-sized documents as well as business cards.

♦ Flatbed scanners can be slower but can take various-sized documents.

♦ Output: It is most desirable if you can directly select OCR'd PDF format (which scans the document into a dual-layer PDF and allows you to search the document as it recognizes words in a separate layer as opposed to a single-layer PDF, which is equivalent to a photograph image only).

♦ TWAIN compliance is often cited as an important consideration as you can then open a scanned document in any software application that supports TWAIN. If the scanner is not TWAIN compliant, you may have to save the document separately before opening it in your application of choice. (Personally, I have never really found this to be a barrier, but some feel otherwise.)

♦ Resolution is important, as is black-and-white and color capability. In most cases, black and white is fine, but you may want to scan some documents in color to preserve the ability to differentiate data that is in different color inks and would be lost in black and white. Resolution is important, as low resolution may lead to being unable to OCR the document or increased OCR errors. I would use a minimum of 300 dots per inch (black and white).

♦ The ability to connect wirelessly is a nice feature, as is full duplex scanning (both sides at the same time). Consider size and weight, and whether you have an Ethernet port to connect it to the network.

## Backup Systems

For anyone who has faced the "blue screen of death" or in Haiku:

*A crash reduces*
*your expensive computer*
*to a simple stone.*

You know the angst and frustration caused by data loss. Moreover, the implications can be long-reaching: Many businesses that have been hit by environmental calamities, fires, and even terrorist activities failed because they could not resurrect their lost data. Moreover, don't underestimate the effect that ransomware such as CryptoLocker can have on a law firm.

Waking up and finding that all your data has been encrypted and you are facing paying the ransom in order to be back in operation is a terrible situation to be in.

Accordingly, it is important that you match your expensive computer system with a good and robust backup system that will preserve your data and allow you to be up and running as quickly as possible. Fortunately, electronic data can be backed up and stored in multiple locations easily once the system is configured and set up. Contrast that with an office with paper files in a single location: If it is hit by fire or flood, the files will be destroyed with no backups.

I recommend that you back up your system to a rugged external hard drive that is resistant to fire and flood (such as the ioSafe SoloPro or, for larger firms, its NAS storage devices) as well as to a cloud-based back-up service.

The reasons are manifold. Your rugged hard drive can be used to restore your network quickly, provided that the hard drive survives (and there is a good chance that it will). However, if the calamity is such that your entire office is destroyed, then the cloud-based backup will be your fail-safe method of preserving your data—paying for cheap insurance vs. going out of business (or even facing a malpractice claim).

TopTenReviews has rated the best backup software for Windows in 2015. The results can be found here at **http://pc-backup-review.toptenreviews. com**. The top three products were as follows:

- ◆ NovaBackup
- ◆ Acronis Backup for PC
- ◆ Genie Backup Manager

### Monitors

Like scanners, there are two camps when it comes to monitors in a paperless office. The benefits of having two (or even more!) monitors on your desk are easily demonstrated. You can have your reference information on one screen (or on one-half of a very large screen) while you craft documents on another. Personally, I always prefer to work on two large monitors as I find the time saved in not having to open windows repeatedly adds up quickly!

Consulting with an ergonomic consultant can help you design workspaces that are comfortable as well as functional (as the writer has done and can say it was well worth it!). Otherwise, improper placement can lead to neck, shoulder, and back issues.

Flat-panel displays are now the current state of the art.

Features to look for in a good monitor:

♦ **Definition:** While most people think that higher resolution is a good thing, it may not be depending on the age of your eyes since increasing the resolution, while it makes thing sharper, also makes things smaller. Most flat-panel displays have a recommended resolution. (In Windows, click on START then CONTROL PANEL then APPEARANCE AND PERSONALIZATION and click on ADJUST SCREEN RESOLUTION—the recommended display resolution should be shown. On a Mac, click SYSTEM PREFERENCES then DISPLAYS and select RESOLUTION: Best for Display). Microsoft has a listing of recommended resolutions based on monitor size as well as instructions on how to set the best resolution for your monitor at windows.microsoft.com/en-ca/windows/getting-best-display-monitor#getting-best-display-monitor=windows-7.

♦ **Dot Pitch:** This is the spacing between different pixels on the monitor. It can range from .30mm to .15mm. Generally speaking, the smaller the distance, the better.

♦ **Brightness and Contrast:** Most monitors have their own controls to set the contrast and brightness of the displays. Windows has a feature called Adaptive Brightness that will adjust the monitor display if your computer has a light sensor installed and enabled. Check for this by going to Power Options in System and Security settings and enabling adaptive brightness. Apple computers has a setting under Displays in System Preferences that allows the automatic adjustment of brightness. You can adjust contrast on external displays if you find that helps. Windows has a feature called ClearType that makes fonts easier to read. This should be turned on and adjusted to your monitor to ease your eyes.

♦ **Size:** Monitors now come in sizes up to 98 inches (NEC X981UHD for $39,999.00, which is 14 inches bigger and $10,000 cheaper than last year's biggest monitor). But most users will want a monitor (or two) that is between 24 and 34 inches. Accordingly you should be able to find a monitor to match your space and size requirements.

♦ **Ports:** Look for multiple ports to match the ones on your computer. Common formats are VGA, DVI (digital display), and HDMI.

You don't want to end up with a monitor that will only accept a DVI cable when your computer only has a VGA port. (I saw that in an office where the poor lawyer was given a brand new monitor only to find out it wasn't compatible with her computer system.)

♦ **Warranty/Reviews:** I would check both the applicable warranty (two to three years is good) that comes with the display as well as online reviews from actual users. Common problems to watch for are failure of the backlight as well as multiple pixel defects. Is there a restocking fee if you return the unit?

Techradar.pro rates the top monitors for 2015 here: **www.techradar.com/us/news/computing-components/peripherals/best-monitor-9-reviewed-and-rated-1058662**.

## A Bit about the Software That You Will Need

### Document Management Considerations

There is much discussion about e-document formats (Adobe Acrobat PDF/A—the archival format—in particular), the media on which the electronic documents are to be stored (locally? backed up onto a remote device? on the cloud?), scanners, remote access, and the like. Some firms choose to use only electronic storage for their closed files, eliminating the expensive cost of storing paper files for years, while others prefer to have all open and closed files in electronic form. Still other firms are concerned about cultural issues around going paperless and the change management process that would entail.

But lost in this discussion is a much more basic issue—one that is fundamental to taking a law firm paperless yet is often overlooked. In the paper world, there are file folders and filing cabinets, both of which help keep the documents organized. The file folder has its brads (places to attach correspondence, pleadings, etc., in date order), and the filing cabinet keeps the file folders organized.

When a law firm goes paperless, however, there typically isn't the appreciation for the electronic equivalent of the brad file folder and filing cabinet. Records—which could be pleadings, correspondence, e-mails, etc.—are usually found in numerous different places on the network. E-mails may be stored in Outlook folders, while documents such as pleadings, research memos, and correspondence may be saved in various Windows folders. Worse yet, Outlook stores sent e-mails in "Sent Items" while incoming e-mails are typically filed in other folders.

Unfortunately, each software application an office uses stores its data in different folders scattered across the network. As the number of electronic files grows, the ability to gather all these disparate bits of information together into a "client file" gets harder and harder. With paper files, the firm would typically print out all this information and store it in the file folder. In that situation, the way in which each application and user names and stores the records on the network and hard drives is largely irrelevant. But as the firm moves to a paperless office, the disorganized nature of electronic recordkeeping starts to become a problem. It is now harder to reproduce "the file" and the collection of folders that would otherwise be found in the steel filing cabinet.

Some firms use indexing and desktop search engines, such as Windows Search or X1 or Copernic or Spotlight on the Mac, to find documents on the network, but this is not a workable equivalent to a good document management application. Other firms claim that their "standardized file-naming and storage convention" is good enough. Unfortunately, this convention only works as long as everyone, at all times, complies. Once someone decides "just this time" not to follow the convention, the system starts to break down. (The second law of thermodynamics basically says that any system, over time, goes from an organized to a disorganized state without the continual addition of energy to keep it organized—otherwise known as *entropy*. In a paperless office system, this means that paperless file/folder naming systems will suffer from entropy unless everyone is dutiful in following the system, every time. In the writer's experience, as the size of a law firm increases, the entropy factor grows exponentially.)

So what should a firm do? The solution is document management software. This software is the equivalent of the steel filing cabinet, organizing all "records"—be they documents, e-mails, pleadings, etc.—into the electronic equivalent of the paper folder. Document management software keeps each folder distinct from the others, offering the organizational ability of the filing cabinet.

With document management software, a document must be "profiled" before it can be saved on the network. Profiling entails keying in some information about the document: nature, author, form (pleading, e-mail, etc.), client, matter, and more. This "metadata" allows the document management software to know how to categorize the document properly. E-mails, pleadings, correspondence, memos, etc., are all organized by client, matter, lawyer, and date created in addition to other criteria.

Document management software also allows searching (including Boolean searches) by keyword, type of document, client name, and other keywords. It offers version control; tracking and audit (who created what version); and other activities around document creation, modification, and the like. Best of all, it offers the ability to draw together in one place on the network all the disparate records that would otherwise be affixed to the brad of a paper file.

Another benefit of moving to a DMS is that remote access is enabled since all documents are already in digital form. Accordingly, it matters not if you are in the office or half a world away since you can sign on to your desktop and access all your files and information. Most DMS applications allow "briefcasing," or mirroring the documents on a laptop with synchronization once you reconnect to the network. This eases the problem of multiple versions of the same document, since changes can't be made to a document that is "checked out."

Entropy is avoided since the user must profile the document *before* it can be saved. This is how the document management software achieves its goal: It imposes order on chaos. While some may chafe at this process, in the long run, this is the only way to keep entropy at bay.

By making a document management system the foundation of your paperless office, you can achieve the degree of rigor, organization, and systemization that will allow you to develop your business even as people change and clients come and go. Otherwise, finding a document on the network is like looking for a needle in a haystack.

What to look for in a good DMS system:

- ♦ The first rule of introducing any new application into an existing system is to determine if it will work well with your existing software and hardware. Particularly with a DMS, you will want to ensure that it works easily with your existing scanners, e-mail system, server, and any other software that you use in the office.

- ♦ Second, it should be easy to use. A DMS that is complicated with a search feature that is difficult to understand will not be well liked in the office. Moreover it should integrate with Microsoft Outlook in order that e-mails are easily brought into the DMS. You should be able to create "profile folders" within Outlook that will automatically profile an e-mail according to predetermined parameters. (This feature will ensure that e-mails are profiled and attached to a client's file automatically once the e-mail is dragged and dropped into the appropriate profiled folder in Outlook.)

♦ Third, it should be able to work with PDF files easily, and it should have the ability to take a PDF document and OCR it—apply Optical Character Recognition— which is to convert a PDF scanned document (which is a single-layer PDF that is equivalent to a photocopy, being black dots on a white page) into a machine-readable form (that can be searched and opened in Word) as well as the image file that you read. The OCR process does what your mind does when it looks at the PDF scan—it recognizes the dots on the page as being text and creates a dual-layer PDF, one that is an image as well as a text file.

♦ Fourth, it should facilitate mobile devices—iPads, smartphones, and laptops–so that you can have staff work outside the office easily.

♦ Fifth, today I think it is important that it support a client extranet. E-mail is dying and insecure. A secure client portal or extranet allows the firm and the client to exchange documents securely and privately without the need to use e-mail.

TopTenReviews has the latest reviews and rankings of DMS software at document-management-software-review.toptenreviews.com.

## Think about the Role of Cloud-Based Services

The Law Society of British Columbia has released a report on cloud computing for lawyers along with a checklist when looking at the cloud.

Cloud computing due diligence guidelines (**www.lawsociety.bc.ca/docs/practice/resources/guidelines-cloud.pdf**)

Cloud computing checklist (**www.lawsociety.bc.ca/docs/practice/resources/checklist-cloud.pdf**)

The following website discusses ethical decisions and offers guidance from numerous bar associations as well as from the ABA: **www.americanbar.org/groups/departments_offices/legal_technology_resources/resources/charts_fyis/cloud-ethics-chart.html**.

Before you move to the cloud, research what may be published in your jurisdiction and what steps you have to take before you jump into the cloud.

The cloud offers many benefits to lawyers in terms of the paperless practice of law and the ability to recover from a natural or human-made disaster, but these have to be balanced against possible privacy, security, ethical, and client concerns. There is no right answer; rather, each firm has to determine the appropriate protections and such for meeting their needs as well as their clients' needs (such as using encryption with cloud applications such as Dropbox).

## Think about Mobile Computing, Remote Access, and Apps

Mobile computing and apps are dealt with in a different chapter in this book. However, it is worth noting that the mobile practice of law does go hand in glove with the paperless practice of law since all your office files are already in digital form. You need to consider how to grant access to your staff and whether this takes place using smartphones, laptops, tablets, or other devices. Consider the policies that you should you put into place (such as not using any insecure public Wi-Fi hotspots, as these are inherently vulnerable to a number of security risks, such as man-in-the-middle attacks that steal user names and passwords) and how you will enforce them. Particularly consider policies that will prevent what is termed the "rogue cloud"—namely staff sending documents home to work on using e-mail or file transfer services that have not been approved by the firm and thus place the integrity and the safety of the office network at risk. Consider, for example, if the home computer in question is used by other persons (possible loss of confidentiality), if it is infected with any malware (placing the office at risk if that document is then subsequently brought back into the office network), or if a document is transferred using a file transfer service that is insecure.

There are any number of applications for the iPhone, Android, and BlackBerry smartphones (such as DocsToGo) that allow you to read, annotate, and in some cases work on documents on the road. With Microsoft Office now available for the iPad along with Office 365 for virtually any device that hosts a browser, the ability to work remotely has never been better. The enhanced ability to work remotely on virtually any device, wherever you can access an Internet connection, is definitely one of the strongest reasons for fully implementing the paperless office.

## Setting New Business Processes to Align with Your Goal(s)

There is an expression tossed around in IT circles about "paving the cow paths." AgileConnection's website states:

> In the IT world, "paving cow paths" means automating a business process as is, without thinking too much about whether or not that process is effective or efficient. Often business process automation initiatives require figuring out entirely new ways of doing business processes–impossible prior to automation (for example, work flow automation and digital image processing)–defining more effective and efficient process highways.

If you are making the transition to paperless, you need to give some thought about how you can rework your business processes to make them more efficient and effective. An example of this is going to centralized conversion of paper documents to PDF. If you have a small group do this, then you ensure that all documents are converted to digital form quickly and consistently. You are not waiting for certain people to take the piles of papers on their desks and bring them into the DMS system—with all the resultant tensions and delays as people wonder when the laggards in the office are going to "get with the program."

Accordingly, don't just pave your cowpaths. Think about how you can make your systems better and faster by eliminating outdated ways of working and taking advantage of the new technologies in the office. A good consultant who has taken law firms down the paperless path can be worth his or her weight in gold. He or she will guide you in the software, hardware, and processes best suited to implementing the paperless practice in your firm.

## How Will You Transition to Paperless?

There are two recognized ways of bringing the existing paper files into the paperless system. One could be called the brute force method; the other could be called the accretion method. Which one you adopt depends on the size of your office and the willingness of your staff to pitch in and do the conversion all at once.

The brute force method typically involves the availability of a long weekend. On Friday, the office closes; from that point onwards the sole task of everyone is to use as many scanners as possible, take every open file, scan and OCR the contents, and bring them into the DMS system. You can see that you need a dedicated team to throw everything that they have at the conversion of the files so that when you open again for business, every file is now in paperless form.

The accretion method takes a different approach. Here, the first time you need to "touch" a file on or after the stated conversion date, you stop everything and scan and OCR the contents to bring it into the DMS. With this approach, the most active files are brought in first—with the least active files last. The disadvantage is that the time to convert files may take a while and laggards have the opportunity to drag their feet.

Also consider if you have legacy servers and data and how you will bring that data into your DMS. Some firms adopt a policy that the legacy servers can continue to be accessed but you cannot save any new information into them—all document saves must take place within the DMS. This way the important information on the legacy servers can be brought into the DMS when needed.

Which approach you take depends on the culture of the firm, the commitment of your staff to take a long weekend for work purposes, and the ability of everyone to pitch in.

## Getting Buy-In from Your Team Members (Leading the Change)

### Change Management

Let's discuss the change management aspects of what you are contemplating in going paperless.

### Awareness about the Nature of Change

Before you start, think about and come to an understanding of the scope or magnitude of this change toward paperless that is being introduced. How many people, structures, systems, etc., will be impacted by the introduction of change? Will people in the firm regard this change a voluntary one or not? How do you deal with people who feel that this change is being thrust upon them rather than change being led from within? Notice that in most cases, law firms deal with change from outside the organization. Now, however, you are being a catalyst of change from within and you need to make your staff and lawyers appreciate that this will result in a better and more efficient and effective organization once the change is implemented!

## The Three Levels of Change

There are three levels of change that you will deal with: procedural, structural, and cultural. What are the implications of each in your change to paperless?

Procedural change means the rules or policies around handling, storing, searching, and retrieving documents will change. Structural change means that the office will no longer look or feel the same. Paper will disappear, documents will be scanned and stored, files will be only electronic, and the like. Cultural change means that people will have to adapt to living and working in a paperless world and that new entrants will have to learn and become part of the new system.

## Management of Change

The old expression states that you never get a second chance to make a first impression. Accordingly, it is vitally important to give considerable thought to the plans for the introduction of the change as well as for people and organization's first exposure to the new system. Identify the roadblocks and strategies to cope with them well ahead of time. Identify tactics to deal with issues before they appear. Bring people into the process early on and let them shape the eventual systems, policies, and procedures. Listen to their concerns and respond accordingly.

## Focus on Who Matters Most

The third step recognizes that if everyone openly adopted change, there would never be any need to be concern with implementing change. However, there will always be three groupings of people and organizations when change is involved:

- ◆ Enthusiasts: Those who recognize the benefits of the new system and line up to help spread and support the new system
- ◆ Backbones: The large majority of people who are solid performers and support the change since they are reliable workers
- ◆ Resisters: Those who oppose change either due to a perceived loss of power, status, money, or some other attribute or who simply do not wish to expend the time and/or energy to change

Obviously, you need as many people as possible in the first two camps and as few as possible in the last one. You may have some hard decisions to make. For example, if someone who stands in the way of the change consistently opposes you, you may have to decide if that person's future lies outside the firm.

### Celebrate the Successes

Every project has its milestones, setbacks, and successes. By positively communicating your successes you help keep the momentum going and the change process positive. You also need to have strategies in place to deal with the setbacks in order to avoid having your project derailed by the naysayers.

### Learn

Every successful change management process lays the groundwork for the next. Learn how to gather the takeaways that form the institutional learning for future growth. This is known as transforming your law firm into a "learning" organization that is better adapted at dealing with change.

## Learning from Your Experience and Continuing to Improve Your Systems

A learning organization is one that has adopted a culture of continually evaluating and learning from its change processes. Adopting the paperless practice of law is a perfect time to implement learning concepts into the firm. As each step is achieved in a change process, ask your teams these questions: What went right? What went wrong? How can we do this better? Keep a record of what you have learned and draw on that each time you need to implement a change in the firm.

When you recognize that leading, dealing with, and managing change is one of the most important skills that any person or organization can develop, then you have taken the first step toward implementing a learning (or change management) culture in your organization. Seek to build on this and instill it into the culture of your firm. You—and your law firm—will be stronger, will be more adept, and will have a greater capacity to absorb the changes that are thrust upon it as a result.

## Conclusion

OK you have now read all the advice that I can give you on going paperless. As you stare over the abyss, recall that anticipation is almost always worse than reality. The process can be managed by properly planning, anticipating, executing, adjusting, and learning.

Don't forget to involve everyone in the project at the start—and to celebrate with them at the end! The firms that have gone paperless all say the same thing: It is cost-effective, it enables remote work and greater work-life balance, and it allows you to carry your documents with you and access them on multiple remote devices wherever you may be. You can take your case to court and present it with ease. Moving to e-filing in government registries and tribunals is eased. It is easier—and cheaper—to store documents electronically than on paper. Moreover, it results in tangible benefits to the law firm, to the environment, and to the work culture in the law firm.

So take a deep breath . . . and take that first step . . .

# CHAPTER TWENTY-NINE

# Tomorrow in Legal Tech

*"Even if you're on the right track, you'll get run over if you just sit there."*
—Will Rogers

*"We are stuck with technology when what we really want is just stuff that works."*
—Douglas Adams

## Introduction

Ah, if we could only see beyond the horizon. But just as in the real world we can only see so far physically, we can only see so far in the digital world as well. And sometimes what is just over the horizon is a surprise. Who would have dreamt that Apple (remember how Steve Jobs HATED styluses?) would announce the Apple Pencil in 2015? But here we are.

After the wobbly start of Windows 8, who would imagine that businesses would glom onto Windows 10 (and where did 9 go?) with fervor? And who would think that right after Apple announced its eagerly awaited new products, its stock price would drop?

This visionary business is for the birds. But Will Rogers was right, even if we've done our best with legal technology up until the present, we can't wash our hands of it. We are never done, and we will get run over if we don't do our best to keep up with it.

Douglas Adams was right too. We need to learn about technology, but the average lawyer doesn't do that. The typical lawyer just wants stuff that works. It's no wonder the words *plug and play* have such allure.

While this book isn't exactly "plug and play," it has the same motivation—to make your life simpler. We don't cover every product or technology—there are way too many choices, way too many vendors hawking their wares, and way too much data to ingest if you try to learn it all yourself. So we try to give "best of breed" advice with the solo/small firm lawyer in mind. I should have said "best of breed and budget conscious" advice because that is what the solo/small firm lawyer always wants.

## Trending Now . . .

One of our favorite resources is the *ABA 2015 Legal Technology Survey*. Some of the stats suggest where the legal profession is heading—and with what technology:

### Tablets
- 42 percent using for legal work (40 percent in 2014)
- 78 percent using Apple iPad (84 percent in 2014)
- Windows Surface 12 percent (only 5 percent in 2014)
- Samsung Galaxy 11 percent (10 percent in 2014)

### Smartphones
- 79 percent using for law-related tasks (77 percent in 2014)

### IT Staff
- 42 percent of firms have no IT support staff at all locations combined
- 12 percent of firms have one IT staff member
- 8 percent of firms have two IT staff members

### Operating System
- Windows 7 47 percent (54 percent in 2014)
- Windows 8 26 percent (15 percent in 2014)
- 10 percent still using Windows XP (14 percent in 2014)
- 8 percent using a Mac OS

### E-mail
- Microsoft Outlook 75 percent
- Web-based e-mail 17 percent
- Outlook Express 11 percent
- Apple Mail 7 percent

### Instant Messaging Software
- 31 percent using for law-related tasks (30 percent in 2014)

The top three being used were:

- ♦ iChat 24 percent (20 percent in 2014)
- ♦ Google Chat 22 percent (25 percent in 2014)
- ♦ Microsoft Messenger 19 percent (20 percent in 2014)

### *Time and Billing Software*

The top four remain the same as in 2014:

- ♦ QuickBooks 13 percent
- ♦ Timeslips 12 percent
- ♦ PCLAw 9 percent
- ♦ TABS3 2 percent

### *Case Management Software*

- ♦ 45.4 percent reported that case/practice management software was available at firms (made us wonder if they were using it)
- ♦ 15.4 percent didn't know if it was available

### *Security Software*

Personally used for law-related tasks (remember that some would be managed environments):

- ♦ Antivirus (this is how the survey titled it, but I am assuming they were security suites protecting against malware, phishing, etc.) 79.4 percent
- ♦ Encryption 30.8 percent, although 50 percent said that encryption software was available at their firm (I do not believe that the percentage would be as high for e-mail encryption software, which is less common than hardware encryption).

### *Hardware Manufacturer Winners*

- ♦ Dell wins for desktops (57.2 percent), laptops (37.5 percent), and servers (45.4 percent)
- ♦ The smartphone winner is Apple iPhone 77.4 percent
- ♦ The winning tablet is Apple iPad 77.9 percent

### *Cloud Computing Software*

The top three:

- ♦ Dropbox 51.4 percent
- ♦ Google Docs 39.1 percent
- ♦ iCloud 21.4 percent

A couple of points we found interesting: 37 percent of the respondents are using metadata removal software. The figure was 39 percent in 2014. This is a remarkably low percentage.

Although 31 percent reported using cloud computing for law-related tasks, 16 percent reported using no precautions/security measures. Alarming but not surprising.

For the third year in a row, the most popular legal app was Fastcase, with 40.6 percent of respondents using it. And with the rollout of a new (and terrific) version of Fastcase, that number is likely to rise.

## Big Data

Lawyers frequently forget just how much data they (and everyone else) is managing. So let's remind ourselves—because the future is going to continue to result in explosions of data volume.

Hat tip here to David J. Walton, who included these fun factoids in an article entitled "Litigation and Trial Practice in the Era of Big Data" in the ABA's summer issue of Litigation magazine.

> *"From the beginning of the world through 2003, humankind created five exabytes of data. By 2010, we were creating five exabytes of data every two days.*
>
> *For $60, you can now buy enough memory to store all the music ever created in the world.*
>
> *It is estimated that by 2016, the gigabyte equivalent of all movies ever made will cross global IP networks every three minutes.*
>
> *The average smartphone now has more computing power than all of NASA in 1969, the year Neil Armstrong landed on the moon."*

With big data comes big data analytics. And big data is having a huge impact on trial practice, some of which we see clearly (like technology-assisted review), but many more impacts may be beyond our ability to see. Consider that one company, Lex Machina, is already using big data to predict outcomes in IP cases.

In ten years, we'll look back astonished at the power of data analytics and how it affected the practice of law. Add artificial intelligence to the mix (see the end of this chapter) and the practice of law will undoubtedly undergo a revolution of sorts.

## Microsoft Windows 10

It looks as though Microsoft Windows 10 is going to be BIG. Seventy-five million downloads were recorded in the first month after its release. And most businesses surveyed said they were planning on upgrading to Microsoft Windows 10 at some point—this year or next. There is a lot of information on the specifics of Microsoft Windows 10 in this book (just use the index to find it), but we want to remind you that we recommend waiting three to six months after a major operating system release before installing it.

Anecdotally, we've seen a lot of lawyers who are, as we write, unhappy that they clicked on the "download now" message. Microsoft Windows 10, like all new releases, has its glitches and sometimes doesn't play well with certain hardware or software.

Mind you, we are thinking of moving to Windows 10 and bringing clients there too, probably in the beginning of 2016, when most of the bugs should be gone. The application developers should have supported versions for Windows 10 by that time as well.

It is truly amazing how many people clung to Windows 7 and refused to adopt Windows 8. Windows 9 was "skipped over," an invisible OS, and Windows 10 looks to be a winner in the same way that Windows 7 was a winner. Just be careful—keep reading to see what issues may exist and make sure you talk to your IT provider before you make the move. Chances are that by the time you see this book, it will be time to make the move if you haven't already done so.

## Data Breaches and Cybersecurity

More than half of all Americans had their private data exposed in the year before we began drafting this chapter. The OPM breach was huge and the Ashley Madison breach grabbed headlines, but there were a lot of breaches.

The 2015 Verizon Data Breach Investigations Report revealed that 2014 had 2,122 confirmed data breaches and 79,790 security incidents in which data was compromised.

In 60 percent of the cases, attackers were able to compromise an organization within minutes.

23 percent of recipients open phishing messages, and 11 percent click on attachments. Yes, in law firms too.

50 percent open e-mails and click on phishing links within the first hour after transmission.

Out of tens of millions of mobile devices, the ones infected with truly malicious exploits was negligible, only 0.03 percent. (That surprised us, but look for that number to rise markedly.)

One lesson from the report was crystal clear: Humans need to be trained—and trained again—in safe computing and social engineering! If you aren't doing this, you are writing an engraved invitation to hackers.

2015 was the year in which Citigroup issued a report chiding law firms for not disclosing data breaches. The reluctance of law firms to discuss or acknowledge data breaches has frustrated law enforcement and clients for years. The report indicated that law firm security is often below the standards for other industries.

Federal authorities are urging law firms to be more open about reporting incidents. Good luck with that. We have frequently observed that law firms are loathe to admit to data breaches, no doubt having nightmares involving a massive client exodus after the revelation of a breach. Without a law that has teeth, we don't expect that to change even though the law firms may be ethically required to report the breaches to clients. They don't seem to fear the bar disciplinary authorities nearly as much as they fear the loss of clients.

Breaches are going to continue to plague law firms—not much by way of news there. It is appalling that in 2015, we saw another law firm breach reported in California. It was a garden variety story of a stolen laptop while an attorney was on the MTS Trolley in San Diego. The firm would not have had to report the theft if the laptop had been encrypted, so it obviously wasn't.

The information on the laptop included names, addresses, telephone numbers, Social Security numbers, and possibly certain financial information or medical records. The firm offered recipients of the notification letter a free year of identity theft protection and credit monitoring services. The notification letter states "We have no reason to believe that the laptop was stolen for the information it contained." It also said "We also have no information indicating that this information has been accessed or used in any way."

Undoubtedly that is true. But oh why are lawyers traveling anywhere with unencrypted mobile devices? It is a lesson we seem never to learn. Let's hope that law firms get smarter with mobile devices in 2016.

If law firms didn't have enough to worry about with respect to cybersecurity, the Third Circuit Court of Appeals ruled in 2015 that the Federal Trade Commission (FTC) could proceed with a lawsuit alleging that hotel chain Wyndham Worldwide Corp. shoulders some of the responsibility for three breaches from 2008–2010 in which hackers allegedly stole more than 619,000 credit and debit card numbers.

Since our moribund Congress hasn't managed to pass comprehensive data security laws, the FTC has stepped in, bringing more than fifty data-security cases based on its authority to take action against unfair and deceptive business practices.

The FTC alleged that Wyndham failed to implement reasonable safeguards, including leaving consumer data unprotected by firewalls and using outdated software that couldn't receive security updates. (This is where those of you using Windows XP and other outdated software should pay attention.)

Large firms are indeed paying attention to cybersecurity, boarding a fast-moving train that is unlikely to slow down.

By way of proving that, The Legal Services Information Sharing and Analysis Organization (LS-ISAO) Services for law firms has been launched with the help of the financial services industry whose fifteen-year-old Financial Services Information Sharing and Analysis Center (FS-ISAC) is considered one of the most mature ISAC/ISAO groups today.

Initial applications to become members of the group were sent to about 200 law firms (mostly large firms). Membership is $8,000 per year.

"We're providing [to the legal ISAO] the infrastructure to disseminate and receive cybersecurity threat and vulnerability information," says Cindy Donaldson, vice president of products and services with FS-ISAC.

ISACs and ISAOs provide an official mechanism for sharing information about the latest cyberattacks and threats spotted targeting specific industries, for instance, and include databases of the threats and vulnerabilities for their members. They also provide conferences and other ways for members to interact and share their experiences to better collaborate in fighting cybercrime and cyber espionage actors. Among the industries with ISACs and ISAOs are the aviation, the defense industrial base, emergency services, IT, maritime, nuclear energy, real estate, public transportation, retail, and water utilities.

Initially, the LS-ISAO will offer members access to intel-sharing list servers with threat information and advisories from vendors and government agencies as well as member-to-member threat sharing and other resources. Ultimately, it will evolve to offer portal services for members to share threat intelligence securely and anonymously, as well as the Holy Grail of intel-sharing—automating the use of the information into the member's internal security tools and networks.

While we're happy to see the beginning of a legal ISAC, we hope it will travel down from the major leagues to the minor leagues, where it is also sorely needed.

Experiencing a data breach is not an "if"—it is a "when." Just ask the IRS and the Office of Personnel Management. Mind you, their approach to information security was sloppy. Lawyers cannot afford, ethically, to have slipshod security when protecting confidential data.

If you haven't been breached yet, you will be. It doesn't take a fortune teller to read these tea leaves. Breaches are and will remain an epidemic. The Ashley Madison breach may have driven that point home to people who never imagined that they would be caught up in a breach. At least it served to offer up a valuable lesson.

It is imperative that you be ready for a data breach. This means you need a plan, which tends to be called an Incident Response Plan (IRP), often focused on data breaches, but "incidents" can refer to responding to ransomware, fighting attempted hacks, or an insider accessing data without authorization.

Most large firms now have these plans in place, but many smaller firms do not. More and more, we are seeing clients and insurance companies asking to see your Incident Response Plan. In the face of ever-escalating data breaches, now is a good time to come up with a plan. After all, football teams don't get the playbook on game day!

The problem with all plans is that they don't survive first contact with the enemy. That's OK. Far worse is having no plan at all and reacting in panic with no structure to guide your actions. We see that all the time. The first hour you spend with a client after the client knows he or she has been breached is often called "the upchuck hour." It is not a happy time.

Don't go in search of a template IRP. No two law firms are set up exactly the same, and all have different business processes, network infrastructures, and types of data. You need a plan customized to fit your firm. The smaller you are, the shorter the plan is likely to be. While a book could be written about IRPs, we are going to give you a condensed and, we hope, digestible overview. Perhaps 2016 should be your year to take serious action on the security front. Here are some of the elements of an IRP:

♦ Name the position titles that will be responsible for the functions listed in the IRP. Don't use names since people come and go. You need a broad-based team if you are a firm of any size—management, IT, information security, human resources, compliance, marketing, etc. Have a conference call bridge line identified in case a breach happens at night or on the weekends and include home/cell phone numbers and personal as well as work e-mail addresses. This list will need to be updated regularly as people join and leave the firm.

♦ Identify the contact information for a good data breach lawyer—many large firms now have whole departments working with data breaches. Don't think you can handle this without an attorney who specializes in data breaches. Your data breach lawyer (if you selected a good one) will be an invaluable quarterback for your IRP team, and he or she may be able to preserve under attorney/client privilege much of the information related to the breach.

♦ Identify the location of your insurance policy (which darn well better cover data breaches). You need to make sure you are covered before you start and list the insurer's contact information because you are going to need to call your insurer as soon as you are aware of a possible breach.

♦ Identify the contact information for law enforcement (perhaps your local FBI office), often the first folks called in.

♦ Identify the contact information for the digital forensics company you would want to investigate and remediate the cause of the breach. Generally, you will have been breached for six months or more before you discover the breach; it will take time to unravel what went on. You'll want to know if all data that should have been encrypted was indeed encrypted in transmission and in storage. If it was, this may lessen your notification burden. Identify any PII (Personally Identifiable Information) that may have been compromised.

♦ If you have intrusion detection or data loss prevention software, those logs should be provided to your investigators immediately and preserved. If you don't, you may want to think about implementing such software.

- Identify the contact information for your bank in case your banking credentials have been compromised.

- (Optional but often useful) Identify the contact information for a good public relations firm. If you are not required to make the breach public, you may not need one, but if it does go public, you may need to do some quick damage control. Your insurance coverage may provide for this, in which case the insurance company will put you in contact with the appropriate firm.

- How will you handle any contact with clients and third parties, remembering that you may wish not to "reveal all" and yet need to achieve some level of transparency? Be forewarned that this is a difficult balance. You will feel like the victim of a data breach, but your clients will feel as though you have breached their trust in you. A data breach that becomes public can cause a mass exodus of clients, so work through your notification planning with great care. Be wary of speaking too fast before facts are fully vetted. This is common mistake, trying to limit the damage and actually increasing it as the scope of the breach turns out to be far greater than first known.

- How will you handle informing employees about the incident? How will you ensure that the law firm speaks with one voice and that employees do not spread information about the breach in person or online? How will your social media cover the breach, if at all?

- If you have a data breach notification law in your state (and almost all do), put it right in the plan along with compliance guidelines. You may be required to contact your state attorney general. These laws vary widely, so be familiar with your own state law.

- If you have HIPAA, HITECH, or other regulated data that may be impacted, make sure the relevant data breach regulations are referenced in the plan and attached to it.

- Does the breach require that IT and information security policies be changed? Does what you learned from the breach require that the IRP itself be revised? The IRP should mandate an annual review even without an incident.

You need dress rehearsals for a data breach. Add and subtract factors. Add a terrorist threat, subtract key personnel who are on a cruise, yada, yada. This is most often done as a tabletop exercise, one that should take place at least annually.

You will find that your needs and responses to a breach may evolve over time. For instance, as ransomware saw a *4000 percent increase* in 2014 (yikes), it became apparent that many backup systems needed to be reengineered so that they wouldn't be impacted by CryptoLocker, CryptoWall, and their many variants. The threats will no doubt morph over time—as will the defenses.

Make no mistake about it. The most successful attack against law firms is spear phishing, a targeted attack where the attacks have done some reconnaissance. They may know what cases you're involved in, who the opposing counsel is, the nickname of a senior partner, etc. This makes it easy to send what looks like a "genuine" e-mail, which in reality contains a malicious hyperlink or an attachment. After all, much of the information about your cases and the firm are public records.

Training employees to be skeptical and to refrain from being click-happy and to think about the e-mail they see in their inbox is invaluable. We've seen firms that have successfully avoided a breach simply because an employee had enough sense to question whether a very well-done phishing e-mail was real.

If you question the monies spent on training or the loss of billable time, stack those costs up against the financial damage of a data breach and you'll see the absolute need for annual training. According to Verizon's 2015 Data Breach Investigations Report, almost 30 percent of data security incidents were due to human error. Persuaded yet?

The security of third-party vendors that have "hooks" into your network is critical for you to understand. Just ask Target, which got compromised because an HVAC contractor was breached and the contractor had administrator access to Target's network. Make sure you understand a vendor's information security and don't permit vendors to have access to any data they don't need. A vendor management policy is now a key law firm policy. (We only started seeing these in the last year or two.) If you don't have one, this too should be high on your priority list.

Complacency and inaction are not your friends when it comes to data breaches. Lawyers love risk management. The surest pathway to data breach risk management is to be prepared.

## Ransomware and Phishing

Ransomware and phishing are related to data breaches, because they are so often the vehicle for the breaches. But they deserve their own heading!

The FBI warned businesses in 2015 to be alert for phishing e-mails. These are often targeted attacks in which e-mails appear to come from a colleague or trusted supplier.

The FBI calls this family of scams "Business Email Compromise" (BEC) scams. Since October 2013, BEC scams have cost businesses around the world over $1.2 billion according to the agency. While losses in some eighty countries were tallied up, U.S. businesses were hit the hardest. Seven thousand U.S. businesses have reported $747 million in losses, with an average loss of $130,000.

The scammers, who appear to be members of organized crime groups operating out of Africa, Eastern Europe, and the Middle East, are targeting businesses that work with overseas suppliers or regularly make wire transfer payments. But instead of sending funds to legitimate suppliers, the money transfers end up in bank accounts controlled by the criminals, mostly with banks based in China.

The scammers succeed by compromising legitimate e-mail accounts through social engineering or malware that steals account credentials. They then use access to e-mail accounts to gather information about billing and invoices that won't raise the suspicion of employees who send transfer payments.

BEC e-mail scams are proliferating rapidly—up 270 percent since the beginning of 2015. Law firms seem to be hit by many of these scams.

What to do? Naked Security and Sophos expert Paul Ducklin offers the following tips:

- Revisit your outbound e-mail filtering rules to prevent sensitive information from going out to inappropriate destinations.
- Require multiple approvals for overseas wire transfers.
- Incorporate strict controls over changes in payment details or the creation of new accounts.
- Use strong passwords and consider two-factor authentication (2FA) to make it harder for crooks to gather intelligence from your network in the first place.
- Consider a "back-to-base" VPN for remote users so that their online security is kept up, even on the road.
- Have your own "central reporting" system, in the manner of IC3, where staff can call in suspicious messages to prevent crooks from

trying different employees with the same scam until a weak spot is found.

♦ Think twice about publicly posting personnel information that could be abused in phishing attacks.

Remember the good old days of ransomware? You would get an e-mail saying that you owed the IRS money and could pay it via a helpfully included link. Lots of people did this because it was only a couple of hundred dollars. And who wants to duke it out with the IRS? The same dull-witted people fell for the e-mail claiming that someone at their home had downloaded music or movies illegally (much more likely true than the first scenario) and they needed to pay a fine so that no one would come after them (or their spouse/child) for a much greater sum. Again, the price was relatively small, and many people paid.

The likelihood that a lawyer would fall for these primitive versions of ransomware was small. Fast forward to the days of CryptoLocker, which began in 2013. This ransomware Trojan attacked computers running Microsoft Windows, propagating itself by getting a user to click on an attachment or a link contained in an e-mail. If the user clicked on the link or attachment, "Winner, Winner, Chicken Dinner," the malware invisibly downloaded and began to encrypt his or her files. The malware encrypted files stored locally on the computer system as well as on any mapped network drives, such as those files on a server, connected flash drives, and other external USB drives.

The user then got a message on the screen indicating that he or she would be given the decryption key to unlock his or her data for a reasonable sum of $300–$500 (no checks or credit cards though). The payment of choice was and still is usually bitcoins. Curiously enough, there has been considerable honor among this brand of criminal, who normally provides the decryption key once the ransom is paid. Not 100 percent but most victims report that they did get the decryption key, although it took them as much as a week to decrypt all their data.

Before we understood CryptoLocker well, many backups (especially in solo and small firms) were engineered in such a way that they too were easily infected and encrypted. This immediately caused IT folks to reengineer backups so that they were not vulnerable to attack by ransomware, meaning that they could restore the encrypted files from their backup and not pay the ransom. But we still regularly see backups that have not been reengineered, endangering all of the law firm's files. The simple solution for most solo/small firm lawyers? Unplug the external USB hard disk after the backup job completes. Another solution is to use agent-based backup implementations. This is our customary solution.

After some period of time, standard Enterprise Level security suites began to get a handle on CryptoLocker (and its variants) and were able to detect and stop the malware from infecting machines. We began to see less of CryptoLocker.

But along came CryptoLocker's evil cousin, CryptoWall, and the fight to defeat CryptoWall (and all its variants) has proven to be much harder. Frankly, it has had many IT consultants tearing their hair out. Criminals have gotten smarter too, often spoofing sender e-mail addresses that make the recipient think they are receiving the e-mail from a court or a reputable law firm. And the English and grammar are much better too!

The Symantec 2015 Internet Security Threat Report had a lot of meat to digest, including the stat that ransomware (the general kind) increased by 113 percent in 2014. That's bad enough, but what made us reel was the finding that ransomware that encrypts your data and demands money to provide the decryption key rose by 4000 percent in 2014. That's one heck of a percentage!

This is consistent with the deluge of calls from law firms we received in 2015 about data encrypted by ransomware. It is a scourge that shows no sign of abating. Standard enterprise security suites have been unable to slow the tsunami of variants, especially the CryptoWall variants.

Herewith, some guidance on how to fight ransomware, particularly for solo and small firms that cannot afford the wallet-busting protections that large firm utilize.

As we say all the time, **THERE IS NO SILVER BULLET THAT PRO-TECTS AGAINST ALL RANSOMWARE**. Sadly, new variants are released every day.

Besides making sure that your backup is properly engineered as described above, you need a high-quality enterprise security suite installed. We like Trend Micro and Kaspersky, but there are many good suites to choose from—talk to your IT consultant.

Let's suppose, in spite of all you do, that you do get hit by ransomware. Do you have a plan for proceeding? Do you have cybersecurity experts to call in? Do you know what your insurance will and will not cover? And remember that no plan survives first contact with the enemy, so be prepared to revise the plan on the fly.

You might check out CryptoPrevent, software that offers the ability to prevent (in large measure) Windows computer systems from infection by ransomware. This software is relatively inexpensive, costing $15 or less per computer, depending on the number of licenses needed. The configuration of this software has to be customized for each client, depending on the applications that will need to be allowed to run on your systems, which requires input from you. It will take some amount of time and money, as each computer is manually configured.

Another "no software cost" alternative is to configure Windows policies to achieve the same operational restrictions that CryptoPrevent provides. CryptoPrevent is automatically updated, whereas the "no software cost" solution is static. You see the trade-off.

At ABA TECHSHOW, we asked our very knowledgeable faculty colleague, IT consultant Ben Schorr, about CryptoPrevent. He noted that clients (understandably) don't like the manual intervention required by CryptoPrevent to whitelist applications. He had especially run into problems where automated software updates were not permitted by CryptoPrevent, requiring more manual work. Ben shook his head and commiserated with us on the difficulty of advising solo and small firms on how best to defend themselves against this kind of ransomware while keeping costs down.

We became aware recently of four law firms that were successfully attacked by a CryptoWall variant in one month in Northern Virginia. Given that, we have begun recommending the installation of CryptoPrevent—or at least making clients aware that it exists so that they can make the money/aggravation vs. risk decision. We warned firms that they may get pushback from employees who are accustomed to installing any software they want. CryptoPrevent has proven to be quite effective by **disallowing** the installation and execution of software unless it has been whitelisted. You must determine for yourself if the risk of infection is high enough that you believe this kind of precaution is warranted, even as we tell you that no solution has been 100 percent effective.

The most common way that law firms get ransomware? Employees click on an attachment or a malicious link in an e-mail. This brings us to another important point: One of the most often-overlooked aspects of an organization's security readiness is end-user training. It is just as important that your employees know what not to click on as it is to have security software installed to help prevent these types of malware outbreaks. Your best bet is to train your employees every year about what NOT to click on and to educate them about the indicators they might see that should cause them to question whether the e-mail is suspect. And this is something law firms steadfastly refuse to do. Some firms cite the training cost (pretty minimal compared to the risk in our judgment) and others cite the loss of billable time. We have a slide in one of our PowerPoints that says simply "Training, training, training—oh, have we mentioned training?" You can see where we come down on that issue.

Resolve in 2016 to check out the possibility of installing CryptoPrevent and making it a part of your overall business information security protection, which also should include your firewall, IDS/IPS device, physical security, securely engineered backup, security awareness training, etc.

Don't think you can wish this problem away. The new breed of ransomware is a devilish adversary!

## E-mail Encryption

We talked about hardware encryption briefly as part of the data breach topic above, but let's talk about e-mail encryption, which began to gather steam in 2015 and will no doubt continue to expand in 2016.

The times they are a-changing when it comes to the transmission of confidential data by lawyers. In 1999, ABA Formal Opinion 99-413 approved the use of unencrypted e-mail for the transmission of confidential information with the caveat that under circumstances where the information to be communicated is highly sensitive, the lawyer should forgo e-mail, just as he or she would from making a phone call or sending a fax, and consult with the client about the best way to transmit the information.

Most of the opinions from those "early days" took the view that e-mail is appropriate for lawyer/client communication, since it is just as illegal to intercept an e-mail as it is to tap a phone call. A couple of states, including Arizona and Missouri, were a little more cautious.

Then both the ABA Ethics 2000 Commission (E2K) and the Ethics 20/20 Commission expanded the caution, advising in paragraphs 18 and 19 of the Comment to Rule 1.6 Confidentiality of Information that, in effect, the more sensitive the nature of the information that is to be transmitted, the more the lawyer should consider whether it is appropriate to consult with the client about the extent to which additional safeguards should be employed.

An Ethics 20/20 inspired amendment to Rule 1.1 Competence requires lawyers to have a basic understanding of the technology that they use so that they can advise their clients as to the risks and advantages of different means of communication.

Few people think of e-mail as private anymore, given the ease with which it can be monitored by employers and intercepted by hackers and law enforcement.

The pendulum began to swing toward considering encryption with opinions issued by the State Bar of California and the Pennsylvania Bar Association's Committee on Ethics and Professional Responsibility.

And it was big news in 2015 when the State Bar of Texas addressed the issue squarely and provided specific guidance. Opinion 648 (2015) identified several instances where encryption or some other method of security may be appropriate, including:

♦ Communicating highly sensitive or confidential information via e-mail or unencrypted e-mail connections

♦ Sending an e-mail to or from an account that the e-mail sender or recipient shares with others

♦ Sending an e-mail to a client when it is possible that a third person (such as a spouse in a divorce case) knows the password to the e-mail account or to an individual client at that client's work e-mail account, especially if the e-mail relates to a client's employment dispute with his employer

♦ Sending an e-mail from a public computer or a borrowed computer or where the lawyer knows that the e-mails the lawyer sends are being read on a public or borrowed computer or on an unsecure network

♦ Sending an e-mail if the lawyer knows that the e-mail recipient is accessing the e-mail on devices that are potentially accessible to third persons or are not protected by a password

♦ Sending an e-mail if the lawyer is concerned that the NSA or another law enforcement agency may read the lawyer's e-mail communication, with or without a warrant.

Texas is now at the forefront of a swelling movement that lawyers should heed—encrypting e-mail is now so simple and inexpensive that it may be unethical NOT to use it in many instances. If you are not encrypting your e-mail where appropriate, you certainly are not managing risk well and you may find yourself in ethical hot water sooner rather than later. The current Rule 1.1 and Rule 1.6, which have been adopted in fifteen states as of this writing, are enough to potentially sustain a finding of unethical conduct where encryption should have been used and was not. And as state bars begin to issue opinions essentially mirroring the Texas opinion (and they will likely do so), adoption of encryption where appropriate will become an ethical necessity.

## Cyberinsurance

Cyberinsurers may not cover stupidity. This is a message that all law firms should heed. The story broke in 2015 and goes like this . . .

In 2013, California healthcare provider Cottage Health System discovered that security on one of its servers had been disabled, leaving tens of thousands of patients' files potentially open and exposed on the Internet. Those files included patients' names; addresses; dates of birth; and in a few cases, diagnosis, lab results, and procedures performed.

To no one's surprise, Cottage was sued, along with inSync, a company responsible for putting the records in a secure location online. As you might imagine, a lot of money was spent on a forensic investigation, security consultants to get rid of malware, patient notification, credit monitoring, and no doubt attorney fees.

Cottage had cyberinsurance to cover the breach, and Columbia Casualty Company agreed to fund a $4.2 million settlement to a class-action lawsuit brought against Cottage as a result of the breach. After that, Columbia filed a suit of its own stating that it should not be obligated to pay for these damages, pointing to a clause in the policy that effectively said it didn't have to cover the breach because Cottage hadn't followed "minimum required practices" as spelled out in the policy.

Specifically, Columbia claimed that Cottage "stored medical records on a system that was fully accessible to the Internet but failed to install encryption or take other security measures to protect patient information from becoming available to anyone who 'surfed' the Internet."

The patient data had been exposed for about two months starting in October 2013. There was no cyberattack—the data was publicly available; you could just Google it. Pretty tough to know who accessed the data.

Besides the failure to encrypt, Columbia alleges the following security shortfalls:

Cottage and its third-party vendor, inSync, allegedly failed "to continuously implement the procedures and risk controls identified in its application" for the coverage, including

- Configuration and change management for Cottage's IT systems as well as regular patch management

+ Alleged failure to regularly "re-assess its information security exposure and enhance risk controls" and to "deploy a system to detect unauthorized access or attempts to access sensitive information stored on its servers."

AON PLC, the world's largest reinsurance broker, claimed in October 2014 that the cyberinsurance market was at the time growing 38 percent annually, which we can well believe. The large firms all seem to have it, but smaller firms often do not—or think they do, but without full understanding of the policy.

Insurers can dodge covering data breaches for a host of reasons, including:

+ Not paying retroactively.
+ Given that breaches can be discovered months or even years after they begin or end, organizations should carefully consider when coverage starts.
+ Terrorism/act of foreign enemy exclusions.
+ Many cyberattacks originate from outside a country's borders, and many of them are believed to be state-sponsored. Depending on the policy's wording, an organization could be left high and dry. Experts advise negotiating the removal of such exclusions.
+ Lack of coverage for negligence.

Insurers are starting to cover only data theft, not negligence. If an employee loses a laptop with sensitive data, some policies won't cover it.

Amazingly, most folks enter into these policies without a full understanding of what is included and excluded. In 2016, a lot of smaller law firms can or should acquire or review their cyberinsurance coverage.

## Internet of Things

As lawyers, along with the rest of world, sport their smartwatches and adopt IoT (Internet of Things) technology in their homes and offices, they should take note of a 2015 interview with cybersecurity guru Bruce Schneier in which he highlights his "doomsday" view of IoT security. Always blunt, Schneier's remarks are to the point.

As a teaser, here' s a question and answer:

Question: "What should enterprises worry about when it comes to the Internet of things?"

Answer: "Everything."

Elegant in its simplicity and quite likely true. The prolific IoT devices are mostly low-margin and likely to be insecure and to enable surveillance. As Schneier notes, in the computer world of the nineties, no one was paying any attention to security—the IoT world is now much the same. He comments, "it's all really, really bad and it's going to come crashing down."

We loved this bit: "Do you know the way you patch your home router? You throw it away and buy a new one. And that is going to be a freakin' disaster."

Schneier believes, and we agree, that companies will make the next new IoT thing and then the next and no one will do updates—heck, ultimately, no one may know how the thing works. All of the devices will have vulnerabilities, and most of them won't be able to be patched.

If your law office has a smart thermostat that is connected to your network, that could be the entry point for attack.

Will your firm's employees bring their IoT devices to work, thereby presenting another point of vulnerability? Sure.

More vintage Schneier: "They no longer say you can't bring in your own tablet. People would just quit. I think you'll have a hard time enforcing any of those rules because [IoT] is so powerful. If the CEO says, "We're saving 20% of our energy bill" and the security guy says, "But it's insecure," the CEO will say, "Shut up. We're saving 20% on our energy bill. Go away."

## Competence

In 2012, the American Bar Association formally approved a change to the Model Rules of Professional Conduct to make it clear that lawyers have a duty to be competent not only in the law and its practice but also in technology.

The ABA's House of Delegates voted to amend Comment 8 to Model Rule 1.1 to read as follows:

"To maintain the requisite knowledge and skill, a lawyer should keep abreast of changes in the law and its practice, including the benefits and risks associated with relevant technology, engage in continuing study and education and comply with all continuing legal education requirements to which the lawyer is subject."

As we write, fifteen states have adopted the duty of technology competence: Massachusetts, Arizona, Arkansas, Connecticut, Delaware, Idaho,

Illinois, Kansas, Minnesota, New Mexico, North Carolina, Ohio, Pennsylvania, West Virginia, and Wyoming.

Some states, while they haven't formally adopted the change to their rules of professional conduct, have nonetheless acknowledged a duty of lawyers to be competent in technology. And some have changed (slightly) the wording of the ABA Model Rule.

It is increasingly clear that competent lawyers must have a basic understanding of the technology they use.

In 2015, California stirred up a ruckus when it became the first state to specifically require a lawyer to be competent in e-discovery. The California State Bar's Standing Committee on Professional Responsibility and Conduct issued Formal Opinion 2015-193 on June 30.

The digest for the opinion lays out the essence of the document:

> "An attorney's obligations under the ethical duty of competence evolve as new technologies develop and become integrated with the practice of law. Attorney competence related to litigation generally requires, among other things, and at a minimum, a basic understanding of, and facility with, issues relating to e-discovery, including the discovery of electronically stored information ('ESI'). On a case-by-case basis, the duty of competence may require a higher level of technical knowledge and ability, depending on the e-discovery issues involved in a matter, and the nature of the ESI. Competency may require even a highly experienced attorney to seek assistance in some litigation matters involving ESI. An attorney lacking the required competence for e-discovery issues has three options: (1) acquire sufficient learning and skill before performance is required; (2) associate with or consult technical consultants or competent counsel; or (3) decline the client representation. Lack of competence in e-discovery issues also may lead to an ethical violation of an attorney's duty of confidentiality."

As anyone who lectures on e-discovery knows, the majority of attorneys still lack a baseline understanding of e-discovery, including the technology involved—and it is critical that there be some understanding of the technology.

We believe that other states will look at California's opinion and perhaps come up with similar ethical opinions. Frankly, even those attorneys who do not litigate need to have a basic understanding of e-discovery because virtually all attorneys are involved in the creation and/or management of data that may become subject to discovery. It will be interesting to see if other states go down this road in 2016—more on that next year.

## Ross, the Super Intelligent Lawyer (The Rise of the Machines)

This is probably the most radical prediction of this edition of our book. By way of setting the stage . . .

In 2011, many TV viewers (including us) were glued to the screen watching *Jeopardy*. Three episodes made television and science history as IBM's Watson, a computer with artificial intelligence, took on two of the best players *Jeopardy* had ever seen.

Ken Jennings had the longest unbeaten run at 74 appearances, and Brad Rutter had won the largest prize—$3.25 million.

It was a fascinating night. Watson was in a back room with his answers piped into the studio. He couldn't be in the studio because he consisted of ten racks of ten Power 750 servers and his cooling system roared a bit. He was represented at the podium by an avatar of IBM's Smarter Planet logo; its moving lines would turn green when he was right and orange when he was wrong.

Watson wasn't perfect. He was a little shaky on his Harry Potter knowledge, but the upstart player rattled his human counterparts almost from the beginning. In the end, Watson decisively won the game with $77,146, leaving Rutter and Jennings eating his dust with $21,600 and $24,000, respectively. As the grand winner, he received the first-place prize of $1 million.

Jennings, knowing defeat was certain, appended his Final Jeopardy answer with the words "I for one welcome our new computer overlords."

Author Nelson was transfixed and noted to author Simek, "They're going to bring Watson to the legal sector one day—and it's going to play hell with the practice of law." Author Simek agreed, and this story and our thoughts about it have been simmering ever since.

Watson has many children now in many sectors. Some bear his name, and some do not. If you scan IBM's Watson website, you'll see that Watson has moved into social services, the health industry, data analytics, wearable technology, the banking sector, and even fantasy football.

IBM certainly knows that Watson's progeny will make Big Blue a fortune and has sunk a lot of money into expanding Watson's capabilities. It took five years to build Watson before he wowed audiences around the globe. Four years later, we began to see Watson's children in many arenas. In 2011, the Watson business unit was created, joined by 107 Watson staffers.

Watson's entourage knew from the beginning that they would tackle the healthcare industry first, and they correctly judged that any information-intensive industry was ripe for Watson's talents. And yes, that means the legal industry. The team moved fast. In the first year, Watson became 240 percent faster. Once the size of a master bedroom, Watson was now 18 inches wide and 36 inches deep and weighed 100 pounds.

The healthcare industry began to use Watson as a tool to diagnose and treat patients. There were glitches, some of them comical. After Watson was "fed" the Urban Dictionary, he answered one researcher's query with the word *Bulls\*\*\**. The dictionary was quickly removed so that Watson would display the right professional business behavior.

Where Watson was wrong, medical specialists corrected him. He learned—again and again. For those familiar with technology-assisted review in e-discovery, you will recognize the "wash, rinse, repeat" nature of teaching machines.

Citibank began to use Watson to improve customer experiences and to let Watson decide whether potential customers were likely to repay loans and to ferret out probable cases of fraud and identify theft. And those were just the early days.

At its core, Watson is a question-answering system. He (how easy it is to personify a machine) takes a question expressed in everyday language, seeks to understand the question in detail, and then returns a precise answer to the question.

The first time we learned Watson had a lawyer son was when we read news reports that IBM was moving into the legal vertical. The stories reported on the Watson University Competition, at which a group of University of Toronto students built a legal application on top of the Watson platform. The "son of Watson" was called "Ross, the super intelligent attorney." The students placed second in the IBM contest.

IBM supplied the Ross team with continued access to Watson's cloud platform. The students created Ross by loading a huge volume of public legal documents and used the subject matter experts on their team to calibrate

Watson to provide useful answers about the documents. What makes Watson so powerful is its ability to learn. So the more lawyers use it, the better it gets.

Ross has a huge volume of knowledge to rely upon from the public records that have been loaded on to it. The team is looking to strike deals with courts so that they can feed more legal documents into Ross as soon as they become available.

Ross, by taking advantage of the natural language and cognitive computing platform that Watson offers, can predict the outcome of court cases with a confidence rating, assess legal precedents, and suggest readings to prepare for cases. Ross, who his creators say has "gone to law school," is now being funded by Dentons, a global law conglomerate with over 6,000 lawyers. As they put it, Ross has landed a job, and they expect he "will become a senior partner in every single practice area."

You have to start somewhere. As of August 2015, Ross was learning everything there is to know about U.S. bankruptcy law. The former students are now the entrepreneurs behind Ross Intelligence. And Ross is being piloted in a number of elite law firms.

As for Dentons, it has an undisclosed investment in Ross Intelligence, Inc. The company will make use of the law firm's NextLaw Labs, a project aimed at developing new technology for the legal industry. Dentons also announced a partnership with IBM to provide legal startups (like Ross Intelligence) working within NextLaw Labs access to a technology platform using IBM's cloud computing resources. Y Combinator also has an undisclosed investment in Ross Intelligence.

Recently, lawyer/blogger Lee Rosen wrote "Paralegals have largely been replaced by technology. If you're still using them, then you should be carefully examining their function and looking at tech options for solving the problems the paralegals are solving now. Bring in the technology and dispatch the paralegals."

Lee was talking about case management, document management, and other currently available tech tools. But if you take Lee's position to the future, Watson would largely eliminate the need for paralegals.

Without question, Watson can replace some lawyers. Who needs an army of associates to do legal research when you can just ask Watson? On the other side of the equation are lawyers who are irreplaceable because of whom and what they know and their expertise in "custom" law—negotiating, strategic planning, litigation skills, etc.

Hold on to your hats because the stats from the Altman Weil 2015 "Law Firms in Transition" Survey may blow you away. It indicates clearly that legal leaders increasingly anticipate that work handled by human beings in 2015 will inevitably be handed over to intelligent systems.

In 2015, when legal leaders were asked whether or not they could envision a law-centric artificial intelligence (AI) system replacing workers in their offices within five to ten years, 47 percent said paralegals could be replaced by AI in that time, 35 percent said that first-year associate work could be offloaded, and 19.5 percent indicated that intelligent systems would be able to handle work done by third-year associates within that time frame.

Leaders still believe senior associates, those with four to six years of experience, will remain largely irreplaceable. Only 6.84 percent agreed that their work could be replaced within five to ten years.

The belief that AI will be able to handle these tasks has increased considerably since Altman Weil asked that question in 2011. Those who believe that paralegal and first-year associate work could be done by an intelligent system have increased by over 12 percent in those four years. Perhaps more telling, the percentage of leaders who believed "computers will never replace human practitioners" has dropped dramatically from 46 percent in 2011 to only 20.3 percent in 2015.

So yes, Ross is a threat to lawyers. We see Ross—and his inevitable siblings and progeny—as a replacement for a lot of paralegals and young lawyers over time, particularly if he masters form-based lawyering and document review, which he certainly will. And if Ross should go commercial outside the law firm environment, a lot of people with garden-variety problems are going to question whether they need human lawyers at all. And here we were worrying about competition from LegalZoom, Rocket Lawyer, and Avvo . . . we just weren't looking far enough into the future!

# Glossary*

**Active Directory (AD)** is an implementation of Local Automatic Data Processing (LADP) directory services by Microsoft for use primarily in Windows environments. Its main purpose is to provide central authentication and authorization services for Windows-based computers. Active Directory also allows administrators to assign policies, deploy software, and apply critical updates to an organization. Active Directory stores information and settings in a central database. Active Directory networks can vary from a small installation with a few hundred objects to a large installation with millions of objects.

**ActiveSync** is a synchronization program developed by Microsoft. It allows a mobile device to be synchronized with either a desktop PC or a server running Microsoft Exchange Server, PostPath Email and Collaboration Server, Kerio MailServer, or Z-Push.

**Advanced technology attachment (ATA)** is a standard interface for connecting storage devices such as hard disks and CD-ROM drives inside personal computers. The standard is maintained by X3/INCITS committee T13. Many synonyms and near-synonyms for ATA exist, including abbreviations such as IDE and ATAPI.

**Adware** is any software package that automatically plays, displays, or downloads advertising material to a computer after the software is installed on it or while the application is being used. Some types of adware are also spyware and can be classified as privacy-invasive software.

**AppleCare Protection Plan** Apple's warranty with a new product is 90 days' complimentary telephone support and a one-year hardware guarantee. These can both be extended to a three-year (for computers) or two-

---

*This glossary was compiled from definitions available online at Wikipedia (**www.wikipedia.org**).

year (for iPods and iPhones) warranty and telephone support (inclusive of the initial support) through the AppleCare Protection Plan packs, which can be purchased separately within the initial one-year warranty or simultaneously with new Apple products, mainly Macs, iPods, and iPhones.

**Auto Document Feeder (ADF)** is a feature in multifunction or all-in-one printers, fax machines, photocopiers, and scanners that takes several pages and feeds the paper one page at a time into the scanner, allowing the user to scan (and thereby copy, print, or fax) multiple-page documents without having to replace each page manually.

**Boot Camp** is a utility included with Apple's Mac OS X v10.5 Leopard operating system that assists users in installing Microsoft Windows XP or Windows Vista on Intel-based Macintosh computers. Boot Camp guides users through nondestructive repartitioning (including resizing of an existing HFS+ partition, if necessary) of their hard disk drive and using the Mac OS X Leopard disc to install Windows drivers. In addition to device drivers for the hardware, the disc includes a control panel applet for selecting the boot operating system while in Windows.

**Broadband** is any high-speed Internet access that is always on and faster than traditional dial-up access.

**Byte** (pronounced "bite," IPA: /ba_t/) is a unit of measurement of information storage, most often consisting of 8 bits. In many computer architectures, it is a unit of memory addressing.

**Category 5e Cable (Cat5e)** is an enhanced version of Cat 5 that adds specifications for far-end crosstalk. It was formally defined in 2001 in the TIA/EIA-568-B standard, which no longer recognizes the original Cat 5 specification. Although 1000BASE-T was designed for use with Cat 5 cable, the tighter specifications associated with Cat 5e cable and connectors make it an excellent choice for use with 1000BASE-T. Despite the stricter performance specifications, Cat 5e cable does not enable longer cable distances for Ethernet networks: Cables are still limited to a maximum of 328 feet (100 meters) in length [normal practice is to limit fixed ("horizontal") cables to 90 meters to allow for up to 5 meters of patch cable at each end]. Cat 5e cable performance characteristics and test methods are defined in TIA/EIA-568-B.2-2001.

**Category 6 Cable (Cat6)**, commonly referred to as Cat 6, is a cable standard for gigabit Ethernet and other network protocols and is backward compatible with the Category 5/5e and Category 3 cable standards. Cat 6 features more stringent specifications for crosstalk and system noise. The cable standard provides performance of up to 250 MHz and is suitable for 10BASE-T/100BASE-TX and 1000BASE-T (gigabit Ethernet). It is expected to suit the 10GBASE-T (10 gigabit Ethernet) standard, although with limitations on length if unshielded Cat 6 cable is used.

**Cathode Ray Tube (CRT)** is an evacuated glass envelope containing an electron gun (a source of electrons) and a fluorescent screen, usually with internal or external means to accelerate and deflect the electrons. When electrons strike the fluorescent screen, light is emitted.

**CD-ROM** is a compact disc that contains data accessible by a computer. While the CD format was originally designed for music storage and playback, the format was later adapted to hold any form of binary data. CD-ROMs are popularly used to distribute computer software, including games and multimedia applications, although any data can be stored (up to the capacity limit of a disc).

**Central Processing Unit (CPU)**, or sometimes just processor, is a certain class of logic machines that can execute computer programs. This broad definition can easily be applied to many early computers that existed long before the term *CPU* ever came into widespread usage. However, the term itself and its initialism have been in use in the computer industry since at least the early 1960s (Weik, 1961). The form, design, and implementation of CPUs have changed dramatically since the earliest examples, but their fundamental operation has remained much the same.

**Client Access License (CAL)** is a kind of software license, distributed by Microsoft, to allow clients to connect to its server software programs.

**Code Division Multiple Access (CDMA)** employs spread-spectrum technology and a special coding scheme (where each transmitter is assigned a code). In communications technology, there are only three domains that can allow multiplexing to be implemented for more efficient use of the available channel bandwidth, and these domains are known as time, frequency, and space. CDMA divides the access in signal space.

**Computer Monitor** is a piece of electrical equipment that displays viewable images generated by a computer without producing a permanent record. The word *monitor* is used in other contexts, in particular in television broadcasting, where a television picture is displayed to a high standard. A computer display device is usually either a cathode ray tube or some form of flat panel, such as a thin film transistor liquid crystal display (TFT-LCD). The monitor comprises the display device, circuitry to generate a picture from electronic signals sent by the computer, and an enclosure or case. Within the computer, either as an integral part or a plugged-in interface, there is circuitry to convert internal data to a format compatible with a monitor.

**Computer Virus** is a computer program that can copy itself and infect a computer without permission or knowledge of the user. However, the term *virus* is commonly used, albeit erroneously, to refer to many different types of malware programs. The original virus may modify the copies, or the copies may modify themselves, as occurs in a metamorphic virus. A virus can only spread from one computer to another when its host is taken to the uninfected computer—for instance, by a user sending it over a network or the Internet or by carrying it on a removable medium such as a floppy disk, CD, or USB drive. Additionally, viruses can spread to other computers by infecting files on a network file system or a file system that is accessed by another computer.

**Contrast Ratio** is a measure of a display system, defined as the ratio of the luminosity of the brightest color (white) to that of the darkest color (black) that the system is capable of producing. A high contrast ratio is a desired aspect of any display, but with the various methods of measurement for a system or its part, remarkably different measured values can sometimes produce similar results.

**DAT72 Backup Tapes** stores up to 36GB uncompressed (72GB compressed) on a 170-meter cartridge. The Digital Audio Tape (DAT) 72 standard was developed by HP and Certance. It has the same form factor and is backward compatible with DDS-3 and DDS-4.

**Database Application** A computer database is a structured collection of records or data that is stored in a computer system. A database usually contains software so that a person or program can use it to answer queries or extract desired information. The term *database* refers to the collection of related records, and the software should be referred to as the database management system (DBMS).

**DDR2 SDRAM**, double-data-rate two synchronous dynamic random-access memory, is a random-access memory technology used for high-speed storage of the working data of a computer or another digital electronic device.

**Digital Copier** In recent years, all new photocopiers have adopted digital technology, replacing the older analog technology. With digital copying, the copier effectively consists of an integrated scanner and laser printer. This design has several advantages, such as automatic image quality enhancement and the ability to "build jobs," or scan page images independently of the process of printing them. Some digital copiers can function as high-speed scanners; such models typically have the ability to send documents via e-mail or make them available on a local area network.

**Digital Subscriber Line (DSL)** is a family of technologies that provides digital data transmission over the wires of a local telephone network.

**Digital Visual Interface (DVI)** is a video interface standard designed to maximize the visual quality of digital display devices such as flat-panel LCD computer displays and digital projectors. It was developed by an industry consortium, the Digital Display Working Group (DDWG). It is designed for carrying uncompressed digital video data to a display.

**Display Resolution** of a digital television or computer display typically refers to the number of distinct pixels in each dimension that can be displayed. It can be an ambiguous term, especially as the displayed resolution is controlled by different factors in CRT and flat-panel or projection displays using fixed picture-element (pixel) arrays.

**Domain Controller** On Windows Server Systems, the domain controller (DC) is the server that responds to security authentication requests (logging in, checking permissions, etc.) within the Windows Server domain.

**Dots Per Inch (dpi)** is a measure of printing resolution, in particular the number of individual dots of ink a printer or toner can produce within a linear 1-inch (2.54 cm) space.

**DVD** (also known as digital versatile disc or digital video disc) is a popular optical disk storage media format. Its main uses are video and data storage. Most DVDs are of the same dimensions as compact discs (CDs) but store more than six times as much data.

**E-mail Spam** is the practice of sending unwanted e-mail messages, frequently with commercial content, in large quantities to an indiscriminate set of recipients.

**Encryption/Decryption** is the process of transforming information (referred to as plaintext) using an algorithm (called cipher) to make it unreadable to anyone except those possessing special knowledge, usually referred to as a key. The result of the process is encrypted information (in cryptography, referred to as ciphertext). In many contexts, the word *encryption* also implicitly refers to the reverse process, decryption (e.g., "software for encryption" can typically also perform decryption), to make the encrypted information readable again (i.e., to make it unencrypted).

**Enhanced-Definition Television** Enhanced- or extended-definition television, or EDTV, is a Consumer Electronics Association (CEA) marketing shorthand term for certain digital television (DTV) formats and devices. EDTV generally refers to video with picture quality beyond what can be broadcast in NTSC or PAL but not sharp enough to be considered high-definition television (HDTV). A DVD player with progressive output is considered the lower end of this class when playing a progressively encoded disc. (The maximum EDTV frame rate of 60 per second is not possible from a DVD.) The common implementations of EDTV are 480- or 576-line signals in progressive scan, as opposed to 50–60 interlaced fields per second (see NTSC or PAL and SECAM). These are commonly referred to as "480p" and "576p," respectively. In comparison, a standard-definition television (SDTV) signal is broadcast with interlaced frames and is commonly referred to as "480i" or "576i." EDTV can also refer to a display device that has a maximum resolution of 480p or 576p.

**Extensible Markup Language (XML)** is a general-purpose markup language. It is classified as an extensible language because it allows its users to define their own elements. Its primary purpose is to facilitate the sharing of structured data across different information systems, particularly via the Internet. It is used both to encode documents and serialize data.

**Firewall** is a network security system that monitors and controls the incoming and outgoing network traffic based on predetermined security rules. A firewall typically establishes a barrier between a trusted, secure internal network and another outside network, such as the Internet, that is assumed to be not secure or trusted.

**FireWire** is Apple's brand name for the IEEE 1394 interface (although the 1394 standard also defines a backplane interface). It is also known as i.LINK (Sony's name). It is a serial bus interface standard for high-speed communications and isochronous real-time data transfer, frequently used in a personal computer (and digital audio/digital video).

**FireWire 400** can transfer data between devices at 100, 200, or 400 Mbit/s data rates.

**FireWire 800** (Apple's name for the nine-pin "S800 bilingual" version of the IEEE 1394b standard) was introduced commercially by Apple in 2003. This newer 1394 specification (1394b) and corresponding products allow a transfer rate of 786.432 Mbit/s via a new encoding scheme termed beta mode. It is backward compatible to the slower rates and six-pin connectors of FireWire 400. However, while the IEEE 1394a and IEEE 1394b standards are compatible, FireWire 800's connector is different from FireWire 400's connector, making the legacy cables incompatible. A bilingual cable allows the connection of older devices to the newer port.

**Gigabyte** (derived from the SI prefix giga-) is a unit of information or computer storage meaning either exactly 1 billion bytes ($1000^3$, or $10^9$) or approximately 1.07 billion bytes ($1024^3$). It is commonly abbreviated as Gbyte or GB.

**Global System for Mobile Communications (GSM)** is the most popular standard for mobile phones in the world. Its promoter, the GSM Association, estimates that 82 percent of the global mobile market uses the standard. GSM is used by over 2 billion people across more than 212 countries and territories. Its ubiquity makes international roaming very common between mobile phone operators, enabling subscribers to use their phones in many parts of the world. GSM differs from its predecessors in that both signaling and speech channels are digital call quality, and so it is considered a second-generation (2G) mobile phone system. This has also meant that data communications were built into the system using the 3rd Generation Partnership Project (3GPP).

**Hard Disk Drive**, commonly referred to as a hard drive, hard disk, or fixed disk drive, is a nonvolatile storage device that stores digitally encoded data on rapidly rotating platters with magnetic surfaces. Strictly speaking, *drive* refers to a device distinct from its medium, such as a tape drive and its tape or a floppy disk drive and its floppy disk.

**Hash Function** is a reproducible method of turning some kind of data into a (relatively) small number that may serve as a digital "fingerprint" of the data. The algorithm "chops and mixes" (i.e., substitutes or transposes) the data to create such fingerprints. The fingerprints are called hash sums, hash values, hash codes, or simply hashes.

**High-Definition Multimedia Interface (HDMI)** is a licensable compact audio/video connector interface for transmitting uncompressed digital streams.

**High-Definition TV (HDTV)** is a digital television broadcasting system with greater resolution than traditional television systems (NTSC, SECAM, PAL). HDTV is digitally broadcast because digital television (DTV) requires less bandwidth if sufficient video compression is used.

**Hub** is a device for connecting multiple twisted pairs or fiber-optic Ethernet devices together, making them act as a single network segment. Hubs work at the physical layer (layer 1) of the OSI model, and the term *layer 1 switch* is often used interchangeably with *hub*. The device is thus a form of multiport repeater. Network hubs are also responsible for forwarding a jam signal to all ports if it detects a collision.

**The Institute of Electrical and Electronics Engineers, or IEEE** (read *i* triple *e*), is an international nonprofit professional organization for the advancement of technology related to electricity. It has the most members of any technical professional organization in the world, with more than 360,000 members in around 175 countries.

**Intel Core 2 Duo Processor** The Core 2 brand refers to a range of Intel's consumer 64-bit dual-core and MCM quad-core CPUs with the x86-64 instruction set and based on the Intel Core microarchitecture, which derived from the 32-bit dual-core Yonah laptop processor.

**Intel Corporation (Intel)** is the world's largest semiconductor company and the inventor of the x86 series of microprocessors, which are found in most personal computers.

**Internet Information Services (IIS)** is a set of Internet-based services for servers using Microsoft Windows. It is the world's second most popular web server in terms of overall websites, behind Apache HTTP Server.

**Internet Protocol Address** An IP address (Internet protocol address) is a unique address that certain electronic devices currently use to identify and communicate with each other on a computer network utilizing the Internet protocol standard (IP)—in simpler terms, a computer address. Any participating network device—including routers, switches, computers, infrastructure servers (e.g., NTP, DNS, DHCP, SNMP), printers, Internet fax machines, and some telephones—can have its own address that is unique within the scope of the specific network. Some IP addresses are intended to be unique within the scope of the global Internet, while others need to be unique only within the scope of an enterprise.

**Intrusion Detection System (IDS)** is a piece of hardware that detects unwanted manipulations of computer systems, mainly through the Internet. The manipulations may take the form of attacks by crackers. An

IDS is used to detect several types of malicious behaviors that can compromise the security and trust of a computer system. This includes network attacks against vulnerable services; data-driven attacks on applications; host-based attacks such as privilege escalation, unauthorized logins, and access to sensitive files; and malware (viruses, Trojan horses, and worms).

**IPsec (IP security)** is a suite of protocols for securing Internet protocol (IP) communications by authenticating and/or encrypting each IP packet in a data stream.

**iSight Camera** is a webcam developed and marketed by Apple. The iSight was sold retail as an external unit that connects to a computer via FireWire cable and comes with a set of mounts to place it atop any current Apple display, laptop computer, or all-in-one desktop computer. The term is also used to refer to the camera built into Apple's iMac, MacBook, and MacBook Pro computers.

**Keyboard** In computing, a keyboard is a peripheral partially modeled after the typewriter keyboard. Physically, a keyboard is an arrangement of rectangular buttons, or keys. A keyboard typically has characters engraved or printed on the keys; in most cases, each press of a key corresponds to a single written symbol. However, to produce some symbols requires pressing and holding several keys simultaneously or in sequence; other keys do not produce any symbol but instead affect the operation of the computer or the keyboard itself.

**Laser Printer** is a common type of computer printer that rapidly produces high-quality text and graphics on plain paper. Like photocopiers, laser printers employ a xerographic printing process but differ from analog photocopiers in that the image is produced by the direct scanning of a laser beam across the printer's photoreceptor.

**Light-Emitting Diode (LED)** is a semiconductor diode that emits incoherent, narrow-spectrum light when electrically biased in the forward direction of the p-n junction, as in the common LED circuit. This effect is a form of electroluminescence.

**Lightning** (connector) is a proprietary computer bus and power connector created by Apple Inc. to replace its previous proprietary 30-pin dock connector and is used to connect Apple mobile devices like iPhones, iPads, and iPods to host computers, external monitors, cameras, USB battery chargers, and other peripherals. Using eight pins instead of 30, Lightning is significantly more compact than the 30-pin dock connector and can be inserted with either side facing up.

**Linear Tape-Open (LTO or LTO2)** is a magnetic tape data storage technology developed as an open alternative to the proprietary digital linear tape (DLT). The technology was developed and initiated by Seagate, Hewlett-Packard, and IBM. The standard form factor of LTO technology goes by the name Ultrium.

**Liquid Crystal Display (LCD)** is a thin, flat display device made up of any number of color or monochrome pixels arrayed in front of a light source or reflector. It is often utilized in battery-powered electronic devices because it uses very small amounts of electric power.

**Macintosh AirPort** is a local area wireless networking brand from Apple based on the IEEE 802.11b standard (also known as Wi-Fi) and certified as compatible with other 802.11b devices. A later family of products based on the IEEE 802.11g specification is known as AirPort Extreme. The latest family of products is based on the draft-IEEE 802.11n specification and carries the same name.

**Macintosh/Macs** Macintosh—or, for newer models, Mac—is a brand name that covers several lines of personal computers designed, developed, and marketed by Apple Inc. The original Macintosh was released on January 24, 1984; it was the first commercially successful personal computer to feature a mouse and a graphical user interface (GUI) rather than a command line interface. Apple consolidated multiple consumer-level desktop models into the 1998 iMac, which sold extremely well. Current Mac systems are mainly targeted at the home, education, and creative professional markets. They are the aforementioned (although upgraded) iMac and the entry-level Mac mini desktop models, the workstation-level Mac Pro tower, the MacBook, MacBook Air and MacBook Pro laptops, and the Xserve server.

**MagSafe Power Adapter** is a power connector introduced in conjunction with the MacBook Pro at the Macworld Expo in San Francisco on January 10, 2006. The MagSafe connector is held in place magnetically. As a result, if it is tugged on—for instance, by someone tripping over the cord—it comes out of the socket safely, without damaging it or the computer or pulling the computer off its table or desk.

**Media Access Control Address (MAC)** address is a quasi-unique identifier attached to most network adapters. It is a number that acts like a name for a particular network adapter; so, for example, the network interface cards (NICs, or built-in network adapters) in two different computers will have different names, or MAC addresses, as would an Ethernet adapter and a wireless adapter in the same computer and as would multiple network cards in a router.

**Megabyte** is a unit of information or computer storage equal to either 106 (1,000,000) bytes or 220 (1,048,576) bytes, depending on context. In rare cases, it is used to mean 1000 × 1024 (1,024,000) bytes. It is commonly abbreviated as Mbyte or MB.

**Message-Digest Algorithm 5 (MD5)** is a widely used cryptographic hash function with a 128-bit hash value. As an Internet standard (RFC 1321), MD5 has been employed in a wide variety of security applications and is also commonly used to check the integrity of files. An MD5 hash is typically expressed as a 32-character hexadecimal number.

**Microsoft Exchange Server** is a messaging and collaborative software product developed by Microsoft. It is part of the Microsoft Servers line of server products and is widely used by enterprises using Microsoft infrastructure solutions. Exchange's major features consist of electronic mail, calendaring, contacts and tasks, and support for the mobile and web-based access to information, as well as supporting data storage.

**Microsoft SQL Server** is a relational database management system (RDBMS) produced by Microsoft. Its primary query language is Transact-SQL, an implementation of the ANSI/ISO standard Structured Query Language (SQL) used by both Microsoft and Sybase.

**Microsoft Windows** is the name of several families of software operating systems by Microsoft. Microsoft first introduced an operating environment named Windows in November 1985 as an add-on to MS-DOS in response to the growing interest in graphical user interfaces (GUIs). Microsoft Windows eventually came to dominate the world's personal computer market, overtaking Mac OS, which had been introduced previously. At the 2004 IDC Directions conference, IDC vice president Avneesh Saxena stated that Windows had approximately 90 percent of the client operating system market. The most recent client version of Windows is Windows 10. The current server version of Windows is Windows Server 2008. The successor to Windows Server 2003, Windows Server 2016, is currently being beta-tested.

**Modem** (from modulator-demodulator) is a device that modulates an analog carrier signal to encode digital information and also demodulates such a carrier signal to decode the transmitted information. The goal is to produce a signal that can be transmitted easily and decoded to reproduce the original digital data.

**Mouse** In computing, a mouse (plural mice or mouses) functions as a pointing device by detecting two-dimensional motion relative to its supporting surface. Physically, a mouse consists of a small case, held under one of the user's hands, with one or more buttons. It sometimes features other elements, such as "wheels," which allow the user to perform various system-dependent operations, or extra buttons or features that can add more control or dimensional input. The mouse's motion typically translates into the motion of a pointer on a display.

**MP3** MPEG-1 audio layer 3, more commonly referred to as MP3, is a digital audio encoding format. This encoding format is used to create an MP3 file, a way to store a single segment of audio, commonly a song, so that it can be organized or easily transferred between computers and other devices, such as MP3 players.

**Network Address Translation (NAT)** is a technique of transceiving network traffic through a router that involves rewriting the source and/or destination IP addresses and usually also the TCP/UDP port numbers of IP packets as they pass through.

**Network Card/Adapter** Network adapter, LAN adapter, or NIC (network interface card) is a piece of computer hardware designed to allow computers to communicate over a computer network.

**Optical Character Recognition (OCR),** usually abbreviated OCR, is the mechanical or electronic translation of images of handwritten, typewritten, or printed text (usually captured by a scanner) into machine-editable text.

**Peripheral Devices** In computer hardware, a peripheral device is any device attached to a computer to expand its functionality. Some of the more common peripheral devices are printers, scanners, disk drives, tape drives, microphones, speakers, and cameras.

**Personal Digital Assistants (PDAs)** are handheld computers that have become much more versatile over the years. PDAs are also known as small computers or palmtop computers. PDAs have many uses: to do calculations; to use a clock, calendar, and address book; to access the Internet and send/receive e-mails; to do video recording, typewriting, and word processing; to make and write on spreadsheets; to scan bar codes, use as a radio or stereo, play computer games, and record survey responses; and to use a Global Positioning System (GPS). Newer PDAs also have both color screens and audio capabilities, enabling them to be used as mobile phones (smartphones), web browsers, or portable media players. Many PDAs can access the Internet, intranets, or extranets via Wi-Fi, or wireless wide-area networks (WWANs). Many PDAs employ touchscreen technology.

**Portable Document Format (PDF)** is the file format created by Adobe Systems in 1993 for document exchange. PDF is fixed-layout document format used for representing two-dimensional documents in a manner independent of the application software, hardware, and operating system.

**Private Branch Exchange (PBX)** is a telephone exchange that serves a particular business or office, as opposed to one that a common carrier or telephone company operates for many businesses or for the general public.

**PS/2 Connector** is used for connecting a keyboard and a mouse to a PC compatible computer system. Its name comes from the IBM Personal System/2 series of personal computers, with which it was introduced in 1987. The PS/2 mouse connector generally replaced the older DE-9 RS-232 "serial mouse" connector, while the keyboard connector replaced the larger 5-pin DIN used in the IBM PC/AT design. The keyboard and mouse interfaces are electrically similar, with the main difference being that open collector outputs are required on both ends of the keyboard interface to allow bidirectional communication. If a PS/2 mouse is connected to a PS/2 keyboard port (or if a PS/2 keyboard is connected to a PS/2 mouse port), the mouse (or keyboard) will not be recognized by the computer.

**Radio-Frequency Identification (RFID)** is an automatic identification method that relies on storing and remotely retrieving data using devices called RFID tags or transponders. An RFID tag is an object that can be applied to or incorporated into a product, an animal, or a person for the purpose of identification using radio waves. Some tags can be read from several meters away and beyond the line of sight of the reader.

**RAID 5** A redundant array of independent disks (RAID) 5 uses block-level striping with parity data distributed across all member disks. RAID 5 has achieved popularity due to its low cost of redundancy. Generally, RAID 5 is implemented with hardware support for parity calculations. A minimum of three disks is generally required for a complete RAID 5 configuration.

**Random-Access Memory (usually known by its acronym, RAM)** is a type of computer data storage. Today, it takes the form of integrated circuits that allow the stored data to be accessed in any order—i.e., at random. The word *random* thus refers to the fact that any piece of data can be returned in a constant time, regardless of its physical location and whether or not it is related to the previous piece of data.

**Ransomware** is a type of malware that restricts access to a computer system that it infects in some way and demands that the user pay a ransom to the operators of the malware to remove the restriction.

**Redundant Arrays of Independent Disks** is the most common definition of RAID. Other definitions of RAID include redundant arrays of independent drives and redundant arrays of inexpensive drives. RAID is an umbrella term for computer data storage schemes that divide and replicate data among multiple hard disk drives. RAID's various designs balance or accentuate two key design goals: increased data reliability and increased I/O (input/output) performance.

**Remote Desktop Protocol (RDP)** is a multichannel protocol that allows a user to connect to a computer running Microsoft Terminal Services. Clients exist for most versions of Windows (including handheld versions) and other operating systems such as Linux, FreeBSD, Solaris, and Mac OS X. The server listens by default on TCP port 3389. Microsoft refers to its official RDP client software as either Remote Desktop Connection (RDC) or Terminal Services Client (TSC).

**Revolutions Per Minute (abbreviated rpm, RPM, r/min, or r•min$^{-1}$)** is a unit of frequency: the number of full rotations completed in one minute around a fixed axis. It is most commonly used as a measure of rotational speed or angular velocity of some mechanical component.

**Rootkits** is a program (or a combination of several programs) designed to take fundamental control (in Unix terms, "root" access; in Windows terms, "administrator" access) of a computer system without authorization by the system's owners and legitimate managers. Access to the hardware (i.e., the reset switch) is rarely required, as a rootkit is intended to seize control of the operating system running on the hardware. Typically, rootkits act to obscure their presence on the system through subversion or evasion of standard operating system security mechanisms. Often they are Trojans as well, thus fooling users into believing they are safe to run on their systems. Techniques used to accomplish this can include concealing running processes from monitoring programs or hiding files or system data from the operating system.

**Router** is a piece of hardware that connects two or more different networks (e.g., LAN to WAN) to route data between them.

**Scanning Resolution** describes the detail of the scanned image. The term applies equally to digital images, film images, and other types of images. Higher resolution means more image detail.

**Secure Sockets Layer (SSL)** is a cryptographic protocol that provides secure communications on the Internet for such things as web browsing, e-mail, Internet faxing, instant messaging, and other data transfers.

**Serial Advanced Technology Attachment (SATA)** is a computer bus primarily designed for transfer of data between a computer and storage devices (like hard disk drives or optical drives). The main benefits are faster transfers, ability to remove or add devices while operating (hot-swapping), thinner cables that let air cooling work more efficiently, and more reliable operation with tighter data integrity checks than the older Parallel ATA interface.

**Serial Attached SCSI (SAS)** is a computer bus technology primarily designed for transfer of data to and from computer data storage devices such as hard drives, CD-ROM and DVD tape drives, and similar devices. SAS is a serial communication protocol for direct attached storage (DAS) devices. It is designed for the corporate and enterprise market as a replace-ment for parallel SCSI, allowing for much higher speed data transfers than previously available and is backward compatible with SATA drives.

**Server** is an application or a device that performs services for connected clients as part of a client-server architecture. A server application, as defined by RFC 2616 (HTTP/1.1), is "an application program that accepts connections in order to service requests by sending back responses." Server computers are devices designed to run such an application or applications, often for extended periods of time, with minimal human direction. Examples of d-class servers include web servers, e-mail servers, and file servers.

**Service Set Identifier (SSID)** is a name used to identify the particular 802.11 wireless LANs to which a user wants to attach. A client device will receive broadcast messages from all access points within range advertising their SSIDs and can choose one to connect to based on preconfiguration or by displaying a list of SSIDs in range and asking the user to select one.

**SHA Hash Functions** are five cryptographic hash functions designed by the National Security Agency (NSA) and published by the NIST as a U.S. Federal Information Processing Standard. SHA stands for secure hash algo-rithm. Hash algorithms compute a fixed-length digital representation (known as a message digest) of an input data sequence (the message) of any length. The five algorithms are denoted SHA-1, SHA-224, SHA-256, SHA-384, and SHA-512. The last four variants are sometimes collectively referred to as SHA-2. SHA-1 produces a message digest that is 160 bits long; the number in the other four algorithms' names denotes the bit length of the digest they produce.

**Shadow Copy (also called Volume Snapshot Service, or VSS)** is a feature introduced with Windows Server 2003 and available in all releases of Microsoft Windows thereafter that allows taking manual or automatic backup copies or snapshots of a file or folder on a specific volume at a specific point in time. It is used by NTBackup and the Volume Shadow Copy service to back up files. In Windows Vista, it is used by Windows Vista's backup utility, System Restore, and the Previous Versions feature.

**Small Computer System Interface (SCSI)** is a set of standards for physically connecting and transferring data between computers and peripheral devices. The SCSI standards define commands, protocols, and electrical and optical interfaces. SCSI is most commonly used for hard disks and tape drives, but it can connect a wide range of other devices, including scanners and CD drives. The SCSI standard defines command sets for specific peripheral device types; the presence of "unknown" as one of these types means that in theory, it can be used as an interface to almost any device, but the standard is highly pragmatic and addressed toward commercial requirements.

**Smartphone** is a mobile phone offering advanced capabilities beyond a typical mobile phone, often with PC-like functionality.

**Solid-State Drives (SSD)** are solid-state storage devices that use integrated circuit assemblies as memory to store data persistently. SSD technology primarily uses electronic interfaces compatible with traditional block input/output (I/O) hard disk drives, which permit simple replacements in common applications.

**Spyware** is computer software that is installed surreptitiously on a personal computer to intercept or take partial control over the user's interaction with the computer without the user's informed consent. While the term *spyware* suggests software that secretly monitors the user's behavior, the functions of spyware extend well beyond simple monitoring. Spyware programs can collect various types of personal information but can also interfere with user control of the computer in other ways, such as installing additional software, redirecting web browser activity, accessing websites blindly that will cause more harmful viruses, or diverting advertising revenue to a third party. Spyware can even change computer settings, resulting in slow connection speeds, different home pages, and loss of Internet or other programs.

**Stereophonic Sound (stereo)**, commonly called stereo, is the reproduction of sound using two or more independent audio channels through a symmetrical configuration of loudspeakers to create a pleasant and natural impression of sound heard from various directions, as in natural hearing. It is often contrasted with monophonic (or "monaural," or just mono) sound, where audio is in the form of one channel, often centered in the sound field.

**SuperDrive** is a term that has been used by Apple for two different storage drives: from 1988 to 1999 to refer to a high-density floppy disk drive capable of reading all major 3.5-inch disk formats and from 2001 onwards to refer to a combined CD/DVD reader/writer. Once use of floppy disks started declining, Apple reused the term to refer to the (originally Pioneer-built) DVD writers built into its Macintosh models, which can read and write both DVDs and CDs. As of December 2006, SuperDrives are combination DVD ±R/±RW and CD-R/RW writer drives offering speeds of 4x-36x and supporting the DVD-R, DVD+R, DVD+R DL, DVD±RW, DVD-9, CD-R, and CD-RW formats along with all normal read-only media.

**Switch** is a computer networking device that connects network segments. Low-end network switches appear nearly identical to network hubs, but a switch contains more "intelligence" (and comes with a correspondingly slightly higher price tag) than a network hub. Network switches are capable of inspecting data packets as they are received, determining the source and destination device of that packet, and forwarding it appropriately. By delivering each message only to the connected device it was intended for, a network switch conserves network bandwidth and generally offers generally better performance than a hub.

**Tagged Image File Format (TIFF)** is a container format for storing images, including photographs and line art. Originally created by the company Aldus for use with what was then called desktop publishing, it is now under the control of Adobe. The TIFF format is widely supported by image-manipulation applications; by publishing and page layout applications; and by scanning, faxing, word processing, OCR, and other applications.

**Tape Drive** is a data storage device that reads and writes data stored on a magnetic tape. It is typically used for archival storage of data on hard drives. Tape generally has a favorable unit cost and long archival stability.

**Terminal Services** is a component of Microsoft Windows (both server and client versions) that allows a user to access applications and data on a remote computer over any type of network, although normally best used when dealing with either a Wide Area Network (WAN) or local area network (LAN). Ease and compatibility with other types of networks may differ and vary. Terminal Services is Microsoft's implementation of thin-client terminal server computing, where Windows applications, or even the entire desktop of the computer running terminal services, are made accessible from a remote client machine.

**Time Machine** is a backup utility developed by Apple that is included with Mac OS X v10.5.

**Universal Serial Bus (USB)** is a serial bus standard to interface devices. USB was designed to allow peripherals to be connected using a single standardized interface socket and to improve plug-and-play capabilities by allowing devices to be connected and disconnected without rebooting the computer (hot-swapping). Other convenient features include providing power to low-consumption devices without the need for an external power supply and allowing many devices to be used without requiring manufacturer specific, individual device drivers to be installed.

**UNIX** is a computer operating system originally developed in 1969 by a group of AT&T employees, including Ken Thompson, Dennis Ritchie, and Douglas McIlroy, at Bell Labs. Today's Unix systems are split into various branches developed over time by AT&T as well as various commercial vendors and nonprofit organizations.

**USB Thumb (flash) Drive** are NAND-type flash memory data storage devices integrated with a USB connector. They are typically small, lightweight, removable, and rewritable.

**Video Card/Graphics Adapter**, also referred to as a graphics accelerator card, display adapter, graphics card, and numerous other terms, is an item of personal computer hardware whose function is to generate and output images to a display.

**Video Graphics Array** The term *video graphics array (VGA)* refers to an analog computer display standard; the 15-pin D-subminiature VGA connector, first marketed in 1988 by IBM; or the 640 × 480 resolution itself. While this resolution has been superseded in the computer market, it is becoming a popular resolution on mobile devices.

**Virtual Private Network (VPN)** is a communications network tunneled through another network and dedicated for a specific network. One common application is secure communications through the public Internet, but a VPN need not have explicit security features such as authentication or content encryption. VPNs, for example, can be used to separate the traffic of different user communities over an underlying network with strong security features.

**Web 2.0** is a trend in web design and development and can refer to a perceived second generation of web-based communities and hosted services—such as social networking sites, wikis, and folksonomies—that aim to facilitate creativity, collaboration, and sharing between users. The term gained currency following the first O'Reilly Media Web 2.0 conference in 2004. Although the term suggests a new version of the World Wide Web, it does not refer to an update to any technical specifications, but to changes in the ways software developers and end users use webs.

**Wi-Fi** is a wireless technology brand owned by the Wi-Fi Alliance intended to improve the interoperability of wireless local area network products based on the IEEE 802.11 standards. Common applications for Wi-Fi include Internet and VoIP phone access, gaming, and network connectivity for consumer electronics such as televisions, DVD players, and digital cameras.

**Wi-Fi Protected Access (WPA)** is a class of systems to secure wireless (Wi-Fi) computer networks. It was created in response to several serious weaknesses researchers had found in the previous system, wired equivalent privacy (WEP). WPA implements the majority of the IEEE 802.11i standard and was intended as an intermediate measure to take the place of WEP while 802.11i was prepared.

**Windows Recycle Bin** is temporary storage for files that have been deleted in a file manager by the user but not yet permanently erased from the physical medium. Typically, a recycle bin is presented as a special file directory to the user (whether or not it is actually a single directory depends on the implementation), allowing the user to browse deleted files, undelete those that were deleted by mistake, or delete them permanently (either one by one or by the Empty Trash function).

**Windows SharePoint Services**, or Windows SharePoint, is the basic part of SharePoint offering collaboration and document management functionality by means of web portals by providing a centralized repository for shared documents, as well as browser-based management and administration. It allows creation of document libraries, which are collections of files that can be shared for collaborative editing. SharePoint provides access control and revision control for documents in a library.

**Wired Equivalent Privacy (WEP)** is a deprecated algorithm to secure IEEE 802.11 wireless networks. Wireless networks broadcast messages using radio, so they are more susceptible to eavesdropping than wired networks. When introduced in 1999, WEP was intended to provide confidentiality comparable to that of a traditional wired network.

# Index